The Emergence
of the Arab Movements

The Emergence
of the Arab Movements

Eliezer Tauber

Bar-Ilan University

Routledge
Taylor & Francis Group

LONDON AND NEW YORK

First published 1993 in Great Britain by
Routledge
2 Park Square, Milton Park, Abingdon, Oxon, OX14 4RN
270 Madison Ave, New York NY 10016

Transferred to Digital Printing 2008

British Library Cataloguing in Publication Data

Tauber, Eliezer
Emergence of the Arab Movements
I. Title
909.82

ISBN 0-7146-3440-9

Library of Congress Cataloging-in-Publication Data

Tauber, Eliezer,
The emergence of the Arab movements / Eliezer Tauber.
    p.   cm.
Includes bibliographical references and index.
ISBN 0-7146-3440-9 (hardback)
ISBN 0-7146-4084-0 (paperback)
    1. Nationalism—Arab countries—History. 2. Arab countries—
Politics and government. I. Title.
DS63.6.T39   1993
    320.5'4'09174927—dc20   92-8131
                                                    CIP

ISBN 0 7146 3440 9
ISBN 0 7146 4084 0 (paperback)

Typeset by Regent Typesetting, London

Publisher's Note
The publisher has gone to great lengths to ensure the quality of this reprint but points out that some imperfections in the original may be apparent.

Published in cooperation with
The Harry S. Truman Research Institute
for the Advancement of Peace
The Hebrew University of Jerusalem

The Harry S. Truman Research Institute for the Advancement of Peace, established in 1966, conducts major research on the growth, and political and social development of the non-Western world, with particular emphasis on the Middle East. Its Middle East unit studies Israel and the territories, Turkey and Iran, and the Arab countries of the Middle East in the modern and contemporary period, with reference to problems relating to peace prospects in the area.

Contents

PART III: The Arab Societies: An Analysis

Acknowledgements

I wish to express my sincere gratitude to the Truman Institute of the Hebrew University, which has rendered me financial help both at the research stage preceding this book and during its translation into English. Additional financial help was rendered to me by the Faculty of Jewish Studies at Bar-Ilan University and my sincere thanks for it are hereby acknowledged. Naomi Goldblum of the Hebrew University translated this book from the original Hebrew.

The Syrian Central Society, dealt with in chapter 11, was first discussed in the introductory part of "Four Syrian Manifestos after the Young Turk Revolution", *Turcica*, 19 (1987), pp.195-213. An enlarged version of chapter 16, dealing with Rashid Rida, was published as "Rashid Rida as Pan-Arabist before World War I", *The Muslim World*, 79 (1989), pp.102-112. An earlier version of chapter 20, dealing with Sayyid Talib, appeared as "Sayyid Talib and the Young Turks in Basra", *Middle Eastern Studies*, 25 (1989), pp.3-22.

A final note of appreciation goes to my mother, whose devotion has long been a source of strength to me.

Eliezer Tauber

Tishrey 5751
Bar-Ilan, Israel

Abbreviations

A.A. = Awswärtiges Amt
AB = *Arab Bulletin*
AN = Archives Nationales
BD = *British Documents on the Origins of the War 1898-1914*
Cd'O = *Correspondance d'Orient*
C-in-C = Commander-in-Chief
CPC = Correspondance Politique des Consuls
CUP = Committee of Union and Progress
CZA = Central Zionist Archives
d = despatch
FO = Foreign Office
FSI = Secretary to the Government of India in the Foreign and Political Department
GFM = German Foreign Ministry
Guerre = Guerre 1914-1918
IJMES = *International Journal of Middle East Studies*
IO = India Office
ISA = Israel State Archives
JB = *Journal de Beyrouth*
l = letter
L/P&S = India Office, Political and Secret Departmental Records
MAE = Ministère des Affaires Etrangères
memo = memorandum
MEJ = *Middle East Journal*
MES = *Middle Eastern Studies*
MG = Ministère de la Guerre
MW = *Muslim World*
NS = Nouvelle Série
PRO = Public Record Office
r = report
RMM = *Revue du Monde Musulman*
SSI = Secretary of State for India
Syrie-Liban = Levant 1918-1929, Syrie-Liban-Cilicie
t = telegram
WO = War Office

Introduction

In the period following the Young Turk revolution in 1908 and
before the outbreak of World War I, some twenty Arab societies
seeking solutions to the plight of the Arabs in the Ottoman
Empire were founded within and beyond the Empire's confines.
These societies entered the history of the modern Middle East as
"the Arab national societies": that is, they were considered
organizations striving for the goals of a single Arab national
movement that supposedly existed in that period. This label was
derived primarily from George Antonius' book, *The Arab Awakening*, where, for propagandistic purposes and perhaps also for
lack of knowledge, the societies were presented in this light.
Written in English and therefore widely read by European
researchers and writers, that book was long considered the "official history" of Arab nationalism. Only several decades after its
publication did researchers begin to dissociate themselves from
it. Many important episodes in the history of modern Middle
East nonetheless still continue to be presented as Antonius
described them. Among them is the saga of the Arab societies.
  This book presents a completely different picture. It proves
that these societies fell into four ideological categories: Arabism
(societies such as *al-Fatat* and *al-'Ahd*), which began as moderate and not clearly defined, was carried to extremes in response
to the Turkification policy of the Young Turks and even developed in a very few cases into a pan-Arab ideology; Lebanonism
("The Lebanese Revival"), with its origins in the Lebanese
desire to maintain the special status of their mountain; and Syrianism ("The Decentralization Party"), which began in the second half of the nineteenth century, but expanded in response to
the rapid decline of the Empire at the start of the twentieth century. One can also discern early signs of Iraqism in this period.
The Egyptians, outside the Empire and forming an independent
nationalism of their own, were unconnected to any of these
trends, and are therefore beyond the scope of this study.
  The book is divided into three sections. "Beginnings"
describes precursors of the various national trends in the Arab
Middle East during the second half of the nineteenth century
and the first eight years of the twentieth century. It begins with
the Syrian thinker Butrus al-Bustani, whom I consider the first
Syrian nationalist of modern times. The second and major

section, "The Arab Societies 1908-14", gives a narrative account of the history of the Arab societies without commentary. The purpose is to describe history "as it actually happened"; "*wie es eigentlich gewesen*", to cite Ranke's words. "The Arab Societies: An Analysis" then examines ideological, political and sociological aspects of these societies. It analyses their characters and activities, explaining how all were integrated into a single albeit multi-nuanced system. This section tries to reach an understanding of the ideological trends which emerged in the pre-war period and were represented by the said societies. It explains how and why the societies became a turning point in the history of the modern Middle East, their impact reaching beyond the period under discussion, to some degree extending even to this very day.

The book is based on documents from the Archives du Ministère des Affaires Etrangères and the Archives Nationales in Paris; the Archives du Ministère de la Guerre, Service Historique de l'Armée de Terre in' Vincennes; the Public Record Office at Kew; the Foreign and Commonwealth Office, Library and Records Department, and the India Office Library and Records in London; and the Central Zionist Archives and the Israel State Archives in Jerusalem. In these archives I found many original documents of the societies and also examined documents of French and British ambassadors and consuls, as well as, to a lesser degree, those of German and Zionist representatives. These diplomats and their assistants worked actively among the members of the societies, and had an impressive knowledge about them.

This book, however, does not focus on the attitudes of the European states towards the Arab question, but on the Arab point of view itself. In order to understand this point of view, I examined many memoirs by participants in the societies, as well as the press in Arabic and other languages. I examined these books and newspapers in the Israel National Library in Jerusalem; the Tel Aviv and Bar-Ilan University Libraries and that of the University of Haifa; the Bibliothèque Nationale in Paris and Versailles; the library of the Ecole Nationale des Langues Orientales Vivantes of Paris; and the British Library in London.

I attempted to see the chain of events through the eyes of those who lived them, and not from the retrospective of a researcher living three-quarters of a century after these events had taken place. This influenced the way I translated the original Arabic documents when translation was needed. Eventually, I decided to translate Arabic words and terms in the way they were used by the players of the period, and in relation to the events recounted. Thus, for example, I translated the Arabic term *milla* as "nation", when I assessed that as being its meaning in a certain placard, even though this term is usually translated differently in dictionaries. Such examples of independent translation are numerous, and I mention particularly here the two terms *wataniyya* and *qawmiyya* which are usually rendered as 'patriotism' and 'nationalism'. I rejected these common translations in the context of the period, as discussed in the chapter on the ideology of the societies.

The utilization of many original documents, which were known only in part to previous researchers on this subject, explains why the conclusions of this book are so different from those of earlier studies. Its chapters describe and clarify the historical processes that took place in the Arab Middle East during the first decade and a half of the twentieth century. My intention is, in fact, to present a new and different history of the emergence of the Arab movements on the eve of the First World War.

Part I

BEGINNINGS

Chapter 1

BUTRUS AL-BUSTANI

From the beginning Butrus al-Bustani (1819-83) did not fear expressing his own mind. He was born in the village of Dabya in the Lebanon and graduated from the Patriarchal School in 'Ayn Waraqa, but in 1840 he left the Maronite faith for Protestantism and fled to Beirut, fearing death from emissaries of the Maronite Patriarch, who had put a price on his head. He began then to assist in the activities of American missionaries in the Levant and worked for a time as an interpreter in the American and French consulates in Beirut. The 1860 massacres in the Lebanon and in Damascus constituted a turning point in his life. He left missionary activities and began to work for greater Arab cultural homogeneity among the Syrians, which he hoped would lead to the creation of a common consciousness and then patriotic feelings among the Syrians.[1]

Following the 1860 massacres, al-Bustani began publishing a weekly paper called *Nafir Suriyya*, which called upon the Syrian people to unite and cooperate in reconstructing their ruined land. In 1863 he founded, with the aid of British and American friends, the *al-Madrasa al-Wataniyya* (National School), where he served for 12 years as an educator for youngsters of all communities and regions of Syria, teaching them religious tolerance and national ideals. He contributed to the Arabic language—which for him was not merely a means but a basis for national identity—by publishing the dictionary *Muhit al-Muhit*, to which he devoted ten years of his life, and for which he received a prize of 250 liras from the Ottoman sultan and a decoration. Another contribution by al-Bustani was writing the encyclopaedia *Da'irat al-Ma'arif*, intended to include all information pertaining to the Eastern world; he managed to publish six volumes of this encyclopaedia before his death.[2]

Al-Bustani disseminated his ideological notions through a series of newspapers he published, beginning with *Nafir Suriyya*, and continuing, in 1870, with *al-Jinan* (headed by the verse *hubb al-watan min al-iman* — the love of one's fatherland is the edict of faith), *al-Janna*, and *al-Junayna*.

In *Nafir Suriyya* al-Bustani wrote: "Syria . . . is our fatherland

... and the population of Syria, whatever their creed, community, racial origin or groups are the sons of our fatherland." Those who replaced love of the fatherland by sectarian fanaticism were not worthy of belonging to Syria and were enemies of the fatherland.[3] He believed that religious solidarity should be replaced by patriotic solidarity;[4] for by spreading weakness and disagreement, and dividing the nation into many sects concerned only with their own interests, religious solidarity was leading the nation into disaster. Therefore Syrians desiring progress must abandon religious solidarity and strive for national identity.[5] A nation for al-Bustani was a people united by its *jinsiyya*, like the French or the Germans, who fulfilled the commonly accepted criteria for nationhood: living in one land and speaking one language. In his opinion the Syrians were a nation, according to these criteria.[6]

In addition to his nationalist ideology, al-Bustani strove for individual rights, religious freedom, equality and liberty. The people, in his opinion, would not permit a tyrannic and arbitrary regime. They were ready to be imprisoned rather than submissively accept repression. The nation created the state (*dawla*) to serve its own interests and therefore the interests of the state and the interests of the nation must be reconciled.[7]

Al-Bustani's attitude towards the West was ambivalent. On the one hand he claimed that the East must recover by exploiting the knowledge of the Europeans. The achievements of the West should not be ignored, and what Europe had accomplished over a long period of time should be adopted quickly in the East. On the other hand he believed that the West should not be imitated blindly. The Arabs should choose what was suitable for them in order to build their new culture, obviously taking from Europe the idea of national unity.[8]

Al-Bustani saw himself as an Ottoman subject and did not strive to cut himself off from the Empire. Nevertheless he saw Syria as his basic fatherland within the Empire—his *watan*. The expressions *hubb al-watan* and *bilad Suriyya*[9] appeared for the first time with their modern meanings in al-Bustani's writings. Butrus al-Bustani may therefore be considered the first of the Syrian nationalists in the modern age.

An alternative ideology to that of al-Bustani, an Arab ideology, was espoused by his contemporary Ibrahim al-Yaziji (1847-1906), a Greek Catholic from Beirut, who called in 1868 for a national awakening of the Arabs. He extolled the splendour of the Arabs in the past and saw them as a nation that within a short time had achieved more than any other nation. In his opinion, the Europeans had succeeded in progressing quickly only because they had borrowed their knowledge from the Arabs. The Arabs themselves had begun to degenerate only after non-Arabs (meaning the Turks) had gained control over them. In order to bring back the days of their splendour the Arabs must rid themselves of strangers and fanaticism. Only in this way would they succeed in regaining their previous position.[10]

Chapter 2

THE INDEPENDENCE MOVEMENT IN SYRIA

At the same time that Butrus al-Bustani and others were crystal-lizing their ideologies, there were those who were not satisfied with ideas and turned to action. The first rallying cry against the Turkish regime in Syria came from Aleppo. The British consul there reported in 1858 on a readiness among the Muslim popu-lation in the ports of northern Syria to secede from the Ottoman Empire and to establish a new Arab state under the sovereignty of the sharifs of Mecca. He also reported that there was an atmosphere of incitement against the authorities in Aleppo and that a number of incidents had occurred there.[1]

A broader and much more significant independence move-ment began in Syria at the time of the Ottoman-Russian War in 1877-78. During this period the Ottoman Empire seemed on the verge of disintegration. Several of the national groups in the Empire, such as the Montenegrans and the Serbs, demanded greater autonomy. The Albanians demanded that their country be protected from foreign occupation. The Armenians demanded administrative reforms. Austria-Hungary strove to gain control of Bosnia and Herzegovina. Russia strove to conquer regions in Northeast Anatolia. The Syrians, who had begun to worry about the fate of their country, started discussions about ways of protecting it from foreign occupation. Very soon these discus-sions crystallized into an active movement centred in Beirut.

Ahamd al-Sulh, the founder of the movement, was a Muslim from Beirut. He gathered together a number of his friends and they began discussing appropriate means to deal with the situ-ation. At the next stage contacts were made with Sidon and Jabal 'Amil and the founders stayed in Sidon for two months to discuss the situation further. From Sidon the founding group turned to Damascus and there made contact with some of the city's notables, telling them of their fears for Syria's fate were the Ottoman Empire to disintegrate. From Damascus the members of the group turned to Amir 'Abd al-Qadir al-Jaza'iri, an Alge-rian leader who had fought against the French occupation in Algeria until 1847, and then had been exiled and in 1854 arrived in Syria. For three days they stayed with him and discussed the situation in the country and ways of rescuing it. Then they returned to Beirut.

From Beirut al-Sulh began a correspondence with many leaders in various Syrian towns and invited them to come to Beirut for consultations. For this purpose Munah al-Sulh, Ahmad's son, and Ahmad 'Abbas al-Azhari,[2] a Muslim who was a graduate of al-Azhar, were also sent to the towns of northern Syria, to Aleppo, Homs, Hama and Latakia, where they met with the town leaders and with the heads of the 'Alawi tribes. Afterwards they went south to Damascus and from there to the Harwan and the Druze mountain, and invited their leaders for consultations in Beirut. At the appointed time they all gathered together in Beirut and conducted secret sessions to discuss the means they should employ for the defence of their country. After 20 days of consultations a decision was reached to meet again in a sort of secret congress in Damascus and to complete the discussions there.

The congress was organized towards the end of the Ottoman-Russian War, in 1878. It was attended by some 30 leaders and notables, among them representatives of the Shi'ites from Jabal 'Amil and Sidon. The congress participants formulated a plan for the secession of Syria from the Ottoman Empire as an independent state that would control the regions now called Syria, Jordan, Lebanon and Israel. As ruler of this state the congress participants chose Amir 'Abd al-Qadir al-Jaza'iri, who had great authority in Syria at that time, because of his respected family background, because he was a national hero and a statesman of great stature in their eyes, and because he had already established a strong Arab state in Algeria and had fought to defend it from French occupation. It is noteworthy that the fact that he was an Algerian and not a Syrian did not bother the congress participants.

The day after the session in which al-Jaza'iri was chosen, Ahmad al-Sulh went to his palace in Dumar to tell him of the decision. Al-Jaza'iri raised three reservations: He insisted that the spiritual connection between Syria and the Ottoman caliphate must remain and that the Ottoman caliph must remain the caliph of the Muslims; he demanded a *bay'a* (loyalty oath) from all residents of Syria; and he wanted a definition of what sort of independence the congress participants were striving for. Most of the participants supported his stand concerning the caliphate and all of them supported the idea of the *bay'a*. As to defining the type of independence, it was decided that they supported the idea in principle, but they would put off the discussion of its scope until the end of the Ottoman-Russian War, when the exact situation of the Empire would be known.

The Syrian congress participants followed with great interest the Berlin Congress which took place after the war ended. They decided that if it became clear during the Berlin Congress that one of the Powers wanted to take control of Syria, they would demand complete independence. If, however, there was no such danger, they would only demand self-government, as Egypt and some of the Balkan countries had. In order to prepare the ground for this, it was decided that al-Jaza'iri would tour various regions in Syria and that a delegation would be sent to Europe to gain the support of the European states for this movement.

At this stage the movement's plans were revealed to the Ottoman authorities, who immediately took steps against the members of the movement. Some of them were followed, some were exiled to distant parts of Syria, and some were forced to leave the country. Moreover, contact between 'Abd al-Qadir al-Jaza'iri and Ahmad al-Sulh was forbidden. The steps taken by the authorities, as well as the results of the Berlin Congress, in which the European countries prevented Russia from conquering Istanbul and destroying the Empire, made it impossible for the plans of the independence movement to be carried out.[3]

But it was not only the fears of a foreign power gaining control over Syria that had led to these separatist tendencies. In July 1878 the French representative in Damascus reported on the increasing bitterness among the population because of the acts of injustice perpetrated by the tyrannical authorities. This bitterness was expressed in the appearance of placards plastered on the walls of houses in the city during the night, which publicly denounced the behaviour of the authorities. The French representative noted that this means of expression had not been customary before, and might be a sign of awakening among a people that had long accepted subordination. He included in his report translations of two placards that he had managed to obtain. The first included a call to the Syrian population to remove the yoke of oppression and the second included a sharp and direct attack on the Vali and listed a series of unjust acts that he had perpetrated. The French representative added that one of the notables of Damascus had already spoken to him in similar language and had said that the corrupt officials that were sent from Istanbul must be removed. Moreover, the notable asked rhetorically if the local people were not capable of administering Syria.[4]

A later echo of the independence movement in Syria appeared

in a report by the French consul-general in Beirut. He reported in October 1879 that the British ambassador, who was touring Syria at the time, had asked the Vali Midhat Pasha if there was any truth in the reports of a great Arab conspiracy with branches in Aleppo, Mosul, Baghdad, Medina and Mecca. Midhat answered that he had also heard of such a conspiracy. A senior official in the vilayet told the French consul-general that as far as he knew this conspiracy was planning the establishment of an Arab state which would unite the provinces of Aleppo, Damascus, Baghdad, Yemen and others, and that this state would be headed by an Arab sultan, apparently Amir 'Abd al-Qadir al-Jaza'iri. The senior official mentioned that until then no practical steps for this plan had actually been carried out.[5]

During the Ottoman-Russian War of 1877-78 there was some correspondence on the subject of the secession of the Arabs from the Ottoman Empire between Yusuf Karam, the exiled Maronite leader from North Lebanon,[6] and Amir 'Abd al-Qadir al-Jaza'iri. In a letter sent to the amir from his exile in Rome, Karam expressed his opinion that in order for the Arab countries to be rescued, they must be united under the leadership of al-Jaza'iri. If it would not be possible to find a solution to the problem by cooperating with the Ottoman authorities, then there would be no alternative to the secession of the Arab countries from the Ottoman Empire.[7] In this letter as well as others Karam used quite modern terminology to define his ideas:

> It would be better, my honored master, that you cut the Arab countries free from the Ottoman government, countries which naturally long to revive the power and the rights of the race (jins) and the fatherland (watan), than to watch the downfall of us all . . . No other way is left for the Arab race to defend itself from the attacks of the ambitious ones except by giving the bow to the one who is shooting with it and the amirate to the one who is worthy of it.[8]

In another letter Karam suggested to al-Jaza'iri that the structure of the regime in the Arab countries and the connections between them after their secession from the Empire should be based on a confederation:

> You will appoint independent amirs over the Arab territories, and they will transfer money to you according to what will be decided, and they will unite their ranks under your standard against any attack . . . This is the sort of policy that the Prussian government saw fit to take and it used this policy in organizing Germany out of independent territories that were united into a confederation.[9]

And in another letter Karam wrote:

> There is no escape now from the kindling of the spirit of racial friendship (*ulfa jinsiyya*) for the emancipation of the Arab countries, in order to made clear to the other countries of the world that our race is demanding its essential rights.[10]

'Abd al-Qadir al-Jaza'iri apparently supported the idea of an Arab confederation, but he did not want to work for this idea openly, apparently because he had not forgotten that he himself was a political refugee in Damascus. He expressed willingness to meet with Yusuf Karam, but the end of the war, which did indeed harm the Empire but did not destroy it, also ended these contacts.

Chapter 3

THE SECRET SOCIETY OF BEIRUT

At the same time that Muslims from all parts of Syria were working for the realization of their independence plan, a small group of Christians was active in Beirut, also secret and no less revolutionary, but motivated by fierce hatred for the oppressive Ottoman rule rather than by the fear of Syria's occupation by a foreign power

The Secret Society of Beirut[1] was established as a result of the preaching of Elias Habbalin,[2] a Maronite who taught French in the Syrian Protestant College of Beirut from 1871 to 1874. Habbalin, who had been influenced by French revolutionary ideas, preached to his students at the College to revolt against the Turks and against the injustice and corruption of the government. In 1875 Habbalin left for Egypt, but the ideas he had planted in the minds of his students took root and it was these students who established the society in the same year.[3]

The society began its activities with a founding nucleus of 12 members,[4] Christians, mostly graduates of the Syrian Protestant College, such as Faris Nimr, Ya'qub Sarruf, Shahin Makaryus, and the poet Ibrahim al-Yaziji.[5] At their first meetings they used to cite a phrase attributed to the Turks: "*Inna al-Turki fawqa al-Muslim wal-Muslim fawqa al-Masihi*" (the Turk is above the Muslim and the Muslim is above the Christian)—meant to express their degradation at the hands of the Turks. But these young people soon understood that they needed the cooperation and assistance of the Muslims in order to create a broader front against the Turks. They understood that in order to achieve their goal they must build a movement based on what they had in common with the Muslims—"Arabism" (*'uruba*). They tried to foster the cooperation they hoped for by including Muslims in the Freemason branch in Beirut. And indeed, some Muslims joined the Freemasons and then the society as well, which included about 70 members at its peak. But even these Muslims agreed to cooperate with the Christians only in the struggle against the injustice and tyranny of the Turks and did not agree with the ultimate goal of the society: the removal of the Turks from the vilayet of Syria and from the autonomous sanjaq of the

Lebanon. This was an expression of the essential difference in the attitudes of the Christians and the Muslims towards the Ottoman Empire. While the Christians did not consider the Turkish government as their own the Muslims were able to consider the Muslim empire as their state.[6]

At first the members of the society were content with the secret evening meetings on the rocky coast of South Beirut, at which they discussed their revolutionary ideas and ways of achieving their goals. After three or four years they decided that they must disseminate their ideas by distributing placards. The members of the society began to go out into the streets of Beirut by night and put up their placards on the walls of buildings, especially near the foreign consulates. In order that the authorities would not be able to identify them, the authors altered their handwriting and sometimes inserted deliberate grammatical errors into their texts. On the morning after the distribution of the placards the members of the society would mix with the crowds that were reading them, listen to their reactions and formulate the following placards accordingly. It seems that there were supporters of the society's ideas in other Syrian cities as well, since similar placards were also distributed in Damascus, Tripoli and Sidon. Even in Dayr al-Qamar a similar nucleus was founded by the young Maronite Salim 'Ammun, who had been influenced by Alexandre Dumas' book *The Three Musketeers*. Together with two of his friends he tried to imitate the musketeers and set up a secret society for the liberation of the Lebanon from the Turks.[7]

At the beginning of June 1880 placards appeared in the streets of Beirut and Damascus and were immediately removed by the police. They described the magnificent past of the Arabs and demanded autonomy for Syria.[8] A few days later additional placards appeared in Beirut and were again confiscated by the authorities. Headed by a picture of a sword, they called upon the Syrians not to flinch from activity against the Turks and not to remain their bonded slaves. At the end of June placards appeared for a third time, this time only two or three of them. Also headed by a picture of a sword, they called upon the Syrians not to rely on the reforms of the Turks, to fend for themselves and to take their fate in their hands. The authors of the placards expressed their readiness to sacrifice themselves for the fatherland.[9]

The British consul-general in Beirut, who hastened to report the appearance of the placards, noted that they had very little influence on the population, which treated them as curiosities.

Even the Vali Midhat Pasha was apathetic towards the phenomenon and did not react. The purpose of this, according to the consul-general, was to prove the sad state of the vilayet and the need to give him more authority. He ruled out the possibility that Midhat Pasha himself was the author of the placards, since it would be too dangerous for him. The consul-general noted that for five years a secret society had been active in Syria, and was striving for administrative autonomy. Its members agreed that the Sultan should be recognized as their sovereign, but if the authorities would not agree to some of their demands they would strive for complete independence. It was possible, he added, that it was the members of this society who had distributed the placards.[10]

In late December 1880 additional placards went up in Beirut, Tripoli and Sidon. This time headed by a picture of two swords, they were addressed to the "sons of the fatherland (*watan*)". The placards attacked the tyrannic regime of the Turks, who were enslaving the Arabs, and announced that after consultations that had taken place throughout the country it had been decided that a series of demands should be put to the authorities, and if these demands were not accepted there would be no alternative to the use of the sword. The demands were:

Firstly: Independence, in which we will be partners with our brothers, the Lebanese, since our national interests unite all of us. Secondly: The Arabic language will be official in the land, and its speakers will have full freedom to publish their opinions, writings and newspapers, in accord with the obligations of humanity, progress and culture. Thirdly: Our soldiers will be limited to the defence of the fatherland alone and will be released from serving the Turkish commanders.

This proclamation included verses of a poem composed several years earlier by Ibrahim al-Yaziji.[11]

The British consul-general who reported the appearance of the placards also noted that the Beirut notables hastened to hand the Vali a petition in which they expressed their loyalty to the Sultan and deprecated revolutionary movements. In Sidon it was mainly the Christians who paid attention to the placards, and several who were suspected of posting them on the walls were arrested. In Damascus the secret police arrested two Christians, and they were expelled from the country. From the fact that the placards appeared simultaneously in a number of places the consul-general deduced that this was not a matter involving only a few individuals but a coordinated activity of a secret society, with branches in various cities in Syria, and from the style he deduced that their authors were educated people. The consul-general also reported suspicions that had been raised concerning the "Society of Good Intentions" (*Jam'iyyat al-Magasid al-Khayriyya*), a philanthropic organization, which was rumoured to be responsible for the placards. Though a number of Christian notables from Sidon had written to the Vali that it was this society that was responsible, at this point no steps had been taken against it. In the consul-general's opinion it was probable that the placards were distributed by a revolutionary society that had united with the Society of Good Intentions at its foundation a year and a half earlier and was now doing its work through this society.[12]

The question that aroused the interest of the population and the foreign diplomatic representatives in Syria, and later also the authorities in Istanbul, was the question of the involvement or lack of involvement of the Vali Midhat Pasha in the appearance of the placards.[13] Midhat Pasha (1822-83), one of the initiators of the 1876 constitution, had been appointed by Sultan 'Abd al-Hamid II as the Vali of Syria a short time after being discharged by him from his position as Grand Vizier. The period of his service as Vali of Syria was marked by tense relations with the Sultan and by the attempts of Midhat to prove that he should be granted more authority in the administration of the vilayet. The placards appeared for the first time in June 1880, at approximately the same time that Midhat Pasha offered the Sultan his resignation for the second time, with the claim that he did not have enough authority. His attempt to resign was rejected by the Sultan and it may be assumed that it was in Midhat's interest to increase the existing tension in order that his demands would be met.[14]

It should be noted that in 1879 Midhat had already told the British ambassador, who was visiting Syria at the time, that there were secret societies in Syria and that he expected trouble if the Sultan continued with his present policy. When the ambassador asked him if he knew about an Arab-Muslim conspiracy originating in Mecca or Medina and its intention to revolt against the Ottoman government, Midhat preferred for his own reasons to confirm the story, and he even added that as far as he knew the organizers of the conspiracy had already mobilized 100,000 people in the cities and towns of Syria to carry it out. These words of course impressed the British ambassador, and he asked Sultan 'Abd al-Hamid to grant Midhat broader authority to institute reforms, lest a movement demanding autonomy and even independence and secession from the Empire should grow in Syria.[15] And so it was in Midhat's interest to continue to create an intentional atmosphere of crisis and political instability in order to put pressure on the Sultan to give him the authority to strengthen his position and to realize his reform plans. The fact that Midhat Pasha did not seem particularly troubled by the appearance of the placards starting in June 1880 only contributed to the spread of the rumours that he was the active force behind them.[16]

On the other hand, it should be remembered that all of Midhat's reform plans had an Ottoman and not a separatist basis, and so it is implausible that he would have had connections with a society having Syrian separatist goals. Furthermore, in the reports of 'Abd al-Hamid's spies, who followed Midhat's activities, there is no mention of any connections of his with a separatist movement of this sort. Even those reports that dealt with the placards attributed them only to Midhat and his circle, and not to any cooperative activity on his part with local Syrians.[17]

It appears that the placards distributed in 1880 came from two different sources. While some of them, whose contents were described above, were indeed written by the Christian Secret Society of Beirut, there were also others that were not. In August 1880 the British vice-consul in Damascus reported the appearance of proclamations written in Qur'anic language that called upon the masses "to rise and shake off the rule of those who set the precepts of the Koran to nought; act as infidels; and have brought misery and ruin upon the true believers of Syria". He expressed the opinion that they were composed by 'ulama' (religious sages).[18] It can therefore be hypothesized that such proclamations were distributed by the Muslim Society of Good Intentions, with the encouragement of Midhat Pasha for the reasons mentioned above.

At any rate, Midhat Pasha's opponents, who were numerous, began to spread rumours that he was interested in being the ruler of Syria. 'Abd al-Hamid decided not to take any more risks, and with the appearance of the first placards in Damascus he sent a commission of enquiry to Syria. The commission was headed by Husayn Fawzi Pasha, a general who had been appointed Mushir (field-marshal) of the Fifth Army in Syria. The commission arrived in Beirut unexpectedly and without prior announcement on 29 July 1880, and three days later it had reached Damascus. It began its investigation immediately. It discovered that Midhat was not liked by the population, especially by the Muslims, who were ready to confirm the Sultan's worst suspicions concerning Midhat's ambitions. Husayn Fawzi reported this immediately to the Sultan, who sent Midhat a telegram on 4 August 1880, discharging him from his position as Vali of Syria and appointing him Vali of Smyrna.[19] In contrast to Midhat Pasha's ignoring the appearance of the placards, the new Vali Hamdi Pasha ordered a general search for the authors after the next wave in December 1880. This search ended in arrests, not necessarily of the right persons.[20]

The reaction expected from the population to the call of the Secret Society of Beirut did not occur. In the wake of the increased pressure of the Ottoman security services the society stopped its activities in 1882-83 and burned its papers.[21] Some of its members emigrated to Egypt.

It was not only in the cities of Syria that revolutionary placards appeared. In May 1881 "A Manifesto to the Arab Nation (*umma*)" appeared in Baghdad, put out by the Society for the Protection of the Rights of the Arab Nation (*milla*). It was addressed to both the Muslims and the Christians of Syria. To the Muslims the proclamation said:

> For centuries the Arab nation, Muslim and Christian, has suffered from all manner of troubles and iniquities at the hands of the Turks, until all of our land has become desert and waste ... Look at how the Turks sold our land to the Russians, to the Montenegrans and to the Bulgarians ... Look at the Serbs and the Bulgarians [who had achieved independence] ... Where are you and where are they?! Which of you is now an Amir, which of you is now Vizier, and which of you is now a Mudir? Every one of you is poor. Your greatest, like your lowest, is despised, and your property and hopes are in the hands of the Turks ... You are now neglecting your rights ... and if you will continue in this neglect you will regret it.

The proclamation called upon the Christians of Syria to unite with the Muslims in order to achieve liberty, since they had common interests. It ended as follows:

> Our success and our emancipation from the Turks are conditional on the event that one opinion, one hand and one goal will emanate from you ... Do not give the Turks any of your men or a dirham of your money, since the Turks are acting to sell your land.[22]

This look at the independence movement in Syria and the Secret Society of Beirut shows that there were separatist movements at that time both among the Muslims and among the Christians in Syria. It seems that the Muslim Syrian independence movement had a broader base and the people who participated in it had a higher status than those who took part in the Christian Secret Society of Beirut. The motivations of the two movements were different. While the Muslim Syrian independence movement feared the occupation of the land by a Christian foreign power, the Christian Secret Society of Beirut acted out of opposition to the Muslim Ottoman regime of oppression.

Chapter 4

AL-AFGHANI AND 'ABDUH

Among the most outstanding thinkers of the Middle East in the second half of the nineteenth century were Jamal al-Din al-Afghani and Muhammad 'Abduh.[1] The Persian al-Afghani (1839-97) was not an Arab nationalist but a pan-Islamist, or perhaps an Islamic nationalist, meaning that for him the nation was based on religious rather than ethnic unity.[2] The Egyptian 'Abduh (1849-1905) was not an Arab nationalist either, and, if he was a nationalist at all, which is doubtful, then he was an Egyptian one. Nevertheless both of them made a certain contribution to the design of the nationalist movements in the Arab Middle East. Their contribution (especially that of al-Afghani) was expressed in the design of the framework for these movements, that is, the call for revolutionary activism that would be expressed in a struggle against European imperialism as well as against tyrannical local governments.

Al-Afghani's activities and preaching contributed to the spread of a new revolutionary spirit and a new activist approach to the politics of the Middle East. He was in favour of political assassinations, if these were essential for the realization of his goals. When he reached the conclusion that it was necessary to get rid of Khedive Isma'il, he suggested an attack on his life when he was passing in his carriage on his daily ride on the Qasr al-Nil bridge. 'Abduh supported the idea enthusiastically. Though the plan was abandoned because they could not find a suitable person to carry it out, the two of them continued to contrive plans for deposing Khedive Isma'il. Later they decided that in order to achieve a representative assembly in Egypt and to implement reforms it was necessary to get Khedive Tawfiq out of the way. In his book on "Islam and Christianity" 'Abduh wrote explicitly that it was necessary to depose a ruler if he was not worthy and harmed the public interest. As a civilian ruler, he was under the control of the *umma* and it had the right to remove him. The two thinkers also said in an article in their newspaper *al-'Urwa al-Wuthqa* (the Indissoluble Tie) that if an evil tyrannical ruler arose over a nation, then it was the nation's obligation to depose him and to put a new, better ruler in his place.[3]

In Egypt, from 1871 to 1879, al-Afghani taught his students theology and philosophy, but at the same time he warned them of the danger of European intervention and of the need for national unity in order to oppose it. In an article that al-Afghani wrote in the 1880s, "The Philosophy of National Unity Based on Race and Linguistic Unity", he expressed his opinion that there were two kinds of connections in the world, the connection of language, on which nationalism and national unity were based, and the connection of religion. In his opinion, there was no doubt that linguistic unity was more capable of existing for a long time than religious unity. A nation kept its language and its nationalism for a thousand years, while it changed its religion two or three times. The change of religion would not destroy a nationalism based on language. Therefore, he added, connections and unity stemming from linguistic unity were more influential than religious connections in most of the events in our world.⁴ Yet, in spite of these positive words by al-Afghani on nationalism, it should be remembered that in general his attitude towards nationalism based on race and language was characterized by articles of the sort that he published in al-'Urwa al-Wuthqa, in which he wrote: "Whoever holds fast to the Islamic religion will, when his faith is deeply rooted, forget about his race and his people."⁵

Muhammad 'Abduh was aware that the common history and identity of interests of people living in the same country create ties between them in spite of differences in religion. The importance of unity, which influenced his opinion regarding the Islamic reform, also influenced his opinion in regard to the nation. He considered unity paramount in political life. The strongest form of unity existed, in his opinion, between those who shared the same land, not only in the geographical sense but also as the centre of their civil rights and obligations and as the object of their love and honour.⁶

The two thinkers reached the peak of their joint activity in spreading their ideas in Paris in 1884, when they founded a secret society called al-'Urwa al-Wuthqa, whose members were strict and educated Muslims from India, Egypt, North Africa and Syria. The purpose of the society was "to unite the Muslims, to awaken them from their sleep, to inform them of the dangers threatening them and to guide them on the path they must take in order to withstand these dangers". Every new member of the society swore "that he would invest whatever he could for the revival of Muslim unity . . . that he would search for means for the strengthening of Islam", and so on. Branches of the society were to arrange conferences, and at the end of each the participants would donate money anonymously for the common fund. It seems that the society's newspaper of the same name, which was for the most part distributed without charge, was funded by these donations.

The newspaper appeared for 18 editions between 13 March and 16 October 1884, having been edited in a small Paris attic. Ideas for the articles were inspired by al-Afghani, while the formulation and publishing were the province of 'Abduh.[7] One of the newspaper's primary goals was arousing the people of the East against foreign occupation. It fought assiduously against foreign occupations of Islamic countries and especially against the British occupation of Egypt. One of the articles claimed, "The British government is very hostile to the Muslims". Another article argued that "It would be more appropriate for the Ottoman army to clash with the English than to serve them . . . The Egyptians, both felaheen and bedouins, should know that the British aspire to enslave them . . ."[8] The response to such articles was that the British authorities in Egypt and India forbade the entry of the newspaper into those countries. In July 1884 the Egyptian government announced a ban on bringing it into Egypt and the imposition of fines from five to 25 Egyptian pounds on anyone who was caught with a copy in his possession. Soon the Ottoman Empire also announced a ban on bringing the newspaper into its territory.[9] Owing to the constant surveillance that was placed on the newspaper and the barring of distribution in the countries for which it was intended, it ceased publication.

Shortly afterwards 'Abduh left Paris and went to Tunisia, where he propagandized for the society. Later he visited a number of other countries, where he worked to strengthen the society's branches. But 'Abduh gradually began to separate from al-Afghani's revolutionary inspiration, and in 1885 he went to Beirut, where he began a new stage of his life, the stage of Islamic reform.

Chapter 5

'ABD AL-RAHMAN AL-KAWAKIBI

Al-Afghani and 'Abduh are identified with the pan-Islam and Islamic reform movements. 'Abd al-Rahman al-Kawakibi (1854-1902), a Muslim from Aleppo, took another step forward towards the Arab movement, calling for the renewal of the Islamic world by moving its centre of gravity to the Arabs. Yet he was not an Arab nationalist. He did indeed awaken Arab consciousness with his ideas, but for him the Arabs were not the goal but only the means to achieve the renewal of the Islamic world.

'Abd al-Rahman al-Kawakibi[1] was born to a noble family of Kurdish origin, graduated from a traditional school run by his father and by the age of 22 was appointed editor of Aleppo's official newspaper. Two years later he began publishing his own newspaper, in which he called for the implementation of reforms and criticized the activities of the Vali of Aleppo. The price of this criticism was the closing of the newspaper, and the same fate befell his second newspaper, which he began publishing a year later. Al-Kawakibi then began to engage in politics and received various administrative and governmental positions. But his opinions once again led to tension in his relations with the Vali, which finally caused his resignation. Al-Kawakibi then decided to open an independent law office, but here too he found himself surrounded by the Vali's spies.

At this point al-Kawakibi was no longer willing to tolerate the situation, and together with other residents of Aleppo he complained about the Vali to the central government in Istanbul. As a result an emissary was sent from Istanbul in 1885 to investigate, and al-Kawakibi organized the presentation of the residents' complaints about the Vali before the emissary. The Vali on his part reacted by throwing al-Kawakibi and his supporters into prison on the false charge that they were involved in a plot against his life. Only due to the intervention of the emissary from Istanbul were they freed a few days later.

These events increased al-Kawakibi's popularity in the city, and in 1892 he was appointed to the position of mayor of Aleppo for a short time. After a number of attempts to implement reforms in the city he resigned from this position and went to Istanbul to see the nature of tyranny at close range. Upon his return to Aleppo he attempted to enter the tobacco trade, but he failed. He once again returned to the administrative system, this time in the position of head secretary of the Shar'i court in Aleppo, but he was dismissed as the result of an intrigue against him between the Vali and the qadi. He was appointed to other positions and again entered into confrontations with the authorities because of his opinions. The Vali increased his plottings against him, and incited Armenian residents of the city to raid his fields.

At that time Al-Kawakibi's book *Umm al-Qura* (The Mother of Villages—Mecca) was ready for publication, and he decided to publish it even if he would have to leave the Empire in order to do so. In 1889 al-Kawakibi left Syria secretly and went to Egypt. A few days later the Egyptian newspaper *al-Mu'ayyad* began to publish sections of his other book, *Taba'i' al-Istibdad* (The Nature of Tyranny). Shortly afterwards both books appeared in print and aroused much commotion. A sultanic command forbade bringing the books into the Empire. The Egyptian khedive 'Abbas Hilmi, of whom it was said that he desired the caliphate, was impressed by al-Kawakibi's powers of expression and hired him for 50 Egyptian pounds a month to write propaganda. For this purpose al-Kawakibi went on a six-month journey in 1901 to the Arabian Peninsula, East Africa and India, returning to Cairo three months before his death. He managed to write sequels to his two books, but he died before he was able to publish them.[2]

'Abd al-Rahman al-Kawakibi was a revolutionary by nature. He was once heard to say, "If I had an army at my command I would overthrow 'Abd al-Hamid's government in 24 hours."[3] He did not have an army, but his book *Taba'i' al-Istibdad* was clearly directed against the oppressive regime of the Sultan, in spite of the facts that 'Abd al-Hamid's name was not mentioned explicitly in the book, and that al-Kawakibi declared at the beginning that the book was not intended against any specific tyrant.[4] In its pages al-Kawakibi attacked the tyrannical ruler who related to his subjects as to a cow to be milked. The subjects must not make peace with this situation because the ruler was to serve the people and not vice versa. An intelligent society would know how to revolt against a tyrannical ruler, and the latter, when he saw the oppressed people opposing him, would cease his evil actions.

According to al-Kawakibi, political tyranny stemmed from

religious tyranny. While most religions tried to enslave the people to the holders of religious office, who exploited them, the original Islam was built on the foundations of political freedom standing between democracy and aristocracy. In the original Islam religious leaders did not control the people, and the existing situation, contrary to the spirit of Islam, was the cause of the sorry situation of the Muslims at the time.[5] The tyrannical ruler was afraid of knowledge. He preferred that his subjects remain ignorant, because ignorance made his rule easier. "Between tyranny and knowledge there is a continual war . . . and there is no doubt that the tyrant fears the revenge of his subjects more than they fear his power, since his fear derives from knowledge while their fear derives from ignorance . . ."[6] Tyranny led to extortion of the public's money. The government officials enjoyed the money of the public, and with the authorization of the ruler they harmed the rights of the public. Tyranny led to corruption in ethics. People cared only about their own interests and about pleasing the authorities. They lost their faith in one another and fear controlled them.[7] Tyranny also harmed culture, because culture depended on intelligence—to which the tyrant was opposed—"and everything that culture builds, in spite of its weakness, the tyrant destroys with his power". For the same reasons, tyranny also prevented progress.[8]

Al-Kawakibi called upon Muslims and non-Muslim Arabs to unite and to work together against tyranny. He called upon them to imitate the United States, which had achieved national unity (*ittihad watani*) rather than religious unity. "Let us take care of our lives in this world and let the religions rule in the next world."[9] In the last chapter of his book al-Kawakibi presented a series of rhetorical questions to his readers:

What is a nation or a people? Is it a heap of creatures . . . slaves of a king? Or is it a community connected by ties of race, language, fatherland and common rights?! What is a government? Is it a man and his assistants who gain control over people . . . and do whatever they want, or is it a political trust that is given by the nation for the administration of its common general interests?! What are the rights of the public? . . . What is equality of rights? . . . What are the rights of the individual? . . . Is the best government an unrestrained despotism, or . . . a presidential regime for life, or for a limited time?! . . . How should one legislate laws? . . .[10]

Al-Kawakibi summarized his book with three principles:

1. A nation that does not feel, in its entirety or in its majority, the

tortures of tyranny is not worthy of freedom; 2. Tyranny should not be fought with power but flexibly and gradually; 3. Before one fights tyranny one must prepare what will take the place of the tyranny.[11]

Al-Kawakibi's second book, *Umm al-Qura*, became publicly known when Rashid Rida serialized it in his periodical *al-Manar*, from April 1902 to February 1903. The subtitle of the book was "The protocol of the discussions and decisions of the Islamic Revival Congress which took place in Mecca in 1316" (1898/99 CE). Through this subtitle and by various means, including writing parts of the book in cipher, al-Kawakibi attempted to convince his readers that the congress he described and the society that was founded as a result were established facts and not merely the fruit of literary imagination.

Al-Kawakibi told his readers that he had decided to find the causes of the sorry state of Islam at the time and so he established the society, which included 22 educated members besides himself, from all parts of the Islamic world. This society met in 1316 in Mecca to discuss the necessary means for bringing about an Islamic revival. A scholar from Mecca was elected president of the society, while the author was elected as its secretary.[12] The first speaker at the society's congress was the president from Mecca, who described the decline of Islam, censured the ignorance that brought this about, and called for a return to the ways of the *salaf* (the early generations of Islam). He extolled the Arabs of the Arabian Peninsula, "who are between seven and eight million people, all *salaf*ist Muslims by belief."[13]

Then, during the following sessions of the congress described by al-Kawakibi, each of the other scholars expressed his opinion about the causes of the inferiority of the Islamic world at that time. Thus, for example, the Syrian scholar claimed that it was the dogmas which had entered Islam that had destroyed it.[14] The scholar from Jerusalem said that the cause of Islam's weakness was that the Muslim states had ceased to be representative democracies and had become absolute governments.[15] The Tunisian attributed the weakness of Islam to the fact that its rulers were ignorant despots,[16] while the representative from Istanbul said that not all the blame should be attributed to the rulers, who were only a few people, but rather that all the Muslims were ill in that "we have lost our freedom and we do not know what freedom is".[17] The scholar from Fez said that the disintegration of the Islamic world derived precisely from the weakness of the religious ties, which led to the weakening of the political ties.[18] The scholar from Medina, on the other hand, was of the opinion that the guilty ones were the religious extremists, in error and causing others to err, who had confused the minds of the masses.[19] According to the Kurdish member the decline was caused by the fact that the Muslims had stopped acquiring secular knowledge, such as mathematics and natural sciences, while these sciences were progressing in the West.[20] The Tatar said that the lack of leadership was responsible for the present state; there was no one to guide the nation.[21] The Najd member was of the opinion that Islam itself was responsible for the present situation "because the religion existing now . . is not the religion that characterized the *salaf*".[22]

At the seventh session of the congress the author's turn to speak arrived, and he listed 86 causes for the inferiority of the Islamic world. Among them were: fatalism; fruitless discussions about religious dogmas; religious rifts; intolerance; the insertion of distortions into religion; abandoning the way of the *salaf*; absolute government; the ban on freedom of speech; injustice and inequality; the control of the ignorant over religious offices; the stupidity of the rulers; the public's neglecting to stand up for their rights; the preference for defence and services over industry; uncritical acceptance of the written word; hostility towards the sciences; disorganization and inefficient use of time; lack of striving for perfection; imbalance between ability and willingness to act; neglect of women's education; and apathy.[23]

Al-Kawakibi also added a number of causes peculiar to the Ottoman Empire, which had led to the loss of two-thirds of its area over the past 60 years: uniform laws and uniform punishment throughout the Empire in spite of the differences between its various nations; clinging to centralized administration; lack of control over the actions of the administrative heads and the valis; giving authority in the provinces to unsuitable people so that they would be hated by the population, which would thus not cooperate with them against the Empire; discrimination among the nations of the Empire; lack of thought for the future; intrigues against enlightened thought out of the desire to prevent its development; administration of the Empire's affairs without consultations or discussions; a policy of silence; and others.[24]

At the following sessions the participants in the congress discussed the the society's programme, meant to lead to the renewal of the Islamic world. The introduction to the programme included the following:

1. The Muslims are in a state of general weakness. 2. This weakness must be cured quickly . . . 3. The cause of this weakness is the

negligence of the rulers, the 'ulama' and the amirs. 4. The germ causing the disease is absolute ignorance . . . 5. The most harmful sort of ignorance is the religious sort. 6. The remedy is: first, illumination of religious ideas; and second, finding a stimulant for progress in the minds of the youth. 7. The means to the remedy is the founding of certified study societies. 8. The scholars, the enlightened people among the leaders and the 'ulama' have the obligation to carry this out. 9. The ability to gradually eliminate this weakness exists particularly among the Arabs . . .[25]

According to its programme, the society had 100 members. The proposed centre of the society was in Mecca. The society would absolutely not intervene in political matters. It would not belong to, or even be associated with, any specific government, nor would it belong to any religious school or faction. It would work for general literacy, improvement in the basics of teaching the Arabic language and religious studies, and uniformity in the basics of teaching and in the textbooks. The society would publish an Arabic religious journal every month. It would work to hold an official congress of Muslim kings and amirs in Mecca.[26]

At the closing session of the congress the members of the society added to the protocol a declaration that by virtue of a number of unique characteristics which they possessed, the hopes of the society for the improvement of the situation of Islam were pinned on the Arabs of the Arabian Peninsula. The 26 reasons for this included the following: The light of Islam shone from the Arabian Peninsula; the Ka'ba was there; the peninsula was halfway between the Muslims of Western Africa and those of Eastern Asia; the region was freer than other Islamic lands from foreign influence; because of the poverty of the region, its people were free of desires and ambitions, and it was therefore fit for free people; the Arabs of the peninsula were the most learned in the laws of the religion because they had been practising it longest; they were the most fanatic in preserving Islam; there were no distortions in their religion; they were the most willing to tolerate suffering in order to realize their goals; they had not assimilated with foreigners; they were the most zealous for their freedom and independence, and they opposed oppression; their language, Arabic, was the richest of all the Muslims' languages, was known to all Muslims, and 100 million Muslims and non-Muslims spoke it; the Arabs had the longest history of all nations in keeping the principles of equal rights and consultation in public matters and communal life; as in the past, the Arabs were the most suitable religious authority for Muslims.[27]

In an appendix to the book al-Kawakibi presented a dialogue between the Indian member of the society and an amir. The amir expressed his opinion that "religion is one thing and the government is another . . . the administration of religion and the administration of the government were absolutely never united in Islam, except during the periods of the Rashidi caliphs and 'Umar ibn 'Abd al-'Aziz . . .". Afterwards the caliphate was separated from the secular government. The amir therefore suggested the following plan: an Arab caliph of Quraysh descent (from the tribe of Muhammad) would be set up in Mecca; his political authority would be limited to the Hijaz; the caliph would work for the establishment of an advisory council with 100 members from all the Islamic countries, which would concentrate only on religious matters; the oath to the caliph would become void if he transgressed certain conditions; the oath would be renewed every three years; the election of the caliph would be in the hands of the advisory council; the caliph would not intervene in political and administrative matters of other Islamic countries; the caliph would not have any sort of military force under his command; and internal security in the Hijaz would be in the hands of a military force of two to three thousand men, under the command of a Muslim from another state and defending the advisory council.[28]

Al-Kawakibi ended his book with the declaration that *Umm al-Qura* was an established fact and would continue to exist forever.[29] There were indeed those who believed this. One who went quite far was the French minister in Cairo, who reported, at the time that the book began to appear, that the *Umm al-Qura* Society had been founded 20 years earlier with the intention of deposing the caliph and replacing him with the former khedive of Egypt, Tawfiq. According to the minister, a branch of this society had been founded in Mecca, and after Tawfiq's death the society was disbanded, its Meccan members becoming supporters of the Grand Sharif there. The minister added that remnants of the society who were allies of the Young Turks now wanted to frighten the Sultan and to make him believe that the society still existed, with supporters who were carrying out conspiracies against him. However, the minister assured his readers that the society no longer existed and that it had no basis in Egypt.[30]

The *Umm al-Qura* Society was the fruit of al-Kawakibi's imagination, but the book's influence was not imaginary at all. The members of the Arab societies that were established at the beginning of the twentieth century read the book and were influenced by it, and some of them considered the *Umm al-Qura* Society the spiritual mother of the Arab societies founded afterwards.

Chapter 6

NAJIB 'AZURI AND THE LIGUE DE LA PATRIE ARABE

The Muslim 'Abd al-Rahman al-Kawakibi saw the improvement of the Islamic world as his goal and the Arabs as the agents for achieving this. The Christian Najib 'Azuri, on the other hand, saw the Arabs themselves as the goal. He was the first to advocate publicly their secession from the Ottoman Empire and the establishment of a new pan-Arab empire, in which religion would be absolutely separate from the state. (His solutions to the problems of religion and state were remarkably similar to those suggested by al-Kawakibi in the appendix to *Umm al-Qura.*) 'Azuri was thus the first person who merits being described as a pan-Arab nationalist—although a careful study of his activities from the time he was a senior official in the Ottoman Empire until his death in exile in Cairo raises the question of whether his ideology was really intended to advance Arab interests or whether it was simply a means for advancing his own.

Najib 'Azuri[1] (1873?-1916)[2] was born in Syria, studied at the School of Political Science in Paris and afterwards entered the School of Administration in Istanbul. In 1898, after he agreed to cease his activities among the Young Turks and declared his loyalty to the Sultan, he was appointed assistant to the governor of the sanjaq of Jerusalem. In Jerusalem 'Azuri married the sister of the wife of the governor's dragoman, and he soon began to cast his eyes on his new brother-in-law's position. When he did not succeed in obtaining this position, he tried to get that of director of the tobacco régie in Jaffa. Having failed in this attempt as well, he quarrelled with the governor and began to plot against him. The governor became angry and 'Azuri fled to Cairo in May 1904, leaving his wife and small son in Jaffa. In early June 1904 'Azuri initiated a series of savage propaganda attacks in the Arab newspaper *al-Ikhlas* against the governor of the sanjaq of Jerusalem, accusing him of corruption and taking bribes. It seems that these attacks infuriated the governor, and he asked the French consul-general in Jerusalem to bar distribution of this newspaper through the French postal system, since its entry into the Empire and distribution there had been banned. The consul-general complied with this request.

But 'Azuri's grudge against the governor was great, and in a book he wrote later he accused him of ignoring the quarantine requirements on travellers from Egypt during the great cholera epidemic in Egypt in August and September of 1902. 'Azuri claimed that the governor had allowed merchants from Egypt to enter the Jaffa market in return for 200,000 francs in taxes, and that as a result of this a cholera epidemic broke out a week later and killed 20,000 people. 'Azuri accused the governor's dragoman of permitting the release of a murderer for a bribe of 20,000 francs, 5,000 of which he pocketed while using the rest to bribe other officials. Only in this way, explained 'Azuri, did the dragoman succeed in accumulating 500,000 francs at a time when his salary was only 100 francs per month. In the wake of such attacks in the press, which continued after 'Azuri left Cairo for Paris, on 31 July 1904 he was put on trial in the criminal court in Istanbul. He was sentenced to death in absentia "because he left his position without permission and went to Paris, where he devoted himself to carrying out acts that harm the existence of the state".[3]

When he arrived in Paris 'Azuri founded the Ligue de la Patrie Arabe. This league consisted of 'Azuri himself and a Bordeaux-born Frenchman called Eugène Jung, who had previously held governmental positions in Indo-China.[4] In December 1904 and January 1905 the league published two manifestos in French and in Arabic that were distributed during the following months via the French postal system throughout the Ottoman Empire.

The first manifesto of the league, entitled "The Arab Lands for the Arabs", was addressed to "the enlightened and humane nations of Europe and North America" and declared that a great change was taking place in "Turkey". The Arabs, until then tyrannically ruled by the Turks, had now discovered their national, historic and ethnic homogeneity and wanted to secede from the Ottoman Empire and establish an independent state. This state would extend from the Tigris and Euphrates valley to the Suez Canal (that is, not including Egypt!) and from the Mediterranean Sea to the Sea of 'Uman. The new state would be headed by an Arab sultan as a liberal constitutional monarch. The vilayet of the Hijaz, together with the city of Medina, would form a separate independent state whose ruler would be the religious caliph of all the Muslims. "Thus the great difficulty of separating the civil authority from the religious authority in

Islam will be solved." The proclamation promised that all foreign interests in Arab countries would be honoured, as well as the autonomy of Mount Lebanon and the status quo of the Christian institutions in Palestine and the independent principalities of Yemen and the Persian Gulf. The liberation of the Arabs would be the sign of the beginning of the liberation of the rest of the oppressed nations of the Empire, which would soon follow in their footsteps. The manifesto ended with the claim that 12 million Arabs were now ready to revolt.

The second manifesto, headed by the same banner and dated 3 January 1905, was addressed to "all the inhabitants of the Arab fatherland who are oppressed by the Turks". It opened with a description of the sorry state of the Arabs in the Empire, oppressed by "these barbarians who came from Central Asia". The Arabs, who had once conquered the East and the West in less than a century, who had excelled in science, literature and the arts, and who had led world culture for centuries, had since the capture of the caliphate by the Turks become the poorest people in the world. The proclamation argued that only through Arab soldiers were the Turks succeeding in controlling the Empire, and reminded its readers that in Nizib 40,000 Syrians under the leadership of Ibrahim Pasha had prevailed over 120,000 Turks. And the Arabs' reward for helping to maintain the existence of the Empire was to be called "dirty Arabs", kept out of senior positions and oppressed without mercy. The Arabs provided two-thirds of the Empire's budget and in return they were discriminated against and neglected, and their lands were taken by Sultan 'Abd al-Hamid for his personal use.

Now, the manifesto announced, the Ligue de la Patrie Arabe had been founded in order to end this situation and to liberate the fatherland. The league had already had great success in the previous months and had opened branches in all the large cities of Palestine, Syria, Mesopotamia, Egypt and Europe. The proclamation reported that all the enlightened powers regarded this movement positively and promised it their sympathy. As detailed here, the league's plan was identical to that described in the first manifesto (except for the paragraph about honouring foreign interests. . .). Additional articles promised that all Arab functionaries would keep their positions and that 'Abd al-Hamid's private property would be distributed among all those who contributed to the league's success. The proclamation also promised a general amnesty for all criminals without exception, and claimed that carrying out this plan would not require any bloodshed, but only the will of the Arabs to be liberated, since in all the Arab lands there were only 500 to 600 Turks, as opposed to 12 million Arabs. The proclamation asked the inhabitants to remain calm and obey the Arab governors who would replace the Turkish Valis and Mutasarrifs. It also requested the Arab soldiers to obey the Arab officers who would replace the Circassian officers on the appointed date.[5]

The confident style of these manifestos provoked anxiety among the authorities when they reached most of the notables, consuls and hotels in Adana in early February 1905. Several days later, when the manifestos reached Jerusalem, the governor asked the French post office not to distribute them. A large number of copies also reached Beirut and aroused a certain amount of excitement there, with most readers expressing support for their content. Distribution outside Beirut was obstructed because the Ottoman postal system confiscated the copies intended for the interior. In Beirut, and in Jaffa, the authorities responded to the appearance of the manifestos by arresting local notables and carrying out a general search of the home of Hafiz al-Sa'id, a wealthy resident of Jaffa.[6]

Soon afterwards, 'Azuri published his book *Le Réveil de la Nation Arabe dans l'Asie Turque* (The Awakening of the Arab Nation in Turkish Asia), in which he summarized his ideas about the future of the Arab movement, his attitude towards the various European states and his attitude towards the Jews. He began the introduction by quoting the first manifesto and then went on to address the Jewish problem. He mentioned that the book was complementary to another work which he was about to publish, under the name "Le Péril juif universal: Révélations et études politiques" (The universal Jewish peril: Revelations and political studies—it, in fact, never appeared). These works, he wrote, were both based on the six years he had spent in Palestine, during which he became aware of the Arab problem and of the quiet but harmful efforts of the Jews in this land. The Arab movement, according to 'Azuri, had arisen just at the time when the Jews were closest to success in their plot to gain control over the world:

> Two important phenomena of the same nature, but at the same time opposite to each other, which have not yet attracted anyone's attention, are occurring at this moment in Asiatic Turkey. These are the awakening of the Arab nation and the latent efforts of the Jews to re-establish the ancient kingdom of Israel on a broader scale. These two movements are destined to fight each other until one of them will prevail over the other. The fate of the entire world is dependent on

the final outcome of the struggle between these two nations, who represent two contrary principles.[7]

'Azuri devoted half the book to expressing his opinions about the various European countries. Russia, in his opinion, did not believe that the Arabs should be granted emancipation, and its occupation of the Arab lands would be merely the replacement of one oppression by another. However, Russia's schemes would not succeed, because the Arabs, aware of their identity, were preparing a national revolution that would surprise the world with its swiftness and its pacifist spirit. When the British, on the other hand, took control of an area, they respected its institutions and customs and allowed the old laws and functionaries to remain. Thus their colonial rule was not felt so much. Britain, in 'Azuri's opinion, did not then intend to gain control over Syria and Mesopotamia. Its aim was to rule over the Asiatic bank of the Suez Canal and to prevent the Russians from advancing to the Dardanelles, to the Euphrates valley and to Syria.

"France," he wrote, "of all the European powers, is the only one that offers its generous and spontaneous assistance to the oppressed and unfortunate nations . . . The uncountable services that it has rendered civilization at all times give it the right to the sympathy and gratitude of all the Easterners regardless of race or religion . . . France is the nation which possesses the most rights and interests in the whole Ottoman Empire." Thus France was the only nation whose rule would be welcomed in the Arab countries. And 'Azuri added that since the Arabs were planning to rid themselves of the corrupt government of the Turks in a revolution that would take less than 12 days, he expected that France would act in accordance with its generous tradition and would support the Arab movement. Concerning Germany 'Azuri wrote that it was trying to gain control over Austria, the Balkans and Macedonia, and then to advance to Asia Minor, thus establishing a vast German Empire from the North Sea to the Persian Gulf. "Under the hands of the Germans Asia Minor will become an entirely German country within a few years." The Germans would completely Germanize this region, as they had done to their villages in Palestine. "This is the most colonizing nation in the world." As for the Italians, who themselves had long been under subjugation, 'Azuri was certain that they would display sympathy for the Arab movement as soon as it arose. He also expected the moral and diplomatic assistance of the United States.[8]

The last part of 'Azuri's book was devoted to the Ottoman Empire. Sultan 'Abd al-Hamid was the worst Turkish ruler in history. His rule had brought disaster on the country, and the Empire had lost Romania, Serbia, Montenegro, Kars, Batum, Cyprus, Egypt, Tunisia, Eastern Rumelia, Thessalia and Crete during his rule—altogether more than half its area.[9] 'Azuri went on to repeat ideas that he had already expressed in his manifesto: The Arabs were the greatest nation in the Empire; before they were oppressed by the Turks, they had led world culture; the Turks had robbed them of the caliphate; only by virtue of Arab soldiers had the Turks managed to maintain control of the Empire.[10] But nothing would help the Turks and their tyrant. The oppressed nations of the Empire would together revolt against them. The Arabs would proclaim a Sultan in Damascus, the Albanians would also proclaim their own king, and the Armenians would set up a temporary government.[11] Twelve million Arabs would not need, in 'Azuri's opinion, more than 12 hours to banish the 12 hundred Turks who had exploited them. 'Azuri claimed that the Arabs already had three societies in Europe and America, two societies in Egypt, and societies in all the central towns of Syria and Mesopotamia that were all now waiting for the final united action.[12]

The detailed plan of the league described in the final pages was virtually identical to that of the manifestos. 'Azuri added that Egypt would not become part of the future Arab Empire "because the Egyptians do not belong to the Arab race". He contended that the Egyptians originated from an African Berber family and their language before Islam was not like Arabic at all. There was a natural boundary between Egypt and the Arab Empire, and the Arab caliphs had never succeeded in reigning over the two lands at the same time for a long period.[13]

'Azuri concluded his book with a series of attacks on Sultan 'Abd al-Hamid — that he was not fit for the position of caliph, because despite his advanced age he had never made a pilgrimage to Mecca; because he stole from his subjects; because he did favours for criminals; and because he was kicked by all the ambassadors. In all the Arab countries there was not one Muslim who did not curse him a hundred times a day. 'Azuri expressed his hope that 'Abd al-Hamid would nevertheless continue to rule for a long time, as his actions would only hasten the division of the Empire and would lead the populace to join the Arab movement. The more decorations and glorifications that the Sultan gave out after each loss of part of the Empire, the more ridiculous he would appear in the eyes of his subjects.[14]

'Azuri's book was written in French and therefore was able to bring the Arab problem to the awareness of the European nations. This advantage at the same time was also a drawback. In French it did not have much influence among the Arabs. It also failed to gain support because 'Azuri's plan was too extreme for its time; Muslim Arabs were not yet ready to harm the last Muslim empire in the world.

In the ten years following the publication of *Le Réveil de la Nation Arabe* 'Azuri engaged in intensive contacts with many European representatives of various ranks, trying vainly to convince them of the seriousness of his plans. He returned to Cairo and in January 1906 sent a letter to Christian, the manager of the national printing house in Paris with whom he had established contact, proposing to incite a pro-French revolt in Syria if he could be given the sum of "only 100,000 francs". He asserted that the transferring of this sum would bring industrial and national groups, with whom he was already in contact, to join the financing of the revolt. In another letter to Christian two weeks later he wrote that he had discovered a dangerous plot against France's position. This information, he claimed, was very delicate, and therefore he requested the French to pay his expenses for a return trip to Paris, as well as living expenses for a month for himself, his wife and son, so that he would be able to report about the plot directly. In return for this service to France, 'Azuri requested that the sum of money he had asked for in his previous letter, which was needed to carry out the first steps of his plan, be transferred to him.[15] 'Azuri did not get the sum he requested.

The next stage for 'Azuri in drawing the attention of the Europeans to the Arab problem in general and to the two members of the league, 'Azuri and Jung, was the publication of the journal *L'Indépendance Arabe*, which was published from April 1907 to September 1908. The manager of the journal was 'Azuri, the editor-in-chief was Jung, and most of its writers were Frenchmen, Orientalists and members of the colonialist circles. In the first issue of the journal an article that was signed "le Comité" (the Society) expressed satisfaction with the development of events as had been predicted by 'Azuri's book. . .[16] In another issue a newspaper article was quoted that reported that the league's influence had reached Port Sudan. In yet another issue 'Azuri repeated his theory that the Arabs and the other nations of the Ottoman Empire were about to be liberated from the "wormy tree".[17] A crushing attack appeared in the journal on the Egyptian nationalist Mustafa Kamil, "the anti-European anglophobe" who had "no right to proclaim himself the head of any party", for he was "only seeking financial profit in the agitation he fomented" and his patriotism "was nothing but that of a charlatan".[18] The anti-Ottoman 'Azuri had a clear ideological reason to attack the Egyptian nationalists, who were pro-Ottoman and had Islamist tendencies.

"Managing" the journal from Cairo, 'Azuri continued his contacts with foreign diplomats. In January 1908 the French chargé d'affaires in Cairo reported that 'Azuri had had contacts with the German Baron Oppenheim, that his Paris newspaper was financed by the British and that he had also turned to the French delegation in Cairo. 'Azuri, in short, "offered his services to the various diplomatic delegations and most adroitly attempted to exploit his relations with each of them to carry out intrigues."[19]

In the last issue of his journal, which was published in 1908, after the Young Turk revolution, 'Azuri wrote:

> In the light of the latest events we must carry out the promises that we have always pledged our friends, the Young Turks: to abandon arms and to cooperate with them in the rehabilitation of the Ottoman Empire on the day when our common efforts to force a constitution upon Sultan 'Abd al-Hamid will succeed ... If later on the parliament will show evidence of vitality and enlightened liberalism, we will cease our struggle and work in constitutional ways for the establishment of a regime of administrative autonomy in our country.[20]

Indeed, when elections were held for the first parliament of the constitutional period, 'Azuri was a candidate for the sanjaq of Jerusalem. His electoral platform did not mention his nationalism or the Jewish problem in Palestine, but this did not help him with the representatives of the Zionist movement, as well as the Jews in general, who considered him an anti-Semite and probably did everything in their power to oppose him. His request to the French consul-general to assist his candidacy was rejected.[21] 'Azuri was not elected to the parliament and he returned to Cairo to continue his contacts with diplomatic representatives. At the same time he became the foreign secretary of the Young Egyptian Party, which was founded by Idris Raghib, the owner of the newspaper L'Egypte where 'Azuri worked. This party promoted the creation of a representative government in Egypt in cooperation with the British[22] (another explanation for 'Azuri's hostility to the Egyptian National Party).

In February 1912 'Azuri asked the Italian chargé d'affaires in Cairo, Count Grimaldi, to give him 100,000 rifles with 200 bullets apiece for his revolutionary plans, as well as means of transporting them. In March he was asked to return to the Italian legation and there he was told that his demands were excessive. 'Azuri replied that he would make do with only 2,000 rifles as a preliminary stage. The Italians' reply was negative and 'Azuri concluded that "Italy will not go with us".[23]

In November 1912 'Azuri sent a letter to Jung, which the latter transferred to the French foreign ministry. In this letter he warned of Britain's increasing prestige in Syria and requested France's assistance for his movement in order to deal with this: "We do not request extraordinary assistance . . . 600,000 francs . . . will be sufficient."[24] Jung enclosed a letter of his own, in which he requested, in addition to the 600,000 francs, 4,000 rifles and two million bullets as well. The requests were denied.[25]

In December 1912 'Azuri sent another letter through Jung to the French foreign ministry, in which he warned of the increase in British propaganda in Syria. In a similar letter sent in March 1913, he wrote that the Syrian Muslim notables had requested from Lord Kitchener that Syria should be annexed to Egypt or be granted independence. And 'Azuri added: "It was I who aroused the Arab decentralization movement which you read about in the Paris newspapers and which pressed for the establishment of the society in Cairo" (meaning the Decentralization Party).[26] This was another attempt by 'Azuri to steal someone else's thunder. On the eve of the Paris Congress (described below), 'Azuri sent an express letter to Jung in which he denounced such organizers as Shukri Ghanim, who according to 'Azuri had been a servant of the Young Turks and had abandoned them in favour of the Arab movement only after he had been disappointed by the salary they offered of 400 francs a month. 'Azuri asked Jung to try to persuade the initiators of the congress to postpone it to July or even to September, so that he would be able to get to Paris in the meantime and tell them "some truths"[27]—a revealing request. Jung did not succeed in having the congress postponed.

In February 1914 'Azuri wrote to Jung that the situation in Syria was ripe for a revolution and the Arab officers were only waiting for someone to support them. There was a need for 100,000 rifles and ammunition "for everything". This request, which was transmitted to the French authorities, was also rejected.[28] In November 1914 'Azuri wrote to Jung that he had asked General Maxwell, the commander-in-chief of the British forces in Egypt, to assist him in organizing a revolt in Syria. Maxwell had replied that the British were not interested in allowing the conflict to spread at this point beyond the Arabian Peninsula. 'Azuri added that he hoped that the battles would spread to Syria anyway and he expressed his wish to land in Syria "in order to fight the Turks".[29]

Jung, for his part, turned to the French foreign ministry at the outbreak of the war, with plans for an uprising in the Levant against the Ottomans. He wrote that "one of the principal leaders" of the Arab movement, Najib 'Azuri, who was now serving as manager of the newspaper *L'Egytpe*, was planning an action and therefore it was important that they should recognize him as the leader of Arab nationalism.[30] The letter was not answered, and therefore Jung turned to the British embassy in Paris and tried to convince them of the seriousness of his plans. He claimed that the French took his plans seriously and that they had recommended that he speak to the British because this area was their responsibility. Jung told the British that 'Azuri's movement had branches throughout Syria, Palestine and Mesopotamia and that 'Azuri had specific plans for carrying out his proposals. After Jung left the embassy, the British investigated in the French foreign ministry to find out who he was, and were told that the French had not sent him to them at all, that Jung was not a serious person, that he should be treated carefully, and that at one time he had been dismissed from service in the French foreign ministry in circumstances which were better not repeated.[31]

Jung continued in his appeals to the French foreign ministry, and 'Azuri even encouraged him, in a letter of March 1915, not to despair and to continue to turn to the French foreign minister, as there was no doubt that eventually the Arab problem would receive a reasonable and appropriate solution and that the Arab countries would be able to develop normally under the supervision of France and Britain.[32] In August 1916 Jung announced in a letter to the French president that on 23 June 1916 Najib 'Azuri, "the great friend of France", had died. He took advantage of this letter to offer himself once again as an emissary on behalf of the French government to the Arabs, who had begun the Arab revolt of Sharif Husayn of Mecca two months earlier.[33]

Chapter 7

THE SOCIETY OF THE ARAB REVIVAL

The Society of the Arab Revival[1] (al-Nahda al-'Arabiyya) was the first true Arab society of the twentieth century. Unlike previous groups and societies, which had been limited initiatives, sometimes by only a few people, without long-term effects, this new society endured for eight years with a fixed structure and institutions. In that those who left it joined, and in some cases founded, almost all the Arab societies that arose in the period from the Young Turk revolution to the outbreak of World War I, it may be considered the mother of the Arab societies of that period.

At the time of Midhat Pasha's rule in Syria, Sheikh Tahir al-Jaza'iri[2] (1851-1920) was appointed general supervisor of education in the vilayet. An Algerian scholar who had previously belonged to the entourage of Amir 'Abd al-Qadir al-Jaza'iri, his activities at that time were concentrated on bringing education to the Syrians. For this purpose he established the "Society of Good Intentions" (Jam'iyyat al-Maqasid al-Khayriyya) of Damascus, a semi-official philanthropic society that invested money received from both the government and rich local notables in the establishment of schools and a printing house for the publication of textbooks in Arabic. After Midhat Pasha's removal from Syria and the advent of a new Vali, Hamdi Pasha, the society still continued its activities; the new Vali even helped Sheikh Tahir realize his great dream of establishing the al-Zahiriyya library in Damascus to collect the thousands of manuscripts and ancient books previously scattered throughout the city.

This activity continued during 1880-82, and then the Sultan, displeased by Sheikh Tahir's excessively independent activities, commanded him to leave the society. During this period a circle (halqa) for the study of modern science, Arab history and Arab traditions began to form around the Sheikh in Damascus. The circle believed in keeping religious customs while at the same time drawing from the best of Western secular culture. Among the participants in Sheikh Tahir's circle were Jamal al-Din al-Qasimi (1866-1914), 'Abd al-Razzaq al-Bitar (1834-1916), and

Salim al-Bukhari (1851-1928), all three Damascene 'ulama' who had called for religious reform. A number of younger Muslims subsequently joined the circle, including Rafiq al-'Azm, Muhammad Kurd 'Ali, Shukri al-'Asali, 'Abd al-Wahhab al-Inklizi, 'Abd al-Hamid al-Zahrawi, Salim al-Jaza'iri, 'Abd al-Rahman al-Shahbandar, and Muhibb al-Din al-Khatib — all future leaders of the Arab societies in the period before World War I. The members of the circle would meet with Sheikh Tahir, some after Friday prayers and some on other occasions, to hear his lectures on the latest scientific, philosophical and political developments.

Muhibb al-Din al-Khatib, the youngest of his students, related that Sheikh Tahir "believed that [the lot of] Islam and the Muslims, especially the Arabs, will never be improved except by those who managed their affairs in the period of the *tabi'un*" (the generations after Muhammad; that is, the Arabs). Such ideas did not please the Sultan. When someone informed on him claiming that he had distributed placards on behalf of the Young Turks, Sheikh Tahir was forced in 1905 to flee secretly to Egypt. The movement he had begun in Damascus did not cease with his flight.[3]

Some of the members of Sheikh Tahir's circle, such as his nephew, the officer Salim al-Jaza'iri, and the civilians Faris al-Khuri, Shukri al-'Asali, and 'Abd al-Wahhab al-Inklizi, joined Turkish officers and notables in a joint secret society whose aim was to fight against the tyrannical regime of Sultan 'Abd al-Hamid. The members of this society were in contact with the Young Turks.[4] Younger people gathered around Muhibb al-Din al-Khatib, who in 1903 founded the Small Circle of Damascus (*Halqat Dimashq al-Saghira*, so called to distinguish it from the Large Circle of Damascus, that is, Sheikh Tahir's circle).

Muhibb al-Din al-Khatib (1886-1969) was the son of the secretary of the al-Zahiriyya library in Damascus. After his father had died, Sheikh Tahir al-Jaza'iri took the eleven-year-old into his care ("Sheikh Tahir took me in hand and turned me towards the true Islam"). Muhibb al-Din studied at Maktab 'Anbar secondary school in Damascus (from which many Syrian notables emerged) and in order to broaden his horizons in Islamic subjects, was employed at the same time by Sheikh Tahir to care for manuscripts. When he finished his own studies, Muhibb al-Din would go to Sheikh Tahir's circle to listen to his lectures. During this period he reached the conclusion that the Arabs were the first ones to be responsible for the spreading of Islam in every place and at every time. He kept this idea throughout his life and it was the motive behind his future activities. During this period he also happened upon 'Abd al-Rahman al-Kawakibi's book *Umm al-Qura*, which he read and handed on to his friends in the Small Circle of Damascus, such as 'Arif al-Shihabi, Salah al-Din al-Qasimi, Salih Qunbaz, Lutfi al-Haffar, Rushdi al-Hakim, 'Uthman Mardam, and his two cousins Zaki and Sayf al-Din al-Khatib. (Some of these later became statesmen of the first rank in Syria.)

The members of the Small Circle of Damascus would meet in the Maktab 'Anbar school and study Arabic history, language and literature. Their secret goal was to spread Arabism (*'uruba*) among the Arab youth in Damascus. Nevertheless, they did not seek to secede from the Ottoman Empire, but rather to bring about a decentralized regime in which the rights of the Arabs in the government would be assured and Arabic would be considered an official language in schools, courts and the government offices of the Arab vilayets.[5]

When he was in the sixth class of secondary school, Muhibb al-Din was caught with forbidden books in his possession, among them a book by the Turkish poet Namiq Kemal on the right to freedom. The books were confiscated, his grade in conduct was reduced by two points, and after an attempt was made to fail him in the final examination he had no choice but to transfer to the secondary school of Beirut. He and other students who transferred to Beirut with him, among them all the Shihabi amirs, were in contact with the students at the Syrian Protestant College and with the students of Sheikh 'Abbas al-Azhari's college, among them 'Abd al-Ghani al-'Uraysi, Muhammad al-Mihmisani, and 'Adil Arslan. In 1905 most of the young men went on to advanced studies in Istanbul. On the ship there Muhibb al-Din met a young Shi'ite by the name of 'Abd al-Karim Qasim al-Khalil,[6] who was to play one of the key roles in the Arab movement, before being hanged by Jamal Pasha in 1915.

While he was a law student in Istanbul, Muhibb al-Din noticed that the Arab students were ignorant of their language and preferred to speak Turkish. In order to impress upon them that the Arabs also had a language and a literature of their own, he wrote to Muhammad Kurd 'Ali, who was then in Egypt and had begun to publish the periodical *al-Muqtabas*, and asked him to send various newspapers, via the French postal system. Young Arabs such as 'Abd al-Karim Qasim al-Khalil, the Shihabis, Fa'iz al-'Azm, Shukri al-Jundi, and Mazhar Raslan would gather together in his room in Istanbul and read these newspapers, forbidden in the Ottoman Empire, in secret. These youths were soon persuaded to learn the basics of Arabic language and literature. Muhibb al-Din and 'Arif al-Shihabi, a Damascene who was a native of Hasbaya, divided the youths into two groups, and each of them provided instruction gratis to those who lived nearest to him. Muhibb al-Din's method was first to teach the theoretical rules of the language and afterwards to ground them through the use of texts that would arouse nationalist and Islamist feelings.

On 24 December 1906 Muhibb al-Din assembled selected students from the two study groups, explained to them that the activities they were carrying out were actually "revival" (*nahda*), and suggested that they unite in a framework to be called the Society of the Arab Revival. Muhibb al-Din was elected leader of the society and 'Arif al-Shihabi its secretary. The members of the society continued to meet at first as before, although they wrote a secret temporary constitution and began to collect donations for the society at their meetings. As the number of members in the society began to grow, Muhibb al-Din decided that it was necessary to find a permanent centre for meetings. For this purpose he chose a café near a central crossroads in the capital, and with the money collected by the society new furniture and a gramophone with Arab records were brought there. The café soon became a gathering place for Arab youth in Istanbul. Then Muhibb al-Din decided to hold a party at which all the members of the society could meet at the same time and get to know one another. This was not at all simple during the reign of 'Abd al-Hamid, "when walls had ears", and so it was decided to hold the party on a small island near the capital, in a garden owned by Ahmad Pasha al-Zuhayr, an Arab notable from Basra, far from the eyes of the Hamidian secret police. The party was held on 13 July 1907, but in spite of the security precautions taken these activities began to draw the attention of the authorities.[7]

The Hamidian detective system had no difficulty in discovering that the centre of this activity was Muhibb al-Din's room, and one evening a senior police official appeared at the doorway. However, Muhibb al-Din was extraordinarily lucky, because the official, Farid Pasha al-Yafi, who had been put in charge of this investigation, was married to the sister of his cousin Sayf al-Din al-Khatib, also a member of the society. Farid Pasha, who knew nothing about these activities of his relative, was just as surprised to see Muhibb al-Din as the latter was surprised to see him. He looked at the forbidden books and newspapers in the room and immediately invited Muhibb al-Din for a confidential conversation. He explained that the room had been under the surveillance of the police for some weeks, that he had actually come with an order to arrest the participants in the meetings, and that the building was surrounded by policemen who were just waiting for the command to enter and arrest those present. He could not arrest him, however, because of their family relationship, and he would report to his superiors that no forbidden activities were taking place in the room, but Muhibb al-Din must immediately destroy all the forbidden material in his room and stop the gatherings, or else it would be bad for both of them.

'Abd al-Karim al-Khalil took it upon himself immediately to get rid of the books and newspapers, while Muhibb al-Din and Fa'iz al-'Azm went to warn the participants of the meetings at 'Arif al-Shihabi's apartment. Deciding that it was too dangerous for him to remain in Istanbul, Muhibb al-Din returned to Damascus at the end of the academic year. The society in Istanbul ran afterwards into trouble, both because of the surveillance of the authorities and because of conflicts among its members.[8]

Muhibb al-Din related that the goal of the society's founders was "to make the intellectual Arab youth aware of their Arabism and to encourage them to cooperate in improving Ottoman society, whose righteouness was dependent on that of Arab society from the Taurus mountains to Bab al-Mandib". Arabism ('uruba), in their view, was the noblest element in Islamic society, chosen because of its unique characteristics by Allah to carry the trust of Islam during the first period, and they believed that it was now once again responsible for carrying the message of Islam and the renewal of its youth. This was in accordance with Sheikh Tahir al-Jaza'iri's teaching, that "if any barrier is placed between Islam and Arabism, Arabism becomes like a body without a soul and Islam like a soul without a body".[9]

While he was still in Istanbul Muhibb al-Din asked Salah al-Din al-Qasimi and Lutfi al-Haffar to set up a branch of the Society of the Arab Revival in Damascus. Returning from Istanbul, Muhibb al-Din made the Damascus branch the centre of the society. Shortly afterwards he decided to go even further away from the capital, and he accepted the position of interpreter that was offered him by the British consulate at Hudaida in Yemen. During the last days before he went there, he worked to stabilize the centre of the society in Damascus, together with two of its members there, the brothers Jamil and 'Uthman Mardam.[10] After Muhibb al-Din left for Yemen (where he founded another branch of the society), the society continued to develop, with Salah al-Din al-Qasimi becoming its prominent activist.

Salah al-Din al-Qasimi (1887-1916) lost his father at the age of 12, and his older brother Jamal al-Din al-Qasimi took him under his wing. Throughout his life he was influenced by the philosophy of his brother, an 'alim with a reformist viewpoint. He studied in government schools and then entered medical college, from which he graduated in 1914. Salah al-Din was the youngest member of the society, but nevertheless was appointed its first secretary. At the bi-weekly meetings that he began to organize at night, members donated small sums of money for the society. A small library was later set up with the funds that had accumulated. The society became very influential at that time, especially among the students of the Maktab 'Anbar secondary school, many of whom had relatives in the society.[11] Then the Young Turk revolution occurred.

The members of the society, who participated in the festivities in honour of the promulgation of the constitution, felt safe enough to bring the formerly secret activities of the society into the open. The society's centre in Khan al-Jumruk in Damascus was opened with a large ceremony.

In November 1908 Muhibb al-Din returned from Yemen to Damascus, since he now felt reasonably secure. He decided that the society should now act only within the framework of the law, and he presented the society's constitution to the authorities for authorization, an essential step in making the society official. But the authorities refused to authorize the constitution, though its avowed aims were all purely cultural. Someone had taken the trouble to inform the authorities that the society had political aims as well. As it was not officially recognized, the society's meetings were illegal. It continued to meet secretly for some time, but it was eventually obliged to change its constitution in order to pacify the authorities and adapt it to the new societies' law (described below). The most important adjustment was the change of name from "The Society of the Arab Revival" to "The Society of the Syrian Revival". The authorities did not like the word "Arab", as they had begun their policy of Turkification. Even the new constitution was accepted by the authorities only after a long debate. Shortly afterwards Muhibb al-Din himself became involved in the publication of a satiric-critical newspaper and was forced to flee again, to Istanbul and from there to Egypt.[12]

After the revolution the society obtained a three-room house to expand its library. Arabic lessons were conducted there as well, twice a week. The society thus fulfilled Article 2 of its constitution, which called for the "propagation of the Arabic language". By 1912 it already had about 1,000 books on history, social science and literature. To raise money for the upkeep of the reading rooms, the society presented plays whose earnings were earmarked for this purpose. But its financial situation was difficult, as some of its members had gone to Beirut, Istanbul and even France and Britain for higher education, and the membership dues were nominal, only a quarter of a majidi per month, so that poor people would not be prevented from joining.[13]

The authorities suspected that the society's activities were not purely cultural but also nationalist, and put on trial some of the Syrian 'ulama' who were suspected of participation. The following was reported by Jamal al-Din al-Qasimi in his diary (28 September 1909):

> I was invited today to the investigation department at the court. A summary of what informers told the authorities . . . that the Society of the Syrian Revival was formed with our encouragement and we are among its leaders, and that it is a branch of societies in Yemen and Najd, is striving for administrative independence and wants to throw domestic affairs into disorder, by demanding an Arab government . . .[14]

Did the society really engage in political activity? 'Ali Rida al-Rikabi, who was the Muhafiz (governor) of Medina in 1911, was sure that this was the case. He reported to the interior and war ministers on the treason of Sharif Husayn, who was supported in his plans by "the revolutionary Society of the Arab Revival", founded in Egypt [sic] with the aim of establishing an Arab caliphate for which it considered Husayn a suitable candidate. This society, according to al-Rikabi, held meetings under the leadership of Sheikh Tahir al-Maghribi (he meant al-Jaza'iri), who had fled Damascus and settled in Egypt. It had branches in Damascus, Beirut and other towns. Al-Rikabi also reported that two years earlier the former judge of Tripoli, Selkezadeh Kamal, had opened an investigation of the members of the society in Damascus, but they had immediately threatened him with assassination. While he was on leave in Istanbul the judge had been dismissed from his position through the influence of members of the society, and all the reports on the investigations that he had managed to carry out disappeared and were destroyed. Al-Rikabi noted that he himself intended to continue the investigation, and he added that as far as he knew the members of the society were also encouraging Sayyid al-Idrisi of 'Asir to be an Arab caliph, and Imam Yahya of Yemen to head a Zaydi imamate. The success of their plans, he predicted, would lead to a general Arab uprising in the Hijaz, Iraq, Syria and Palestine.[15]

It is difficult to know where truth ends and imagination begins in Al-Rikabi's report. The evidence brought by the society members contradicted his statements and presented the society as having only cultural aims. What is clear is that many members of the society did indeed join and even establish secret societies, which became more and more separatist with time. Four years later some of them became fellow members of al-Rikabi himself in the secret society *al-Fatat*.

Chapter 8

THE SOCIETY OF THE OTTOMAN COUNCIL

The oppressive regime of Sultan 'Abd al-Hamid II caused many Syrian intellectuals to flee the Empire. Some emigrated to America, while others went to Egypt, where they could express their opinions relatively freely. Among those who fled were Sheikh Tahir al-Jaza'iri and many members of his circle, such as Muhammad Kurd 'Ali, Rafiq al-'Azm, and 'Abd al-Hamid al-Zahrawi, as well as others who would later dominate the development of the Arab societies in the period before World War I, such as Rashid Rida and Ibrahim Salim al-Najjar.

The activities against Sultan 'Abd al-Hamid's tyrannical regime were coordinated during this period by the Young Turks. While some of the Syrian émigrés in Cairo were members of this movement, they felt themselves pushed to its outskirts, as it became more and more Turkish. Two of the Syrian émigrés in Cairo, Rashid Rida and Rafiq al-'Azm, therefore decided in early 1907 to set up an Ottoman-oriented society, in which all the nationalities of the Empire could participate equally. Thus the Society of the Ottoman Council (*Jam'iyyat al-Shura al-'Uthmaniyya*)[1] was founded in Cairo, with the participation of Arabs, Turks, Albanians, Kurds and Armenians, both Muslim and Christian. The society's aim was to unite all the nationalities of the Ottoman Empire in a joint action to replace 'Abd al-Hamid's tyrannical rule with a constitutional regime. According to Rashid Rida, when 'Abd al-Hamid found out about the establishment of this society, he was so disturbed that he was unable to sleep for three nights, until his spies discovered who its founders were.[2]

Rashid Rida was elected president of the administrative council of the society, Rafiq al-'Azm was elected treasurer, his cousin Haqqi al-'Azm was elected Arab secretary, and 'Abdallah Jawdat was elected Turkish secretary. According to Rida, even the official Ottoman representative in Cairo was in favour of the establishment of the society, and it was he who told Rida about the Sultan's hostile attitude towards it.[3]

The first articles of the society's constitution began as follows:

A society will be established for all residents of the Ottoman Empire, called the Society of the Ottoman Council, and this is its constitution:
Art. 1: The purpose of establishing the society is to turn the Ottoman regime into a de facto constitutional and parliamentary regime.
Art. 2: The society will invest whatever effort is necessary to achieve this purpose by any legal means.
Art. 3: The Society of the Ottoman Council will include Ottoman subjects regardless of religion or nationality.[4]

Branches of the society were set up in the Arab countries and it distributed its programme among them, as well as proclamations in Arabic and in Turkish, which attacked 'Abd al-Hamid's oppressive regime. The society's proclamations even reached Turkey itself, by means of Russian ships that sailed the Black Sea. In late January 1907 the society founded a newspaper with the same name and it too was distributed throughout the Empire. The Arabic half of the newspaper was written by Rafiq al-'Azm, while the Turkish half was written by Haqqi al-'Azm.[5]

The members of the Committee of Union and Progress (CUP) of the Young Turks became interested in the society, and they sent one of their leaders, Ahmad Rida, from Paris to Cairo, to try to persuade the members of the society to unite with the CUP. The administrative council of the society turned down the request; Rashid Rida declared that as long as the two societies were striving for the same goal there was no harm in having more than one. He also added that there was an essential difference between the two societies, in that the CUP was a Turkish society while his was Ottoman and was of the opinion that the struggle for a constitution should include all the nationalities of the Empire. Though Ahmad Rida replied that according to the CUP constitution non-Muslims could also join, Rashid Rida rejected this argument, claiming that this was not applied in practice, and the proof was that there were no Armenians or Christian Syrians in the society. Nevertheless, Rashid said that his society was prepared to cooperate with the CUP in the struggle against 'Abd al-Hamid's tyranny and oppression, and in striving for a constitutional government headed by a parliament.[6]

It seems that the society had practical success particularly in Yemen. On his way to Yemen in November 1907 Muhibb al-Din al-Khatib travelled from Damascus to Cairo, where he met with the heads of the society. They told him that the society already had 13 branches in the Arab countries and it was agreed that when he arrived in Yemen he would set up the fourteenth branch of the society there. In Yemen Muhibb al-Din was employed as interpreter by the British Consulate in Hudaida, and he began to form connections with officials and officers who served in the port. At the casino of Hudaida's port he met town commandant Shawqi al-Mu'ayyad of the al-'Azm family and became friendly with him. A short while later he described to him his plan to set up a branch of the society in Yemen. Al-Mu'ayyad not only read the society's platform and expressed his wish to join, but was even elected president of the Hudaida branch, which consisted mostly of army officers.

Yemen's governor-general ignored the news about the Young Turk revolution when it broke out in 1908, but word reached Muhibb al-Din through a member of the society who brought him telegrams about it. He hurried to tell the officers who were members of the society, and also telegraphed to the members of the society in San'a and other Yemenite towns with the permission of the manager of the local post office, a sympathizer of the society. Then Muhibb al-Din, Shawki al-Mu'ayyad, and other officers decided to establish a fait accompli by holding all the ceremonies for the promulgation of the constitution. Thus the constitution was proclaimed in Hudaida in opposition to the will of the authorities, and not long after, in San'a.[7]

After the CUP took over the government, it offered the members of the society another opportunity to join forces. The society responded with a list of conditions that were not acceptable to the CUP, and the negotiations failed. But in the end, Rafiq and Haqqi al-'Azm joined the CUP as individuals, and with this the matter was practically closed for the society. In Yemen Muhibb al-Din took matters into his own hands when he heard about the contacts between the society and the CUP, and declared the society's branch in Hudaida to be a local CUP branch.[8]

Chapter 9

THE YOUNG TURK REVOLUTION

The first organized opposition group against Sultan 'Abd al-Hamid II was established in 1889 in the Military Medical School in Istanbul and was shortly afterwards named "The Committee of Union and Progress" (CUP). The group's attempt to overthrow the Sultan in 1896 failed, and the centre of gravity of the opposition to the Sultan moved to Europe. In 1902 the first congress of the Young Turks was held in Paris, its aim being the preparation of a military revolution against 'Abd al-Hamid. A revolution did not emerge from this congress, but the ideological differences of opinion that broke out there led to the formation of the two main forces within the Young Turks: the CUP, headed by Ahmad Rida and his supporters, who were considered Turkish nationalists, and Prince Sabah al-Din, who was considered a liberal Ottoman and founded the League for Private Initiative and Administrative Decentralization. Afterwards other groups of Young Turks were set up, the most important of which were the officers' groups in Damascus and Salonika.

In 1907 a second congress was held in Paris in an attempt to unite the supporters of Ahmad Rida and those of Sabah al-Din. At about the same time the officers' groups from Damascus and Salonika joined with the CUP in Paris, transforming it into the dominant force in the movement. However, by now the activities in Paris were no longer important, and the course of events had begun to be determined by the Young Turks within the Empire. In 1908 a wave of strikes and revolts spread throughout Asia Minor. In June 1908 a young officer in Salonika by the name of Enver decided to flee to the mountains rather than go to the capital for "promotion". He was followed by another officer, Niyazi. Army battalions that were sent to suppress the revolutionaries joined them instead. The army in Macedonia began vigorously demanding that the Sultan restore the 1876 constitution. On 23 July 1908 the constitution was independently proclaimed in Monastir. A day later 'Abd al-Hamid was forced to comply with the demands and renew the constitution.[1]

The restoration of the constitution and the conclusion of the tyrannic era of the Sultan caused a mighty wave of joy throughout the Empire. In the words of contemporary observers:

> The entire Empire burst forth in universal rejoicing . . . cities and towns were decorated, Muslims were seen embracing Christians and Jews and inviting one another to receptions and feasts.[2]

> Greeks, Turks, Armenians and Jews fraternized, and on one occasion I saw a Mollah effusively embraced by a long-haired and bearded Greek priest. He took it very well.[3]

> All barriers seemed to have been levelled by one overwhelming feeling — mutual gratulation on the achievement of a common deliverance.[4]

These descriptions reflected not only what was happening throughout the Empire, but what was happening in its Arab provinces as well. The city of Beirut was decorated festively and a gala party was held with the participation of 15,000 people. Similar reactions were seen in Haifa and Jerusalem as well. In Damascus more than 25 meetings were held, attended by thousands of demonstrators who denounced tyranny and praised freedom and the constitutional regime. Among the Ottoman émigrés in Cairo the news aroused "considerable enthusiasm" and "Christians and Muslims fell into each other's arms with mutual felicitations."[5] Many members of the various Arab societies and circles of the pre-constitutional period now joined the CUP, among them Rafiq al-'Azm and 'Abd al-Rahman al-Shahbandar. Rashid Rida wrote in his periodical al-Manar: "Today the Ottomans breathed the air of political and social life and tasted the sweetness of liberty . . . The difference between the past and the present is like the difference between day and night."[6]

But not everyone agreed. In a letter that 'Arif al-Shihabi sent from Istanbul to Muhibb al-Din al-Khatib, who was then in Yemen, he wrote: "The promulgation of the constitution is a decisive blow to our nationalism, because those who hated the tyrannical absolute rule would have responded to our call, and now, with the constitution proclaimed, they are satisfied with that and will no longer walk with us."[7]

'Arif al-Shihabi was worried needlessly. The Ottoman honeymoon in the wake of the renewal of the constitution was soon to end. While the various nationalities of the Empire, among them the Arabs, were anticipating participation and equality within the framework of the Empire, the members of the CUP had other plans, plans that would soon muddy the waters of Arab-Turkish relations. The first sign of this was at the parliamentary elections that were held in late 1908. Of the more than 250 members of parliament who were elected, there were more than 140 Turks and only 60 Arabs. The Arabs, who believed that their numbers in the Empire were greater than those of Turks, saw this as acute discrimination.[8] Even those Arab representatives who succeeded in being elected were mostly supporters of the CUP. The few who opposed the CUP, such as Shafiq al-Mu'ayyad, Rushdi al-Sham'a, 'Abd al-Hamid al-Zahrawi and Shukri al-'Asali, lost their seats in the 1912 parliamentary elections.

On 12 April 1909 an uprising headed by the Muhammedan Union (an extremist religious organization that had been founded a few days earlier) broke out in Istanbul, and soldiers, mostly Albanians, took control of the capital the next day, vigorously demanding the abrogation of the constitution and the return of the shari'a (religious law). 'Abd al-Hamid announced that he was accepting the demands of the rebels. News of the counter-revolution reached Salonika by telegraph, and the Action Army, headed by General Mahmud Shawkat, advanced on the capital and conquered it on 24 April. The counter-revolution was suppressed, the constitution was saved and Sultan 'Abd al-Hamid was deposed. From then on the CUP was the true ruler of the Empire and began realizing the guiding ideas of some of its members.

In 1911 Ziya Gökalp said: "The country of the Turks is not Turkey, nor yet Turkestan. Their country is a broad and ever-lasting land—Turan." Some of the Young Turks were then striving to bring about the assimilation of all the nationalities of the Empire within Turanian nationalism. In their view the Ottoman Empire was a Turkish empire and all its other nationalities should be assimilated and become Turks, whether they wanted to or not. To this end there were those who wanted to translate the Qur'an into Turkish, to introduce the study of Turanian history in higher education, and to remove the names of the Rashidi caliphs from the mosques, replacing them with the names of Genghis Khan, Hulagu and Timerlane.[9] They angrily attacked those who opposed their ideas, and they had special plans for the Arabs who stubbornly insisted on remaining Arabs. The editor of the newspaper Tanin wrote: "The Arabs do not stop prattling in their language and they are total ignoramuses in Turkish, as if they were not under Turkish rule. The government is obligated in such a case to force them to forget their language and to learn the language of the nation that is ruling them."[10] The Turkish writer Jalal Nuri wrote in his book *Ta'rikh al-Mustaqbal*:

> The government is obligated to force the Syrians to leave their homes and to turn the Arab countries, especially Yemen and the Hijaz, into Turkish settlements in order to spread the Turkish language, which must become the language of religion. In order to protect our existence we have no alternative except turning all the Arab lands into Turkish lands.[11]

The Turkish nationalists did not stop at words. They began a process of Turkification (*tatrik*) of the Empire, of which the Arabs considered themselves the major victims. Within the framework of the governmental reorganization following the restoration of the constitution, 15 Arab mutasarrifs were removed from their positions. In the foreign ministry, where there had been 12 Arab officials out of 600, only one remained. In the treasury ministry as well, only one Arab remained. A member of the Arab societies who was staying in Istanbul at this time listed as follows the Turkish attempts to repress the Arabs: 1. Removal of Arabs from the positions they held. When the Turks made lists of their officials, they wrote down an *'ayn* (the initial letter of *'arabi*) next to the name of every Arab, so they would be able to identify them for appointments and dismissals. 2. Arabs were not invited to meetings whose purpose was the thawing of relations between the nationalities of the Empire. 3. Arab members of the CUP were not included in the Central Committee of the CUP in Salonika. 4. Arab members of the CUP did not attend its political discussions. 5. The CUP was transformed from an Ottoman society to a purely Turkish society. 6. The Awqaf (Islamic religious endowments) ministry was transferred from an Arab minister to a Turkish minister. 7. Arab valis, mutasarrifs and qadis were replaced by Turks, and Arabic speakers were not appointed to positions in Syria and Iraq. 8. The CUP opposed all educational and scientific plans in the Arab provinces and took action against the Society of the Syrian Revival. 9. The Turks opposed the Arabic language.[12]

The attention of the Arabs during that period was focused on the debate about the Arabic language. Courses of study were held in Turkish. Even courses in Arabic grammar were taught to Arab students by Turkish teachers using Turkish textbooks. Turkish became the only permitted language in the courts and government offices in the Arab provinces. Businessmen were forced to follow judicial processes in Turkish, which most of them did not understand, and the use of Arabic when applying to the authorities was prohibited. The Arabs felt that not only their language but also the language of Islam was being harmed. In 1910 Rashid Rida called upon the Turks to remember that "Arabic is the language of the Qur'an and the Sunna . . . Most of the people in the Empire are Muslims and need Arabic . . . The Islamic shari'a . . . is in Arabic . . . The Arab Ottoman element is the largest element [in the Empire] and the furthest from knowing the official language [Turkish]."[13]

Even in the army and in the military academy in Istanbul the Arab officers perceived discrimination. In one of the lessons a Turkish lecturer told them: "Be certain that Turkish is better for us than Islam and that racial zealotry is one of the best things in society." One of the Arab cadets responded: "Turkification (tatrik) of Ottoman elements . . . will lead to their secession from the Empire and the disintegration of the state." The lecturer answered mockingly: "Know that your Arab extraction does not prevent you from being Turkish, since your country is only a colony that the Turks have conquered with their swords and you must all know that you are Turks." In 1912 Arab officers found a letter that had been sent by a CUP leader to a Turkish officer, in which was written: "Put the Arabs facing the bullets of the enemy, and endeavour to get rid of them, since their death will benefit us."[14]

Such insults by the Turks—whether real or imaginary—caused a counter-reaction among some of the Arabs. These Arabs promoted their own interests, local or general, against Turkish nationalism. The severe defeats suffered by the Empire—at the hands of the Italians in Libya in 1911 and in the Balkan War in 1912-13—only strengthened the feeling of some Arabs that the Turks no longer had the power to control the non-Turkish regions of the Empire. In order to protect their own interests, both general and local, and the Arab lands, wholly or in part, they founded the Arab societies.

Part II

THE ARAB SOCIETIES 1908-14

Chapter 10

THE ARAB-OTTOMAN BROTHERHOOD

The Arab-Ottoman Brotherhood (*al-Ikha' al-'Arabi al-'Uthmani*), considered the first of the Arab societies that were founded after the Young Turk revolution, was actually established by functionaries of the deposed Hamidian regime. Now worried about their status, their purpose was to defend it by presenting themselves as the protectors of Arab interests in the Empire. This becomes evident in examining the nature of the activities of the society's founders in the periods before and after the promulgation of the constitution.

The founders, in order of their importance within the society, were:

Shafiq Bek al-Mu'ayyad al-'Azm: a Muslim from Damascus, related by marriage to the former Grand Vizier Jawad Pasha. For some years he was an interpreter in the Hamidian palace and was an imperial commissar in the Caisse de la Dette. In 1908 he served as the imperial commissar of the tobacco régie in Istanbul. In 1910 he was accused in the parliament of being a spy for 'Abd al-Hamid.[1]

Nadra Bek Mutran: a Greek Catholic from Ba'albek, visited Istanbul frequently during 'Abd al-Hamid's reign and was friendly with 'Izzat Pasha al-'Abid, who was close to the Sultan. According to the French he was loyal to the Sultan and a spy for him.[2]

Shukri Bek al-Husayni: a Muslim from Jerusalem, was the society's treasurer. Previously chief accountant for the Ottoman education ministry, he was a member of 'Izzat Pasha al-'Abid's circle and became rich as a result of his relationship with him.[3]

Yusuf Bek Shatwan: a Muslim from Tripoli (Libya), was one of 'Abd al-Hamid's men. In 1910 he was accused in the parliament of being a spy for the Sultan. Later he joined the supporters of the CUP, became an opponent of the reform movement in the Arab provinces and denounced the congress that the members of the Arab societies held in Paris in 1913.[4]

'Arif Bek al-Mardini: a Muslim from Aleppo. The CUP people tried to buy him at the beginning of 1909 by appointing him Vali of Basra. After the deposition of 'Abd al-Hamid he moved

to Cairo. He came to terms with the CUP at the beginning of
1913 and was appointed Vali of Damascus, where he began
forcefully to repress the reform movement through arrests and
newspaper closures. When the Paris Congress was held he
organized the propaganda against it in Syria.[5]
Shukri Pasha al-Ayyubi: a Muslim from Damascus, was a general in the Ottoman army and the manager of a carpet factory
near Istanbul. He was said to be one of the heads of the Hamidian espionage system.[6]
Sadiq Pasha al-Mu'ayyad al-'Azm: a Muslim from Damascus. In
1910 he was assessed by the CUP as completely loyal to them
and was sent to spy on the separatist and nationalist activities of
the Arab activists.[7]
Sharif Ja'far Pasha: the grandson of a former amir of Mecca. He
became a collaborator of the CUP, opposed the reform movement and joined the denouncers of the Paris Congress in 1913.[8]
Muhammad Pasha al-Makhzumi: a Muslim from Beirut, was a
member of the Education Council in Istanbul during the Hamidian regime. In 1913 he participated in a meeting against the
Paris Congress.[9]

The society was established by this group of functionaries and
spies in the aftermath of a consultation that took place in Prin-
kipio, near Istanbul, on 5 August 1908, following attacks on the
houses of Arabs who had served in the old regime. There were
no such attacks on the houses of Turks who had taken positions
similar to those of the Arabs. The group was joined by a number of Arab students who apparently had some doubts about the
motivations of the founders, but nevertheless felt the need to
support any group that declared itself to be Arab. Two of these
students, 'Abd al-Karim Qasim al-Khalil and Jamil al-Husayni,
distributed the society's proclamations, which announced its official opening conference in the capital on 2 September 1908.
Representatives of the CUP were also present at this conference,
which was held with the participation of many Arabs who lived
in Istanbul, and a CUP officer delivered a speech approving the
society's programme without reservations.[10]

The goals of the society, according to its programme, were:

1. Guarding the constitution and protecting it from any distortions
   that might harm it. All the members of the Society swear to sacrifice their lives and their property for this goal.
2. Explaining to the Arabs in particular and to the other Ottomans
   that all parts of the Ottoman Empire are the body of Ottoman
   nationalism (*wataniyya*) and it is their duty to protect them, and if

necessary even to sacrifice life and property for them, and to repudiate anyone who would bring about a schism between the various Ottoman races.

3. Every Ottoman has the obligation to believe that every piece of land in the Empire is his fatherland, and that every Ottoman person, without regard to race, belief or language, is his brother. Therefore the Society considers it its duty to remind the Arabs that they are the brothers of the other Ottoman nationalities and to encourage them to unite and to reach agreement with them.

4. Since the Ottoman throne represents the strongest tie between the various races and areas of the Ottoman Empire, the Society considers the Arabs to be obligated to adhere to this tie, as long as the Sultan keeps the constitution.

5. Obviously all the above will not prevent each race in the Empire from taking care of its own private concerns, especially the Arab race with its esteemed Qur'anic language and magnificent history. The Society will therefore try to enhance the dignity of Arabism and the Arabs within the general Ottoman union, so that the Arabs, regardless of religion or aspiration, will benefit from constitutional equality expressed in the attainment of offices, positions and other legitimate rights.[11]

The society was headed by an administrative committee, and it was decided that there would be no president. It was also decided at this conference that any Arab could join the society, provided that he was of good character, that he had not been convicted of a criminal offence and not deprived of his rights as a citizen. An Arab was defined as one who had been born in the Arab countries and considered them his fatherland (watan)—there was no reference here to ethnic origin! It was further decided that the society would publish three newspapers, in Arabic, Turkish and French, in order to create unity between the Arab provinces and the centre in Istanbul and disseminate the society's decisions. At the first session of the society the participants were already asked to donate money for this purpose. Ahmad Pasha al-Zuhayr, a member of the administrative committee of the society, collected 150 Turkish liras, and beginning on 1 October 1908 he published the French newspaper La Constitution in Salonika. On 21 January 1909 Shafiq al-Mu'ayyad began publishing the Arabic newspaper al-Ikha' al-'Uthmani in Istanbul.[12]

The society's printed platform reached Syria by November 1908 and branches of the society were set up there. The society was especially successful in Aleppo, where 900 people joined, among them Muslim and Christian notables. In its early days the society also obtained large donations, and a Christian Arab who lived in America pledged thousands of dollars to its treasurer, Shukri al-Husayni.[13]

The first confrontation between the society and the CUP occurred in Damascus, when members of the local branch of the Arab-Ottoman Brotherhood supported opponents of the CUP in the parliamentary elections. Shafiq al-Mu'ayyad, the most prominent member of the society, was elected representative of Damascus in the parliament, to the great resentment of the CUP. CUP members tried to invalidate his election, as well as the election of Yusuf Shatwan as representative of Benghazi in the parliament, with the claim that they had used illegal methods during the election campaign. Outraged, the Arab students in Istanbul began to distribute literature and to give speeches against the injustice, and in the end the CUP retreated. Afterwards, as a demonstrative measure, the students organized a reception when the Arab representatives to the parliament arrived in the capital. The students welcomed them at the port and brought them in procession to the society's building. In the parliament itself an attempt was made by the society to set up an Arab parliamentary party. The attempt was not particularly successful, nor was an attempt by representatives of the society to protest the beginning of the process of dismissing Arab officials in the framework of Turkification.[14]

The society did not succeed in obtaining popular support. The first months after the July revolution constituted a honeymoon period in Arab-Turkish relations. The government promised repeatedly to grant equality to all elements in the Empire, and Arab intellectuals believed in the need to work together with the Turks for the sake of the Empire. Indeed the society was also in favour of this goal, but the very fact that it was established on an Arab basis and for the advocacy of Arab interests was not appreciated by many of the Arab activists in this period. Rafiq al-'Azm, who believed that the CUP should be allowed to work alone and without disturbance for the progress of the Empire, sent a letter to his cousin Shafiq al-Mu'ayyad sharply denouncing him for establishing the society.[15]

Rashid Rida related that when he was travelling in Syria in October 1908, Nadra Mutran arrived in Damascus and began to propagandize for the society and to arouse the racial consciousness of the Arabs there, cursing the Turks and the CUP. Upon hearing that the society had been founded with the encouragement of the Sultan, in order to assist him against the CUP, Rida exhorted the inhabitants that it was absolutely forbidden to arouse hostility between the Arabs and the Turks "and whoever tries to separate us from them is our enemy".[16] Nadra Mutran too described the sharp response encountered by the members of the society, especially in Damascus—a response justified by the need to defend the Young Turks. Many protests against the society were then sent to Istanbul by Arabs.[17] Among those who denounced the society was the pro-Turkish author and journalist Jurji Zaydan, who viewed the members of the society as sympathizers of the era of tyranny.[18]

The Turks suspected that the members of the society were acting secretly against the government and that they had secret plans to separate the Arabs from the Empire. After the repression of the attempt at a counter-revolution in April 1909, the newspaper *Tanin* explicitly accused the society of connections with reactionary elements working to overthrow the constitution. The society denied these accusations. Yet many of those belonging to the society's branches in the Arab vilayets were supporters of the counter-revolutionary effort, even if not within the framework of the society. The upshot was that after the repression of the counter-revolution the authorities decided to close the society's branches and its newspaper.[19]

The society received its death blow with the publication on 23 August 1909 of the "Law of Societies", which was passed by the parliament after stormy and prolonged debate, by a majority of 90 to 69. The key articles of this law were as follows:

Art. 3: It is forbidden to set up societies which are founded on an illicit basis and which are opposed to the prescriptions of the law and the public morality, or which aim to bring about political dissension between the various elements of the Empire . . .

Art. 4: It is forbidden to set up political societies on the basis of nationalism or incorporating the names of races.

Art. 5: The establishment of secret societies is absolutely forbidden . . .[20]

It was Article 4 that aroused most of the debates during the discussion of the law in the parliament, since this article affected all attempts at gathering together on a nationalist basis. This article also made illegal every society in whose name the word Arab appeared, including, of course, the Arab-Ottoman Brotherhood.

Chapter 11

THE SYRIAN CENTRAL SOCIETY

At the time that Nadra Mutran was roving between Syria and Istanbul, spreading propaganda for the Society of the Arab-Ottoman Brotherhood, his two brothers were living in Paris, adhering to a totally different ideology, an ideology that in the terms of that period was considered revolutionary.

Rashid Mutran, a Greek Catholic from Ba'albek, had left the Empire before the revolution and had moved to Paris, where he had commercial connections with the French. In early 1909 he was described by the Beirut newspaper *La Liberté* as "one of the more fervent auxiliaries of the Hamidian regime and corruption". His younger brother, Nakhla Mutran, also engaged in commerce in Paris at that time. There were those who thought he was the head of Sultan 'Abd al-Hamid's secret police in Paris. Be that as it may, he had contacts with the Ottoman ambassador to Paris and also served as secretary at the Ottoman embassy for a time.[1]

In late 1908 the two founded the "Comité Central Syrien"[2] with Rashid the self-appointed president. On 25 December 1908 the society published a manifesto which declared that all Syrians within and outside the Empire stood behind it and that it expressed their aspirations. It negated the possibility of a constitution in the Western sense on the grounds that because the Empire was made up of many different nationalities with diverse aspirations, it would inevitably be split and fall apart. If indeed a liberal regime came into existence, it could only be a hybrid regime vulnerable to the same arbitrariness as in the past. Since the purpose of the society was to protect Syria against such an eventuality, it accepted the constitution promulgated by the Sultan with the reservation that Syria should have the right of self-government, strong enough to protect itself from possible intervention by the central government. The manifesto continued by claiming that although all the European powers supported a liberal regime in the Empire, it would be reduced to naught by the Turks, who would never cease striving to rule the other races of the Empire and would not display the tolerance necessary to grant to others their legitimate aspirations. Since

Syria was the most important part of the Empire, due to its strategic and geographic position, and since none of the European powers could allow another power to rule it, the society suggested that they support the demand that Syria be granted self-government within the framework of the Empire. In a proclamation that was attached to this manifesto the society called upon the Ottoman parliament to grant Syria self-government.

The manifesto and the proclamation were given first to the French foreign ministry and to the British embassy in Paris and later distributed in the Empire.[3] The first to respond to it was Shukri Ghanim, who was then president of the Ottoman Chamber of Commerce in Paris and had good relations with the Young Turks. He sent a telegram to the CUP centre in Salonika and to the parliament in Istanbul, attacking the activities of the Mutrans and claiming that they lacked all importance. He also sent a letter to Sulayman al-Bustani, a member of parliament from Beirut, informing him that the Syrians were neither separatists nor autonomists but were loyal to the Empire. (Several years later, Shukri Ghanim did an about-face and advanced opinions not very different from those of the two Mutrans.)[4] Nadra Mutran too published a derogatory statement against his brothers in the newspaper *Istanbul*. Rafiq and Haqqi al-'Azm joined the opposition from Cairo and accused the Mutrans of causing injury to the Empire. All these individuals declared their loyalty to the Ottoman idea.[5] The manifesto reached Damascus in the second half of January 1909, and was greeted with general ridicule and criticism. Telegrams signed by hundreds of the city's notables were sent to the Grand Vizier and to the parliament, condemning the proposals of the society and pledging loyalty to the Empire and its unity.[6] In Beirut, the manifesto appeared in the press and was sent to local notables and foreign consulates, but was received with indifference.[7]

On 10 February 1909, the Grand Vizier Kamil Pasha, who was identified with the old regime, appointed two of his own people to be war minister and the minister of the marine. There were those who considered this a dictatorial act. These appointments were not acceptable to the CUP and a government crisis followed. On 13 February the parliament passed a vote of no-confidence in Kamil Pasha and he was removed. In his place, Husayn Hilmi Pasha was appointed Grand Vizier.[8] Following these events the society felt the need to issue two new manifestos. The first manifesto explained that it was the CUP that had saved the Empire from the attempts of Kamil Pasha to harm the constitutional regime and that they would be the ones to save it from similar attempts in the future by continuing to keep an eye on the government. The problem was that Europe and the civilized world saw the behind-the-scenes supervision of the activities of a legitimate government by an organization such as the CUP as an infraction of the constitution that would lead to anarchy. Since it was impossible to continue under these conditions and impossible to forgo the supervision of the CUP that prevented the return of tyranny, the society expressed its opinion that the only escape from this dilemma was administrative independence. Granting this status to the various vilayets would so bind them together that they would be able to repel any potential tyrant. A tyrant who would take over the capital (which would be only the centre of the union of vilayets) would perhaps be able to abolish the constitution and to disperse the parliament, but his power would not exceed the borders of the capital. Only through administrative independence could true liberty and a constitutional regime be preserved; all the elements in the Empire would win their rights and their equality, and the constitutional regime would be maintained. This independence not only would not cut the vilayets off from the centre of the Empire but would strengthen their ties with it.

In the second manifesto, administrative independence was explained for those who had opposed it out of misunderstanding. It meant a state with one flag, with each part ruling its own internal affairs and developing its own culture in its own way. This type of political system has been adopted by all the multiracial states, such as the United States, Germany and Austria-Hungary. The Ottoman Empire was also a country of many races and tongues, but the Turks, who were definitely not the largest element, had taken possession of the government. Only administrative independence for each vilayet could keep them an inseparable part of the Empire. The society therefore demanded that Syria be granted the status of administrative independence; that Arabic be recognized as an official language within it; that its governors, officials and policemen be natives; that its development be in the hands of its own administrative council and municipalities; that a third of its income be used for its own welfare; and that those Syrians who served in the army should serve in Syria itself.[9]

These two manifestos were also distributed in the Empire, and in March 1909 they reached Baghdad and were distributed to the Muslim notables of the city in order to convince them to join the movement for administrative autonomy. 'Abd al-Rahman al-Kaylani, the Naqib of Baghdad, proved his loyalty to the authorities by delivering one of these manifestos to the Vali.[10]

After the issuance of these two manifestos, the society ceased its activities. It would appear the number of its followers never exceeded the two original founders, Rashid and Nakhla Mutran, and its entire activity can be summed up in the publication of its manifestos. While the ideas and the claims of the society in 1909 received no support whatsoever, four years later in 1913, with the Turkification policy of the Young Turks at its height, the demands of the society were brought forward anew by others and this time received support from considerable portions of the Syrian populace.

Chapter 12

THE LEBANESE REVIVAL

In the wake of the massacres of Christians that took place in the Lebanon and Damascus between April and July 1860, France, which considered itself the traditional protector of the Christians in the Levant, sent a force of 6,000 soldiers to restore quiet to the region. In addition to punishing the rioters and compensating the Christians of Damascus and the Lebanon, it was decided that the administration of Mount Lebanon be reorganized. An international committee including representatives of the European powers decided that Mount Lebanon should now be an autonomous sanjaq under a Christian Ottoman governor-general. The boundaries of this sanjaq were narrowed to exclude the city of Beirut, the Biqa' and a number of other towns and villages. All the regulations concerning the special status of this sanjaq were summarized in a protocol that was signed by the representatives of the European powers on 9 June 1861 and was called the règlement organique of the Lebanon. The period that followed, until the outbreak of World War I, saw endless confrontation between the Ottoman authorities, who tried to diminish the rights of the autonomous sanjaq, and the residents of the Lebanon, who tried to preserve them by various means— primarily by asking the European powers to defend the règlement organique.

The problematic nature of Mount Lebanon's special status in the Empire came to the fore after the Young Turk revolution. News of the revolution led to fears among the populace that impending changes would affect this special status. This anxiety grew with the beginning of the election campaign for the first parliament, when many residents of Mount Lebanon adamantly opposed sending representatives to the parliament, a step which they felt would harm its autonomous status.[1] The framework of the demands that the Lebanese would raise from then on was outlined in Paris by Bulus Nujaym, a Maronite lawyer, and author of the book *La Question du Liban* under the pseudonym M. Jouplain. In this book he spoke of the Lebanese nation which had existed from the dawn of history, and called for the return of territories to Mount Lebanon that had been unjustly separated from it by the 1861 règlement organique, and without which it could not develop: the areas of Beirut, Tripoli, the Biqa' and Sidon. He also called for political reform in the Lebanon's regime, a reform which would suit the democratic ambitions of its residents and would block the Young Turks' intention to abrogate its autonomy. He pinned his hopes for the realization of these aspirations on France, the traditional protector of the Lebanese Christians for hundreds of years, to whom the Lebanese now looked for salvation.[2]

Similar and even more extreme demands were presented during the following six years by a series of Lebanese societies inside and outside Mount Lebanon, most with the same Arabic name: The Lebanese Revival (al-Nahda al-Lubnaniyya). They were independent of one another, but they worked towards the same goals and there was some coordination among them.

THE SOCIETY IN THE LEBANON AND IN BEIRUT

On 12 September 1908, while the governor-general of the sanjaq of the Lebanon, Yusuf Franku Pasha, was in his summer home in Bayt al-Din, a large number of Lebanese notables gathered in Beirut and decided to send a delegation to him to present a list of demands concerning the situation in the Lebanon. The most eminent of those initiating this meeting was Salim 'Ammun, a Maronite from Dayr al-Qamar who was the former qa'imaqam of the Kisruwan district and had been dismissed by the governor-general at the end of 1907. As a result of differences of opinion that broke out among the conference organizers, and also because of his personal indecisiveness, he drew back at the last moment and decided not to join the delegation that was leaving that day for Bayt al-Din.

When the delegation reached the governor's palace, its member Habib al-Sa'd presented the governor with the demands of the Lebanese, which were: (a) that the representatives to parliament from the Lebanon should not have the right to discuss matters connected with the Lebanon's special status. Such matters should be decided upon by the Lebanese themselves; (b) that the Lebanese Administrative Council should be dissolved and new members should be elected in accordance with the will of the Lebanese people; (c) that corrupt functionaries should be removed from the Lebanese administration; (d) that some new taxes should be abolished.

The governor refused even to listen to this and left the room.

The delegation responded that it would not leave the palace until its demands were heard. When the governor wanted to set his soldiers against the delegation, he discovered that the local soldiers were sympathetic to it; their Turkish officers tried to persuade him to enter into negotiations with the delegation. On the following day, after the palace had been surrounded by many Druzes from the neighbourhood, the governor agreed to talk to the delegation and even accepted some of its demands. A number of officials and functionaries who were not accepted by the inhabitants were dismissed, and it was decided that a new Administrative Council would be set up, whose vice-president would be Salim 'Ammun. While the latter was indeed accepted by most of the people, there were those who held a grudge against him because he had not participated in the delegation and they considered this a lack of resolution on his part. When difficulties also manifested themselves over the procedures for choosing the members of the new Administrative Council, several Lebanese despaired of improving the situation of the Lebanon from within, and they therefore decided to found the Society of the Lebanese Revival.[3]

The initiators of the society were Maronites of the al-Khazin family of Juniyya. The members of this family had extended connections with France, and during the seventeenth and eighteenth centuries members of the family held the position of Vice Consul of France for 100 years. The two most prominent people from this family at the beginning of the twentieth century were the brothers Philippe (1865-1916) and Farid (1869-1916) al-Khazin, both honorary dragomans at the French consulate-general in Beirut.[4] Other prominent members of the society were Rizq Allah Arqash, a Greek Catholic journalist and lawyer; Khalil Zayniyya, a Greek Catholic journalist and author; and Bishara al-Khuri, who became the first president of independent Lebanon.

The first activity of the society was to protest against sending Lebanese representatives to the parliament. The society organized a conference in Beirut with the participation of Christian and Druze notables from all the districts of the Lebanon. At the conclusion of the conference they sent a telegram to the governor-general in which they announced their opposition to sending "whoever it might be" to parliament. At that time the society was headed by a committee of 25 people whose task, according to the society's programme, was to supervise the activities of the governor and the Administrative Council; to call them to order if they should perform activities harming the special status of the Lebanon or the public welfare; to uncover corrupt officials; and to send the proposals of the society for essential changes in the règlement organique to the government in Istanbul and to the representatives of the foreign Powers.[5]

During 1909 the society crystallized the ideology that directed it until the outbreak of World War I. By this time its members were dissatisfied with maintaining the status quo and defending the special status of the Lebanon, and they demanded an increase in its autonomy, extension of its borders, and coverage of the deficit in the Lebanon's balance of payments by the Imperial Treasury in accordance with the règlement organique (1864 version, Article 15). They also opposed new taxes that had been imposed, the closing of the Lebanon's ports by the Ottoman authorities, a ban on enlarging the salt mines of the Lebanon, and the enforcement of the laws concerning the Lebanon that had been passed by the Ottoman parliament. Their belief was that the Empire had no more right to the Lebanon than the European powers who had signed its règlement organique and guaranteed its special status, and that therefore the Empire did not have the right to introduce any changes in this status without the agreement of those Powers.[6]

In February 1910 Philippe al-Khazin published a pamphlet entitled *Perpétuelle Indépendance Législative et Judiciaire du Liban depuis la Conquête Ottomane en 1516* (Perpetual Legislative and Judicial Independence of the Lebanon since the Ottoman Conquest in 1516), in which he employed extensive documentation to try to prove that the Lebanon had always been legislatively and judicially independent, and that this independence was guaranteed it by the Powers. This independence, which placed administrative, judicial, military and financial matters in the power of the Lebanon, actually made it an autonomous state. At the end of the pamphlet he pointed an accusing finger at the representatives of the Lebanon who were not fighting for the preservation of this status, and claimed that the governor-general of the Lebanon wanted to destroy what was left of the Lebanon's special rights. He called upon the Powers who were the guarantors of its status to intervene on its behalf.[7]

Al-Khazin gave a copy of this pamphlet to the French representative in Beirut, who expressed the opinion that such a thesis had no chance of being accepted; that even if al-Khazin succeeded in proving that the Lebanon had had a certain degree of independence in the past, his claims regarding the Lebanon's present independence were not convincing.[8] A short while later al-Khazin sent a copy of the pamphlet to the Speaker of the

British House of Commons. In an accompanying letter, he presented a series of complaints and claims concerning injuries to the status of the Lebanon, and requested the assistance of the Speaker in the struggle against them. The letter was transmitted to the British ambassador in Istanbul, who rejected al-Khazin's claims one by one. He maintained that, in contrast to what al-Khazin had written, the règlement organique of the Lebanon did not provide it with the right of legislation, and therefore al-Khazin's claim that the authorities were trying to force the Lebanon to send representatives to the parliament was incorrect. The ambassador disposed of the claim that the authorities had closed the Lebanon's ports by asserting that they had not been opened. As to the claim that the Lebanese who were living outside of the Lebanon were worried that they would be drafted into the army, such drafting was reasonable and not in opposition to the règlement organique. The ambassador also rejected al-Khazin's demand that the Lebanese should be able to legislate laws for their own internal administration as absolutely exceeding the provisions of the règlement organique.[9]

In June 1910 the government conducted a population census in the Lebanon. At the head of the forms that were prepared in Istanbul for the residents was printed, whether by mistake or not, "The Vilayet of Lebanon" instead of "The Mutasarrifiyya of Lebanon". The Lebanese saw this as an affront to the special status of the Lebanon, as if it were being regarded as one of the ordinary vilayets of the Empire, and the society immediately advised the residents of Mount Lebanon not to fill in the forms. A wave of protests began streaming into the governor's office from all parts of the Lebanon. They included that of Shahin al-Khazin, one of the society's activists, who summarized the demands of the society as follows:

2. To stop any census as long as the government is not constituted in conformity with the règlement organique.

3. To abolish all illegitimate laws that offend the Lebanon . . .

4. To abolish all new customs duties and collections of taxes.

5. To organize the government in strict conformity with the règlement organique, with the faculty of legislating permanent laws. Without this faculty . . . the government would be incapable of administering the country.

7. To restore to the Lebanon the territories that had been expropriated from it . . .[10]

These demands approached that of establishing a truly independent Lebanon, merely under Ottoman suzerainty, and therefore they could not be accepted by the Ottoman govern-ment. The Lebanese nonetheless continued to despatch similar claims and demands to the representatives of the European pow-ers. In June 1911 Farid al-Khazin gave the French consul-general in Beirut another list of complaints concerning the Lebanon. The present governor's term of office was about to expire, said al-Khazin, and this was the time for the Powers to improve the situation. He complained about the tyrannical authority of the governor of the Lebanon and about the fact that the Powers could not depose him in the present situation. It was his opinion that the governor of the Lebanon should be a local Christian, and if circumstances were not yet ripe for this, a European prince from a neutral country should be appointed to this position. Al-Khazin also complained about the burden of taxes that were imposed on the Lebanese and argued that no one had the right to take out more money for the administration of the country than had been agreed upon in the règlement orga-nique, thus creating the need to impose more taxes. He also voiced the perennial Lebanese complaint over not being permit-ted to use the ports of the Lebanese coast. He concluded his list with the key sentence: "It should be mentioned here that the Powers have never recognised the Sublime Porte's right of *sover-eignty* over the Lebanon but only its *nominal suzerainty*" (emphases in the original). He therefore requested that the Pow-ers that had signed the règlement organique of the Lebanon should protect it from harm. A month later Farid al-Khazin was in Paris on an official visit on behalf of the Maronite Patriarch. He took advantage of this opportunity to present the French foreign ministry with a translation of the petition of the Leba-nese living in Beirut protesting the government's demand that they choose between being drafted into the army or paying a ransom.[11]

The fact that the governor of the Lebanon's term of office was about to expire motivated not only Farid al-Khazin and the members of his society to compose petitions. During May 1912 another society, "The Cedars of the Lebanon" (Les Cèdres du Liban), which had been founded in 1910 and which strove for the administrative independence of the Lebanon under the aegis of France, presented a list of "the demands of the Lebanese" to the representatives of the Powers that had signed the règlement organique of the Lebanon. They demanded first and foremost that the authority of the new governor to arrive in the Lebanon should be limited, and also that the independence of the Admin-istrative Council of the Lebanon be secured. They also demanded improvements in the method of electing the council, by increasing the number of electors in order to decrease the impact of the corruption of any one of them, and of course they also demanded the dissolution of the present Administrative Council. They demanded further that the independence of the officials of the judicial system in the Lebanon should be preserved by their being granted immunity; that a limit should be set on the amount of taxes that could be imposed on Mount Lebanon; that there should be an immediate improvement in the ability of the local militia to preserve the public security; that the residence of the governor-general should be moved from Beirut to the interior of the Lebanon; and that a business court should be set up in the Lebanon.[12]

In 1912 the Society of the Lebanese Revival underwent a process of expansion. Ibrahim Salim al-Najjar, a Maronite journalist and one of the most prominent activists of the society outside of the Lebanon, returned to Mount Lebanon from the United States, where he had founded a branch of the society in New York. He now wanted to set up a branch of the society in every qa'imaqamiyya in Mount Lebanon. He set up two branches in Biqfaya and Zahla, but when he tried to mobilize funds he encountered refusal, which discouraged him from continuing his activities there.[13] At any rate, the increase in the political activity of the Lebanese and the defeat of the Empire in the Balkan War, apparently encouraged the Lebanese so much that some of them went to the French representative in Beirut in October 1912 and declared their belief that the moment had come to remove the yoke of the Turks and to proclaim independence under the aegis of France. The French representative was compelled to throw cold water on their enthusiasm.[14] The demands of the society for the widening of the Lebanon's borders also began to spread beyond the circles of the society and to become popular sentiment at that time.[15]

Although the hopes of the Lebanese for independence then had no chance, their efforts towards the end of the term of the Lebanon's governor did finally bear some fruit. France began negotiations with the Ottoman authorities, which ended on 23 December 1912 with the signing of a new protocol for Mount Lebanon that introduced a number of changes and reforms into its règlement organique. It was decided to set up two ports on the Lebanese coast, one of them in Juniyya. It was also decided that the power of the local gendarmerie should be increased. Ohanes Kuyumjian, an Armenian Catholic who had previously been a senior official in the Ottoman foreign ministry, was appointed to be the new governor.[16]

When the negotiations concerning the new protocol were drawing to an end, the French premier, Raymond Poincaré, gave a speech to the Foreign Committee of the French senate, declaring that France would protect its interests in the Levant. The Lebanese considered this public announcement to be a strengthening of their position, and the society in Beirut sent Poincaré a letter thanking him and expressing Lebanese loyalty to France.[17] However, the society was not entirely satisfied with the new protocol, and in a session that took place on 16 January 1913 it decided to present the representatives of the signatories of the règlement organique with exactly the same proposal that had been presented by Farid al-Khazin in 1911: that from now on the governor of the Lebanon be a native of the region who would be elected by the inhabitants of Mount Lebanon, or alternatively a European governor recommended by the Powers. The society also demanded that the Lebanon be given absolute financial autonomy, that its natural and historic borders be restored, and that the rights of Lebanese residents be preserved even when they left the country. These decisions of the society in Beirut were approved by the president of the society in Cairo, Iskandar 'Ammun, and the secretary of the society in Paris, Khayrallah Khayrallah, and they were sent afterwards by Bishara al-Khuri, the secretary of the society in Beirut, to the French foreign minister.[18]

In April 1912 the Lebanese gendarmerie started a revolt for the improvement of its pay conditions that caused utter chaos. Bishara al-Khuri suggested that a national assembly be set up in the Lebanon, which would have the authority to impose a new tax on the population and use this money to finance the gendarmerie. Finally, after discussions, the society presented the sanjaq's council with a list of reforms that it considered essential for the improvement of the situation in the country. Among other things it called for (a) the establishment of police academies ("so that the Lebanese police will be educated people who will know what their duty demands of them for the public security"); and (b) increasing the salary of the police and of the judges "in accordance with their honour" so that they would be able to resist bribes.[19]

This list of reforms was quite moderate, but the society was also active at this time in spreading its more revolutionary ideas through propaganda in the newspapers. From this standpoint its situation was very comfortable, as it could take advantage of the special status of Mount Lebanon. When the Turks would close one of Beirut's newspapers because of its propaganda, the same propaganda would continue to be published ten minutes away, in Mount Lebanon, without the authorities being able to do anything about it. One of the most prominent members of the society, Rizq Allah Arqash, worked efficiently to gain control of many newspapers in Beirut and turned them into organs of his society. Arqash placed a Christian member of the society, Sa'id 'Aql, as editor of the extremist Islamic newspaper *al-Ittihad al-'Uthmani*, which was owned by Sheikh Ahmad Tabbara, and from then on the newspaper began to promote a pro-French policy. Afterwards Arqash transferred 'Aql to the editorship of the newspaper *al-Ahwal* and introduced another editor at *al-Ittihad al-'Uthmani*. Subsequently *Al-Ahwal* as well began to display pro-French tendencies. Another newspaper under Arqash's influence was *al-Nasir*, and it also expressed a Lebanese, anti-Ottoman and pro-French standpoint. Khalil Zayniyya, another member of the society, was the editor of the decidedly pro-French newspaper *al-Thabat*. The Turks suspected that all these newspapers received monetary support from the French, and they believed that Arqash had connections with the French foreign ministry, through Khayrallah Khayrallah, a member of the Paris branch of the society, and that the French were providing him with money and information for the activities of the society.[20]

The members of the society also infiltrated nearly all the other societies of the period, even those with entirely different goals, and acted from within them to promote the Lebanese idea and pro-French sentiment. Their numbers were especially large in the Reform Society of Beirut and in the Decentralization Party.[21]

When World War I broke out in Europe the Lebanese were already willing to revolt openly against the Ottomans. In early August 1914 a number of Maronite leaders had approached the British, French and Russian consuls-general and requested the assistance of British and French soldiers and a supply of arms and ammunition for an uprising against the Ottomans. They expressed their belief that the Syrian Muslims would join such an uprising. The British consul advised the Maronites who had approached him against revolt, because they did not have the power to withstand the Ottoman army alone, and warned them not to expect Russian or French assistance.

Georges Picot, the French consul-general in Beirut, on the other hand, expressed positive interest, but since he could not yet promise France's active assistance, in the light of its policy of avoiding war with the Ottoman Empire, he approached the

Greek consul-general on his own initiative with the request that the Greek government supply the Lebanese with arms. The Greek government expressed its willingness to give 15,000 rifles and 2 million bullets. Meanwhile the war broke out with the Empire as well, and Picot moved to Egypt, where he continued in his contacts with the representatives of the Greek government in Alexandria. He also sent a telegram to the French foreign minister, stressing the necessity for action in order to preserve French prestige in the Levant, and mentioned that as far as he knew 30,000-35,000 Lebanese would join a landing force coming to liberate them from the Ottomans.

A delegation of Lebanese, Maronites and Orthodox, arrived in Athens shortly afterwards seeking arms to start a revolt against the Ottomans or to assist an Allied landing on the Lebanese coast. The Greek prime minister agreed to give them 3,000-4,000 rifles with ammunition and a small ship to transfer them to the Lebanon, but only on condition that this be done with the agreement of the French government. At this stage the French foreign minister expressed his consent, but the British, who had found out about the plan, expressed sharp reservations. They argued that such a small quantity of arms would not be sufficient, and since the Allies were not in a position to provide active assistance, an abortive revolt would result in severe reprisals on the part of the Ottoman army against the Lebanese. Because according to plan the arms were to be sent to the Lebanon by way of Cyprus, then under British occupation, it was necessary to obtain their approval. Additional discussions were held, and in the end the British agreed, but with open reluctance and with a warning to the Lebanese to be aware of the danger they were getting themselves into. At this point it was the French foreign minister who, on second thoughts, changed his mind and decided that France must concentrate on the western front and not get involved on another front in the Levant.[22] The Lebanese apparently lost their opportunity to revolt and to realize their aspirations for independence, but it can realistically be assumed that the British view was correct and that such a Lebanese revolt would have been doomed to failure.

THE SOCIETY IN CAIRO

Among the Ottoman emigrants who for various reasons left the Empire for Egypt were many Lebanese. They included Antun al-Jumayyil (1887-1948), a Maronite who was an editor at the newspaper *al-Ahram*. Visiting the Lebanon in 1909, he came into contact with members of the Lebanese Revival and was influenced by their ideas for improving the situation in the Lebanon and protecting its rights. When he returned to Cairo he organized a conference, held on 21 November 1909, for the purpose of establishing a Cairene branch of the society. About 200 Lebanese participated. There al-Jumayyil recounted such offences by the Ottoman authorities against the Lebanon's status as the closing of its ports to steamships and imposing taxes. A speech followed by Da'ud Barakat, the editor-in-chief of *al-Ahram*, who called for Lebanese solidarity. It was decided that a society should be set up in Cairo, and to emphasize its independence it was called, in Arabic, not "The Lebanese Revival" but "The Lebanese Union" (*al-Ittihad al-Lubnani*; in French, l'Alliance Libanaise). Iskandar 'Ammun (1857-1920), a Maronite lawyer from Dayr al-Qamar, who had long served in the judicial system of the Egyptian government, was elected president of the society. His brother Da'ud (1867-1922), who was engaged in financial speculation and had lost most of his wealth two years earlier, also joined. After the opening conference and before the outbreak of World War I the participants did not again meet together; the activities of the society were carried out by a limited group of about ten people, most of them Maronites, with a few Druzes.[23]

In April 1912 the society's activists formulated a list of demands concerning the Lebanon, which was to be presented to the Sublime Porte and to the representatives of the signatory powers of the Lebanon's règlement organique. These included the demand to deny the governor of the Lebanon the power to remove members of the judicial service and functionaries in the government; and a demand for precise and valid application of all the arrangements proclaimed in the previous protocols, as well as all those that would come in the future. This list, given to Da'ud 'Ammun to present to the French government in Paris, was quite moderate.[24] But in November 1912 the society's activists met again and sent the following telegram to the foreign ministers of the signatory Powers of the Lebanon's règlement organique:

> The Alliance Libanaise, in the name of the Lebanese people, repeats its solicitation for reforms, as previouly formulated: first and foremost, the establishment of an effective and autonomous constitutional government; proportional representation with legislative power; reintegration of the ancient territories, especially the Biqa'

and Beirut; the appropriation of the rights [to control] of customs, the postal system, and the telegraph. . . . The Lebanese await your protection . . .[25]

In December the society heard rumours that the Ottoman government was about to carry out reforms in the Lebanon under pressure from the Powers. But these reforms did not seem sufficient to the society, and they sent another telegram to the Sublime Porte and to the ambassadors of the Powers in Istanbul:

> Only reforms based on effective autonomy and territorial extension can restore tranquillity to the Lebanon and stop the ruinous emigration. All reforms on any other basis will be sterile.[26]

In 1913, when the Decentralization Party was established in Cairo, several members of the society joined it, among them its president, Iskandar 'Ammun. They had a great influence on the party, and the two groups coordinated their activities to a certain extent on the eve of World War I.[27] The society continued to be active during and after the war, until the establishment of Greater Lebanon by the French in 1920. During these years it underwent a number of ideological changes, the most significant one being the ending of the pro-French tendency that had characterized it.

THE SOCIETY IN PARIS

When Da'ud 'Ammun, the Cairo society's delegate, arrived in Paris in mid-May 1912, he immediately requested an interview with the French foreign minister to present him with the society's demands. The French did not take him seriously, considering him an unknown without a recognized mandate to represent the Lebanese.[28] 'Ammun therefore turned to Shukri Ghanim, who had access to the French foreign ministry, and asked him to mediate for him.

Shukri Ghanim (1855-1932), a Maronite author and playwright who was a native of Beirut, had moved to Paris in 1888 after a short career in the administration of Tunisia. At the time of the Young Turk revolution he was the president of the Ottoman Chamber of Commerce in Paris. Together with Georges Samné, a Greek Catholic doctor who was a native of Damascus, he founded the Ligue Ottomane, whose purpose was to support the new regime. This society disbanded a short time later, after the true aims of the Young Turks were revealed. Ghanim then became one of the founders of the French colonialist society, "Amis de l'Orient", later called the "Comité de l'Orient", whose purpose was to strengthen the connection between the Orient and France, and to participate in solving the problems of the Orient. From then on, Ghanim became involved in French political circles and even gained a certain fame after a play he had written was performed in 1911 at the Odeon in Paris.[29]

When 'Ammun turned to Ghanim, the latter gathered together about 20 Lebanese who lived in Paris for a conference on 1 June 1912. It began with a speech on the situation in the Lebanon by Khayrallah Khayrallah, a Maronite who had been a functionary in the Lebanon and later moved to Paris, becoming the editor of the newspaper *Le Temps*. Then it was decided to set up the "Lebanese Society of Paris" (Comité Libanais de Paris). Shukri Ghanim was elected president of the society and Khayrallah Khayrallah was elected secretary. It is not clear to what extent Ghanim actually represented the opinions of the Lebanese. Scrutiny of his later career shows that he stood for the establishment of a Syrian federation and did not consider the Lebanon to be independent, as did the other Lebanese. At any rate, the Lebanese who participated in the conference gave him and Khayrallah the authorization to represent their demands. Among others who joined the society later were Charles Dabbas, a Greek Orthodox lawyer and journalist who later became president of Lebanon, and an eccentric who called himself "le Comte Cressaty de Damas" and hoped for the annexation of Syria to France.[30]

With this backing, Ghanim felt able to recommend Da'ud 'Ammun to the foreign ministry. He used this opportunity to request a meeting with Premier Poincaré, which 'Ammun and Khayrallah would also attend, at which they could present the premier with their proposals for changes and improvements in the Lebanon's status, on the occasion of the expected end of the term of office of the Lebanon's governor, Yusuf Franku Pasha. The foreign ministry was not enthusiastic, as they questioned Ghanim's mandate to represent the Lebanese as well. At first they wanted to arrange a meeting for the three only with a member of Poincaré's bureau, but eventually, so as not to endanger France's image in the eyes of the Lebanese, they agreed to organize a quick meeting of the three with Poincaré himself.[31]

On 29 June 1912 Ghanim, Khayrallah and 'Ammun arrived at the meeting with the premier. Ghanim explained that the situation in Lebanon in 1860 was not the same as that of 1912, and therefore the règlement organique that had been established then did not suit the present and needed to be changed. He added that the Lebanon did indeed see itself as part of the Ottoman Empire, but only with the preservation of its privileges, which were essential to its existence. The members of the delegation expressed their hope that France would take action on behalf of the Lebanon, and they gave Poincaré a "Memorandum on the Lebanese Question" (Mémoire sur la Question du Liban). Poincaré answered that the Lebanon was always under the patronage of France, which would protect its interests, and he promised to read the memorandum carefully.[32]

The memorandum, written by Khayrallah and signed by him and by Ghanim in the name of the societies of Paris, Cairo and New York, began with a description of the incessant offences by the Ottoman authorities against the special status of Mount Lebanon and the continual erosion of the provisions of its règlement organique. It then discussed the current plight of the Lebanon and the defects of its government, which had led to the emigration of its population. The last part of the memorandum was devoted to the demands of the Lebanese for improvements in the situation on the basis of broad decentralization and division of authority: that the governor of the Lebanon confine himself to his real task, as chief supervisor of the administration of the country, and not have the power to dismiss officeholders without the decision of a disciplinary committee; that a Grand Council (Grand Conseil) be set up which would enjoy immunity and have the necessary authority for the internal administration of the Lebanon; that the Council would be chosen either by a general referendum or by a two-stage election, that is, by the election of electors. It would be replaced every six years and would consist of 19 members: seven Maronites, four Greek Orthodox, four Druzes, two Greek Catholics, one Mutawali Shi'ite and one Sunni. A General Assembly (Assemblée générale) would also be set up, which would include the Grand Council, the members of the civil and the criminal courts, and the heads of the services, and which would present and approve plans for the improvement of the Lebanon's situation. The administration of the Lebanon would be reorganized and it would be divided into 13 administrative divisions. The heads of the services in the central administration would be appointed by the president of the Grand Council. Since the Lebanon's income was not sufficient, the customs and the postal and telegraph systems, which had been taken away from it, should be returned. The return of the Biqa' and Ba'albek, as essential parts of the

Lebanon, was also demanded, as well as the ports of Tripoli and Sidon or the port of Beirut. The memorandum ended with a call to the signatory Powers of the Lebanon's règlement organique to act for the realization of this plan.[33]

There was no chance that the Ottoman government would agree to these demands, which in practical terms were meant to transform the Lebanon into an almost entirely independent state. The French themselves virtually ignored it.

Besides the memorandum, Khayrallah wrote a long article called "La Syrie", which was later published as a book, in which he revealed an interest in all of Syria and not just the Lebanon. He spoke of the Syrian nation and expressed his hope that in the future "one unified Syria" would arise, based on the principles of democracy, secularism and decentralization. It would be a federation of districts, each of which would be based on a religious or ethnic unit of the population, and the cooperation among these districts would be based on Syrian nationalism, which would develop gradually. He also stressed the strong connection existing between the French and Syrian cultures.[34]

The end of the term of the Lebanon's governor continued to occupy the society until late in the year. In November Ghanim sent Poincaré a request from the societies in Paris and New York not to be satisfied merely with appointing a new governor, but to take the opportunity to implement reforms in the Lebanon at this time. The societies also suggested that a local Lebanese, Habib al-Sa'd, should be appointed to the position. While no one bothered to consider this recommendation, another issue that Ghanim had raised—the fear of an increase in British influence in the Levant—did bring him some satisfaction, as Poincaré declared in the senate in December that France would not abandon its interests in the Levant. Following this declaration the society sent Poincaré congratulations in its own name and in the name of the societies of Egypt, New York and São Paulo.[35]

Khayrallah Khayrallah, the secretary of the society, now decided to become more active. In a speech delivered to a group of French statesmen, he warned of the outbreak of an Arab revolt against the Turks if the Turks continued their present policies. He reported to one of the officials in the French foreign ministry that a revolt against the authorities in northern Lebanon was very probable, and asked him what the French attitude would be towards such a revolt. Shortly afterwards the members of the society decided to send Khayrallah on a mission to the Levant. Khayrallah, who was working for the newspaper Le Temps, had taken advantage several times of the opportunity to tour Cairo, Syria and the Lebanon as a journalist, and to coordinate the activities of the Lebanese societies in those places. Thus he left Paris again and arrived in Damascus in January 1913, afterwards proceeding to Beirut. On this journey he disseminated pro-French propaganda and encouraged the activities of the societies in the Lebanon. The Turks believed that Khayrallah's journey was funded by the secret expense fund of the French foreign ministry and that he received 20,000 francs for the assistance of the society in the Lebanon.[36]

In June 1913 the members of most of the Arab societies that existed at that time held a joint congress in Paris (see below). At this congress there were also participants from the Society of the Lebanese Revival: Iskandar 'Ammun, who came as a delegate of the Decentralization Party; Khalil Zayniyya and Ayyub Thabit, who came as delegates of the Reform Society of Beirut; Na'um Mukarzal, president of the Society of the Lebanese Revival in New York; 'Abbas Bijani, a member of the society in Paris who represented the Arabs in Mexico at this congress; as well as Shukri Ghanim, Khayrallah Khayrallah and Charles Dabbas, who came in the name of the Arab community in Paris. A total of one third of the participants in the congress were members of various branches of the society, although only one of them (Mukarzal) came as its official delegate.

This was a rare opportunity for so many important members of various branches of the society to be together, and the society in Paris took advantage of it to come to a joint decision. At a meeting held three days after the congress, they decided to send the foreign ministers of France and Britain a protest "against the plots aimed at dissolving the Administrative Council of the Lebanon, despite its immunity accorded by the règlement organique and confirmed by the last protocol of December 1912" and "against the imposition of new taxes for covering the Lebanon's budget deficit, which Turkey refuses to cover despite its engagements and the international conventions".[37]

The problem of the Lebanon's budget greatly disturbed the Lebanese societies. In 1913 the situation of the Lebanon's balance of payments was most difficult and the Ottoman Treasury refused to assist it, even though it was obliged to do so according to the règlement organique. According to Article 15 of the règlement the Ottoman Treasury was required to cover the Lebanon's expenses whenever these exceeded its yearly income, up to a maximum of 30,000 Turkish liras. But since 1878 the Ottoman Treasury had refused to do so. In June 1913 an international committee was set up in Paris to deal with the problems that had been created following the Balkan War. When the society in Paris saw that the representatives of the Empire who had presented a list of the Ottoman floating debt to the committee had not included in it the sums of money that were supposed to be paid to the Lebanon, they sent a sharp protest letter to the president of the international committee, in their own name and in the name of the societies of Cairo, New York and São Paulo, pointing out the financial obligations of the Empire to the Lebanon according to the règlement organique.[38]

In December 1913 Khayrallah sent the French premier another protest letter in the name of the Lebanese societies, to which he appended 40 protest letters that he claimed had been formulated by more than 300,000 Lebanese, and that were approved by 113 Lebanese mayors and 17 municipal councils. He stated that the Lebanon would be in danger of turning into a desert due to the emigration of its people, unless the Powers intervened. The signatories of the protest letters from the Lebanon claimed that the Ottomans were making a joke of the concessions that had been made in the Lebanon in the wake of the 1860 massacres, that is, the opening of its ports and its right to administer its own budget. The Ottomans were operating the ports themselves and were therefore also receiving the income from them. They were also administering the Lebanon's budget themselves, in such a way as to ensure an artificial balance between expenses and income, so that they would be able to evade Article 15 of the règlement organique. Therefore the Lebanese demanded, in order to improve their situation: (a) the return of the Biqaʿ region to the Lebanon, thus restoring it to its natural and historical boundaries; (b) the return of its customs duties and postal and telegraph systems.[39]

When World War I broke out in Europe, Ghanim informed the French foreign minister that the Lebanese had decided to defend themselves against an invasion of Mount Lebanon by the Ottoman army. He requested that the French consul-general in Beirut, Georges Picot, remain in the Lebanon even if the Empire joined the war on the side of the Germans, since his "moral support" would help the local residents.[40] Picot, however, did not remain in the Lebanon. The society in Paris continued to exist until 1915, when it disbanded after a quarrel between Ghanim and Khayrallah.

THE SOCIETY IN NEW YORK

In 1911 one of the roving activists of the Society of the Lebanese Revival, the Maronite journalist Ibrahim Salim al-Najjar (1882-1957), arrived in New York from Paris and established a local branch of the society. The society chose to call itself, in English, the Lebanon League of Progress. Na'um Mukarzal (1863-1932), a Maronite journalist who had already been living in the United States for many years, was elected president of the society.[41]

In the newspaper *al-Huda*, which he owned, Mukarzal published the principles of the society (46 articles), the most important of which were as follows:

1. Rallying the Lebanese in the religion of nationalism (*wataniyya*)
   . . .
3. Requesting a foreign amir from the six European nations that are guarantors of the Lebanon's independence . . .
5. Extending the Lebanon's borders, that is, restoring its original natural boundaries . . . to include Beirut, Tripoli, Sidon . . .
9. Placing a representative in Europe to represent the Lebanese and demand their rights . . .[42]

With the outbreak of World War I, a delegation of members of the society presented the French ambassador in Washington with a memorandum on the future of the Lebanon. The ambassador organized a meeting for them with the British ambassador and a representative of the Russian embassy as well, for the purpose of presenting their viewpoint. The memorandum expressed the faith of the members of the society that they could always count on protection by Britain, France and Russia against Turkish oppression, and added that they now wished to do them a favour in return. They were, of course, also motivated by the wish to be rid of the Turks and to gain their independence. They noted that the Lebanon had strategic significance because it was located halfway between Asia Minor and Egypt, it possessed ports and it was a natural place for the location of an invading army. From this strategic vantage point it would be possible to dominate all the nearby Turkish territories. The Lebanese Christians, who constituted 80 per cent of the population, now wanted to stand at the side of the Allies and help their invading army defeat the Turks—the natural enemy of the Lebanese. The aspiration of the Lebanese was that the parts of the Lebanon that had once belonged to it would be reannexed and that they would be ruled by a European prince. For this purpose they were willing to make sacrifices, and therefore, as soon as the Allied army invaded Lebanon, a general revolt against the Turks would break out there. For the purpose of this revolt the writers of the memorandum were requesting arms, ammunition, and training officers. They claimed that 150,000 Lebanese backed the society and that it maintained contact with branches in South and Central America, Egypt and the Lebanon. Thousands of Lebanese from the United States would be willing to return to the Lebanon to fight if they would only be provided with appropriate transportation. The British ambassador answered that he did not think the Lebanese Christians were capable of defending themselves in the current circumstances.[43]

Another alternative for the Lebanese and Syrian émigrés who were living in New York was the "Syrian Union Society" (*Jam'iyyat al-Ittihad al-Suri*), which strove for Syria's unity. Its first president was Rizq Haddad and the next Da'ud Hudayri. One of its prominent activists was Najib Diyab, a Greek Orthodox who had been publishing the daily newspaper *Mir'at al-Gharb* for many years. Diyab had also been one of the society's delegates at the Paris Congress, at the end of which he announced that the society intended to hold a congress for Syrians living in the United States to discuss the reforms that Syria required. Delegates from Canada, Mexico and the West Indies were also to participate in this congress, as Syrians living in the New World who wanted to identify with the demands of their brothers in the Ottoman Empire.[44] The congress was never held. The society continued in existence during World War I.

THE SOCIETY IN SAO PAULO

In late 1912 a local branch of the Society of the Lebanese Revival, the Centro Renascença do Libano, was set up in São Paulo in Brazil with Asad Bishara as president. The ideology that guided its members was expressed in an article published in the local newspaper *Abu al-Hawl* under the title "I am a Lebanese":

> A nation becomes truly a nation, an entity of strength, only if a strong feeling of love for the fatherland (*watan*) develops in the heart of most of its people . . . We, the community of Lebanese, do not dream of fighting or revolting against Turkey. But the time has come for us to try to strengthen our national union (*jami'atina al-qawmiyya*) and to put together a nation that will be recognized by the civilized world as the 'Lebanese nation' . . .[45]

At the end of 1912, as the governor of the Lebanon's term of office drew to a close, the society sent a letter to the French premier Poincaré, conveying the demands of the Lebanese for freedom and autonomy. The letter attacked the Ottoman government, which was preventing the Lebanon from developing economically and causing its people to emigrate to foreign countries, and it expressed hope and faith that France, "the liberator of oppressed peoples", would intervene for the Lebanese, as it had done in 1860.[46] After the Lebanon's new protocol was signed, the society joined the societies of Paris, Egypt and New York in protesting against it and characterizing it as insufficient.[47]

When the war broke out, Yusuf Lutayf, a new president of the society, sent letters to the foreign ministers of France and Britain, protesting strongly that the Empire wanted to take advantage of this opportunity to abolish the Lebanon's independence according to its règlement organique. The Empire had already sought to harm the Lebanon when it deprived it of its fruitful territories, closed its ports and took control over its customs, postal and telegraph systems. If the Empire was to abolish the Lebanon's independence completely, the Lebanese were prepared to take up arms in order to defend their existence. Since, however, their means were meagre in comparison with those of the Empire, they expected the Allies to intervene on their behalf. "Long live France/Britain, long live the Allies, long live the Lebanon," concluded the letters.[48]

Chapter 13

AL-FATAT

The Society of the Lebanese Revival was not a secret society not even within the Lebanon, although it did conspire against the sovereignty of the Empire. The first secret Arab society established after the Young Turk revolution was *al-Fatat*.[1]

Four days after the promulgation of the constitution, following the Young Turk revolution, two Arab students, Ahmad Qadri of Damascus and 'Awni 'Abd al-Hadi of Nablus, were walking through the streets of Istanbul. A large crowd was gathering around a Turkish officer who stood on a wagon and extolled the constitution. When he went on to denounce the "Arab traitors" 'Izzat Pasha al-'Abid and Abu al-Huda al-Siyadi, both of whom were loyal to Sultan 'Abd al-Hamid, Qadri and 'Abd al-Hadi took offence. There were many Turks who had served 'Abd al-Hamid just as loyally, and the officer had not denounced them. And even if he did denounce 'Izzat Pasha and Abu al-Huda, why mention the fact that they were Arabs? The two students broke through the crowd and began a stormy debate with the officer. Once home they agreed that the lesson of the incident was clear: the Young Turks were Turkish nationalists who sought domination over the other nationalities of the Empire. Their conclusion was that they must set up a secret society on the model of the Young Turks, for the protection of the rights of the Arabs. When Qadri told another student who was a friend of these two, Rustum Haydar of Ba'albek, about their idea, Haydar agreed enthusiastically. Thus the first nucleus of *al-Fatat* was created.[2]

Shortly afterwards 'Awni 'Abd al-Hadi and Rustum Haydar went to Paris to complete their studies. From there they corresponded with Qadri about the society they decided to establish. Qadri responded that they should carry out their plan and that he would soon join them. In Paris 'Abd al-Hadi and Haydar contacted two other students, Tawfiq al-Natur and Muhammad al-Mihmisani of Beirut, and together with another student who arrived somewhat later, Rafiq al-Tamimi of Nablus, they founded the society on 14 November 1909. All the founders were Muslims.[3] For a short time the society was called "The

Society of *Dad* Speakers" (*Jam'iyyat al-Natiqin bil-dad* — named for the Arabs, who speak a language which they believe is the only one containing the consonant *dad*). Afterwards it was decided that the name of the society would be "The Society of the Young Arab Nation" (*Jam'iyyat al-Umma al-'Arabiyya al-Fatat*). Later the word "nation" dropped out of the society's name and it became "The Young Arab Society" (*al-Jam'iyya al-'Arabiyya al-Fatat*). Finally, out of fear that a name which included the word *'arabiyya* would attract the attention of the CUP, it was decided to shorten the society's name to "*al-Fatat*".[4]

The Society's constitution read:

The Arab nation is behind the other nations socially, economically and politically. Its youth are therefore obliged to dedicate their lives to awakening it from this backwardness, and they must consider what will lead to its progress, so that it will attain the meaning of life and preserve its natural rights. According to this basic principle, a group of young Arabs contracted an alliance in Europe, on 14 November 1909, in order to carry out what nationalism (*wataniyya*) imposes on them: to strengthen the [Arab nation's] social, economic and political status in accordance with what the nature of reality demands. The line of action will be as follows:

1. This group will be called "The Young Arab Society", and its goal is to place the Arab nation in the ranks of living nations.
3. All its members must obey the decisions of the Supreme Committee, even against their will.
4. The members of the Society will be divided into three ranks: (a) all the members; (b) the Council; (c) the Supreme Committee.
7. The Supreme Committee consists of seven members; they are the source of the Society's activities and everything will be done according to them. . . .
12. The Supreme Committee will have a secretary, a clerk and a treasurer, which it will choose from among its members.
17. If one of the members suggests a candidate for membership, the Supreme Committee will decide whether to accept him, by a majority of two-thirds.
18. If three members meet in one town, it will be up to the Supreme Committee to decide whether to allow the establishment of a branch in that town.
21. The funds of the Society consist of yearly dues, amounting to 20 francs for each member, and of dues imposed by the Supreme Committee on those who join the Society.[5]

The society thus acted to preserve the "natural rights" of the Arab nation and to place it "in the ranks of living nations". In contrast to the impression created later, the society did not work at this time for the independence of the Arabs or for their secession from the Ottoman Empire. According to Qadri, "At the beginning the society did not harbour any hatred towards the Empire." Tawfiq al-Natur also related many years later that the idea of Arabism was not yet strong during that period; the Arabs merely wanted the same rights and duties in the Empire that the Turks had.[6]

Eventually the institutions of the society took shape in a slightly different way than what its constitution detailed. The society was headed by an Administrative Committee, which was elected by those members of the society who had undergone a trial period of six months. New members of the society, who in principle were not supposed to know the other members, had an inferior status. In order to be accepted into the society a new member had to be a person "who knows how to keep a secret and who believes in the faith of Arab nationalism (qawmiyya)". In order for a new candidate to be accepted, a previous member had to recommend him. If the candidate was not known to the members of the society or they did not approve of his character, they would appoint a member of the society—not the one who had recommended him—to investigate him. After this investigation they would start to reveal basic details about the society to the candidate, but in such a way that they could retreat and dissociate themselves from him if necessary without this affecting the society's secrets. After the Supreme Committee had finally decided to accept him, the recommending member and another member would adjure the candidate "to obey the decisions of the society, to preserve absolute secrecy and to sacrifice life and property for aggrandizing the glory of the Arab nation and placing it in the ranks of living nations". At this time the new member of the society would know only the two members who had sworn him in, and the society would pass on its instructions to him through them. Other security precautions were giving a number to each of the members and using a cipher for correspondence.[7]

In 1911 Ahmad Qadri went to Paris to complete his higher education. Together with 'Awni 'Abd al-Hadi, Rustum Haydar, Tawfiq al-Natur, Muhammad al-Mihmisani, Rafiq al-Tamimi and an Iraqi student, Sabri al-Khawja, he established the first Administrative Committee of the society. At the beginning of 1912 'Abd al-Ghani al-'Uraysi arrived from Beirut and joined the society. His joining gave the society the means for public expression of its ideas—the newspaper al-Mufid which he owned and edited. Later on the students Jamil Mardam (a future premier of Syria), Subhi al-Hasibi and Mustafa al-Shihabi, all of Damascus, as well as Tawfiq Fa'id of Beirut and Ibrahim Haydar of Ba'albek, arrived in Paris and joined the society. During the 1912 summer vacation Qadri and al-Natur returned to Damascus and Beirut, and on their way they passed through Istanbul. There Qadri decided to bring three of his friends from the Literary Club (see below) into the society: Sayf al-Din al-Khatib of Damascus, Rafiq Rizq Sallum, a Greek Orthodox from Homs (the first Christian in the society), and Yusuf Mukhaybar Sulayman Haydar of Ba'albek. He handed their names to the Administrative Committee of the society, and after it was decided that they should be accepted, the task of swearing them in was given to al-Natur. Sallum described it thus:

> Tawfiq al-Natur . . . said to me: "We have set up a secret society in Paris and its founders are myself, Muhammad al-Mihmisani, 'Awni 'Abd al-Hadi, Tawfiq Fa'id and 'Abd al-Ghani al-'Uraysi. No nation achieves its rights and its independence except through its educated youth. We, the youth who have decided to study in Europe, will reach this goal together with the other educated youth. Be with us." And I agreed and entered.

The president of the Literary Club, 'Abd al-Karim al-Khalil, also wanted to join the society, but was rejected "because of his tendency to love publicity". On the other hand, Tawfiq al-Suwaydi (a future premier of Iraq) was later accepted into the society in Istanbul, and during the same year he moved to Paris and joined the members of the society there. At the beginning of 1913 additional members joined the society by correspondence: Rashid al-Husami, who was then an official in the judiciary system in Karak; 'Arif al-Shihabi and Tawfiq al-Basat of Damascus; 'Umar Hamad of Beirut; and Muhibb al-Din al-Khatib, then living in Cairo.[8]

Muhibb al-Din asked to see the programme of the society he had joined, and al-'Uraysi answered from Paris that a new member of the society could only see its programme after a trial period of three months. Nevertheless, he informed him that the principle of the society was "the liberation of the Arab nation in accordance with circumstances and conditions, gradually, using all means, legal and illegal".[9] This principle was not the principle of the society appearing in the first article of its platform, and it apparently represented a development following the deterioration of the Empire's situation and its loss of territory in Libya and the Balkans.

The members of the society in Paris regularly held secret meetings, and in early 1913 they decided to carry out the society's largest project during this period. Five members—'Abd al-Hadi, Mardam, al-Mihmisani, al-'Uraysi and Fa'id—suggested holding a congress in Paris, at which delegates of the various Arab societies would participate, in order to spread the society's ideas. The realization of the project was to be the responsibility of the first four, and they contacted other Arab activists in Paris for this purpose. At the beginning of April the congress activists contacted the Decentralization Party in Cairo. From then on the contacts were made through the *al-Fatat* representative in Cairo, Muhibb al-Din al-Khatib, who was the second secretary of the Decentralization Party and the one who persuaded the party to join the congress.[10]

Seven members of *al-Fatat* (about a third of the members of the congress), participated in the congress itself, but none of them identified himself as a delegate of that society. The four organizers of the congress on behalf of the society participated in it as representatives of the Arab community in Paris. Rustum and Ibrahim Haydar participated as representatives of Ba'albek, and Tawfiq al-Suwaydi as a representative of Iraq.

Following the congress and the agreement that was signed after it with the Ottoman government (see below), the authorities took a number of steps to appease the Arabs. But the society considered these steps marginal, insufficient and an evasion of the major problems. The society therefore accepted the following resolution: "It is obligatory for us not to be shifted from our principal demands by the steps taken by the Turkish government, and the Arabs must show their true feelings by not accepting any solution that is not in accordance with the resolutions of the Paris Congress." The president of the congress, 'Abd al-Hamid al-Zahrawi, eventually accepted a position offered by the authorities, contrary to the resolutions of the congress. Therefore the society transferred this resolution to its members in Istanbul, Sayf al-Din al-Khatib and Rafiq Rizq Sallum, who were among the heads of the Literary Club there, and requested them to act accordingly. This they did, though not with any great success.[11]

Shortly after the Paris Congress most of the members of the society's Administrative Committee returned to their homes in the Levant, having completed their studies, and together with them the centre of the society moved to Beirut, with a branch in Damascus. Muhammad al-Mihmisani was elected secretary-general of the society's centre, while Ahmad Qadri headed the

Damascus branch. During this period the society's ranks were broadened somewhat by the addition of new members, among them Shukri al-Quwwatli (a future president of Syria) and Kamil al-Qassab, an 'alim who was the principal of a secondary school in Damascus and was to become a key figure in the Arab movement in future years. A more significant broadening of the society's ranks occurred when it consolidated its membership with that of the Ten Brothers Society (al-Ikhwan al-'Ashara—named after the first ten sahaba of Muhammad), which had been founded in 1912 by Muhammad al-Shurayqi of Latakia and had members in Beirut, Damascus, Latakia and Tripoli. Following negotiations between the latter and Muhammad al-Mihmisani, the societies were united, and al-Shurayqi was granted the status of one of the founders (mu'assisun) of al-Fatat.[12]

The centre of the society in Beirut met once a week, and the content of the meetings was written down in a special protocol by Muhammad al-Mihmisani and his brother Mahmud. The contacts between the centre and the members were conducted in such a way that they could not know where the centre was located and who its members were. The centre's letters were sent out from the address "The Desert" (al-badiya). In March 1914 the members of the centre held a meeting in the office of the newspaper al-Mufid in Beirut. Through the French postal system Muhammad al-Mihmisani reported on this meeting to Muhibb al-Din al-Khatib in Cairo:

... "Ata'" [the code name of al-Fatat] also decided at its last meeting that its flag would have three colours symbolising the three Arab states [the Umayyad, the Abbasid, and the Fatimid]: green, white and black. It also decided to ask you to prepare a seal for it, with the letters 'ayn, fa [the initials of al-'Arabiyya al-Fatat], with a drawing of a palm tree, leaving the choice of the design of this seal to your good taste.

Muhibb al-Din showed this report to his friends in the Decentralization Party, and the party secretary, Haqqi al-'Azm, announced in a letter to Muhammad al-Mihmisani that the party members had decided to adopt this flag. The members of al-Fatat began distributing badges in the three colours of the flag in Beirut.[13]

In August 1914 the society sent Muhammad al-Mihmisani to Cairo to consult with the leaders of the Decentralization Party concerning the Arabs' attitude towards the approaching war (which had not yet broken out in the Middle East), before the routes between Syria and Egypt were cut off. He stayed there for two days, and after discussions were held it was decided that they should not take any independent decisions, without coordination with the Arab amirs of the Arabian Peninsula. In addition, the party members told al-Mihmisani about contacts that had been begun with the British. Afterwards al-Mihmisani hurried to return to Beirut, with the intention of joining the Ottoman army and defending the fatherland against its enemies.[14]

When the Empire entered the war, contrary to the society's hopes, Damascus became the headquarters of the Ottoman Fourth Army and Syria's centre of gravity. The society's centre moved there at the end of October 1914. From Damascus the society tried to organize its branches in the other Syrian towns and to make contact with the other Arab countries and the outside world. As a result of al-Mihmisani's report on his discussions in Cairo, the society now decided to send Kamil al-Qassab there. At this stage the supporters of independence had the upper hand in the society, and instructions were given to al-Qassab to find out the nature of the contacts with the British and inform those involved that the activists in Syria would not be satisfied with less than full independence for the Arab countries. Al-Qassab left Damascus for Beirut and there paid a sum of money to an Italian sailor who agreed to help him stow away on an Italian ship that was sailing to Alexandria. He was arrested by the British upon arrival, but was freed immediately through the intervention of Rafiq al-'Azm and Rashid Rida. In Cairo he met with the members of the Decentralization Party, without significant results, and also with the British, whom he told that most of the Muslims were prepared to reach an understanding with Britain, based on the establishment of an independent Arab state and on condition that Syria would not be occupied by France. The British did not respond to his suggestion. Al-Qassab returned to Damascus and was arrested by the authorities, who had found out about his trip. But when they interrogated him, he succeeded in convincing them that its whole purpose had been to purchase equipment for his school, and he was released. In fear of his life, he then seized the first opportunity to escape to the Hijaz.[15]

Apparently the lack of response on the part of the British, and perhaps also the relative freedom that the Arabs still enjoyed in Syria at that time, before Jamal Pasha's regime, led the society to decide finally to cooperate with the Ottomans. At a special session that was held on this matter in Damascus the Supreme Committee of the society resolved:

In consequence of Turkey's entry into the War, the fate of the Arab provinces of the Ottoman Empire is seriously imperilled and every effort is to be made to secure their liberation and independence; it being also resolved that, in the event of European designs appearing to materialise, the society shall be bound to work on the side of Turkey in order to resist foreign penetration of whatever kind or form.[16]

A few days later Jamal Pasha arrived. The reign of terror that he established in Syria in mid-1915 completely changed the attitude of the society towards the Empire, and it decided to work for the independence of the Arab countries, with the help of Britain.

Chapter 14

AL-QAHTANIYYA

At about the same time that *al-Fatat* took shape in Paris, another secret society was established in Istanbul, for reasons not much different from those that led to the idea of *al-Fatat*. During and after the Young Turk revolution, many Arab officers joined the CUP in the hope that a new era was beginning in the Empire. Some of them discovered, through declarations of CUP members and through documents in the central office of the CUP in Salonika, that Jawid Bek, Dr Nazim, Niyazi and other members of the CUP had deposited a large sum of money (400,000 liras, it was said) with Jews in Salonika, with the intention of using this money to help establish a centralized government which would impose itself by force over the other nationalities of the Empire.[1] These officers, in cooperation with a number of civilians, established the *al-Qahtaniyya* society in Istanbul at the end of 1909. The society was named after Qahtan, the legendary forefather of the Arabs, perhaps in imitation of the yearning of some of the CUP members for Turan, the legendary land that the Turkish tribes came from.

The most prominent of the society's founders were a civilian, Khalil Hamada, and an officer, Salim al-Jaza'iri. Hamada was a Muslim from Beirut who had lived in Egypt for many years and was employed there by the Egyptian government. He had been sent by them to the Ottoman government to act as a consultant, and in 1909 he held the position of Awqaf minister in the Ottoman government.[2]

Salim al-Jaza'iri (1879-1916), born in Damascus, was of Algerian origin. His father died when Salim was a child, but he was cared for by his uncle, Sheikh Tahir al-Jaza'iri. The uncle felt that his nephew had a talent for a military career, and when he had completed his elementary education enrolled him at the Military Academy in Istanbul. Salim al-Jaza'iri studied afterwards at the Staff Academy and at the School for Land Engineering. In 1906 he began to teach mobilization and military mobility at the military academies in Damascus and in Istanbul. He joined the opponents of the tyrannical regime of Sultan 'Abd al-Hamid, and at the time of the Young Turk revolution he became a member of the CUP. He also participated in the suppression of the counter-revolution in 1909. To his military academy students he presented examples from Islamic history and from the victories of past Muslim leaders, while emphasizing the military strategies of the Arab leaders. This did not please the Turkish nationalists, and they began to limit his activities. As a result of his disappointment with his comrades in the CUP, and after he began to sense that some of them sought to assimilate the Arabs, not only was he among several Arab officers who left the CUP, but he decided that there was a need to set up secret Arab societies that would encourage cooperation among the Arabs and emergence from their centuries-old stagnation.[3]

These two were joined in the establishment of the society's centre by 'Abd al-Hamid al-Zahrawi, an 'alim from Homs who was then a representative of Hama in the parliament, and 'Aziz 'Ali al-Misri, an Egyptian-born officer who was later to play an important role in the development of the Arab movement in this period. Al-Misri later expressed reservations about the multiplicity of the Arab societies, and he claimed that it would be better to concentrate on developing and strengthening a single society. Salim al-Jaza'iri opposed this approach and argued that the many societies had a right to exist simultaneously, even if they were striving for the same goals. In his opinion this was the only way to compete with the Turks, who also had many societies. Other prominent men who joined the society were the civilians Haqqi al-'Azm, Shukri al-'Asali, 'Izzat al-Jundi, Amin and 'Adil Arslan (cousins), Hasan Hamada, 'Abd al-Karim Qasim al-Khalil, 'Arif al-Shihabi, Ibrahim Salim al-Najjar, Salim Thabit and Da'ud al-Dabbuni; and the officers Amin Lutfi al-Hafiz, 'Ali al-Nashashibi and Isma'il al-Saffar.[4]

The goals of the society, to which every member had to swear, were to raise the cultural, social and economic level of the Arabs, and to induce them to act through solidarity and to demand their rights in the Empire. The society demanded equal rights for Arabs and Turks within the framework of the Empire, and claimed that present injustice towards the Arabs stemmed only from the fact that they did not stand up forcefully for their rights. It was therefore a duty for every member of the society to arouse the Arabs to do this, albeit as loyal Ottomans. If the government were to reject their just demands, then the society would have to take the appropriate steps. The society did not specify the type of steps it intended to take in this case, and it did not express any definite aspiration for Arab secession from the Empire.[5]

In order to enlarge its ranks, the society decided that every member would be obliged to enrol another member even without the authorization of the centre. The society attempted to spread its ideas among the members of the Literary Club, which was founded in Istanbul a short while after it. The society also attempted to enrol additional members from among the army officers, and from then on officers began to be involved in the Arab movement. The military wing of the society was headed by Salim al-Jaza'iri, assisted by Amin Lutfi al-Hafiz. Al-Jaza'iri was very strict about carrying out commands and stressed orderly activity, in the belief that only what was done in an orderly manner (*nizam*) would succeed. For security reasons the society did not distribute proclamations, but transmitted its messages orally. Other security measures were the use of identification signals and passwords of varying degrees of secrecy.[6]

The society had a few branches of various sizes outside the capital, with 'Arif al-Shihabi adminstering its affairs in Damascus and in Beirut. In April 1910 'Abd al-Hamid al-Zahrawi founded the newspaper *al-Hadara* in Istanbul, to serve as an organ for spreading the society's ideas. At this time, however, the society had already passed the peak of its activity, less than half a year after it was founded. In June 1910 one of its founders, Khalil Hamada, died. The officers al-Jaza'iri and al-Misri were sent to fight in Yemen. Al-Zahrawi left Istanbul because of the increased pressure of the CUP. Haqqi al-'Azm moved to Syria in the position of Awqaf inspector. 'Izzat al-Jundi also left the capital. In the absence of all its senior members from Istanbul the society disintegrated without ever formally disbanding.[7]

It seems that the last attempt at a coordinated activity by the members of the society was undertaken by Shukri al-'Asali and Salim Thabit, two members who arrived in Cairo at the end of 1911 or the beginning of 1912. The two presented various Egyptian politicians (among them Ahmad Lutfi al-Sayyid, the leader of the Nation Party) with an idea that was not at all related to the ideology of *al-Qahtaniyya*: the annexation of Syria to Egypt. The Egyptian politicians rejected this idea. Nevertheless, when Thabit returned to Beirut, he related that everything was ready for this plan.[8]

Chapter 15

THE LITERARY CLUB

Among the young activists of the Society of the Arab-Ottoman Brotherhood was a Shi'ite student from Jabal 'Amil in the Lebanon, 'Abd al-Karim Qasim al-Khalil. When this society was closed by the authorities he undertook to establish a new society to fill the void, which would be run by people more suited than their predecessors to dealing with the problems of the Arabs. Al-Khalil had arrived in Istanbul in 1905 and studied there in the schools of administration and law. He was one of the first members of the Society of the Arab Revival and afterwards of the secret society al-Qahtaniyya. But he believed that a new open group was also needed, so that the Arab students living in Istanbul could meet and discuss their culture and their heritage, rather than, as he saw it, wandering around idly in the streets of the city and trying to be like the Turks, out of contempt for the Arabs' past and their culture.[1]

Al-Khalil wrote a constitution for such a club and presented it for consideration to Rashid Rida, then in Istanbul. Rida not only approved the idea but suggested that al-Khalil present it to Khalil Hamada, the Awqaf minister, who dealt with clubs of this type. Hamada, who already knew al-Khalil from the ranks of al-Qahtaniyya, greeted the idea enthusiastically, encouraged him to carry it out, made a number of changes in the constitution and even suggested that the club be called the Literary Club (al-Muntada al-Adabi). The minister also promised to allocate 500 Turkish liras per year for the new club from the Awqaf budget, in the expectation that the club would be a kind of educational institution with a lecture series, a library and a number of rooms set aside for Arabs who lacked the wherewithal to stay at a hotel in the capital. When Shukri al-Husayni, the former treasurer of the Society of the Arab-Ottoman Brotherhood, learned of al-Khalil's activity, he transferred to him the 60 liras that remained in the society's fund after it was shut down, and he also gave him all of the society's furniture. Other people who sent donations to the new club were Sayyid Talib al-Naqib and Ahmad Pasha al-Zuhayr, both representatives of Basra in the parliament, as well as the Ottoman crown prince. The money was insufficient for beginning organized activities in the club, and al-Khalil and his friends put on a play called "Salah al-Din al-Ayyubi", which brought them an additional 60 liras. With the combined sums of money they set up the clubhouse. Later the club's administration decided to institutionalize the club's finances and to impose fixed dues.[2]

The opening ceremony for the club was held on 8 February 1910. But the ceremonies soon gave way to controversy. While Al-Khalil had several partners in the establishment of the club—Yusuf Mukhaybar Sulayman Haydar of Ba'albek, Sayf al-Din al-Khatib of Damascus, and Jamil al-Husayni of Jerusalem—he was nevertheless recognized as its president. But when a meeting of the club members was held a week after its opening for the purpose of electing its first Administrative Committee, a number of youths hostile to al-Khalil suddenly stood up and demanded that the constitution be changed and that the names of the founders be omitted. They were headed by 'Abd al-Qadir al-Jaza'iri, the grandson of Amir 'Abd al-Qadir, 'Izzat al-Jundi and Ahmad Qadri (who called al-Khalil "a covetous person who is easily led"[3]). Their intention was to offend al-Khalil, and a fierce argument soon broke out between his supporters and his opponents. The entire programme of the club seemed about to be lost, and several members rushed to 'Abd al-Hamid al-Zahrawi's home to tell him what was happening. Al-Zahrawi hurried to the club, took the chair and suggested that a neutral person acceptable to both sides be elected to the presidency of the club. Husayn Haydar, a doctor from Ba'albek, also hurried to the club and in order to placate the wranglers promised to donate 20 liras for buying books and to buy a plot of land on which to construct a new building for the club. In a vote held later among all the club members, it was decided to keep the constitution as it was, and Mustafa 'Adil, from Tripoli (Syria), nondescript and thus uncontroversial, was elected president. Representatives of both camps were elected to the Administrative Committee: Jamil al-Husayni, 'Abd al-Karim al-Khalil, Yusuf Mukhaybar Sulayman Haydar, Sayf al-Din al-Khatib, 'Izzat al-Jundi, Sami al-Sulh, Ahmad Qadri and 'Abd al-Qadir al-Jaza'iri. A year later, when 'Adil's term ended, some of al-Khalil's opponents had already left the capital. He was elected president of the club in a quiet election and continued to hold this position as long as the club existed. The Christian Rafiq Rizq Sallum of Homs was appointed vice-president.[4]

Most of the Arab students who studied at the various institutions of higher education in Istanbul came to the club. It not only attracted students, however, but also members of parliament, such as al-Zahrawi, Rushdi al-Sham'a, Shafiq al-Mu'ayyad and Shukri al-'Asali; officers, such as Salim al-Jaza'iri, 'Aziz 'Ali al-Misri, and Ja'far al-'Askari (a future premier of Iraq); and other prominent activists, such as 'Abd al-Wahhab al-Inklizi and Haqqi al-'Azm. In a short while the club had over 280 members, and another 500 occasional visitors of all religions and communities.[5]

The apparent purpose of the club was "to favour the intellectual progress of the students of institutions of higher education, by providing them with learning materials, giving them lessons, and organizing scientific, literary and artistic conferences".[6] But as Sayf al-Din al-Khatib related, "The fundamental purpose [of the club] was to gather the youth together in one place and to train their thoughts on the elements of nationalism (*'unsuriyya*) and independence." And Sullam added: "The club had secret instructions that no one except the founders knew about." The secret programme of the club was as follows:

1. Some or all of the founders will tour Beirut, Syria and Mount Lebanon at least twice a year.
2. 'Abd al-Karim al-Khalil and Sayf al-Din al-Khatib will engage in propaganda, in order to attract the students who come to Istanbul for their studies.
3. Proclamations and forms printed for the Society in Egypt or at the *al-Mufid* printing house in Beirut and sent to the club will be distributed among the Arab youth as secretly as possible.
4. This programme must not be revealed to members entering the society, except to those who are absolutely reliable and experienced.[7]

By the time the club had completed its second year, it virtually became an open organization of a secret society called the Arab Youth Society (*Jam'iyyat al-Shabiba al-'Arabiyya*), whose purpose was to bring about the independence of the Arabs by educational means.[8]

Within the framework of the overt activities of the club various courses were offered, among them classes in Turkish and other languages. Lectures were given in a variety of subjects, and the lecturers included, on the one hand, such sworn Ottomans as Sati' al-Husri and, on the other hand, Arab activists such as Rashid Rida, Nadra Mutran, 'Abd al-Hamid al-Zahrawi, 'Aziz 'Ali al-Misri and Salim al-Jaza'iri. While the latter ostensibly lectured on historical topics, they would include ideas about independence in their talks. Turkish notables were also invited to parties at the club, and meetings took place between Arab and Turkish youth as well. Debates were held about the need for reforms, the appropriate measures to combat the Turkification tendencies of the Turkish nationalists, and how to stand up for the rights of the Arabs. At one point Yusuf Shatwan, the representative of Tripoli (Libya) in the parliament, suggested that 50 liras a month from the budget of the education ministry should be allotted to the club for these activities. When the education ministry subsequently sent a supervisor to the club to investigate whether the building and the rooms were appropriate, the club members decided to give up the allotment in order not to be under the supervision of the government. They continued to put on historical plays in order to finance their activities. One of these was "Imru' al-Qays" presented before government officials, members of parliament and other notables, under the honorary presidency of the Ottoman crown prince. The various activities absorbed much of the participants' time, and there were those who complained that the students were neglecting their studies because of their incessant occupation with politics.[9]

The idea of Arab independence led to the students' creation of an Arab flag: four horizontal stripes, the top one white, followed by black, green and red—and they hung such a flag inside the club.[10] Egypt was another topic of discussion and concern, for at that time it was not clear to the Arabs whether Egypt was an Arab country or not. While after lengthy debate, the club members decided that it was indeed an Arab country,[11] this conclusion was not necessarily accepted by the Egyptians themselves.

In March 1910 the Turkish newspaper *Iqdam* published an article on Yemen that was highly insulting to the Arabs, who were characterized as not knowing what honour and loyalty were and as only fit to be camel-drivers. The residents of Yemen were described as "worshipping money. They will sacrifice anything for money, even the honour of women." In response to this article, the Arab students in Istanbul, headed by the club members, held a stormy demonstration against the owner of the newspaper and the writer of the article, smashed the windows of the administrative building of the newspaper with stones, and finally broke into the office, destroyed the furniture and threatened the owner of the newspaper. Not all the Arabs in the capital supported this step; Sulayman al-Bustani, the representative of Beirut in the parliament, denounced it, although he pointed out to the authorities that the article was indeed insulting. Finally Interior Minister Tal'at put an end to the matter by suspending the newspaper, putting its editor on trial and fining him 100 liras. He put the students on trial for disturbing the public order as well and fined them for the damage they caused to the newspaper office.[12]

According to 'Abd al-Karim Qasim al-Khalil, activity aimed at raising the standard of the Arabs was best concentrated in the realm of education, and he thus implemented a plan for reforms in the Arab elementary schools. In June 1911 al-Khalil organized and invited the Arab representatives in the parliament to a conference at which he spoke about the educational situation in the Arab vilayets and its deficiencies. At the beginning of his speech he dwelt on the fact that there was no cooperation among the Arabs themselves: "You see that the Iraqi knows very little about what is happening to the Syrian and the Hijazi does not feel the pain of the Yemenite . . ." In order for the Arab nation to attain its rightful place in the Empire, he claimed it must act together for a definite goal. The Arabs must unite because they had "unity of language, unity of history, unity of fatherland (*watan*) and unity of interests". He presented education as an example of the lack of unity that prevailed in the Arab world, for methods and curricula varied widely from place to place. As a result the Arabs were religious and atheist; Westernized and conservative. To unite them would be as difficult as "to combine fire and water". In order to overcome this problem and to fight ignorance (*jahl*), a new educational system was required, beginning with elementary education, which must become uniform. The members of the club, al-Khalil continued, would be the first to take this project upon themselves. He presented a detailed programme to implement his idea, with the participation of members of the parliament. The programme was accepted sympathetically by the members of parliament, who promised to carry it out. It was later published in the Arab press and al-Khalil went to Cairo to promote it. A special committee with 17 members, Egyptians and Syrians (among them Ahmad Taymur, Rafiq al-'Azm and Shibli Shumayyil), was set up there to implement the programme, yet in the end nothing came of it.[13]

Although initially the club saw itself as part of the Ottoman unity, as relations between the Arabs and the Turks worsened, the club's separatist tendencies increased. In a guest lecture in December 1912 Muhammad Haydar called upon his listeners to follow the example of Tariq ibn Ziyad, who had called to his soldiers "Victory or death". Preaching "love of the fatherland and the nation", he concluded "that a person is commanded to sacrifice himself for his ideology is the first of the principles written on the pages of history. Let us take it on, brothers, because this will give us a great victory."[14] The defeats of the Empire in Libya and in the Balkans only strengthened the feeling of the club members that the Arabs must be capable of defending themselves and no longer depend on the Empire. Thus they formulated the following principles:

1. The Arab nation is one great nation which has lost its magnificence and its independence because foreigners have gained control over it.
2. Because the Arab countries are rich countries, the Powers have ambitions, and strive to dominate them.
3. The Ottoman government, whose weakness and impotence were proven in the wars in Tripoli and the Balkans, will not be able to defend the Arab countries in time of need, should they be attacked by a powerful enemy.
4. The only way to change the situation is by strengthening the Arab element in the Ottoman Empire and turning it into one able to defend its own existence.[15]

In order to strengthen the connections among the various Arab societies, Sayf al-Din al-Khatib went to Beirut in early 1913 to make contacts with the Reform Society there. At the same time al-Khalil went to Cairo for contacts with the Decentralization Party. While there, and as a private initiative, probably to strengthen his position, he set up contacts with a delegation of four German officers, headed by Captain von Hammerstein, which undoubtedly contradicted his friends' fears of foreign infiltration. The purpose of the delegation was to monitor French propaganda in Syria and to set up German intelligence agencies and propaganda centres in Damascus and Beirut. Al-Khalil was to guide this effort. In February 1913 he arrived in Beirut, where he established contacts with the members of the Reform Society.[16]

After the Paris Congress al-Khalil arrived in Paris with a delegate of the CUP and, as described below, facilitated the signing of an agreement between the government and the members of the congress. As a result of this agreement, and the negotiations that 'Abd al-Hamid al-Zahrawi, the president of the congress, held afterwards with officials of the Ottoman government, al-Zahrawi agreed in January 1914 to accept the position of senator. His acceptance was perceived as contrary to the resolution of the Paris Congress that positions should not be accepted until the reforms had actually been carried out, and it aroused great rage against him among the Arabs of Istanbul. But al-Khalil remained at al-Zahrawi's side and defended his decision.

Al-Khalil's involvement in the agreement with the CUP, and his defence of al-Zahrawi, led to the most serious threat to his status as president of the club since the elections for the first Administrative Committee in 1910. The club members met to demand that al-Khalil explain his actions, and a five-member committee was appointed to obtain explanations from him. It was made clear to him that if he refused to discuss the matter with the committee, the members of the club would vote non-confidence in him. At a session that continued far into the night al-Khalil explained his reasoning and why he believed that the CUP was prepared to implement reforms. The committee members were not convinced, but nevertheless, in order to try to heal the breach, which they understood would harm the Arabs more than any others, they finally decided against a vote of no-confidence, instead limiting al-Khalil's activities by appointing a four-member Advisory Committee that he was required to consult in his future political contacts with the government and with the CUP. However, this solution did not satisfy all the Arab activists, and there were those who continued to attack al-Khalil fiercely and to accuse him of responsibility for the disintegration of the reform movement in late 1913 and early 1914.[17]

The CUP members, satisfied with al-Khalil's stands, began to visit the club frequently in order to demonstrate their good intentions towards the Arabs and the correctness of al-Khalil's political conception. Among the visitors were the leaders of the CUP, Tal'at, Enver, Jamal, Fethi and Midhat Shukri. During a speech on one occasion Tal'at declared: "If the Arabs are seduced into believing that they can escape from the Turks, they should know that the Turks will not leave them alone but will follow them like their shadows until they catch them, because the Turks consider the Arabs to be their elder brothers, and it is not easy for a younger brother to leave his elder brother." Tal'at ended with a promise that he would deliver next year's speech not in Turkish but in Arabic.[18] Not surprisingly, not all the club activists were taken in by these fine phrases, and some had already decided that partial solutions such as decentralization were insufficient; that they must strive for absolute secession from the Empire.[19]

In February 1914 the club members were involved in the struggle for the release from prison of 'Aziz 'Ali al-Misri, against whom the Ottoman authorities had brought a list of accusations.[20] At the end of that month the club periodical commenced publication under the same name as the club: *al-Muntada al-Adabi.* This periodical had begun in March 1913 under the name *Lisan al-'Arab*, and was then published by 'Izzat al-A'zami, a student from Baghdad, who was one of the founders of the Green Flag Society, to which the journal first belonged. Al-A'zami, who was also a senior member of the club, now agreed to transfer the periodical to the club and edited it together with another club member, 'Asim Basisu of Gaza. It dealt with Arabism, Arab history, the Arabic language and the rights of the Arabs. Its editorial office also served another purpose, described by Rafiq Rizq Sullam thus: "Proclamations that incited the Arabs against the occupation and in favour of killing the Turks reached us in newspapers that were sent to the manager of the periodical *al-Muntada*, 'Izzat al-A'zami, and to its editor, 'Asim Basisu, and we read them." And Sayf al-Din al-Khatib added: "'Izzat al-A'zami brought in many youths who were studying in the administration and military schools to the office of *Lisan al-'Arab* and *al-Muntada*, and he read these proclamations to them."[21]

At the outbreak of World War I it seemed that al-Khalil's attitude towards the Turks and towards Arab nationalism was changing. Club member Tawfiq al-Basat once asked him, "If we support pan-Islam why are we trying to spread the Arab idea?" Al-Khalil's answer was: "Because the idea of pan-Islam leads to weakness rather than strength, as it distances us from the West while it is incapable of giving the East strength."[22] Nevertheless, when Jamal Pasha invited al-Khalil to persuade the people of Syria to support the government, he hurried to do his bidding. In August he wrote to one of his friends:

> I am about to go to Syria . . . My task in Syria is to bring about the consent of the nation to support the government . . . The government has promised to assist me in this task and to grant any justified requests I will bring them in the name of the Arab nation or in the name of any of its sons. Let us all work together to save the state from the consequences of the European war . . .

Taking the club's last 25 liras, Al-Khalil left for Syria.[23] Following the proclamation of general mobilization in the Ottoman Empire, some club members were mobilized and the rest scattered. In March 1915 the club was closed by the authorities.[24] In August 1915 'Abd al-Karim Qasim al-Khalil was executed by hanging in Beirut, after he had changed his attitude towards the Turks once again and organized a rebellion in the south of Mount Lebanon.

Chapter 16

THE SOCIETY OF THE ARAB ASSOCIATION

The Arab societies that arose within and outside the Ottoman Empire after the Young Turk revolution were divided among those whose goals were particularistic (for instance, the Society of the Lebanese Revival) and those imbued with Arab consciousness (such as the Literary Club), although this consciousness was not defined and the activists did not know how to fulfil their Arab identity. Societies of this latter type had no aspirations, at least at the beginning, to cut the Arabs off from the Ottoman Empire and establish an independent Arab state. They were established to protect the rights of the Arabs; only after this failed did they begin to think about breaking away from the Empire (in the main on the eve of the outbreak of World War I). Even then they had not clearly formulated, even for themselves, what alternative existed to being Arabs in the Ottoman Empire. The first society, perhaps the only one in the pre-war period with a clear and definite aim of establishing a single large, although decentralized, independent Arab state in the Arab countries under Ottoman rule, was the ephemeral society established in Cairo by the Muslim thinker, Muhammad Rashid Rida.[1]

Rashid Rida (1865-1935) was born in the village of al-Qalamun about three miles from Tripoli (Syria). He began his studies with the traditional *kuttab*, continuing at a government school in Tripoli and later entered the Islamic school of Sheikh Husayn al-Jisr where he studied science and philosophy along with religious studies. After having read *Ihya 'Ulum al-Din* by al-Ghazali, he began to lean towards the *tasawwuf* and for a short time joined the Naqshabandiyya order. When, eventually, he understood the spiritual danger of this method he left the order. In 1897 he received a teacher's certificate from Sheikh Husayn al-Jisr and the degree of 'alim. During this stage of his life Rida was influenced both by the advanced ideas taught by Sheikh Husayn al-Jisr and by the copies of *al-'Urwa al-Wuthqa* that fell into his hands. He decided to broaden his knowledge under the tutelage of Jamal al-Din al-Afghani, who was then in Istanbul but died the same year. After suspicions were aroused that the Hamidian regime was responsible for al-Afghani's death, Rida elected to leave the Ottoman Empire for Egypt to join the other man he admired, Muhammad 'Abduh. He travelled first to Beirut and then, penniless, boarded a ship sailing for Egypt. When he arrived in Cairo, he immediately joined Muhammad 'Abduh, thereafter his spiritual teacher. In March 1898 he began publishing *al-Manar* (The Lighthouse), first as a weekly of eight pages and then, a year later, as a monthly periodical. Muhammad 'Abduh's teachings on Islamic reform were its primary subject, though articles on other topics by other writers, such as *Umm al-Qura* by 'Abd al-Rahman al Kawakibi, also appeared. This publication annoyed the Ottoman authorities so much that in 1906 the court of Tripoli issued an order to arrest, wherever he might be, "Muhammad Rashid Rida . . . who had escaped to Egypt and is the owner and editor of the 'vanity filled' paper, *al-Manar*, and is suspected of printing traitorous and slanderous items".

Aside from his work for Islam, Rida was active in politics and was involved in the efforts against the tyrannical regime of Sultan 'Abd al-Hamid II (*Jam'iyyat al-Shura al-'Uthmaniyya*). In September 1908, after the Young Turk Revolution, Rida visited his family in his native village and from there continued on to Beirut, Tripoli and Damascus, preaching for the unity of the Arabs and the Turks in the Empire. In Tripoli he was clubbed by an adversary of the CUP, who even shot at him, but missed. In Damascus he became involved in a religious argument with a conservative sheikh, an argument that caused chaos in the entire town. In spite of these incidents, Rida persisted in his faith in the rosy future of the Ottoman Empire and in the possibility of good relations between the Arabs and the Turks in the era after the revolution.[2]

The starting point of Rashid Rida's ideology was very similar to that of 'Abd al-Rahman al-Kawakibi. He believed that the awakening of the Arabs was an essential prerequisite to the renaissance of Islam that he was working towards. Only through the Arab nation could the strength of early Islam be restored, since in the days of Arab power Islam had achieved its most glorious victories. It was the Arabs who developed the Islamic religion; they were the most superior nation, with the most solid foundations. Islam, according to Rida, was Arabic and it was the non-Arabs who had introduced all the foreign influences and spoiled it.[3] His attitude towards nationalism was ambivalent. In the particular national unit he saw a return to pre-Islamic solidarity, the *'asabiyya*: "and Islam prohibited racial fanaticism . . .

and the prophet prohibited the *'asabiyya* of the *Jahiliyya*".[4] He
believed, however, that while for the rest of the Muslims the
'asabiyya was in opposition to Islam, for the Arabs it stood in
perfect harmony. He was worried about particularistic leanings
that had begun to develop at that time: Turkish nationalism, the
Pan-Turanian idea, Syrian and Iraqi nationalism and Egyptian
nationalism. These ideas brought him into confrontation with
the Egyptian nationalists, who "consider Muslims or Arabs as
foreigners if they are not natives of their country, and therefore
the Sharif of the Hijaz, a descendant of Muhammad, is in their
eyes no better than a Chinese idol worshipper". Their *wataniyya*
"weakened the Islamic brotherhood . . . and this mistaken and
false *wataniyya* even stood against religion itself".[5] Islam, for
Rashid Rida, was a kind of supernationalism, the only true
nationalism for Muslims. Yet, he did recognize certain more limited relationships, such as Arab nationalism based on language
ties. The dilemma in defining the connection between Islam and
Arabism was addressed in an article published in *al-Manar* in
1917:

> I am a Muslim Arab . . . I said that I am a Muslim Arab because I
> am a brother in religion to thousands of thousands of Muslims,
> Arabs and non-Arabs, and a brother in race to thousands of thou-
> sands of Arabs, Muslims and non-Muslims.[6]

His opinion of the term fatherland (*watan*) Rida expressed in
al-Manar in 1909:

> In this world I have two fatherlands: The fatherland of my origin and
> my education, Syria . . . and the fatherland of my activity, Egypt,
> where I have lived for the last eleven years and call for religious,
> social and political reforms.[7]

This declaration of Rida's perhaps best exemplifies his lack of
attachment to a particular territory. His values revolved around
Islam, and therefore also around Arabism.

As a student in Tripoli, Rashid Rida had noticed the influence
of the American missionaries in the town and concluded that the
Muslims should also establish societies and schools like those of
the Mission. The idea continued to work in his mind, but the
opportunity for implementation came only after the Young Turk
revolution. In October 1909 Rida went to Istanbul with two
goals before him: to establish a scientific religious institute in
which true Islam would be taught and whose graduates would
be able to defend the Islamic religion, and "to remove the

misunderstanding that exists between the two great elements of the Empire, the Arabs and the Turks". Tal'at, the interior minister, had promised to meet with him to discuss Arab-Turkish relations, but did not keep his word. And as for the school that Rashid Rida wished to establish in Istanbul, a deeper and more drawn-out disappointment awaited him. At the beginning he showed his plans to Prime Minister Husayn Hilmi, to several other ministers and to several prominent members of the CUP. They expressed their support for the plan and allocated 5,000 Turkish liras for the start of the work. Awqaf Minister Khalil Hamada even promised a grant of 20,000 Turkish liras but before these promises could be carried out the government resigned and the new government of Ibrahim Haqqi took over the reins. Rida renewed his efforts to persuade the new prime minister, who showed considerable interest in the plan, as did the Sheikh al-Islam and the new education minister. At this stage Rida was very optimistic. But all manner of procrastination and delays ensued, and there were those who advised Rida to give up the plan. Rida refused to despair, continued pressuring and finally, after eight months of effort, an agreement was reached allowing the founding of a society for establishing the school. In June 1910 the founding meeting of the society, called the Society of Knowledge and Guidance (*Jam'iyyat al-'Ilm wal-Irshad*), was held.

After the establishment of the society Rida turned to the government, through the Sheikh al-Islam, with a request that the monetary promises be fulfilled. The latter wrote a memorandum to the government in September stating that 3,000 liras were to be given for the founding of the school and that thereafter the school expenses were to be entered into the budget of the Awqaf ministry. The government confirmed the memorandum but with a few reservations: the language of the school must be Turkish; it must be under the supervision and management of the Sheikh al-Islam; and its expenses were to be financed from the education budget of the Sheikh al-Islam. The society met and decided to object to making the Sheikh al-Islam responsible, for that would have made the school an official one, which would then have been considered by the European states as a propaganda tool of the government, and "if politics were admitted, the whole idea would be spoiled". For the same reason, Rida objected to the financing of the school through the Sheikh al-Islam's budget instead of the Awqaf ministry's budget, an arrangement that would lead to its loss of independence. By July Rida had already begun to feel that the Young Turks wanted to turn the school into another tool of their Turkification policy, and he deliberated upon whether it might not be more worthwhile to establish the school in Egypt. In light of the government's demands, he concluded that his year in Istanbul had been used against him in tactics of procrastination and excuses and that he had in fact been ridiculed. Filled with disappointment and bitterness, Rida returned to Egypt at the beginning of October 1910, but not before he had gone to the British embassy in Istanbul and attacked the CUP as a group of atheists and freemasons who hypocritically exploited Islam for their own political ends. He charged that the Young Turks sought to turn the school into a Turkish school and to use it as propaganda tool, in opposition to his aims, which were to remove fanaticism from Islam and to employ modern methods and Western culture while keeping the religion intact. He would open the school in Egypt, for the good of the Islamic world and also as a counterweight against the Egyptian nationalists. Rida never forgave the CUP.[8]

In January 1911 Rida announced in al-Manar that he was going to found in Egypt the Society of Propaganda and Guidance (Jama'at al-Da'wa wal-Irshad), which would establish a school, the House of Propaganda and Guidance (Dar al-Da'wa wal-Irshad). Students from all the Islamic countries would come and learn to be advocates for Islam. The school would have nothing to do with politics and its graduates would be sent to all the Islamic countries (not including the Ottoman Empire). In March 1911 Rida was already able to present in al-Manar the names of the members of the Administrative Council of the society and its constitution. Prince Muhammad 'Ali Pasha of the Khedivial family was elected honorary president of the society, and with that Rida gained the support of the Khedive. The Egyptian nationalists objected to the society, but on the other hand it was supported by some Islamic societies, such as the society "There is no god except Allah" of Alexandria. The meetings of the society were held in the editorial rooms of al-Manar, and in June 1911 it rented the Eastern Palace in Jazirat al-Rawda in Cairo for the school. In October the rules of the school were published, and in March 1912 regular studies began. Students from the entire Islamic world studied there free of charge. The school was financed by Arab philanthropists, by the Khedive and by the Egyptian Awqaf ministry. With the outbreak of World War I the contributions were cut off, as was the assistance from the Awqaf ministry, and the school was closed.[9]

In establishing the school, the House of Propaganda and Guidance, Rida accomplished what he had been unable to do in

Istanbul. Since his return from Istanbul, however, his work had split into two levels, open and secret. His open activity focused upon the school. The secret activity, a result of his disappointment in the Turks and the hatred that he developed towards the CUP, was expressed in the establishment of the Society of the Arab Association (*Jam'iyyat al-Jami'a al-'Arabiyya*). Rida no longer had faith in the Ottoman Empire.

The society had two aims. One was to unify the amirs of the Arabian Peninsula and to prevent dissension between them. The other was to work to achieve cooperation for the development of Arab countries and their protection, and to establish connections between the Arab societies in Syria, Iraq and Istanbul within the framework of their struggle against the CUP.[10] Later Rida defined the purpose of the society as the creation of a union between the Arabian Peninsula and the Arab provinces of the Ottoman Empire.[11] Rida composed an oath to be taken by the amirs and leaders who would join the society:

> I swear by Allah, the mighty, the victorious, the vengeful, the great, who knows my secret and revealed, who can negate all the talents and strengths that were given me, and by the splendid book of Allah, that I will invest all my effort and powers to bring about the cohesion of the Arabs, the unity of their amirs and the founding of a new kingdom for them according to the principles determined by the Society of the Arab Association which I am joining today. . . .[12]

About that time, Rida began a sharp public attack in the pages of *al-Manar* against the CUP, which "invested everything in the Empire . . . to fulfil its aims to intermix the nations of the Empire with the Turkish race". The coup d'état by which they regained power in 1913 he called a "heavy calamity" (*karitha*), and their society he called "the bloody society", "enemy of Arabs and of Islam", which "plots nothing but evil for the Arabs".[13]

In accordance with the aims of his society, Rida corresponded with Ibn Sa'ud of Najd on the necessity of a pact between all the rulers of the Arabian Peninsula in order to strengthen the Arabs, and he sent 'Izzat al-Jundi to Imam Yahya of Yemen and to Sayyid al-Idrisi of 'Asir. They agreed in principle with the aims of the society, though Imam Yahya claimed that he could not come to an agreement with al-Idrisi, because he had once made a treaty with him and later had been betrayed when al-Idrisi made a treaty with the Italians. Ibn Sa'ud asked Rida to send a messenger to him, to explain his plan from the religious and political points of view so that he could persuade his followers. The messenger set out with a case full of religious books, but then World War I broke out; the messenger could not get through and the books were confiscated in Bombay. The war also prevented a continuation of the connection with Yahya and al-Idrisi.

In 1912 Rida had gone on a lecture tour to India on behalf of the Society of Propaganda and Guidance and on the way back to Egypt passed through Kuwait and Masqat, where he contacted Mubarak al-Sabah, the Shiekh of Kuwait, Sheikh Khaz'al, the ruler of Muhammara, and the Amir of Masqat, all of whom he tried to persuade of the necessity of establishing an independent Arab state. In 1914 'Abdallah, the second son of Sharif Husayn of Mecca, passed through Egypt. While he was in Cairo, Rida made him a member of the society and presented him with its programme for a pact among the rulers of the Arabian Peninsula. He suggested a pact in which the rulers of the Hijaz, Najd, Yemen and 'Asir would form a union based on internal independence for each of them and mutual protection against any foreign enemy. Husayn would be the president of the council of his pact, since its meetings would be held in Mecca. 'Abdallah favoured the programme and promised to deliver it to his father, but Husayn turned it down because of his bad relationships with the rest of the rulers of the Arabian Peninsula.[14]

A further reason for the establishment of the society was the fear that the Arab counries in the Ottoman Empire would fall into the hands of the imperialist European states.[15] This fear grew after the defeat of the Empire by the Italians in Libya and its defeat in the Balkan War. Following these two wars, Rida published a pamphlet woven with verses from the Qur'an, calling for solidarity and unity among the Arabs for the salvation of their land and Islam and addressed especially to the amirs and the Arab leaders of the Hijaz, Najd, Yemen and the rest of the tribes of the Arabian Peninsula and the Persian Gulf. It reported the establishment of a Supreme Committee whose aim was to form an Arab Association that would protect the Arabian Peninsula and the Arab nation and would stand up for the honouring of their rights by the Porte. The pamphlet warned the Arabs that foreigners intended to gain control of Syria and the shores of the Arabian Peninsula as a first stage and after that "to destroy the Ka'ba and transport the Black Stone and the ashes of the prophet to the Louvre, museum of antiquities in Paris, capital of France". Therefore, the Arabs should wake up and cease their internal quarrels, putting an end to their hatred at a time so fraught with danger. The Supreme Committee's demands upon the Arabs were as follows:

1. To proclaim the union of all the leaders, amirs and heads of tribes
   . . .
2. To make a provisional peace if necessary . . . between the amirs
   and the leaders who are in conflict . . .
3. To see to it that all Muslim allies unite against any dissident who
   refuses to accept this entente until Allah decides his fate.
4. To prepare all of you to fight so that you will be able to quickly
   answer the first call.

And when the Arabs answered this call they would gain their
honour and independence.[16]

With the outbreak of the war, Rashid Rida published a call to
the Muslims of Syria, ostensibly demonstrating his loyalty to the
Ottoman Empire. But a close examination of the call reveals a
more complicated picture. It turned to the Arabs of Syria for
help for the Empire and even thanked them for their efforts on
its behalf, thus demonstrating that the Arab renaissance led to
progress for the Empire. "But I remind you," Rida continued,
"that the obedience that it is a duty to give the Empire refers
only to its official and legal commands." Secret orders of societies and parties were not to be obeyed, "especially if they trans-
gress the religious law and are contrary to the interests of the
nation and the fatherland, because obedience should not be
given to what has been created by the breaking of the yoke of
the creator."[17] The meaning, of course, was that the CUP should
not be submitted to. With the CUP people then the rulers of the
Empire, this call was not exactly the moral support that the
Empire needed from Muslims outside it. Rida revealed his true
attitude towards the Empire at this time when he assented to a
British request to send messengers to Ibn Sa'ud, Iman Yahya,
al-Idrisi and a number of Syrian leaders to ask them how they
would respond when the war broke out in the Middle East. He
even asked the British for 1,000 Egyptian pounds to finance the
messengers, some of whom left for Syria and the Persian Gulf as
representatives of the Decentralization Party (see below). Rida
wanted to send his cousin, 'Asim Rida, to Yemen, but in the
end this mission did not take place.[18]

A year later, Rida gave to the British his best ordered programme, as far as his ideas about the future Arab Empire were
concerned. It is quite possible, however, that he had prepared
this programme, the "General Organic Law of the Arab
Empire", earlier. The gist of it is paraphrased as follows: 1. The
Arab Empire will be comprised of the Arabian Peninsula, the

provinces of Syria and Iraq and the territory between them. 2. The Arab Empire will be decentralized, its official language, Arabic, and its religion, Islam. . . . 4. Every province in the Empire will be governed by a Vali and a Provincial Council to be elected by the inhabitants. 5. Every province will be independent in its internal administration and will be subject to the central government in its general policy and in matters of common interest to the entire Empire. 6. The general adminstrative policy will be managed by the President of the Arab Government, a Council of Representatives to be elected from the Empire as a whole, and a Council of Ministers to be chosen by the president from among those representatives. 7. The Council of Representatives will elect three of its members as candidates for the presidency, one of whom will be nominated by the Caliph for a five-year term, and will be in charge of civil and political matters. 8. The Caliph will come from the Sharifs of Mecca. He must recognize the "General Organic Law of the Empire" and abide by it. 9. The Caliph will be in charge of all religious matters. . . . 11. The headquarters of the Caliphate shall be in Mecca and the headquarters of the Government and the Council of Representatives shall be in Damascus. . . .[19]

Chapter 17

THE GREEN FLAG AND THE BLACK HAND

At about the same time that Rashid Rida carried out his first missions to the rulers of the Arabian Peninsula, two secret societies were set up in Istanbul, one after the other, inspired by burning hatred of the CUP, as in the case of the Society of the Arab Association. Their initiator was Da'ud al-Dabbuni, a Muslim student from Mosul who was studying medicine in Istanbul. Al-Dabbuni, an ex-member of *al-Qahtaniyya*, had been influenced by Salim al-Jaza'iri's opinion that many Arab societies should be set up, and was not willing to accept the practical elimination of *al-Qahtaniyya*. His hatred for the CUP knew no bounds and soon turned into hatred of all the Turks. According to one account, when a fire broke out in Istanbul—which happened quite often—al-Dabbuni would go up on to the roof of the Medical School, light a cigarette and enjoy the scene, saying, "Ah, how happy I am to see the fire as it destroys the magnificent palaces of Istanbul."[1]

In September 1912 al-Dabbuni met with friends to discuss the necessity of establishing a new secret society, leading to their decision to set up the Green Flag Society (*al-'Alam al-Ahdar*), named after Najd's green flag and symbolizing the founders' view of the independent ruler of Najd, Ibn Sa'ud, as the symbol of hope for the Arab nation. Al-Dabbuni's partners in the establishment of the society were a number of officers, including Isma'il al-Saffar (who had also been a member of *al-Qahtaniyya* and studied in the Medical School with al-Dabbuni), 'Ali Rida al-Ghazali and 'Abd al-Ghafur al-Badri; and civilians such as Fa'iq Shakir and 'Izzat al-A'zami. Naturally, the students in the Literary Club, which was active in Istanbul at that time, were a logical source of manpower for the new society, and some members of this club (besides al-A'zami) did indeed join the new society, such as 'Asim Basisu and Musallam al-'Attar. The society's spiritual authority was Salim al-Jaza'iri.[2]

The society's goal was to strengthen nationalist ties among the Arab students in the institutions for higher education in Istanbul and to encourage them to work for the rescue of the Arab nation from the abyss into which they felt it had fallen. The society claimed to be educating the Arabs politically,[3] though the only practical action it carried out for this purpose was the publication of the periodical *Lisan al-'Arab* in March 1913, under the editorship of al-A'zami. In order to maintain its secrecy, the society's name was not mentioned in the periodical. Articles were written by the members of this society and others, as well as by writers who did not belong to any Arab society. Among the contributors were the poets Ma'ruf al-Rusafi and Jamil al-Zahawi, as well as Muhammad Baqir al-Shabibi, Haqqi al-'Azm, Muhibb al-Din al-Khatib and others from all the Arab countries. The writers concentrated on Arabic and Arabism and called for an Arab awakening, and some of them described the Turks as enemies.

Nine regular issues and one expanded issue of the periodical appeared, and it attracted the attention of the administration of the Literary Club, which also wanted to publish a periodical. The club asked al-A'zami's assent to making the periodical its own organ and changing its name to *al-Muntada al-Adabi*. While the Green Flag members agreed that the periodical could also be the club's organ, they opposed changing its name. A conflict ensued between the club's Administrative Committee and the society, and al-A'zami was torn between his loyalty to the society on the one hand and to the club on the other. When 'Abd al-Hamid al-Zahrawi intervened in the conflict and supported the club's demand, the society agreed to the name change. The periodical began to appear under its new name starting from February 1914 and continued until the outbreak of World War I.[4]

The society also continued to exist until the war began, but it did not carry out any additional activities worthy of note. Da'ud al-Dabbuni, who was disappointed by this inactivity, set up yet another new society shortly after the founding of the Green Flag. This new society was called "the Black Hand" (*al-Yad al-Sawda'*), and its members too were students from the various schools of higher education and from the military academy. The purpose of the society was to assassinate the Arabs who cooperated with the CUP, not out of ideological motivation but in order to strengthen their positions and their personal influence and thus fulfil personal ambitions. Differences of opinion arose among the society members as to the methods of carrying out this purpose and they did not succeed in implementing their plans. The society was dissolved before it was a year old, and in the period preceding World War I al-Dabbuni himself was no longer prominent in Arab activities. At the beginning of the war he was drafted by the Ottoman army and fought against the Russians in Anatolia, where he became sick and died.[5]

Chapter 18

THE DECENTRALIZATION PARTY

By late 1912 the Ottoman Empire had signed an agreement ceding Libya to Italy and was losing the Balkan War. The Syrian community in Cairo was of the unanimous opinion that the Empire would lose additional territories and that Syria would be taken over by a European power. As to the question of which power was preferable, there were differences of opinion. The Syrian émigrés in Cairo held discussions and debates, generally in secret, to decide this question, and it became clear that the Muslims tended towards Britain, perhaps through the annexation of Syria to Egypt, then under British occupation, while the Christians favoured France. Damascene notables such as the brothers Rafiq and 'Uthman al-'Azm and their cousin Haqqi al-'Azm stressed that they preferred the Empire, but if circumstances forced them to choose between British and French occupation, they would opt for the former. They believed that France's attitude towards the Algerians demonstrated that it was the enemy of Islam. At a certain stage a delegation was being organized to approach Lord Kitchener (consul-general in Egypt, 1911-14) and ask him for a British protectorate over Syria. But the idea fell through after Kitchener himself let them know that he would not accept such a delegation. At the head of the Christian propaganda effort in favour of France stood the Protestant Najib Shakur Pasha. Although he had an English mother, had been educated in Britain and worked in the British administration, he believed that only France could grant Syria its fulfilment, as the British would lord it over the Syrians while the French would be their friends.[1]

Rafiq al-'Azm sharply attacked those who tended towards France and were willing to give that country a foothold in Syria: "The Syrians are primarily attached to the Ottoman Empire, and secondarily to the Syrian nation." Therefore, he claimed, France had nothing to look for in Syria.[2] But rumours of French ambitions in the Levant continued and the fear of a French invasion of Syria grew. On 21 December 1912 the French premier, Raymond Poincaré, said in a speech in the French senate:

In the Lebanon and in Syria we have traditional interests and we
intend to have them respected ... The British government has
announced to us in a very amicable manner that it has no intention
of acting in these regions, that it has neither designs nor political
aspirations of any sort. We ourselves are resolved to maintain the
integrity of the Ottoman Empire in Asia, but we will not abandon
any of our traditions there, we will not repudiate any of the sympa-
thies we have acquired there, and we will not allow any of our interests to suffer.[3]

To the Syrians this speech was the decisive proof of France's
plans concerning their fatherland. Among those who had
reached the conclusion that the Empire was no longer capable of
defending its estates was a group headed by Rafiq al-'Azm,
which approached the Ottoman representative in Egypt, Ra'uf
Pasha, to tell of their fears for Syria's fate. Explaining that
France was liable to occupy Syria, as Italy had occupied Libya,
they informed the representative that they had set up a committee for the defence of Syria on their own initiative. Now they
were requesting that he turn to the Sublime Porte to ask how
they could assist Syria's national defence. They also suggested
that arms stores be set up in Syria for use in case of emergency,
to be distributed among the inhabitants if a foreign power
should attack. Ra'uf Pasha did not bother to transmit their
request to Istanbul. The Syrians therefore organized a number
of meetings to discuss the means they would use to defend Syria.
They concluded that it was essential that the country's youth
perform their military service in their own country. But in order
to achieve this aim, they understood that a new type of administration would have to established in the Empire: decentralization. Thus they set up in Cairo at the end of that month the
Ottoman Party for Administrative Decentralization (*Hizb al-
Lamarkaziyya al-Idariyya al-'Uthmani*).[4]

The founders of the party and the members of the first
Supreme Committee were as follows:
President: Rafiq al-'Azm, Muslim of Damascus. Property owner.
Vice-President: Iskandar 'Ammun, Christian of Dayr al-Qamar.
Lawyer.
Secretary: Haqqi al-'Azm, Muslim of Damascus. Cousin of
Rafiq.
Assistant Secretary: Muhibb al-Din al-Khatib, Muslim of
Damascus.
Assistant Secretary: Sami al-Juraydini, Christian of the Lebanon.
Lawyer.
Treasurer: Najib Bustrus, Christian of Sidon. Property owner.

Members: Dr Shibli Shumayyil (Christian), Rashid Rida (Muslim), Da'ud Barakat (Christian), 'Uthman al-'Azm (Muslim, elder brother of Rafiq), Na'man Abu Sha'r (Christian), Dr 'Izzat al-Jundi (Muslim), Khalil Ayyub (Christian), Salih Rida (Muslim, brother of Rashid), Salim 'Izz al-Din (Druze), and Hamid Salah al-Din (Muslim).[5]
The party constitution established the following:

Art. 2 — The purpose of establishing this party is to explain the virtues of a decentralized administration in the Ottoman Empire to the Ottoman nation, which is composed of various races, languages, religions and customs, and to demand by all legal means a government based on the principles of administrative decentralization in all the vilayets of the Ottoman Empire.

Art. 3 — This party is not secret and has no secrets. It publishes its goal, which is based on the demand for broad decentralization, in public, without fear of anyone . . .

Art. 9 — Members of the parliament who belong to the party must strive to the best of their ability to implement the party's plan in the parliament.

Art. 11 — The General Centre of the party is in Cairo. In every city, town or village in which ten residents gather together to support the principle of decentralization, they are authorized to establish a branch of the party and they should inform the General Centre of this.

Art. 12 — The party's Supreme Committee is composed of twenty members, who will elect from among themselves a president, a vice-president, a secretary, two assistant secretaries and a treasurer. . . .[6]

In mid-February 1913 the party held a meeting to decide on its political platform and its demands on the central government.[7] A manifesto of the party's principles was authorized for distribution. The manifesto opened with praise of the idea of decentralization on both the ideological and the practical planes: "The best sort of regime is constitutional and the best sort of constitutional regime is decentralized." This was exemplified by the decentralized government existing in Switzerland as opposed to the centralized regime of the Ottoman Empire, in spite of its variety of nations, races and languages. This regime, the manifesto argued, had caused the Empire to deteriorate into its present state, which was so far gone that the Empire could no longer defend itself, as had been seen in Libya. In order to extricate the Empire from this sorry situation and from this corrupt regime the Decentralization Party had been formed. The Party principles stated:

Art. 1 — The Ottoman Empire is a parliamentary constitutional state. Every one of its vilayets is an integral part of it in all circumstances, and only the administration of these vilayets should be based on administrative decentralization. . . .

Art. 4 — At the centre of each vilayet will be a General Council, an Administrative Council, an Educational Council, and an Awqaf Council.

Art. 5 — All the decisions of the General Council will be valid.

Art. 6 — It will be within the jurisdiction of the General Council of the vilayet to supervise its government and to investigate all the concerns of the local administration . . .

Art. 14 — Every vilayet will have two official languages, Turkish and the local language.

Art. 15 — Education in each vilayet will be provided in the language of its residents.

Art. 16 — The residents of each vilayet will perform their military service in that vilayet, and its army will be ready to defend it during peacetime. The mobilization of soldiers at times of war is in the hands of the war ministry, and then the General Council is obligated to take steps to defend the vilayet.[8]

Two months later an article was published in *al-Manar* to convince its readers of the virtues of decentralization. It deemed this kind of regime essential for the Empire because it had a large population; because the connections between the centre of the Empire and the provinces were not always good; because its residents spoke many different languages and most of them did not know Turkish, the language of its centre; and because the officials sent by the centre did not fit in and the local people were hostile towards them. Therefore each vilayet needed an administration and judiciary system appropriate for its residents' way of life. The article rejected the claim that such a regime would make it easier for foreigners to gain control over the country. It also rejected the claim that with the Empire in the middle of the Balkan War, it was not an appropriate time for such demands. What was endangering the Empire, the author claimed, was the centralization of the CUP.[9]

However, it seems that not all the party members considered a decentralized regime to be the solution for the ills of the Empire. In a referendum held a year later, Da'ud Barakat expressed his opinion that the Empire should be divided into homogeneous regions with administrative independence, each one to be headed by a high commissioner assisted by an advisory council of technocrats. This Empire would be composed of united vilayets (*wilayat muttahida*). Iskandar 'Ammun proposed that each vilayet of the Empire be granted full internal independence, even in legislation, and that the vilayets should be subject to the centre only in general matters. As a model he suggested the United States. Such an Empire would be called the Ottoman United States (*al-wilayat al-muttahida al-'uthmaniyya*).[10]

During the two years before the outbreak of World War I the party succeeded in setting up branches throughout Syria. The Damascus branch was founded by Shafiq al-Mu'ayyad, and among its members were Shukri al-'Asali and 'Abd al-Wahhab al-Inklizi. The Hama branch was founded by 'Ali al-Armanazi and Khalid Agha Darwish al-Barazi, the Homs branch by Qustantin Yani, the Ba'albek branch by the mayor, Salih Haydar, the branch in the Biqa' by Na'if Tallu, and the branch in Jaffa by Hafiz al-Sa'id. Sa'id al-Husayni founded Jerusalem and Nablus branches; the ranks of the latter were filled by the local 'Abd al-Hadi family and it was headed by Hasan Hammad. The Jenin and Haifa branches were founded by Salim al-Ahmad 'Abd al-Hadi, who headed the former, while the latter was headed by Elias Zakka. The Beirut branch, headed by Mahmud al-Mihmisani, had only five members, though the minimum for opening a branch was ten people.[11]

It is possible that it was problems of this sort that led Haqqi al-'Azm to declare, in a letter to a member of the party in June 1914, that four people were enough to set up a branch. The letter also gave instructions for handling the branch's money. It could be deposited in a bank under the names of its president and treasurer, and not withdrawn without the authorization of the branch's Administrative Committee and the signatures of the president and the treasurer. Alternatively, the money could be put into an iron safe with two keys, one of which would be held by the president and the other by the treasurer. Haqqi al-'Azm instructed the recipient to use Muhammad al-Shanti's assistance to set up the branch. A native of Jaffa, al-Shanti was the party's roving agent for establishing branches.[12] In spite of the problems, the number of members of the party in general increased, and the president, Rafiq al-'Azm, decided that there must be liaisons between the centre and the men in the field, so that every ten men would have a "supervisor" (*'arif*), to serve as a link between them and the branch's Committee, and every hundred would have a "guide" (*dalil*), who would be a liaison between the ten "supervisors". Thus the centre would be able to send its decisions quickly to the branch members, and the branch members would be able to express their wishes through their Committee to the Supreme Committee.[13]

Instructions to branches within the Empire, as well as party proclamations that were printed in Egypt, were sent by foreign post and distributed secretly. Haqqi al-'Azm was responsible for the sending of the proclamations. The fact that the party was not recognized as a legal body by the Ottoman authorities forced the branches within the Empire to operate secretly. 'Awni 'Abd al-Hadi, for example, a party activist in Nablus, received the instruction not to sign his letters to the centre on party matters with his name but rather with the number of his membership card.[14]

The decision made by one of its branches not to accept non-Muslim members was another problem that occupied the party. Haqqi al-'Azm wrote to the president of the branch that the Christians were their brothers in race, language, nationality and interests. He strongly rejected the claims that the inclusion of Christians was an act of heresy or of giving over the country to foreigners. He saw such thinking as an act of ignorance and requested, in his own name and that of Rafiq al-'Azm, that the branch president should, on the contrary, work for the inclusion of Christians, Druzes and Jews in the party, so that the party would encompass all the elements in Syria. This was the practice, he claimed, in the other branches. On another occasion a Christian activist from the centre claimed that party positions should be divided equally between Christians and Muslims. This opinion was denounced by the other members of the centre, who considered raising the religious issue as introducing a wedge of hostility between the Christians and the Muslims.[15]

The party had contacts with the Turkish opposition party, the "Party of Liberty and Union", which also had decentralist tendencies. The Ottoman Agency in Cairo reported that a written agreement existed between Sadiq Bey, the leader of the Party of Liberty and Union, and Rafiq al-'Azm, the leader of the Decentralization Party; that the former group promised to help the latter to realize its programme to grant the Arab countries their rights, as detailed in the party's platform, so that they would remain attached to the Ottoman Empire in a decentralized manner; that if the Party of Liberty and Union were to regain power in the Ottoman Empire (it had been the ruling party from July 1912 to January 1913), it would grant the Arab vilayets extensive decentralization, and commit itself to appoint Shafiq al-Mu'ayyad al-'Azm to the rulership of these vilayets; that the decentralists in Egypt and their supporters in the Ottoman Empire commit themselves to work against the CUP and to support the Party of Liberty and Union by all possible means.

These agreements were also supported by Kamil Pasha, the ex-Grand Vizier, whom they designated as the Grand Vizier of the Ottoman Empire.[16]

'Abd al-Karim Qasim al-Khalil, also a member of the Decentralization Party, was appointed secretary of the general centre of the Party of Liberty and Union. The Decentralization Party began to work for the opening of branches of the Party of Liberty and Union both in the Levant and in Egypt, and when the Turkish party was abolished these branches became branches of the Decentralization Party. When Grand Vizier Mahmud Shawkat was murdered in June 1913 and the opposition in Istanbul was liquidated, the connections between the two parties came to an end.[17]

In early 1913 Shafiq al-Mu'ayyad began a tour aimed at convincing the French representatives in the Empire of the importance of the principle of decentralization. When he met the French ambassador in Istanbul in January 1913 he began by asking whether France had sympathy only for the Christians of Syria or also for the Muslims "who have become accustomed to regarding France as a second fatherland". The ambassador, of course, gave a positive answer to the latter, whereupon al-Mu'ayyad went on to discuss the need for reforms in Syria based on decentralization, expressing his opinion that the three Syrian vilayets (Damascus, Aleppo and Beirut) should be transformed into one unit, in which Turks would not be able to hold public office. He also asked the ambassador if France would be willing to despatch armed forces to Syria should the Ottoman authorities send in military reinforcements to strengthen their direct rule there. The ambassador was disconcerted by this direct question. Trying to evade the issue, he answered that it would be best for the Syrians to show the authorities that they were loyal subjects, and that they must understand that the Ottoman government was opposed to decentralization because it suspected that it would lead to the division of the Empire.[18]

In April 1913 al-Mu'ayyad approached the French consul-general in Beirut and complained about the difficulties that the authorities were placing in the way of implementing reforms in Syria (this was after the closing of the Reform Society of Beirut, discussed in the next chapter). He reported his intention to set up a branch of the Decentralization Party in Damascus.[19] In May al-Mu'ayyad approached the French consul-general in Damascus, denounced the Ottoman government as a total failure, and voiced his suspicions about the ambitions of the Powers in Syria. Expressing his hope that France would work for the preservation of Syria's unity, he pointed out that the Syrians refused to be divided: "Syria, until the Euphrates, is a compact unit, an indivisible mass. There is a Syrian patriotism. We demand reforms and decentralization only in order to preserve the whole of Syria. Syria for the Syrians!"[20]

Convening in Cairo after the CUP regained power as a result of the January 1913 coup d'état, the party's Supreme Committee decided that it did not matter who would head the regime: "It would knock on all the gates and use every means to achieve its goals in any manner whatsoever." The new government reacted by instructing all the local post offices to confiscate rather than deliver the copies of the party platform that they received. Nevertheless the platform was published in the Beirut newspapers after it reached them through the foreign post offices.[21]

At this point the party members in Cairo held a variety of opinions concerning Syria's future. Most of the Muslims supported the party's official solution, that is, a decentralized regime in which Syria would be an integral part of the Empire. Others, Rafiq al-'Azm among them, were in favour of granting extensive autonomy to Syria and having it ruled by an Arab prince. Its connection with the Empire would then be that of a vassal state. A third possibility, less acceptable, was to annex Syria to Egypt, bringing it under British rule. On 22 March 1913 a conference of the party leaders was held at the home of the vice-president, Iskandar 'Ammun, to resolve this question. The conference chairman was 'Abd al-Hamid al-Zahrawi. The participants decided at the end of the discussion to adopt the second possibility, which called for transforming Syria into an independent principality ruled by a Muslim prince. Although Shafiq al-Mu'ayyad reported to his fellow participants that France would not help them in practice at the present time, it was decided that if there were a need for foreign protection over Syria, France would be preferred. Michel al-Tuwayni, a party member who was also a dragoman at the French consulate-general in Beirut, was given the task of conveying this to the French. As for who would be chosen to head the Syrian principality, there were differences of opinion among the party members. Rafiq al-'Azm suggested his relative, Shafiq al-Mu'ayyad. Others sharply disagreed and claimed that the Syrians would never agree that one of them should be appointed as their ruler. Some suggested the prince Yusuf Kamal of the khedivial family. Another resolution accepted at the conference called for the inclusion of Mount Lebanon in the Syrian principality.[22] Obviously the party had no means of carrying out these resolutions, whose meaning was the practical secession of Syria from the Ottoman Empire.

In April 1913 two events attracted the attention of the party. The first was the closing of the Reform Society of Beirut. When a new Vali had arrived in Beirut a month earlier, Rafiq al-'Azm had sent a telegram to the Sublime Porte demanding in the name of the party that the new Vali be instructed to carry out the demands of the Reform Society of Beirut.[23] When this same Vali then closed the society, al-'Azm sent a telegram in the name of the party to the Grand Vizier in Istanbul, and demanded the Vali's dismissal. In another telegram to the Vali himself, he demanded the abrogation of the closing decree. In telegrams to the foreign ministers of the European powers and to the important European newspapers, Haqqi al-'Azm protested the closing of the society and called for their intervention on behalf of the Beirutians.[24]

The second event began with a letter from the initiators of the Paris Congress (see below), asking the party for its cooperation and suggesting that one of its representatives at the congress be appointed its president. On 14 April, three days after a conference of the Supreme Committee of the party was held to discuss the question, the party president sent a positive response to the initiators, informing them that the party considered the congress a forum for presenting its principles and that they would therefore send two representatives, whose names were yet to be decided upon, to Paris.[25] Controversy about the representatives, and especially about who was to be the president of the congress, arose among the party members. Rafiq and Haqqi al-'Azm suggested Shafiq al-Mu'ayyad for the position of president, while Rashid Rida, who considered him "a suspicious man", suggested 'Abd al-Hamid al-Zahrawi, the ex-deputy of Hama in the parliament, who was then living in Cairo. Because of the great esteem in which al-Zahrawi was held at that time among the reformists, the latter suggestion was eventually accepted. Party Vice-President Iskandar 'Ammun was chosen as the second representative of the party at the congress.

On 1 May 1913 more than 200 Syrians, Turkish liberals and local and foreign journalists participated in a large meeting held at the Continental Hotel in Cairo, where a public discussion was held on the Paris Congress and the sending of party delegates to it. In addition, a request was formulated to be sent to the Sublime Porte, asking them to stop the persecution of the reformists in Syria. The conference was opened by Rafiq al-'Azm, who discussed the sorry situation of the Empire and contended that its structure and composition meant that only decentralization could save it. "Let no one think that the purpose of our Decentralization Party is to remove the yoke of the Ottoman Empire from our shoulders . . . No! Heaven forbid!" The only goal of the party was "to save the possessions of the Empire from the raptors". And in the next speech Iskandar 'Ammun called for the emulation of other nations that had already adopted this form of government.

In the final speech 'Abd al-Hamid al-Zahrawi demonstrated the weakness of the government's centralization policy through the example of a broken bridge. To fix it for a sum of five liras meant asking permission of the Vali. The Vali then had to request permission from Istanbul. After several months would come the answer that the matter required investigation. The discussions would continue. In the end the damage to the bridge increases and 30 liras are needed to repair it. All the discussions begin again, and before they are finished, the bridge collapses totally. Building a new bridge would cost 500 liras—"and for this Istanbul says there is no money". Al-Zahrawi also attacked Istanbul's educational system, as not appropriate for all the vilayets. With even the elementary studies in Turkish, "it is impossible for the unfortunate pupils to learn, neither Turkish nor Arabic". Al-Zahrawi ended his speech with the fact that, in the present system, the person responsible for the mosque in a remote village could not even buy a bottle without first asking permission from the capital.[26]

After the congress, held in June, an agreement was signed with the Ottoman government (see below). The party waited patiently for the agreed reforms to be implemented. But when it finally became clear that the CUP had no intention of keeping its promises, the Supreme Committee sent instructions to the branches "to renew their activities and to start a new movement, so that the government will know that the opiates of its promises do not affect the Arab nation". Furthermore, the branches were instructed to send telegrams to Istanbul, asking the Sultan to implement the reforms.[27] The party also issued, on 9 October, "A Manifesto to the Arab Nation". The manifesto first returned to the familiar arguments of the sorry state of the Empire deriving from the centralization policy of its government and the need for a decentralized regime. It compared the party platform with the Paris agreement, to demonstrate that even this agreement contained some concessions on the part of the Arabs. It then compared the agreement with the government's announcement of the reforms it intended to implement and with the imperial command that was published on this matter, to show that the government had retreated even from this limited agreement. After exposing the government's bad faith towards the Arabs, the party called on all the Arab societies and on the Arabs in general to unite in their struggle for their rights, inundating the Sublime Porte with telegrams requesting the implementation of extensive administrative decentralization in the vilayets of the Empire.[28]

Early in 1914 al-Zahrawi agreed to accept the position of senator, despite the fact that the resolutions of the congress had forbidden the acceptance of positions before the implementation of the reforms. This aroused great anger among the Arab activists and confusion among the party members. Al-Zahrawi requested the party's retroactive approval for this appointment, and the party agreed to back him, since perhaps through this position al-Zahrawi would be able to contribute to the implementation of the reforms. But al-Zahrawi was requested to come to Cairo, to justify his decision and to explain why he thought the government would finally implement the reforms. There he explained his belief that the government was interested in implementing the reforms but could only do so gradually. The party, however, had to withstand a wave of denunciations, as the moderates accused it of weakness while others accused it of running after office.[29]

The party next became involved in a struggle to free 'Aziz 'Ali al-Misri from prison in Istanbul, described below; they asked Lord Kitchener to intervene and tried to present al-Misri's imprisonment as an offence against the Arabs in general.[30] Following this episode, the party began to think in terms of a second congress. When Muhammad al-Mihmisani, a party member from Beirut, suggested holding it in Cairo, the party leaders accepted the idea enthusiastically. Rafiq al-'Azm instructed Da'ud Barakat, a member of the Supreme Council who was the editor-in-chief of al-Ahram, to publish this in his newspaper. Letters of enquiry were sent to the branches, proposing the following winter as an appropriate time for the congress,[31] but by that time World War I had already broken out and a second congress was never held.

On the eve of World War I the Ottoman authorities tried to take action against the party. The Ottoman representative in Cairo asked the Egyptian government to put Haqqi al-'Azm on trial for the crime of distributing proclamations fomenting rebellion. An official in the Egyptian government, who was close to al-'Azm, informed him, warning that although the Ottoman request had been denied he had best be careful and destroy all documents that could connect him with proclamations of this sort. Al-'Azm went further and also destroyed some reports that had arrived from the branches, thus creating difficulties afterwards in financial accounts. The security measures taken in correspondence between the centre and the branches were increased. Envelopes containing secret or subversive material were marked *f* (for *faransi*, French) and were sent only through the French postal system. For especially restricted material a code was decided upon. Letters sent to the branches during this period stressed that secrecy must be increased beyond what was hitherto customary, and using fictitious names was recommended. It was also recommended that leaders should begin to organize branches in a military structure, so that each ten members would be led by a "commander of ten" and each ten such commanders by a "commander of one hundred".[32]

When the Empire began to mobilize Arab soldiers for the approaching war, the rift between it and the party was already complete. The members of the Beirut branch sent telegrams to the Arab representatives in the parliament demanding that they resign. It was even suggested that the city be closed if the mobilization activities were not stopped. The Supreme Committee also sent a protest to the Sublime Porte. Haqqi al-'Azm sent the following letter to Mahmud al-Mihmisani:

> Woe to us who suffer from the freedom of this Turkish government. Allah! Free us from it, from its freedom and its constitution! Let the curse of Allah be upon it, upon its constitution, upon its freedom and upon the hour in which this cursed constitution was proclaimed . . . What do you think of the arrival of Tal'at and Jawid [two of the CUP leaders] in Syria next month? . . . It seems to me that a strongly-worded proclamation must be distributed immediately, calling upon the Arab nation to welcome these two "heroes" with dynamite and lead, as they deserve.[33]

However, the party was no longer willing to make do with threatening proclamations. It made contact with the Society of the Lebanese Revival through the agency of Iskandar 'Ammun and Da'ud Barakat, and the two societies decided to cooperate if the Empire should enter the war. They planned a rebellion in the Lebanon and they claimed that the French representative in Cairo had promised them 20,000 rifles, three warships to protect them and French officers who would conduct the activities. The centre of the rebellion was supposed to be in Zahla.[34] On 20 August 1914 the following letter was sent to one of the party branches in the Lebanon:

> The fatherland has never needed the help of its sons as much as it does in this difficult time, in which the World War is raging, whose sparks are about to injure the Near East, to burn everything and to destroy the Arabs and the Turks. . . . Inasmuch as this is the appearance of things, it is encumbent upon us, the Arab community, to contemplate the means which will keep our independence from eradication. It is a holy duty of our Party . . . to be at the head of the discussants of this matter and the activists who are are taking steps which will be beneficial for the integrity of the fatherland and the lives of its sons.
>
> Therefore we ask you to respond as soon as possible to the following questions:
>
> 1. What forces do you have that we can depend on in the hour of need in order to carry out a general action?
> 2. Will it be possible for you to collect funds and send them to us, or to hold them until needed? What sums will you be able to collect?
> 3. Can you provide a safe refuge for one or more persons who will be called upon to lead the national (*wataniyya*) movement, and to assure their sustenance?
> 4. Can you send a reliable person who will represent your branch to a place that we will designate, so that he may receive necessary instructions?
> 5. If you cannot send anyone, do you see a need for a special messenger to come to you in order to deliver these instructions?
>
> We ask that you respond immediately, for every minute that passes will be a minute lost to Arab lives. The time has come for us to sacrifice all we have for the sake of national (*wataniyya*) life.[35]

The British in Cairo, unhappy with the contacts of the members of the societies with the French, decided to take the initiative and opened discussions with some of the Muslim members of the party, headed by Rashid Rida and Rafiq al-'Azm. These contacts were arranged without the knowledge of the Christian members of the party. The party members explained to the representatives of the British government their interest in the liberation of the Arab countries from the Ottoman yoke, even at the price of the collapse of the Empire. However, they expressed apprehension about Britain's intentions of annexing parts of the Arabian Peninsula, especially the Red Sea coasts. The decision was reached that they would put their conditions for cooperation with the British into writing to be transmitted to the British government; if the government chose to accept them, it would announce this officially through the Reuter news agency. In return the Arab societies would pledge themselves to stir up rebellions within the Empire. The party members were given 1,000 liras to send messengers for this purpose.[36]

The party members began writing letters to their friends in the Empire, urging them not to join the Turks in the war because this opposed the interests of the Arabs. On 26 October two pairs of party emissaries left for the purpose of inciting rebellion. The first pair of emissaries, Sheikh Muhammad al-Qalqili and 'Abd al-Rahman 'Asim, a pupil in Rida's school, were sent to Syria and Beirut. They arrived at Beirut in an Italian mailboat, just as it became known that the war had broken out in the Middle East. Al-Qalqili panicked and they returned immediately on the same boat to Alexandria.[37]

The second pair, Muhibb al-Din al-Khatib and an Iraqi named 'Abd al-'Aziz al-'Atiqi, were sent to the Persian Gulf, Ibn Sa'ud and Iraq. Leaving Suez for Bombay, they went on to the Persian Gulf. When they arrived in Bushir they were arrested by an intelligence officer of the British army, owing to lack of coordination between the British Foreign Office, which was responsible for their mission, and the India Office, which was responsible for this region. They were transferred to Basra, where they aroused the suspicion of the British officials that they were propagandists for the Turks. Pan-Islamic propaganda and correspondence with Sayyid Talib of Basra were found among their papers. Correspondence between the British Foreign Office and the India Office was conducted at a very leisurely pace, and during the entire period the emissaries remained in prison. Al-Khatib sent a call for help to Rida, and the latter put pressure on the British authorities in Cairo to end the episode. Finally, in June 1915, after seven months had passed, the emissaries were released. Al-Khatib returned to Egypt, while the second emissary chose to remain in Iraq.[38]

While the messengers were still on their way, the British foreign minister told his representatives in Cairo that they should encourage the Arab movement in every possible way. Shortly afterwards Reuter announced that it had learned that the British government had no intention of undertaking any military naval operations in Arabia except to protect Arab interests against Turkish or other aggression or to support attempts by the Arabs to free themselves from the Turkish rule. The party members did not consider this declaration to be sufficient, and they ceased their contact with the British at this stage.[39]

The party continued to exist during World War I, but it became insignificant. Eventually it disintegrated and its members joined new groups, many of them the Syrian Union Party.

Chapter 19

THE REFORM SOCIETY OF BEIRUT

The Decentralization Party in Cairo and the Reform Society of Beirut were established at the same time, in response to the possibility of the Levant's being occupied by a foreign power. But while the primary motivation for the establishment of the Decentralization Party was the fear of the Syrian émigrés in Cairo of such an occupation, the Reform Society of Beirut was established, among other reasons, as a result of the local populace's desire for such an occupation; the Turkification policy and governmental corruption caused the local populace to want to change the situation in any possible way. Thus, in Beirut in late 1912 the differences of opinion among most of the people were not over whether foreign occupation was desirable, but rather over the identity of the desired foreign conqueror.

The Beirut Muslims sought British occupation or the annexation of all Syria to Egypt. At a conference held in November 1912 to discuss the means of realizing this idea, the idea was proposed—though not accepted—of assassinating the British or the French consul in order to force the Powers to intervene. Plans were afoot to send a delegation to Egypt to ask Lord Kitchener for a British protectorate, and a delegation of Druzes and Muslims from the Lebanon and Damascus asked the British consul-general in Beirut for British assistance in the struggle against the authorities. There were rumours that notables from Beirut had sent a letter to the British foreign minister requesting immediate occupation of Beirut by Britain. In Sidon as well a conference was held in favour of British protection and even further south, in Palestine, the local residents leaned towards Britain and the idea of annexation to Egypt. The Christians, on the other hand, especially the Lebanese Maronites, were traditionally in favour of France. However, just as there were also Muslims, in Tripoli for example, who were in favour of French intervention, there were some Christians—mostly Catholics—in favour of British intervention.[1]

The Reform Society of Beirut was founded during the time of the Empire's short rule by the Turkish liberals, headed by the Party of Liberty and Union, the sworn rival of the CUP. The

Grand Vizier was Kamil Pasha, and Adham Bek was appointed as Vali of Beirut in place of Abu Bakr Hazim, who was a CUP member. In December 1912 Salim 'Ali Salam (1868-1938), a rich Sunni merchant who favoured implementing reforms in the government but opposed a foreign occupation, turned to this new, "liberal" Vali to explain the seriousness of the situation in the vilayet and the disposition of its residents to secede from the Empire and be annexed to Egypt or France. When the Vali asked Salam what he thought should be done, he answered that the only solution was to implement an extensive reform plan. Following this discussion the Vali sent a telegram of warning to Kamil Pasha:

> Various groups are pulling the country in various directions. A large part of the population is looking towards Britain or France in the hope of improving the sorry situation. If we do not begin a true reform the country will no doubt slip out of our hands.

Kamil Pasha's telegram of reply informed the Vali of forthcoming discussion of reform in the parliament. Then the representatives of the vilayet would be able to present their demands. The Vali showed this telegram to Salam, but the latter responded that it would be a long time until the parliament convened, perhaps six months, and the situation was too delicate to wait. Though angry, the Vali again asked Salam what he thought should be done. When Salam answered that urgent action must be taken, the Vali responded that he had decided to set up and head a committee which would compile a list of required reforms for presentation to the central government. Despite Salam's warning that because the populace would consider such a committee a governmental body, it would not accept it, the Vali nevertheless established the committee. Composed of two Muslims, Kamil al-Sulh and Ahmad Mukhtar Bayhum, and two Christians, Ibrahim Thabit and Pietro Tarrad, the committee was indeed rejected by the populace—for the people understood reform to mean a massive change in the system of government, while the authorities meant the paving of roads and the draining of swamps.[2]

Following Salam's discussion with the Vali, he and a number of Muslim and Christian notables met to discuss the situation. Despite the fact that he was a member of the official committee set up by the Vali, it was Ahmad Mukhtar Bayhum (1878-1922), a wealthy Muslim of Beirut and Salam's good friend, who suggested founding an independent society that would formulate a

list of reforms and present it to the authorities. A number of
Christian leaders, such as Dr Ayyub Thabit (1875-1947, a future
president of Lebanon) and Pietro Tarrad, a lawyer who was also
a member of the Vali's official committee, joined Salam's initiative, and thus the General Reform Society of Beirut (al-Jam'iyya
al-'Umumuiyya al-Islahiyya al-Bayrutiyya) was founded in late
December 1912. It was based on cooperation between Muslims
and Christians, which certainly had not been very common in
that city before. Several days later Bayhum published the news
of the society's establishment in the newspaper al-Ittihad
al-'Uthmani, which was under the editorship of Sheikh Ahmad
Hasan Tabbara, another founding member of the society. His
article discussed the Empire's loss of territory due to its deterioration, which he attributed to two causes: the policy of centraliz-
ing all authority in the capital and the government's
incompetence. By way of a solution he suggested the two preliminary lines of action agreed upon by the society: setting up a
supreme authority in each vilayet (in other words, decentralization so extensive as to constitute autonomy) and bringing in foreign experts and supervisors to assist all the authorities of the
local administration.[3]

The initiators of the society invited the heads of all the communities in Beirut to sent representatives to the second general
meeting of the society, held on 12 January 1913. On the
appointed day 86 people gathered together at the Beirut City
Hall: 42 Muslim representatives, 16 Greek Orthodox, 10 Maronites, six Greek Catholics, two Protestants, two Armenian Catholics, two Armenian Orthodox, two Latins, two Syrian Catholics
and two Jews. At the head of the main blocs, the Muslim and
the Christian, were the two unofficial heads of these religions in
Beirut, the Muslim Muhammad Bayhum and Greek Orthodox
Yusuf Sursuq, and they were recognized as the presidents of the
society.

Since 86 people were too many to discuss specific reforms,
elections were held for a Permanent Committee (al-lajna
al-da'ima), consisting of 25 people—12 Muslims, 12 Christians
and one Jew—that would be responsible for composing the list
of reforms required by the residents of Beirut, to be sent to the
Sublime Porte. Ayyub Thabit was appointed secretary of the
committee. Sheikh Ahmad 'Abbas al-Azhari, for 18 years principal of the Ottoman College in Beirut, who had been one of the
activists of the Syrian independence movement in his youth, was
appointed, without a vote, to be the head of the committee. A
speech he made at the end of the conference expressed his joy

that representatives of all the religions had gathered for a cooperative purpose: "This is the first time that a meeting of this kind has taken place in Syria. Even if it has no other result, the fact that this meeting of men of all different groupings did take place harmoniously is a fortunate omen for the future."[4]

With much discussion, the committee formulated the list of required reforms. It appointed Salim 'Ali Salam, Ahmad Mukhtar Bayhum and Sheikh Ahmad Hasan Tabbara to present the list to the government, but had no sooner done so than, on 23 January 1913, the CUP carried out a coup d'état, killed the war minister and deposed Grand Vizier Kamil Pasha. The coup d'état was greeted with surprise and despair in Beirut. The population was sure that now the Empire was destined to continue losing territory, and that the new government would oppose, as usual, any call for decentralization. And indeed, a few days later, in a telegram from the Sublime Porte, the Vali was told that although the government recognized the urgency of the reforms, in the present situation, with the fatherland in danger (the Balkan War), it must be made clear to the populace that the existence of the Empire came first. Therefore the Vali was ordered to suppress severely any attempt to cause trouble. The Reform Society nevertheless held a third general meeting on 31 January 1913 at the City Hall to endorse the committee's list of reforms in the presence of all 86 members. Though the Vali actually agreed to accept the list, he was dismissed immediately afterwards by the new government.[5]

The main articles of the list of reforms were as follows:

Art. 1 — The administration of the vilayet will be divided into two sections: The first section will include activities related to the existence and basic interests of the Empire, such as foreign affairs, defence, taxes, the postal and telegraph systems, legislation and customs duties. The second section will include local activities related to the specific internal interests of the vilayet. Decisions and implementation of whatever applies to the first section are the responsibility of the central government. Decisions concerning the second section are the responsibility of the General Council of the vilayet.

Art. 3 — A 30-member General Council, half Muslim and half non-Muslim, will be set up in the vilayet, for a period of four years. . . . The rights and duties of the General Council are: (a) To decide on all internal activities of the vilayet . . . (b) To legislate internal laws . . . (g) The right to ask the Vali for explanations and to request his dismissal. . . .

Art. 4 — The decisions of the General Council are valid unless the

Vali appeals against them, with the authorization of the Council of Advisers, within a week after he has been informed of them, and then the Council will consider the decision again. If the Council upholds the decision with a two-thirds majority, the resolution will become law and the Vali will be required to carry it out.

Art. 6 — . . . The Vali will be dismissed according to decision of the General Council with a two-thirds majority. . . .

Art. 7 — The central government will appoint foreign advisers who know one of the three languages: Arabic, Turkish or French . . .

Art. 8 — The income of the vilayet will be of two types: The first will be transferred entirely to the centre of the Empire, including customs duties, postal and telegraph duties and indemnity for exemption from military service. The rest, that is, all income not mentioned above, will be transferred entirely to the vilayet.

Art. 13 — A council will be set up which will be called the Council of Advisers . . . The duties of this Council are: (a) To interpret the articles of the law which will be legislated by the central government (in accordance with this list) as a constitution for the government of the vilayet and its General Council; (b) To interpret the resolutions and laws that will be legislated by the General Council; (c) To investigate and rule on the necessity of dismissing or not dismissing an official. . . .

Art. 14 — The Arabic language will be recognized as an official language for all matters within the vilayet. It will be recognized as an official language, in conjunction with the Turkish language, in the parliament and the senate.

Art. 15 — Military service will be shortened to two years and will be performed in peacetime within the vilayet. . . .[6]

The CUP government had never had any intention of implementing such a far-reaching reform plan, which would make the vilayet semi-independent. The Ottoman authorities were especially angered by the articles demanding the appointment of foreign supervisors and advisers, and they saw in this a lack of faith in the government, as was indeed the case. But not only the Ottoman authorities opposed this demand. Even a reformist like Rashid Rida sharply criticized the demand for foreign experts and considered it "a huge danger for the future of the country".[7]

As soon as it became known that Abu Bakr Hazim would be returned to the position of Vali in Beirut instead of Adham Bek, the society sent a telegram to Istanbul asking him to speak to the new government about the reforms. The local CUP people sent a counter-petition from Beirut expressing the residents' opposition to the reforms. But as soon as the names of the counter-petition's signatories were published in the newspapers, many of them protested that they were not opposed to the reforms at all, but had been tricked by CUP people who had told them that they were signing a petition for the prevention of the export of grain from the vilayet (the petition was written in Turkish, which they did not understand). Others claimed that they had not signed the petition at all.[8] The Beirut newspapers, which were for the most part in favour of reforms, responded to these CUP attempts by publishing a common article in all the newspapers in March 1913 in favour of the reforms, and a few days later another article in favour of the understanding and agreement between the Christians and the Muslims on this matter. The editors of Muslim newspapers published this article in the Christian newspapers, and vice versa.[9]

Hazim responded to the telegrams of the reformists with the reply that he would not leave Istanbul until he received the endorsement of the authorities for the reforms. But he arrived in Beirut without any such endorsement on 7 March 1913. On 11 March a delegation including almost all the members of the Permanent Committee of the Reform Society met with him, and Kamil al-Sulh gave him three copies of the list of reforms translated into Turkish. Then Pietro Tarrad spoke: "The Arabs feel themselves independent within Ottomanism. All the Muslims, Christians and Jews demand reforms in order to preserve this independence." And Ahmad Mukhtar Bayhum said: "All the difficulties that could arise between the Arabs and their government will not prevent them from regarding the Turks as their brothers; but this is not a reason for us to continue to be silent in our present situation. By the same token, when we claim the rights that have been withheld from us, this legitimate demand does not prevent us from living with them forever as Ottomans." The Vali responded that he had agreed to accept his position only on condition that the reforms be implemented. He told the delegation that a new Vilayets Law would soon be published and that at the end of March the reforms would begin to be implemented. If by that time the government had not endorsed this, he himself would go to Istanbul and would either return with such an approval or not return at all. The delegation left the meeting with new hope.[10]

While these members of the Reform Society tried to advance the reform plan in cooperation with the Vali, six of the Christian members (Michel Tuwayni, Yusuf Hani, Pietro Tarrad, Ayyub Thabit, Rizq Allah Arqash, and Khalil Zayniyya—the last three also members of the Society of the Lebanese Revival) took an entirely different approach. Without the knowledge of their Muslim associates, they wrote a memorandum the day after the meeting with the Vali which society member Khalil Zayniyya presented to the French consul-general several days later. It began with a description of the Christians' situation in the Ottoman Empire, which had worsened as a result of the Balkan War, depicted by the Empire as a war of Muslims against Christians. Christians were now considered enemies of the state, leading to Christian emigration from Syria to America. The memorandum went on to discuss the society's list of reforms, claiming that on the basis of past experience the Christians could no longer believe the government's assertion that it was prepared to implement reforms. The government was using the residents' proposal of reforms as a fig-leaf, so that it would not have to implement the reforms demanded by Europe. The Christians, it was pointed out, had indeed agreed to compile a list of reforms, but only in order to prevent the government from composing this list as it saw fit, and in order to include in it the principle of European supervision over its implementation. The memorandum ended by specifying the Christian Syrians' aspirations, whether or not the reforms were implemented. They were as follows: the occupation of Syria by France; or full autonomy for the vilayet of Beirut, under the protection and the practical control of France; or the annexation of Beirut to the Lebanon and the transfer of both to the practical control of France.[11]

On 17 March, summoned by the Vali, Salim 'Ali Salam learned that the new Vilayets Law would soon be announced and would include some of the reforms demanded by the society. Confronted by the Vali with the choice of waiting for the new law to be announced or sending their list of reforms to Istanbul, the society decided to send the list to the capital. The Vali then demanded that the articles concerning foreign advisers be removed from the list. When the society refused, the Vali refused to transmit the list to the government. Salam resigned in protest from his position as a member of the Administrative Committee of the vilayet, and he also refused to participate in the municipal elections in Beirut, justifying his actions by asserting that he could not agree to hold any position until the reforms were implemented. He was followed by society members Ahmad Mukhtar Bayhum and Muhammad al-Fakhuri, who resigned from the Supreme Committee for the evaluation of structures; Salim al-Bawwab and others, who resigned from the Municipal Council; and all the members of the Chamber of Commerce, who resigned collectively. The atmosphere was filled with tension, which only increased with the proclamation of the new Vilayets Law on 28 March, a law that caused great

disappointment among the reformists. At the end of the month
the society still considered itself strong enough to reject 'Abd al-
Karim Qasim al-Khalil's suggestion to unite with the Decentralization Party; it did not even imagine then what awaited it in the
next month.[12]

On 8 April 1913 two policemen sent by the Vali served notice
to Salam and Tarrad that the society's club was closed and the
society disbanded. The Vali informed the Beirut newspapers at
the same time, with an order that they publish the news the following morning. Meeting that evening, the leaders of the society
decided to call upon the newspapers and the population to demonstrate their support for the reforms.

And so, the next day, 9 April, all the Beirut newspapers, with
the exception of the official vilayet organ, appeared with the
Vali's notice about the closing of the society on the front
page—with the remainder of that page and all of the remaining
ones totally blank. The Vali's notice itself was surrounded by a
black border, like an obituary notice. Armed soldiers burst into
the society's club soon afterwards, ordering those present to disperse, confiscating books, and sealing the doors. A delegation
from the society, two Muslims and two Christians, immediately
went to the Vali with the plea that he cancel the closure order.
They argued with him for hours, but instead of justifying his
step the Vali mocked them and refused to cancel the order.

On 10 April a society manifesto signed by almost all the
members of its Committee was published in the newspapers, distributed in the streets, and sent to the Sultan, the Grand Vizier
and the interior minister. It dwelt on the catastrophes that had
befallen the Empire because of inferior administration, and
argued that the society had been established with the permission
of the authorities to find a cure for the vilayet's ills, with all its
meetings held with the knowledge of the government. It defined
the closure by the Vali as a denial of freedom of assembly and a
choking of the idea of reform, and claimed that this action contradicted the constitution and constituted an offence against freedom of the individual and freedom of expression: if the society's
reform plan was not acceptable to the government it could reject
the plan, but it did not have the right to close the society down.
The society was therefore expressing its protest "in the name of
the fatherland and in the face of history" against the Vali, who
had harmed the interests of the fatherland and the principles of
the constitution.

On 11 April the society began collecting the signatures of city
residents for a petition of "property owners, merchants, bankers,

doctors, lawyers, journalists, publishers, etc.", which was sent to the Grand Vizier and the interior minister. The more than 1,300 residents who signed expressed a protest in the name of all the city's classes against the closure of the society: if its members' demands were really against the constitution, then the Vali should have detailed in his closure order which demands he was referring to, so that it would be possible to cope with this claim. The petition also argued that because the reforms were the will of the people, it was therefore the closure order that was unconstitutional. The Grand Vizier was requested to declare a counter-order cancelling the Vali's order, for the sake of the constitution and for the sake of quieting the population.

The society was not willing to stop at the sending of protest telegrams. On the evening of the same day, at the Syrian Protestant College (considered extraterritorial, so that meetings could be held there freely), the members decided to call upon the entire city to strike and to close all the shops. On the morning of 12 April the society members circulated throughout the city requesting merchants to close their shops. Some of them threatened the merchants if they would not acquiesce. Reacting forcefully, the Vali called in the army and arrested five of the propagandists: the Christians Iskandar 'Azar and Rizq Allah Arqash and the Muslims Zakarya Tabbara, Salim Tayyara and Mukhtar Nassar. (The first four were members of the society.) This action did not exactly ease the situation. All the shops in the city were closed, except for groceries and pharmacies, and the residents declared that they would remain closed until the five were released and the society was reopened. Masses of people began to demonstrate in the streets and to run riot. Some of them put signs around their dogs' necks with the name of the Vali, Abu Bakr Hazim. For a while it seemed that the situation was no longer under the control of either the authorities or the Reform Society.

The Vali did not give up. He instructed the pro-CUP Beirut newspapers *Ababil* and *al-Ra'y al-'Amm* to denounce the reformists and instructed the police to raid the reformist newspapers *al-Mufid* and *al-Ittihad al-'Uthmani*, to confiscate their editions and to stop their activities. But the editors of the two suspended newspapers continued to publish secretly. Ordering the residents to open their shops, the Vali promised that the new Vilayets Law would soon be actively implemented and, accordingly, substantial reforms would be realized. He accused "some interested persons . . . five or six" of inciting the populace to violate the public order, threatening that whoever listened to them would be severely punished and advising the people to preserve peace and quiet. When, however, the Vali's town-crier proclaimed through the streets that anyone who did not open his shop would be brought before a military court, the masses attacked and beat him.

Meanwhile, a telegram arrived from the capital with the response of Grand Vizier Mahmud Shawkat to the telegrams of the reformists sent in the previous days. The Vali hastened to publicize it, for in it the Grand Vizier emphasized that there was only one way to request reforms if the residents wanted them—through their parliamentary representatives. If the majority of the parliament demanded the reforms, then they would be implemented, but the government would not heed requests of residents to set up societies that made illegal demands. The Grand Vizier imposed upon the Vali the task of making it clear to the residents that the government was now engaged in reform legislation, and he instructed him to court-martial anyone who carried out an illegal demonstration and to execute the court's decision "within an hour or two at most".

Meeting that evening at the home of Yusuf Sursuq, one of the society's two presidents, the leaders decided to continue the struggle and the strike until the prisoners were released. Then the fear arose that armed supporters from the Lebanon and even from its gendarmerie would stream into the city. At this stage the French and Russian consuls-general intervened in an attempt to ease the situation. Their discussion with the Vali lasted an hour and a half. The German consul also tried to intervene but was rejected by the reformists. The main brunt of the mediation, however, fell upon the British consul-general. When a delegation of Muslims and Christians turned to him, he agreed to intervene, although not officially. After a number of meetings, both with the society members and with the Vali, an agreement was reached according to which the prisoners would be released on 13 April and the city's shops would be opened the next day.

On 13 April the strike continued. The Vali called a meeting of his government officials to discuss the situation. While the president of the military court, Shakir Bek, argued in favour of forceful action against the strikers and rioters, the Vali in the end kept to his agreement with the British consul-general. He summoned Muhammad Bayhum and Yusuf Sursuq to sign a declaration calling for an end to the strike and the opening of the shops; at 4 pm a delegation of leaders of the society, headed by the two presidents, came to the Vali and asked him officially to release the prisoners in return for their signature on the declaration. The

Vali then sent a telegram to the Grand Vizier seeking permission to release the five prisoners in return for the promise of the city notables to guarantee quiet from then on. He ordered the military court to release the prisoners even before the Grand Vizier's reply arrived.

It was here that a new problem arose. When the court asked the relatives of the prisoners for guarantees in writing that they would not repeat their activities, the relatives refused, arguing that such guarantees were requested only of criminals. Thus the prisoners remained in prison until 10 pm, when the reply telegram arrived from the Grand Vizier, approving the Vali's release of the prisoners in return for the notables' promise to guarantee quiet. The court convened, its president told the prisoners that they were released, and as they left the prison the men were greeted by an enthusiastic mass of people who accompanied them in a "victory parade" to a reception at Sursuq's home. But the delay in their release led to unexpected consequences. During the hours the populace waited for the announcement, more and more people gathered in the city squares. Gradually the rioting began anew. Thus, when the society members tried the next day to keep their part of the agreement and bring about the opening of the shops, they did not succeed.

That morning, 14 April, the third day of the strike, Bayhum and Sursuq distributed a proclamation imploring the residents to end the strike and open the city shops. But the proclamation was of no avail. Even those few merchants who dared to open their shops were forced to close them by the demonstrators, who called for a continuation of the strike until the society was reopened and the reforms were granted. Seeing no choice, Bayhum and Sursuq were forced to hire a carriage to go around the city, trying to persuade the merchants to open their shops. A strike supporter jumped on the carriage as it reached the Iyas market and incited the people not to listen to the two notables. Society member Jamil al-Husami, who was passing, saw the incident and removed the inciter from the carriage, jumped on it himself, and lent his assistance in persuading the residents to open the shops. The success of Salim 'Ali Salam and his friends in other parts of the city was also very limited. The released prisoners also went around the streets and shouted "Open! Open!" — but in such a manner that their hearers did exactly the opposite.

Angered, the Vali announced that if the shops were not opened by noon he would re-arrest the five released prisoners as well as the rest of the members of the Reform Society. The

British consul-general again intervened, and the Vali agreed to extend the deadline until the following morning. The consul-general then told the society members that if the shops were not opened the following morning he would regard it as a personal breach of trust and would no longer accept any responsibility for what might occur. On 15 April most of the shops were opened. By the following day life had returned to normal. But the Reform Society—officially—remained closed.[13]

The Beirut events led to a wave of protests in Basra, Damascus and Cairo. As mentioned, the Decentralization Party sent protest telegrams to the Vali and to the Grand Vizier, calling for the Vali's dismissal, as well as telegrams to European foreign ministers and newspapers requesting assistance for the Beirutians. All the Arab newspapers, both in the Empire and in Egypt, discussed the events and their impact on Arab-Turkish relations. The members of the Paris Congress, in its earliest stages of organization, also sent a protest telegram to the interior minister in Istanbul. They saw in the act of closing the society a continuation of the government's policy to deny the Arabs their rights, and they announced that it confirmed their suspicion that the government really did not want to implement reforms.[14] The CUP, quite surprised by the scale of the popular opposition demonstrated in Beirut, granted several minor concessions to calm the atmosphere. On 19 April the interior minister informed the Vali by telegram that Arabic could be used in courts and local government offices and that it was permitted to teach it in the schools. However, the study of Turkish also remained obligatory and officeholders were required to know it.[15]

The authorities' attitude towards the society convinced its members of the uselessness of trying to achieve reforms in coordination with the government. They decided to turn directly to the European powers for this purpose. The society, which had continued to meet secretly, began a fund-drive to finance a delegation of six members, three Muslims and three Christians, to mobilize support in Europe for their demands for reforms. In the end five people were sent: Salim 'Ali Salam, Ahmad Mukhtar Bayhum, Ahmad Hasan Tabbara, Ayyub Thabit, and Khalil Zayniyya, and they represented the society at the Paris Congress. During the congress the society demonstrated its existence publicly by sending a congratulatory telegram.[16]

Two events agitated the society and the people of Beirut in May 1913. On 12 May at 1 am Zakarya Tabbara came out of a local cinema and entered his car. Before he had managed to drive away an attacker, dressed in white, shot him three times with a gun, killing him. When the murderer was caught shortly afterwards, it became clear that his motive was jealousy because of the relationship between Tabbara and a woman named Fortuna. But because Tabbara was among the society members arrested the previous month by the Vali, tension arose in the city as soon as the murder became known. An accusing finger was pointed at Abu Bakr Hazim. The fact that the CUP was known for political murders only heightened the suspicion that such was the case this time as well.[17]

On the evening of 17 May former Grand Vizier Kamil Pasha visited the city. He was welcomed enthusiastically by the local residents and at a number of dinners that were held for him the main topic was the reforms. Although in a discussion with Salam, who was about to set out for Paris, he agreed that he should have eliminated the CUP while still Grand Vizier, in his public speeches Kamil Pasha disappointed his audience by not displaying enthusiasm for the reform demands, which he claimed were too drastic. He urged the Muslims not to be drawn after the Christians in making demands that no government would be able to accept. When he left the city a large crowd gathered at the port, shouting loudly their demands for reforms.[18]

The society again tried to demand reforms in July 1913, when a new Vali, 'Ali Munif, arrived in the city. A 20-member delegation handed him a petition signed by 1,700 people, demanding decentralization, equalization of the status of Arabic with that of Turkish at all levels of government and in the judicial system, military service of local residents within the vilayet only, except in special circumstances, and the introduction of foreign supervisors into the administration. The delegation asked the Vali's assistance for these and a number of additional requests: abolition of the military regime in the city, freedom of the press and the opening of the society's club, closed by the previous Vali.[19] The demands and requests were not granted.

THE REFORM MOVEMENT IN SYRIA

The Reform Society of Beirut was the first reform society that arose in the Levant, paving the way for further efforts in other towns in Syria and Palestine. The reform movement in Damascus began hesitantly and gradually, through a continuing political struggle with the many CUP supporters in the city. On 5 January 1913 the interior minister sent a telegram to Vali Kazim Pasha, ordering him to convene the General Council of the vilayet and to request that it formulate a reform plan for the vilayet within fifteen days. On 10 January 160 people, including the leaders of all the religious communities in the city and the local supporters of reform, as well as many CUP sympathizers, attended a conference of notables at the City Hall called by the mayor of Damascus to formulate acceptable guidelines for the forthcoming General Council meeting. A committee of 20 people was to be elected to compose the list of required reforms for the General Council and the central government. But as soon as the meeting began 'Abd al-Rahman al-Shahbander, one of the participants, expressed his opposition to the election of the committee members from among those present and demanded general elections for the committee. ("If we really want to implement reforms, this must be a public matter.") Other reformists, such as Shukri al-'Asali and 'Abd al-Wahhab al-Inklizi, backed his view, but the CUP supporters opposed it. Rushdi al-Sham'a, another reformist, then suggested that everyone be allowed to present his own list of reforms to the General Council, which would discuss all the suggestions. In the end the conference disbanded without coming to any conclusions, in the shadow of the fierce controversy between the reform supporters and the CUP supporters.

On 18 January the General Council convened with the Vali as president, while the reformist Ahmad al-Sham'a (Rushdi's father) was chosen as vice-president. Two lists of reforms, one from each of the rival factions, were presented to the Council. The reformists' list was similar to that of their Beirut counterparts, although more moderate. Before the General Council had managed to discuss the lists properly, the CUP coup d'état occurred and a new Vali, 'Arif al-Mardini, was appointed in Damascus.[20]

The closing of the Reform Society of Beirut aroused the Damascus reformists once again. Their newspapers, led by *al-Muqtabas*, protested forcefully, even more fiercely than the Beirut newspapers. The Vali of Damascus received from the Vali of Beirut a copy of the Grand Vizier's telegram ordering him to bring all the rioters to trial, and he sent it to all the Damascus newspapers asking that they print it word for word. *Al-Muqtabas*, for one, refused to do this, arguing that the telegram was intended for Beirut and had the Grand Vizier wanted to send it to Damascus as well he would have done so. Soon after Shukri al-'Asali and Muhammad Kurd 'Ali went to 'Arif al-Mardini to demand that he dismiss the secretary-general of the vilayet, since he had not understood an Arabic petition presented to him and had demanded that it be translated into Turkish. Some Damascus merchants closed their shops in solidarity with the people of Beirut. Al-Mardini, although formerly of the Arab-Ottoman Brotherhood, followed in the footsteps of the Vali of Beirut, closing newspapers, making arrests, persecuting the reformists and, without flinching, flogging his opponents with whips.[21]

In Aleppo the opposition to the Ottoman authorities was radically different in nature from that in Damascus and Beirut, taking a separatist cast. In December 1912 residents began to organize secret meetings to discuss the possibility of a British or French protectorate. The idea was raised of collecting thousands of signatures for a petition asking the British to take on responsibility for the administration of the country. But while some of the Aleppo residents, primarily the Druzes, were in favour of Britain, others, both Muslim and Christian, preferred France. A group of Muslim notables, turning to the French consul, expressed their opinion that the time had come for a revolution that would break out simultaneously in all the Syrian centres, expel the Sultan's representatives and transfer the country to the French.

The CUP coup d'état in January 1913 created considerable anxiety in Aleppo. In March a group of notables brought the British consul a petition signed by many Muslim residents who asked to be under British rule, preferring a regime similar to that of Egypt or India over the rule of the Ottoman government. In April a representative of the Muslim group denounced to the French consul the administration of the Young Turks for creating the miserable economic plight of the country, and he asked for European intervention, preferably French, to improve the situation. The consul maintained that there was then no possibility of active foreign intervention, and it may have been this response that led the local Muslims to turn once again to the British consul a few days later with the request that the British government in Egypt extend its protection over their region. They asserted that they could organize a popular movement in Aleppo in favour of Britain, but they requested a promise in advance that such a movement would actually receive British assistance. The closure of the Reform Society of Beirut, on the other hand, did not arouse emotional reactions in Aleppo as it did in the other Syrian towns.[22]

In Hama there were differences of opinion between the Muslims, who contended that it was not the time to struggle for reforms but rather to assist the Empire in its difficult situation, and the Christians, who favoured France.[23] The Muslims of Tripoli demonstrated a different approach. On the initiative of the local mufti, they decided in January 1913 to set up a society with equal numbers of Muslims and Christians to cooperate with the Beirut Society in trying to achieve administrative autonomy for Syria. Nevertheless, they did not agree with the Beirut Society's demands concerning foreign advisers and supervisors.[24]

THE REFORM MOVEMENT IN PALESTINE

The populace in Jerusalem at the beginning of 1913 was divided between those who aspired to absolute autonomy and those who hoped for occupation by a foreign power, preferably Britain or France. The autonomists, led by the al-Husayni family, aspired to a situation in which, although the country would remain part of the Empire, it would be able to administer its own affairs. In frequent secret meetings held at the homes of members of the al-Husayni, al-Khalidi and al-Nashashibi families, the hatred for the people's common enemy, the Turks, was given expression. Their demands were that all the local income, including customs duties, be used for the improvement of the country's situation; that ten per cent of the taxes collected for the central government be used for common expenses; and that all the officeholders, officers and soldiers in the country be Arabs. Nevertheless they stressed that if the Empire were to be attacked, "all the Arabs would march against the enemies of Islam". In April the residents of the sanjaq presented to the governor a petition asking for reforms similar to those requested in Beirut. Nevertheless, in the light of the Beirut attempt, the reformists were quite pessimistic about the chances that the government would agree to grant these reforms. Thus separatist tendencies arose, and many residents wanted to see the country annexed to Egypt.[25]

A telegram sent in April 1913 to the Grand Vizier and the interior minister by Hafiz al-Sa'id, the leader of the Jaffa branch of the Decentralization Party, in the name of the local reformist notables, expressed sorrow that the Empire was losing its territory due to bad administration and the lack of reforms. In order to preserve the Empire intact and save it from European ambitions, al-Sa'id called for immediate implementation of the list of reforms that had been presented in Beirut. In reaction, an opposing telegram was sent to Istanbul by the mayor of Jaffa, an opponent of the reforms. Immediately after, a third telegram was sent, by the reformists, requesting the implementation of the Beirut reforms in Jaffa and asking the authorities to ignore the opponents of the reforms, who, they claimed, only wanted to fulfil their personal ambitions.[26]

Chapter 20

THE REFORM SOCIETY OF BASRA

The story of the Reform Society of Basra differs somewhat from that of the other Arab societies, in that it is, in effect, the story of one individual, Sayyid Talib al-Naqib, the "strong man" of Basra, who transformed his hometown into the Wild South of Iraq.

The political career of Sayyid Talib al-Naqib (1868?-1929), the young and unbeloved son of Sayyid Rajab, the Naqib of Basra, began in 1899, when his father sent him to Istanbul to complain about the Vali of Basra, hated by both Sayyid Rajab and the Sheikh of Kuwait, Mubarak al-Sabah. Talib succeeded in his mission; the Vali was ousted, and the new Vali appointed in his place was friendly towards both the Naqib family and the Sheikh of Kuwait. Henceforth the Sheikh of Kuwait supported Sayyid Talib and, aided also by the new Vali, Talib began to gain influence and strength and even dared to levy a yearly "tax" on the town notables.

The following year Talib took care of another enemy, an advocate by the name of 'Abdallah al-Ruwanduzi who had represented one of Talib's victims. Initially, Talib despatched some of his henchmen to give the lawyer a beating. Al-Ruwanduzi apparently did not get the message and when he continued his activities against Talib, his assassination was ordered. The removal of the advocate, who had also been hampering Sheikh Khaz'al of Muhammara, was most convenient for this sheikh and pleased him greatly. He befriended Talib and provided him with ample funds to finance his personal bodyguards and improve his extortion methods.

However, 'Abdallah al-Ruwanduzi had been popular in Basra and the murder generated considerable bitterness against Talib. Sensing that his situation was becoming precarious, he turned for help to Abu al-Huda, who had befriended him on his mission to Istanbul and was close to Sultan 'Abd al-Hamid II. In 1902 Abu al-Huda had been instrumental in obtaining for him the appointment of Mutasarrif of Hasa. Shortly thereafter, Talib attacked and burnt down the home of the Sheikh of Qatif, Hajj Mansur Pasha, claiming that ammunition and the British flag were concealed on the property. He also took the opportunity to rob the sheikh of 35,000 (another version says 100,000) Turkish liras. Again there was an outcry against Talib. Forced to give up his position and to return to Basra, he soon resumed his old custom of despatching professional robbers to the homes of notables who refused to pay him protection money. Finally, in 1904 a new and aggressive Vali arrived in the town and ordered his soldiers to surround Talib's home and arrest the entire gang of robbers residing there. The following year he forced Talib to leave town altogether.

Talib proceeded to Istanbul, where for a bribe of 5,000 Turkish liras he was able to persuade 'Izzat Pasha al-'Abid, a man close to 'Abd al-Hamid, to secure him an appointment as a member of the State Council. This appointment Talib used to remove the file containing the complaints of Hajj Mansur concerning the stolen money. Upon the outbreak of the Young Turk Revolution in 1908, Talib hastened to leave Istanbul, fearing revenge from members of the CUP who knew of his connections with Abu al-Huda and 'Izzat Pasha, both of whom they loathed. He returned to Basra by boat, but not before he had set fire to his house in Istanbul in order to collect the insurance on the furniture.[1]

In the parliamentary elections held shortly after his return to Basra, Talib used his influence to ensure that he would be returned to the capital as a local deputy. Taking his parliamentary seat in Istanbul, he made approaches to members of the CUP; however, once it became apparent that he could extract no personal advantage from them, he made contact with Sadiq Bey, thereby becoming one of the founders of the Moderate Liberal Party. His subsequent return to Basra as a declared opponent of the CUP gained him the friendship of the ex-Grand Vizier, Kamil Pasha. Talib was assisted in his activities against the local CUP in early 1909 by the new Vali, 'Arif al-Mardini. But the latter was soon replaced by an activist Vali, Sulayman Nazif, who restricted Talib's activity. Consequently, in 1910 Talib sent off a petition signed by Basra notables to the interior minister, Tal'at, demanding that the Vali be ousted. Tal'at did not accede to the request; indeed, he probably considered Talib's opposition a confirmation of the Vali's qualifications. Sensing which way the wind was blowing, the scheming Talib then organized the riff-raff of Basra to sign a petition requesting the continued service of their beloved and gracious Vali. No sooner did Tal'at receive this petition than he dismissed the Vali. Thus, in his first direct confrontation with the CUP government, Talib emerged victorious, albeit by cunning and duplicity. His prestige in the town soared.[2]

Until the outbreak of World War I, Talib was effectively the ruler of Basra. He roamed the town escorted by an armed guard, and had the newspapers under his thumb to the point that they wrote whatever he dictated. His generosity towards the poor of the town, utilizing money he extorted from the wealthy by threats and blackmail, led him to be dubbed a modern Robin Hood. If all other means failed, Talib did not hesitate to resort to force to obtain the money. However, this was not his only source of income. He owned large palm groves outside the town that returned handsome revenues; his father supported him financially; and he also received monthly salaries of 70 and 50 Turkish liras from the Sheikhs of Kuwait and Muhammara, respectively, for overseeing their considerable holdings in Basra. In this period he sought to enhance his status by making approaches to the British consuls in Basra, Muhammara and Bushir. On one occasion he helped them carry out a secret exploration around Faw; however, a plan to assist a group of British officers on a scouting trip to the neighbourhood of Qarmat 'Ali, without the knowledge of the Ottoman authorities, fell through when one of his associates revealed it to the commander of the Ottoman guard. Talib frequently invited the British consul in Basra to his home in order to impress on him how capable he was of protecting himself against the government, and regale him with tales of his heroic exploits.[3]

On 11 February 1911, while in Istanbul as a member of the parliament, Talib sent a letter to Sharif Husayn of Mecca asserting that since the Turks were "pushing us to the gallows", the Arab members of the parliament would support the Sharif wholeheartedly and would stand by him if he removed the Ottoman yoke from Arab shoulders. He enclosed a declaration, signed by 35 Arab members of the parliament, stating:

> We, the representatives of the Arabs in the parliament, recognize in Husayn the ruler of Mecca and we recognize, in the name of the Arab countries which we represent, that he and only he is the religious leader of the Arab countries. We are ready to take this *bay'a* [loyalty oath] publicly when circumstances require it.

Husayn's reaction to this letter is unknown.[4]

While in Istanbul, Talib also worked to block the central government's plan to confiscate private lands (*mulk*) and place them under state domain (*miri*), thus gaining great popularity among the landowners of Basra. However, in mid-1911, suspecting that his life was not safe in Istanbul and that he might be murdered by CUP men, as others of their adversaries had been, Talib returned to Basra. There, on 7 September 1911, he opened a branch of the anti-CUP Moderate Liberal Party, which later became the Party of Liberty and Union. Talib himself headed the branch, whose members were mainly landowners and notables. As his vice-president he chose Hajj Mahmud Pasha 'Abd al-Wahid, formerly the president of the local CUP branch. Indeed, following the defection of Mahmud Pasha and others, the CUP branch virtually ceased to exist; an attempt to revive it ended in failure when its new president, 'Abd al-Muhsin Pasha al-Zuhayr, also defected to the Party of Liberty and Union.[5]

It was also in 1911 that Talib made his most relentless and sworn enemy, 'Ujaymi ibn Sa'dun, the leader of the Muntafik tribes. 'Ujaymi's father, Sa'dun Pasha, had become the uncrowned ruler of the Muntafik tribes of southern Iraq in 1908, upon his brother Falih's death after a four-year struggle between them over leadership of the Muntafik. Sa'dun became an ardent supporter of the CUP and exploited his connections with them to institute a reign of terror, unmercifully eradicating his enemies and extorting money from others. However, in 1911 he became involved in a campaign against the Shafir tribes which ended in a débâcle. Seizing the opportunity, Falih's two sons rose up against Sa'dun, who, in an effort to maintain his leadership status, sent his son 'Ujaymi to eliminate 15 sheikhs who opposed him. The subsequent chain of murders generated havoc and anarchy in the entire region; in June 1911 the Ottoman authorities appointed a committee of enquiry. The committee held Sa'dun responsible for the situation, and the CUP decided to get rid of him. Thus, in July 1911 the Vali of Basra invited Sa'dun for an "interview". Sa'dun informed Talib that he would be under his "protection" (aman) while in Basra. On 20 July Sa'dun arrived with a 1,500-man guard, but so secure did he feel under Talib's aman that he stationed his men outside the town. Proceeding to the government building, he was informed that the Vali awaited him on the coastguard boat, Marmaris. Suspecting nothing, Sa'dun boarded the ship, but when the Vali failed to appear, he realized that he had been taken prisoner. On instructions from Istanbul, the ship sailed under guard for Baghdad, whence Sa'dun was transferred to Aleppo and imprisoned in that city's fortress. On 25 September, shortly before he was to be sent to Istanbul to stand trial, it was reported that he had died of apoplexy and heart failure. The prevalent opinion was that the authorities had poisoned him. His son 'Ujaymi considered this a breach of trust on Talib's part, and was convinced that the latter had connived with the government. Ever unable to forgive Talib, 'Ujaymi tried to have him killed, even through cooperating with the CUP men who were actually responsible for his father's death.

By January 1912 when the new Mutasarrif for the Muntafik region, Farid Bek, was appointed, 'Ujaymi had already renewed his good relations with the CUP. According to his scale of values, deceit by the government was evidently more legitimate than the breach of trust he ascribed to Talib, for which no forgiveness was possible. In October 1912 'Ujaymi robbed the house of his cousin Mizyad, Falih's son, and thus fell foul of Mizyad's brother 'Abdallah. Talib, who had never been sympathetic to Sa'dun's pro-CUP leanings, and had supported Falih's sons, now proceeded to act according to the adage that "the enemy of my enemy is my friend". He befriended 'Abdallah ibn Falih and assisted his efforts to wrest leadership of the Muntafik from 'Ujaymi.[6]

In 1912 Talib was again elected to the parliament, this time on behalf of the Party of Liberty and Union. Elected with him were another member of the party and two who presented themselves as CUP candidates but were actually from Talib's circle, passing themselves off as sympathizers of the CUP only in order to be elected and further strengthen Talib's position. In the course of the election campaign itself, the Valis of Basra and Baghdad hired a professional "hatchet man" to assassinate Talib for 1,500 liras. Instead, immediately after receiving the money, the hired killer went straight to Talib and told him of the plot against his life. Talib did not take this lying down, and once the Party of Liberty and Union had attained power, in July 1912, he helped the Vali of Basra appointed by the new government, 'Ali Rida al-Rikabi (later a prominent member of al-Fatat), to shadow the local CUP members and hamper their activities. The appointment of Kamil Pasha as Grand Vizier led to the dismissal of the Mutasarrif Farid Bek, a staunch member of the CUP and a great friend of 'Ujaymi. Infuriated, 'Ujaymi decided at the end of the year to attack Basra. However, he was forced to drop his plan when al-Rikabi and Talib organized protection for the town.[7]

Grand Vizier Kamil Pasha had good relations with Talib, and he advised him to strengthen his position by cultivating high British officials. Talib duly visited Egypt that year, meeting both the Khedive and the British consul-general Lord Kitchener, and seeking the latter's support for his position as "strong man" of Basra. He used his return journey to visit India, where he met Lord Hardinge, the Viceroy, and Arthur Henry McMahon, Foreign Secretary of the Government of India. Although these contacts bore no practical fruit, they bolstered Talib's self-confidence to the point where he viewed himself as a leader of international stature.[8]

On 23 January 1913 the CUP returned to power via a coup d'état, and Talib once more found himself at odds with the authorities. His acute political sense telling him that the hour of the Party of Liberty and Union had passed, on 26 January he convened a meeting of notables in his home, who resolved that the Arabs had no interest in the political quarrels between the Liberals and the CUP and would, in the future, concentrate on non-political activity for the exclusive sake of the Empire. In early February an agreement was reached with the local CUP members whereby they would close their clubhouse (which in any case was rarely visited) in exchange for a similar move by the Party of Liberty and Union. However, at this stage Talib had no intention of appeasing the CUP. On the contrary, he decided to follow the lead of the Decentralization Party and the Reform Society, which had been established not long before in Cairo and Beirut. The idea of opening a branch of the Decentralization Party in the town was dropped since it was beneath his dignity to head a mere branch. Instead, he would establish his own reform society. Reconvening the notables in his home on 20 February, he pushed through a decision to send a petition to the capital demanding the establishment of a General Council in Basra which would draw up a list of all the reforms the vilayet required, as had been done in Beirut a month earlier. A second demand was that part of the vilayet's revenues be retained and utilized to improve the miserable and neglected condition of its inhabitants; their situation was the worst in the Empire, it was asserted, and they were anxious to see the reforms accomplished. On 22 February the petition, bearing the signatures of 300 notables, was despatched to the Grand Vizier and the interior minister. Talib himself, for reasons of his own, preferred not to sign the document.[9]

Shortly after the closing of the CUP and Party of Liberty and Union clubs, Talib began preparations to establish the Reform Society of Basra (*Jam'iyyat al-Islah al-Basriyya* or *Jam'iyyat al-Basra al-Islahiyya*). The official opening took place in Talib's home on 28 February 1913, with all past members of the Party of Liberty and Union club in attendance. Besides the notables of

Basra, army officers who were stationed in the neighbourhood joined, among them a Turk named Ahmad Nutqi, who had been invited to join so that he could see with his own eyes that the society was not working against the interests of the Empire. What he saw, however, seems to have convinced him of just the opposite, since he soon left the society and became one of Talib's greatest opponents. By contrast, the joining of the highly influential Mubdir al-Fir'awn, one of the great sheikhs of the Middle Euphrates, was perceived by Talib as a major breakthrough. In general, most of the society's members were to Talib's liking, for example, 'Abd al-Latif Mandil, a rich landowner who exploited every opportunity to expand at his neighbours' expense; 'Abd al-Razzaq al-Ni'ma, a wealthy gambler and drunkard who eventually gambled most of his possessions away; and Sulayman Faydi, a lawyer and journalist and evidently Talib's only true friend, despite his description by the British as "a leech and clinger to patrons".[10]

The upshot of these developments was that the local CUP members decided to try to make peace with Talib. Tal'at told the Valis of Basra and Baghdad to act accordingly. The Vali of Baghdad pressed Rashid al-Khawja, chief of the army staff there (later one of the prominent members of al-'Ahd), to write to Talib along these lines. But after sending this letter, al-Khawja sent another recommending just the opposite. Receiving the two letters at the same time, Talib decided to act according to the second.[11] Moreover, he would step up his demands and not be satisfied only with reforms. In March 1913, at a meeting he initiated in the palace of the Sheikh of Muhammara, with the Sheikh of Kuwait and a high Ottoman official also present, it was decided to demand independence, or at least autonomy, for Iraq. At the same time, 'Ujaymi was gathering a force of 5,000 armed horsemen to storm Basra and finish off Talib.[12]

On 23 April 1913 Talib organized a large group of notables to stage a demonstration before the acting Vali of Basra. He himself did not join the demonstrators. They complained of the lack of security in the area and the numerous robberies and murders, accusing the local gendarmerie of inefficiency and even of collusion in the crimes. The chief of the gendarmerie of Abu al-Khasib, they charged, had the audacity to rob a store in broad daylight, on the pretext of looking for contraband merchandise. In another incident, a fisherman had been shot dead by a gendarme who went unpunished. The demonstrators issued an ultimatum to the acting Vali in the name of the population of Basra: If 'Akif Bek, the commandant of the Basra gendarmerie,

Husayn Hijrani, commander of the gendarmerie *tabur* (regiment) there (both enemies of Talib), and Mulazim Awwal (lieutenant) Ibrahim, chief of the gendarmerie of Abu al-Khasib, were not dismissed within two days, the Arabs would eliminate both the police and the gendarmerie and would see to public security in the region themselves. The acting Vali replied that he could not accept the ultimatum on his own authority, and requested a delay of several days in order to consult with Istanbul. The Basra notables agreed to a week's extension, reiterating that if the officials named had not been dismissed by then, they would rid themselves of them by force.[13]

Towards the end of April 1913, a new Vilayets Law was published according the Vali very broad powers; he could appoint and discharge officials at will, declare emergency conditions and martial law, and even call out the army at his own discretion. He could cancel meetings of the General Council of the vilayet or even request the interior ministry to disband the Council altogether. Indeed, under the new law the General Council had to obtain the Vali's assent to all its decisions.[14] The inhabitants of the Arab provinces, who had anticipated reforms and greater autonomy under the new law, were shocked; it was inconceivable that Talib and his supporters could agree to such a law. On 26 April *al-Dustur*, the local newspaper and Talib's mouthpiece, denounced the new law "as having been passed for the benefit of the Vali and not for the good of the nation", and informed its readers that "the great reformer, Sayyid Talib al-Naqib", had decided to protest this oppressive law. That same night protest cables from Basra streamed into the offices of the Grand Vizier and the interior minister in Istanbul until 3 am. One had 400 signatures, headed by that of Talib. This was followed by an hour-long telegraphic exchange between the Grand Vizier, the interior minister and Talib. The two former begged Talib not to put pressure on the Empire while it was engaged in a war in the Balkans. Talib refused to budge, demanding full administrative autonomy for the vilayet of Basra. In particular, he objected strongly to the articles in the law which extended the jurisdiction of the Vali and diminished the powers of the General Council. He also demanded that the Council be empowered to draw up a list of the reforms required by the vilayet.

The result was that the government decided to increase its military strength in Basra. Talib reacted by despatching letters of incitement to Baghdad, calling on the inhabitants to join in a collective protest against the new law which would enslave the Iraqis to their valis. The notables of Basra decided to break off relations with the authorities and boycott the elections to the General Council that were to be held according to the new law. The bewildered Vali sought the counsel of the interior minister, who instructed him to leave the law intact and to elect a General Council as it prescribed. Outraged, Talib and his followers threatened an armed rebellion. The British Consul requested that a Royal Navy warship be despatched to Basra in order to protect British subjects if necessary. 'Ujaymi began moving his forces towards the town.[15]

At this point the government decided that Talib had to be eliminated at any cost. On 2 May 1913 a new Vali, 'Ala' al-Din al-Durubi, nondescript and lacking authority, was posted to Basra. In the meantime, a secret consultation was held in Istanbul among Najati (the public prosecutor in Baghdad), Tal'at (interior minister), Jamal (military governor of Istanbul), 'Adil (former interior minister and a leading member of the CUP) and 'Azmi (chief of the general security service). Their solution was to send a new military commandant, Farid Bek, the ex-Mutasarrif of the Muntafik, to Basra to kill Talib and everyone else who was demanding reforms, promising Farid Bek that they would appoint him Vali of Basra after he had successfully carried out this mission. The Mutasarrif of the Muntafik Badi' Nuri (the brother of Sati' al-Husri), who was then in Istanbul, was requested to seek the cooperation of 'Ujaymi ibn Sa'dun. He suggested that 'Ujaymi be awarded an honorary decoration, military rank, and a monthly salary of 300 Turkish liras, in order to ensure his support.

Farid Bek well understood the dangers involved in this mission. The night before he left Baghdad for Basra, he sat in on a last poker game, and according to one European who was present, he suddenly threw down his cards and cried out, trembling: "How much longer will Sayyid Talib let me live?" Farid's fears proved well founded. He arrived in Basra on 6 May, took over the military command of the town, appointed Hijrani commander of the gendarmerie, and invited 'Atif, the Muntafik's *tabur* commander, to come there. When Talib demanded an explanation of these developments from the new Vali, the latter answered that he had nothing to worry about because Farid Bek would occupy himself only with military affairs and would not interfere in the administration. For his part, Farid Bek began to make contact with Talib's enemies, including Sheikh Salim al-Khayun, chief of the Banu Asad tribe who was commander of the river police, 'Ujaymi ibn Sa'dun, and his brother Hamed. Badi' Nuri also turned to 'Ujaymi, within the framework of his mission, and 'Ujaymi responded with alacrity, contributing 1,500 horsemen towards Talib's elimination. As a reward, the Ottoman officers promised him the property of some of his own relatives in the town, with whom he had quarrelled, while he himself, as an expression of his loyalty and support for the project, sent 1,000 liras on account to Farid Bek, 100 liras to Hijrani, and 700 liras to the Vali.

On 7 May 'Ujaymi's forces, then only ten hours from the town, began to advance. The Vali, in order to appear to be fulfilling his duty, wired him to halt. 'Ujaymi continued to advance and by the end of the month was positioned close to the town. To justify his activity, 'Ujaymi sent an official telegram to the Grand Vizier and the interior minister in Istanbul, explaining that an investigation he had carried out had proven Talib responsible for the disorder and intrigues that were rampant in Basra, and that he, 'Ujaymi, had brought his men solely to assist the government in suppressing Talib's followers. 'Ujaymi concluded by requesting that Talib be exiled from the town.

Perceiving the course that events would take, Talib began to organize counter-measures. His ally, the Sheikh of Muhammara, sent him a bodyguard of 50 men to be used in an emergency. Farid Bek, apparently wanting to allay Talib's fears and perhaps also to spy on his home, showed unusual courage by visiting him there several times during this period, once even staying overnight. Talib could not refuse him hospitality lest he damage his reputation as a "welcomer of guests". The true motive for these visits was soon revealed, however, when Talib's men discovered—and immediately killed—three assassins hiding in a nearby ruin. This episode led Farid Bek to conclude that Talib could not be disposed of by deceitful means; he therefore decided on a public attack.

It did not take long for the first mistake to be made in the plan to eliminate Talib. At the beginning of June, 'Ujaymi sent a messenger to the Sheikhs of Kuwait and Muhammara, asking them what their attitude would be if 'Ujaymi were to kill Talib. The two, allies of Talib's, immediately informed him of the plan, urging him to leave town until calm was restored. Since Talib's reputation would have been seriously compromised by such a move, he asked instead for the help of the two sheikhs, who responded by supplying him with a large quantity of arms.

On 9 June 'Ujaymi captured the palace of one of Talib's relatives in Shu'ayba, a small town near Basra; its owner's complaint to the Vali remained unanswered. 'Ujaymi made Shu'ayba his headquarters, maintaining regular contact with Farid Bek through Muhammad al-'Usaymi, a native of Zubayr and an enemy of Talib's. On 10 June Badi' Nuri arrived in Basra for consultations and suggested that 'Abdallah ibn Falih be co-opted into the design on Talib's life. This was the plotters' second mistake, for when they related the plot to 'Abdallah ibn Falih, a friend of Talib's, he not only refused to cooperate but probably also revealed the plot to Talib. The planners, at any rate, proceeded, and on 15 June Salim al-Khayun, chief of the Banu Asad tribe, and Hamed ibn Sa'dun, 'Ujaymi's brother, arrived in Basra. They stationed 100 armed fighters in a house purchased by al-Khayun, 80 more in a second house, and 120 more in a nearby plantation, with another 100 deployed outside the town in Kut al-Hajaj. Observing the influx of armed men, the British consul asked for the Vali's intervention, but the latter denied all knowledge of the event, including Farid Bek's role. Yet, on the pretence of fulfilling his duty, he requested Farid Bek to oust 'Ujaymi's men. Farid Bek, for his part, asked 'Ujaymi to advance even closer to the town.

Finally, the culmination of the plot was at hand. On the night of 20/21 June 1913 all Arab officers would be freed from duty and replaced by officers who were members of the CUP. These officers would be stationed throughout the town's quarters, with one officer, Ahmad Nutqi, stationed near Talib's home with a number of other men, who were to open fire. When Talib responded in kind, these men would immediately report that he was causing disturbances in the town. The army and the artillery would then be ordered to move into the area of his palace, capture it, and take Talib dead or alive, even if this entailed burning down the whole neighbourhood. Hamed ibn Sa'dun and Salim al-Khayun would then conquer another part of the town, while 'Ujaymi and his followers entered Basra via the Zubayr gate. At the same time, under the command of Hijrani and 'Atif, gendarmes would surround the houses of twelve of Talib's leading, supporters, order them to come out, and shoot them dead without further ado. A military regime would then be established in the town. To this end, a list of twelve of Talib's supporters was prepared by Farid Bek, among them members of the Reform Society: Sulayman Faydi, 'Abd al-Latif Mandil, 'Abd al-Razzaq al-Ni'ma, Mahmud al-Ahmad al-Ni'ma, Ahmad Chalabi al-Sani', and 'Abdallah Sa'ib (the president of the local criminal court). In a secondary action, probably at 'Ujaymi's request, it was decided to assassinate 'Abdallah ibn Falih, who was to join Farid and Badi' Nuri for a cruise on the coastguard boat *Marmaris*.

All the intricacies of the plot were, however, known to Talib, who, together with Sulayman Faydi, prepared a three-stage counter-plan. All the families of the persons earmarked for elimination would be evacuated from the town; as many armed men as possible would make their way into his neighbourhood; and a surprise attack would be launched on the plot's perpetrators. Talib's plan went like clockwork. After the families were evacuated, armed men were stationed in the homes of those marked for execution. One hundred men were posted in Talib's home alone, and all the key positions in the neighbourhood were held by his supporters. And in the midst of these feverish activities, Talib was even able to find time to send a cable of support to the Arab-Syrian Congress which was then meeting in Paris.

On 19 June Farid Bek, Badi' Nuri, 'Abdallah ibn Falih and a number of Turkish officers boarded the *Marmaris* and sailed to Faw, intending to return the following evening. As the ship set sail, four men could be seen waving a handkerchief. They comprised the gang which was to assassinate 'Abdallah ibn Falih upon the vessel's return. Three of them were Salim al-Khayun's men, and the fourth a slave of Hamed ibn Sa'dun's. Talib now moved to execute the third phase of his plan. On the morning of 20 June a figure dressed in rags and carrying a dirty straw mat on his head emerged from Talib's house. Half an hour later, another man similarly dressed came out, and then two others. The four found cover in an old house overlooking the docks of the Ashar River, where vessels from Basra sailed en route to the Shatt al-'Arab, and took turns watching the river until nightfall. When the *Marmaris* docked at sunset and Farid Bek and others disembarked, Talib's four men opened their mats, drew out rifles, and advanced. Farid Bek leaped on to the steps of the dock and was about to shake hands with a certain Catoni of the Imperial Ottoman Bank, when he and his entourage were surrounded by Talib's men, who opened fire on Farid Bek and Badi' Nuri. Farid Bek was killed on the spot, Badi' Nuri suffered fatal wounds, and one gendarme was wounded. 'Abdallah ibn Falih, who had been with them, came through unscathed. The assassins disengaged quickly, firing behind them as they went and disappearing among the narrow alleys and from there to the nearby date plantations, where they were swallowed up by the darkness.

A series of errors ensued—fully exploited by Talib. Hijrani, commandant of the gendarmerie, who had been present at the scene of the murder, was convinced that the four assassins were the men of Salim al-Khayun and Hamed ibn Sa'dun who were supposed to have killed 'Abdallah ibn Falih but, perhaps because of the darkness, had killed the wrong people. Consequently, he prevented the gendarmes at the site from pursuing the murderers, and instructed a policeman to inform Salim al-Khayun and Hamed that Farid Bek was dead, the plan foiled, and they should "lie low". However, finding it strange that Hijrani did not order the murderers to be pursued, the policeman instead reported the story to the chief of police. In the meantime, confusion reigned in the Turkish camp. While some wanted to continue with the plan in spite of everything, once they realized that the four murderers were actually Talib's men, they decided it would suffice to apprehend them. Patrols were sent to search the date plantations and found. . .the four men of Salim al-Khayun and Hamed. Certain that these were the assassins of Farid Bek and Badi' Nuri, the patrol opened fire. In the ensuing gunfight, one of the four was wounded and all were seized and arrested as suspects in the murder.

Throughout all these events Talib and Sulayman Faydi were sitting in the former's palace, waiting for news. Their main fear was that Farid Bek would escape, and therefore all the ammunition boxes were ordered to be opened. In the neighbourhood, the officer 'Abd al-Jalil al-Shaliji, a member of the Reform Society and a brigade commander, roamed the streets unhampered. Even after receiving the news of Farid Bek's death, Talib still feared that the authorities would pursue the original plan; and his men therefore continued to scour the neighbourhood until morning. In the meantime, the Vali finally decided to intervene. He summoned Hamed ibn Sa'dun, and instructed him to leave Basra immediately. When Hamed refused, the Vali told him that he was acting on instructions from Istanbul, and Hamed's failure to obey would lead him to be treated as a rebel. Immediately thereafter Hamed and Salim al-Khayun were forced to leave the town under guard. The Vali also relayed instructions to 'Ujaymi from the interior minister to leave the region immediately. By 21 June quiet had been restored. The Turkish officers held funeral services for Farid Bek, and at his grave officer Ahmad Nutqi called for a "blood revenge". But the opportunity to eliminate Talib had already been lost.

The judicial system, comprised wholly of Talib's supporters, now went into action. The judiciary insisted on treating the four prisoners as the murderers of Farid Bek and Badi' Nuri. The official investigators determined that the four—it was finally clarified that they were Salim al-Khayun's men—had been sent to kill 'Abdallah ibn Falih, but in the darkness had killed Farid Bek and Badi' Nuri by mistake. The court (whose president, it will be recalled, was one of those on Farid Bek's death list) therefore ordered the arrest of Salim al-Khayun, of Hijrani, who was accused of being an accomplice, and of 'Atif. In a tight spot, the three telegraphed Istanbul, requesting protection. Najati, the public prosecutor of Baghdad, decided to take matters into his own hands and investigate what actually had happened. But, as was brought out in the enquiry, since Najati was one of those who had sent Farid Bek to Basra, Talib hinted to him that he would be endangering his life by coming to Basra. Talib also launched a campaign against Najati by distributing blank papers throughout Basra to be signed by local residents, after which they were inscribed with the demand that the public prosecutor be returned to Baghdad and sent on to Istanbul. Najati nevertheless came to Basra on the *Marmaris*, but before he could disembark Turkish officers went aboard and warned him that if he left the ship he would certainly be killed. Najati returned to Baghdad that same day and wrote a short report in which he absolved Hijrani and 'Atif of guilt and ordered the release of the four prisoners. He also found the Basra court guilty of perverting justice in Talib's favour. In the wake of this report, the government decided to dismiss Baha' al-Din, president of the Basra Court of Appeals. To the justice minister's telegram of dismissal, the astounded judge replied with a cable of his own: "Where shall I go and where am I transferred to?" to which the justice minister retorted: "Go to hell!" In reaction to these events, *al-Dustur* published a sharp attack on the public prosecutor and suggested that the leaders of the CUP lock the doors of their party centre and put up a "For Rent" sign.

Talib could now celebrate his victory, without doubt his greatest in this period. One person who found absolutely no cause to celebrate, however, was 'Ujaymi, frustrated that after all the money he had wasted on the Ottoman officials, among them the Vali, he was now ordered to leave Basra without any return for his efforts. His request for an audience with the British consul, in order to complain about the ingratitude of the Turks, was turned down, the consul maintaining that the government would not be pleased with it. Then suddenly, in a dramatic turnabout, 'Ujaymi announced that he had made peace with Talib and that past differences were forgotten. He fired off cables to all the government authorities, declaring that although his original intention had been to protect Basra from Talib's machinations, his information against Talib had turned out to be false and libellous; henceforth they were friends and would work together to realize the rights of the Arabs. Future events were to demonstrate that 'Ujaymi had not the slightest intention of effecting a genuine reconciliation with Talib, and that his ostensible peacemaking was no more than a tactic on his part. However, Talib now felt secure enough to allow elections to the General Council.[16]

Talib also moved to broaden his support. The officers of the garrison expressed their sympathy for him openly, while the new military commandant, 'Izzat al-Kirkukli, was a friend who had refused to join the plot against him. Indeed, the Vali himself, who at that time commanded the allegiance of no more than 100 Turkish troops, was actually under the control of Talib, by then considered the head of all the tribes from 'Amara to Faw. Although his henchmen were elected to the General Council, Talib did not consider this of significance, warning that public opinion at the moment was more inclined towards *inqilab* (revolution) than *intikhab* (elections). Therefore, he renewed his demands for reforms and self-government, with the threat that if these demands were not met, the inhabitants would not hesitate to fight for them with all the means at their disposal.[17]

On 22 August 1913 the Reform Society of Basra issued its list of demands, which was also published in *al-Dustur*. Tending to extremes, the list of demands included the following:

Art. 2 — No concessions to be made to foreigners in our country. It must be protected against foreign intrigues, and foreign influences must be prevented from infiltrating the country.

Art. 4 — Activities related to the existence of the Sultanate and its basic concerns, which are: foreign policy and security, taxes, post and telegraph, legislation, and the imposition of general taxes, are within the jurisdiction of the central government. Activities related to the internal and administrative concerns of the vilayet, and to the complete fulfilment of all those conditions that are essential for its progress and settlement, are within the jurisdiction of the General Council of the vilayet.

Art. 5 — The Vali executes the decisions of the central government and of the General Council . . .

Art. 7 — The General Council has broad authority to discuss anything that is for the benefit of the vilayet . . .

Art. 8 — The General Council has the power to increase the gendarmerie and the police force and to set up guard stations wherever necessary . . .

Art. 9 — The General Council is completely independent and has complete jurisdiction over the Vali and the other officials. . . .

Art. 14 — The central government has the right to appoint the Vali, on condition that he is an Iraqi . . .

Art. 16 — . . . The Vali may be dismissed by a two-thirds majority in the General Council.

Art. 17 — The income of the vilayet is to be divided into two parts. The first, the income from taxes, post and telegraph, and money paid for exemption from military service, shall be entirely assigned for the headquarters of the Sultanate. The rest, all other income, shall be assigned entirely for the vilayet and be spent within it.

Art. 19 — The local Arabic shall be the official language in all affairs of the vilayet and among its inhabitants. The same shall apply in every courthouse, and all announcements shall be written in Arabic.

Art. 23 — Regular soldiers shall serve in their own vilayet in times of peace, but in times of war the government has the right to send them where it pleases.

Art. 24 — Officers knowing Arabic shall be employed in their own country . . .

Art. 25 — All sciences and arts shall be taught in our schools in Arabic . . .[18]

In late August 1913 the society issued a threatening proclamation directed at the Arab soldiers in Iraq and the tribesmen. Islamic in orientation, the proclamation warned against the selling of the fatherland by the "heretical group" which had robbed the government of the Islamic caliphate and killed hundreds of innocent people. The authorities were accused of selling Bulgaria and Bosnia-Herzegovina, agreeing to the "Zionist plan" to buy Palestine, losing Rumelia, and harbouring a desire to sell lands of Iraq to foreigners. Inter alia, the government was also accused of seeking to "Turkify" the population and aiming to make Sunday the day of rest, as in Europe. The proclamation informed its readers that societies of Muslims and non-Muslims had been established in Basra, Aleppo, Beirut and Syria in order to combat these tendencies and demand that the government grant them decentralization; if this was refused, the Arabs would cease to consider it their legal government. Finally, Arab soldiers were urged to unsheathe their swords and force the government to carry out the decentralization, whether it wanted to or not, since only thus could the country be protected against foreigners. The proclamation was favourably received wherever it was seen. In reaction, Enver instructed the new military commandant to arrest Talib, but since the commandant was on friendly terms with him, he retorted that it was beyond his ability—which was in fact quite true.[19]

At the beginning of October the CUP paid six bedouins from Banu Saʿad 600 Turkish liras to go to Basra and kill Talib. Two of them were caught and sent to prison, their village was burned to the ground and the inhabitants expelled.[20] In November Talib attempted to organize a congress of Arab chieftains to be held early in 1914, in Kuwait or elsewhere, to discuss Arab problems, Arab rights and the need for full coordination when dealing with the government. Representatives of Husayn, Ibn Sa'ud, Ibn Rashid, Sheikh Mubarak of Kuwait, Sheikh Khaz'al of Muhammara and 'Ujaymi were expected. As might have been foreseen, the congress never took place because these chieftains could not overcome their personal differences.[21]

In December the government reopened the enquiry into the murder of Farid Bek, at which point Talib sent a petition to the war ministry signed by over 70 people—not all of them voluntarily—complaining that the government, instead of believing the loyal subjects of Basra, believed the false reports of such intriguers as Hijrani, 'Atif and 'Akif. The signatories expressed their astonishment at this, and stressed that it had greatly undermined their faith in the government. In their minds, a fair government would understand how unjustly Basra was being treated, and would make every effort to remove the misunderstandings. If this were done, justice would prevail in the land. However, the petition concluded, if the government did not act in accordance with the will of the people, the people would take steps, "as long as we have a single man left and a single inch of ground remains to us, to defend our rights and our honour".[22]

Interior Minister Tal'at did not remain indifferent to Talib's arrogance and he ordered all Iraqi officers to be relieved of duty in Basra and stationed in remote locations as punishment for their support of Talib. He also appointed a new Vali to the town, accompanied by Turkish officers and soldiers, and ordered the removal of the military commandant, 'Izzat al-Kirkukli, who was demoted. Talib, who perceived that these developments would imperil his position, opened a correspondence with Tal'at and Enver in which he offered four conditions for peace: (1) restoration of rank to 'Izzat al-Kirkukli; (2) a vow by the two ministers that the Iraqi officers in Basra would not be harmed, even if transferred; (3) that soldiers native to Basra would remain there; (4) a promise by the two ministers to implement all reforms demanded by the Reform Society of Basra. The government accepted the first three conditions to be acted upon immediately, and the fourth to be carried out in stages; in return, the government demanded that Talib mediate between it and Ibn Sa'ud on the question of al-Hasa (which Ibn Sa'ud had conquered several months earlier) and that he undertake to form a committee to assist the Ottoman navy. Talib accepted the government's conditions and began raising money, contributing 500 Turkish liras out of his own pocket towards the purchase of warships. War Minister Enver informed Talib that he had ordered the valis of Baghdad and Basra to consult with him on every action they undertook. At the conclusion of the negotiations, on 2 February 1914, Talib issued the following statement:

> I herewith respectfully announce to all the inhabitants of the vilayet and its environs, that we have agreed to join forces as if we were one soul and one body, to enhance the prestige and the power of our government, which has officially bestowed its friendship upon us. No differences of any kind remain between us and the government. The misunderstandings between us have been smoothed out completely, and we shall work as one unit for the happiness of our eternal state and strive to retain our Ottoman unity with all our strength and to the last man.

Following the announcement, Tal'at and Enver sent Talib congratulatory telegrams.[23]

With the publication of this proclamation, the reform movement in Basra virtually came to an end, although Talib's epic adventures continued until the outbreak of the war. In the 1914 elections to the parliament Talib and the members of his Reform Society won every seat, as expected. However, the CUP manoeuvred to disqualify them, and when Talib learned of this, he ordered the Basra deputies who had arrived in Istanbul to set out for Egypt and await further instructions there. Tal'at urged the CUP to admit these representatives, arguing that new elections in Basra would eventuate in another sweep by Talib's people, as he was the boss in Basra; there was no point in bringing things to the "boiling point" when no advantage could be gained. Thus Talib's men were finally confirmed as elected. Later that year, Talib himself resigned from the parliament, probably having concluded that the position meant nothing to him. In any case, if he valued his life, it was out of the question for him to go to Istanbul.[24]

In order to fulfil his obligation to the government, in April 1914 Talib went to Ibn Sa'ud, ruler of Najd, to mediate between him and the Empire in the case of al-Hasa. The Vali of Basra took advantage of his absence to bring in tens of 'Ujaymi's armed men at the beginning of May, among them two of the latter's brothers. Before his return on 5 May, Talib gathered 250 armed men and with them approached the Vali to warn that if he did not order 'Ujaymi's brothers and their men to leave the town at once, there would be bloodshed. The Vali had to comply, and that very night 'Ujaymi's men were escorted out of Basra under guard.

Negotiations with Ibn Sa'ud were concluded successfully on 15 May when Ibn Sa'ud agreed to recognize the Ottoman flag in exchange for his becoming the de facto ruler of Najd and al-Hasa. A congratulatory telegram to Talib from the Sultan for his part in the success of the affair was followed, at the end of the same month, by a cable from Tal'at suggesting that he become an ambassador, a vali or a senator, whichever he chose. The latter was immediately ruled out since Talib feared for his life in Istanbul. Nor was an ambassadorship to his liking, considering how far this would place him from his armed bodyguards. He opted for the position he had long coveted, Vali of Basra.[25] But when, in July 1914, Tal'at informed the British ambassador in Istanbul that he had decided to appoint Talib Vali of Basra, the ambassador, who was well acquainted with Talib's exploits, and who had also received a cautionary note from the consul in Basra to the effect that this appointment would generate an inevitable clash with 'Ujaymi and chaos in the entire region, persuaded Tal'at to withdraw the appointment. Instead, secret orders were issued to Jawid, the Vali of Baghdad, to send a military column to Basra to arrest Talib. In October 1914 Jawid began to move towards Basra with a large force, but the outbreak of war supervened.[26]

Early in October 1914 Talib met the British consul and expressed a desire for contacts with the British, in the light of the fact that the Empire was about to enter the war. He asked the consul to remind Kitchener (who was already war minister) of their meeting almost three years before and to tell him that "the time has come". The British found themselves in a quandary as to whether they could trust a person whom they regarded as ready to work for any side for personal advantage. They also wondered whether they could use him to incite the Arab soldiers to desert from the Ottoman army and start a rebellion when they attacked Basra. Kitchener thought that Talib might prove useful. Late in October Talib applied to the British representative in Muhammara through Sheikh Khaz'al, requesting a large sum of money and assurance that his position and possessions in the town would remain intact, in exchange for his assistance. He also wished to be appointed as Sheikh or Amir of Basra, under British patronage. Responding more decisively to this offer than had the British Foreign Office, the Indian government informed the consul in Muhammara that no written commitment whatsoever should be given to Talib, as the Indian government was not prepared to recognize him as either Sheikh or Amir of Basra.

By then, Talib's position in Basra was already quite difficult. He knew that a force led by Jawid was nearing the town to arrest him. He therefore decided to leave Basra, ostensibly on a mission to persuade Ibn Sa'ud to cooperate with the Ottomans against the British in the war. Talib arrived in Kuwait on 12 November, after the British had already invaded Iraq, and there met with the British representative to discuss his future. On the instruction of Percy Cox, British Resident in the Persian Gulf and Chief Political Officer of the Indian Expeditionary Force, Talib was told that the British were not prepared to offer him any conditions. Even the Sheikh of Kuwait, no longer interested in supporting Talib, warned the British against trusting him and, after his departure from Kuwait on 15 November, remarked cynically that Talib "now has every door closed against him". Nor was Talib any more successful with Ibn Sa'ud, perhaps because Captain William Shakespear, a British officer close to Ibn Sa'ud, hastened to warn Ibn Sa'ud of possible treachery on Talib's part. Caught in such dire straits, Talib wrote a personal letter to Percy Cox on 12 December, pledging to do all he could for the British and requesting an appointment with him. On 3 January 1915 Talib returned to Kuwait to find Cox's reply saying that he would not meet with him and urging him, for his own good, to proceed to Bombay on the next available ship. With his letter Cox enclosed a passport:

> Certified that the bearer Saiyid Talib Nakibzada of Basra under British protection, has the authority of the undersigned [Cox] to proceed to Bombay and to remain there for the present.[27]

Having no alternative, Talib left for exile in India; he did not see Iraq again until 1920.

Chapter 21

THE NATIONAL SCIENTIFIC CLUB

Basra, the furthest of the three vilayets of Ottoman Iraq from the centre of the Empire, and the nearest to the independent rulers of the Arabian Peninsula and the Gulf, was the leader of the anti-Turkish and reformist movement in Iraq. Mosul, on the other hand, ruled by families that supported the old regime, conservative 'ulama' and Kurds, was the least enthusiastic of the three vilayets about participating in these trends. Baghdad, in the middle, was divided into a number of streams: pro-Turks (CUP members, liberals and supporters of the old regime), religious leaders who focused on pan-Islamic and anti-Christian ideas, and decentralists.

At the time of Sultan 'Abd al-Hamid, in 1902, a secret society called the Secret Club (*al-Nadi al-Sirri*) was established in Kazimayn by 20 merchants, to protect the rights of the Arabs and to oppose the Hamidian tyranny. This society did not strive to bring about the secession of Iraq from the Empire.[1] The Young Turks revolution had a profound effect on the character of Iraqi political thought, leading to freedom of the press, the establishment of societies and party branches, the participation of Iraqis in the administration of the Empire—whether as members of the parliament or in other positions—and the formation of freer relations between Iraq and the outside world, which had not been possible during the time of 'Abd al-Hamid. In Baghdad, however, not everyone was pleased with the new regime after the promulgation of the constitution. The large group of conservatives there, including the Naqib of Baghdad 'Abd al-Rahman al-Kaylani and his friend Sheikh Sa'id al-Naqshabandi (later one of the leaders of *al-'Ahd*), considered the constitution and the new regime a threat to their status. These personages later joined the Moderate Liberal Party, which was the opposition party to the CUP.

In April 1909 the Baghdad newspaper *al-Raqib* published an article entitled "The Parliament, the Arab countries and Arabic", which called upon the Arab members of the parliament to strengthen the Arabic language and to establish it as the language of instruction in the elementary schools.[2] By 1910, however, relations between the populace and the authorities had already deteriorated beyond the question of language. During the night of 17 August some 15 placards fiercely attacking the Vali Nazim Pasha, and accusing the Baghdad residents of lack of patriotism and self-respect in allowing their wives to become the prostitutes of the Vali, were plastered on the walls of Baghdad houses. The police removed the placards immediately and made a number of arrests.[3]

During the same week "Iraq, Iraq", a 26-page booklet of unknown origin, which also attacked the Vali, was widely distributed in Baghdad. The police attempted to locate all the people who possessed a copy of the booklet. "Iraq, Iraq", signed by a Baghdad group called the Committee for the Defence of the Interests of Iraq (*Lajnat al-Difa' 'an Masalih al-Iraq*) and bearing the date 10 Jumada al-Akhira 1328 (17 June 1910), was directed "to the Caliph, the Grand Vizier and his government, the Senate, the Parliament, Ottoman public opinion, the Arabic newspapers in Egypt, Syria, America and Istanbul, all *dad* speakers [that is, Arabs] and especially to Mahmud Shawkat Pasha, the conquerer of Istanbul, a native of Iraq". The booklet opened with an expression of the residents' forceful opposition to the concession that had been granted to the British maritime company Lynch for river shipping between Basra and Baghdad. It claimed that this concession was even worse than the concession granted to the Germans for the railway to Baghdad, and that both concessions would lead to the danger of foreign infiltration into the country. It went on to attack Vali Nazim Pasha fiercely for tyrannical behaviour, including opposition to the Arabic language and prohibiting the receipt of documents in Arabic in the government departments; struggling against freedom of the press in Iraqi towns; ordering the widening of the city streets so that his carriages would be able to pass, instead of eliminating the poverty and ignorance of the Baghdad residents; instead of attempting to act incisively to end the bedouins' raids, angering the tribesmen by imposing taxes on them without consideration of their income, and even asking them to hand over all the weapons in their possession; removing the Arab officers from Iraq and bringing in Turkish officers in their place; and asking the government to remove the irrigation engineer William Willcocks from the region, thus stopping the development of irrigation in Iraq. The booklet ended with: "We are most loyal to the holy Ottoman unity and we stand for the Caliphate's remaining in the Ottoman dynasty", adding that "our brothers in Basra are as tired as we are of the present situation" and that they all wanted "the existence of our Empire to be crowned with equality, freedom and brotherhood, in the full meaning of these words".[4]

The anti-Turkish feelings in the vilayet of Baghdad increased greatly towards the end of that year because of the campaign the authorities were waging against the bedouin tribes there. "Kill the Turk, even if he is your father" (*Uqtul al-turk wa-law kana abuk*) was frequently to be heard during this period.[5] This bitterness against the authorities was exploited by the opposition circles, who set up a branch of the Moderate Liberal Party in Baghdad in September 1911; within a few days some 300 of the city notables had joined. However, because Mahmud al-Kaylani, a son of the Naqib, was elected president of the branch, rival families, such as the al-Suwaydi family, refrained from joining the party in spite of the fact that they too were against the CUP. The branch later became a branch of the Party of Liberty and Union.[6]

In late 1912 another opposition group to the CUP was set up in Baghdad — the National Scientific Club (*al-Nadi al-Watani al-'Ilmi*). The Sunni Muzahim al-Amin al-Pachachi, founder and president of the club, had just completed his law studies in Istanbul and, upon returning to Baghdad, felt the need to rescue the country from its sorry situation. His partners in setting up the club, also Sunnis, were his relative Hamdi al-Pachachi, a teacher of economics and international law at the Law School in Baghdad, who had previously been a member of the Arab-Ottoman Brotherhood, and Ibrahim Hilmi al-'Umar, a journalist. Baghdad intellectuals, members of prominent families, and police and army officers joined the club, as well as some Shi'ites, such as the brothers Muhammad Rida and Muhammad Baqir al-Shabibi. The spirit of the club, and its moral authority, was Yusuf al-Suwaydi, a rich landowner who was the most respected person in Baghdad after the Naqib. One of his sons, Naji al-Suwaydi, at that time the Qa'imaqam of Najaf, also helped in secret and mediated between the activists in Baghdad, those in Najaf, and the tribal chiefs in the Middle Euphrates. When the authorities noticed this activity, they dismissed him from his position.[7]

At first the scope of the club's activities was limited, focusing on reading rooms and the like, but when Sayyid Talib of Basra discovered that the club needed help, he donated large sums of money that allowed it to carry out its aims and open a large library and an evening school in which Arabic, Turkish, French and English were taught. For his donations Talib was made honorary president of the club.[8]

The purpose of the club, or at least its overt purpose, was similar to that of the Literary Club, that is, to awaken the Arabs and to strengthen the relations between them. According to the second article of its constitution, the aim of the club was "to spread knowledge throughout Iraq by establishing various national (*wataniyya*) libraries, spreading national (*qawmiyya*) culture among the youth, helping the needy gain knowledge, sending needy students to Istanbul or to Europe", etc.[9] There were those, however, who claimed that while the overt purpose of the club was literary, it also had a secret political purpose. There were rumours that this purpose was to expel the Turks from Iraq, to establish a form of self-government and to encourage patriotism and pan-Islam. The local authorities attempted to take its measure, and instructions were sent from Istanbul to the Vali to preserve order and to punish whoever caused trouble.[10]

At demonstrations in Baghdad in March 1913, following the activities in Basra, placards denouncing the tyranny of the CUP were carried. A conference of city notables and leaders of the tribes in the area concluded that it was imperative to demand administrative decentralization, for the centralization of the government had led to backwardness and inferiority, and had left the region in danger of intervention from foreign states. Only through decentralization would the local residents be able to manage their own affairs and defend themselves from such dangers. A list of reforms, similar to the Beirut list, emphasized the need to broaden the authority of the General Council. At the end of the month copies of a proclamation were widely distributed in the city. Comparing the past magnificence of the Arabs with their present state, it called for a return to the regime existing at the time of Muhammad and the first caliphs, when the representatives of the provinces had actually been independent rulers and had had to consult their sovereign only in exceptional cases. The proclamation accused the *'ajam*, that is, the Turks, of preferring a centralized tyrannical rule. It differed from other proclamations in that it took a positive attitude towards Europe and claimed that Europe had sympathy for the Arabs and had no intention of causing the partition of Asiatic Turkey. Even if this should occur, Europe would help the Arabs return to the glory of their forefathers. The proclamation ended by calling on the sons of Qahtan (the Arabs) to unite in their demand for decentralization.[11]

After the publication of the new Vilayets Law, the club followed the lead of Sayyid Talib of Basra in protesting it strongly.

Hostility began to develop between the Arab and Turkish officers in the 13th Division, encamped at Baghdad, and quarrels broke out between the Arab and Turkish government officials. On 11 June 1913 Grand Vizier Mahmud Shawkat was assassinated in Istanbul. The CUP seized the opportunity to try to eliminate all opposition, and on 14 June the Baghdad authorities arrested the leaders of the CUP opponents in the city, among them Yusuf al-Suwaydi and Muhammad Kamil al-Tabaqjali, the owner of *Bayna al-Nahrayn*, the newspaper of the Baghdad branch of the Party of Liberty and Union. Two days later most of the detainees were released. The imprisonment did not deter al-Suwaydi and his supporters in their struggle for decentralization.[12]

The populace was divided in its reactions, when, at the beginning of August, the general lines of the agreement between the government and the Paris Congress members became known in Baghdad. Those who were wealthier and enjoyed higher status and participation in the administration of the country, by and large expressed their satisfaction with the agreement. Another group, however, sent an ultimatum by telegram to all the government ministers on 6 August 1913, demanding decentralization and the dismissal of all officeholders of Turkish origin and language. They added that since Iraq was poorer than Syria, the Iraqis would not be satisfied with reforms like those granted to Syria. Two days later one of the pro-reformist Baghdad newspapers labelled the agreement an "anesthetic", a ploy to "sedate" the Arab reformists.[13]

On 3 October 1913 the newpaper *al-Nahda* (The Revival) was first published by the club president, Muzahim al-Pachachi, in order to present the club's political ideas. Eleven issues of this anti-CUP newspaper were published before it was closed by the authorities. Al-Pachachi and editor Ibrahim Hilmi al-'Umar immediately fled to Basra to avoid arrest. There they were protected by Sayyid Talib. Al-Pachachi remained there until the outbreak of the war, while al-'Umar secretly returned to Baghdad after a time. In mid-October the authorities succeeded in arresting Yusuf al-Suwaydi (for the second time), Hamdi al-Pachachi, Sheikh Sa'id al-Naqshabandi and a number of other activists. One of their sympathizers, apparently to draw the attention of British diplomats to the arrests, smuggled a message on to the desk of the first dragoman of the British consul-general in Baghdad: "If you want to know what the Arabs' aspirations are, you can ask 'Abd al-Rahman Haydari, the Naqib Efendi, Yusuf Efendi Suwaydi and the Pachachi family."[14]

THE REFORM MOVEMENT IN MOSUL

In Mosul too an attempt was made to set up a branch of the Moderate Liberal Party in opposition to the local CUP branch. The effort was begun in July 1911 by a number of activists, led by Da'ud Yusufani, a Roman Catholic Chaldean who was a representative of Mosul in the parliament, but it failed within two months because of the active opposition of the Vali and the army. Nor did the populace demonstrate much enthusiasm for joining.[15]

In April 1913 the reform plan of the Reform Society of Beirut arrived in Mosul. That month a proclamation was also distributed in the town, accusing the Turks of incompetence and failure, and calling upon the Arabs to arise and return to their past glory. Although it did not call for secession from the Empire, but only for decentralization, it maintained that if the Empire should disintegrate the Arab countries must remain under Arab control. Under the influence of these events the Mosul notables sent a telegram to the Sublime Porte, saying that they had not previously demanded reforms in order to avoid embarrassing the government in its present difficult situation, but nevertheless they desired reforms no less than Basra and Beirut. By June 1913, at the time of the Paris Congress, the town notables had already decided to present the Sublime Porte with the same demands as Beirut, Damascus and Basra.[16]

In July 1913 Sulayman Faydi, carrying numerous proclamations, was sent from Basra to Baghdad and Mosul to spread nationalist ideas. He made contact with Yusuf al-Suwaydi, Muzahim and Hamdi al-Pachachi and others in Baghdad before continuing on to Mosul. There he found that the number of believers in the Arab idea "was no more than the number of fingers on two hands". Most of the activists were army officers, such as Yasin al-Hashimi, Mawlud Mukhlis, 'Ali Jawdat al-Ayyubi, and 'Abdallah al-Dulaymi, who later became the backbone of the al-'Ahd society. Faydi, who was of Mosuli origin, succeeded with their help and that of others in establishing a secret society in the town to work for the Arab idea. But when the authorities began to take notice of Faydi's activities, a short time later, he left Mosul and returned to Basra. The society disintegrated before accomplishing anything significant.[17]

Chapter 22

THE PARIS CONGRESS

In early 1913 the *al-Fatat* society in Paris decided to organize a
congress, as a vehicle for explaining the Arab problem in
Europe, taking it from the Ottoman to the international arena.
The initiators of the congress hoped to take advantage of the
publicity that the Arab problem would get to put pressure on
the Ottoman government to accept the demands of the Arab reformists. The five society members who conceived the congress,
'Abd al-Ghani al-'Uraysi, 'Awni 'Abd al-Hadi, Muhammad al-
Mihmisani, Jamil Mardam and Tawfiq Fa'id, turned to two
more prominent figures in the Syrian-Lebanese community in
Paris, Shukri Ghanim, the president of the Lebanese Society of
Paris, and Nadra Mutran, in order to spread the idea of the congress outside the narrow circle of their secret society. With the
exception of Fa'id, all of these became part of the eight-member
organizing committee of the congress, as did Charles Dabbas, a
member of Ghanim's society, and Jamil Ma'luf. Al-'Uraysi was
chosen to be the secretary of the committee.

The first problem the organizers faced was the name of the
congress. Since all of them came from Syria (in the sense of
Greater Syria, including the Lebanon and Palestine), it was only
natural to call it the Syrian Congress, and they prepared the congress seal accordingly. But then Tawfiq al-Suwaydi, a Baghdad-
born member of *al-Fatat*, intervened and succeeded in
persuading the organizers to give the congress a pan-Arab flavour by changing its name to the First Arab Congress.[1] The
change in name had no impact on the aims of the congress, as
expressed in the composition of its members and the content of
its discussions. Later the organizers began to use a compromise
name, the Arab-Syrian Congress, even for official purposes.

At a session on 11 March 1913, the organizing committee
decided to call officially upon the Decentralization Party to join
the congress initiative. Their letter of 4 April presented the
planned congress as a means to protect the Arab fatherland and
introduce reforms based on decentralization. The participants
would be delegations from America, Europe and the Empire
itself, and it was suggested that the party should represent the

Syrians living in Egypt and even take upon itself the presidency of the congress. The topics to be dealt with in the congress would be:

1. National (*wataniyya*) life and the struggle against foreign occupation.
2. Arab rights in the Ottoman Empire.
3. The need for reforms based on decentralization.
4. Migration to and from Syria.

The Supreme Committee of the Decentralization Party agreed to accept the offer on 11 April 1913. A reply sent to Paris on 14 April, signed by Rafiq al-'Azm, relayed that the party welcomed the organization of a congress that would represent its ideas about administrative decentralization, and would send two delegates.[2]

On the evening of 16 April a number of Syrians, among them the three Mutran brothers, Nakhla, Nadra and Rashid, and Archimandrite 'Atiyya of the Greek Orthodox Church in Paris, met in a Paris café to discuss the approaching congress. They perceived the purpose of the congress as the protection of the rights of the Syrians, and the discussion centred around the demand for administrative autonomy in Syria, or, if this was not granted, a French protectorate. The participants expressed their confidence that the French people, known for their friendship towards the East, would support the congress.[3] Thus, while the Decentralization Party saw the congress as a forum for raising the idea of administrative decentralization, these people saw the same congress as a forum for raising the idea of administrative autonomy or even of a French protectorate.

Early in May the organizing committee managed to infiltrate a "Manifesto to the Sons of the Arab Nation" into the Empire, condemning the centralized administration of the Empire, which had led to a danger from foreign elements for the Arab vilayets, especially Syria. The Arabs living in Paris had decided, the manifesto announced, "to hold a congress for the Arabs, which will be organized by Syrians and will be attended by delegations of notables from the Arab countries and intellectuals from among the Syrian émigrés in Egypt, North and South America, and the European countries, so that the Arab nation, which is spread throughout the world, will be represented there". The congress was to prove to the nations of Europe that the Arab nation was devoted to its existence and its national characteristics; likewise, it would prove to the Ottoman Empire that decentralization was the basis of the Arabs' lives, as they were "partners in this Empire, partners in military matters, partners in the administration, and partners in politics, but in internal matters partners only of themselves". After listing the topics of the congress, the manifesto called upon the Arabs, and in particular the leaders of the Arab societies, to send delegates to the congress or at least to send telegrams or letters of support.[4]

A number of the future congress participants were present at a conference of the French colonialist society "l'Asie Française" on the Syrian question on 5 May, including Nadra Mutran, Dabbas, Khayrallah and al-'Uraysi. Mutran surveyed the history of the reform movement in Syria for the French politicians, up to the closing of the Reform Society of Beirut, stressing the close cooperation within this movement between the Muslims and the Christians. A discussion centred on the question of whether the reforms demanded at the congress "will have to apply only to the Syrians or to all the Arabs". Khayrallah concluded the conference by pointing out that only the implementation of reforms would prevent European intervention in Syria.[5]

The question of whether the congress was for the Syrians or the Arabs was solved later by Nadra Mutran in his own way. On 1 June he sent a letter to the French foreign minister listing the topics that the congress would discuss, somewhat differently from the letter to the Decentralization Party and the manifesto of the congress committee: the political, economic and administrative interests that must be preserved in Syria for the sake of the Syrians; the rights of the Syrians in the Ottoman empire; the need to achieve decentralist reforms; the emigration of Syrians abroad and the immigration of Turks from Rumelia to Syria.[6]

The Paris Congress created a dilemma not only for French politicians such as the members of "l'Asie Française", but especially for the concerned party, the French government, under whose jusrisdiction it was to be held. France feared the reaction of the Ottoman Empire, as well as the anti-French activities that the opponents of the congress were liable to organize in Syria (as indeed occurred). As early as the end of March Shukri Ghanim had tried to ease the fears of the French foreign ministry with reassurances that the congress did not intend to demand autonomy but only broad decentralization with the assistance of France. He even pretended that the congress was supposed to have been held in London or Berlin—a totally baseless claim—until he, Ghanim, had succeeded in persuading the organizers to hold it in Paris. The congress would benefit France, as the Muslims of North Africa would see that the Syrians were approaching France in particular to request improvements in their situation. In further appeals in May and June Ghanim continued to emphasize his thesis that any unpleasantness that France might suffer as a result of the congress would be much less than the great benefit that would accrue to it from the raising of its prestige in the eyes of the Muslims of the East and of North Africa.[7]

The Committee for Syrian Affairs of the French foreign ministry (established in February 1913 to coordinate French policies in Syria) discussed the congress, and eventually concluded that although unpleasantness was likely to result from it, and they did not approve of all the future participants, they could not prevent its being held without severely injuring French prestige and influence in Syria. Nevertheless, in order to mitigate the damage that might result from holding the congress in Paris, they proposed instructing the newspapers not to give the congress more than minimal coverage, requiring the pro-French participants to present the topics for discussion to the foreign ministry before raising them at the congress, and conveying to Khalil Zayniyya (considered by the French to be their most enthusiastic supporter among the congress participants) the points that interested France.[8]

Zayniyya was one of the members of the delegation sent to the congress by the Reform Society of Beirut. By April al-Fatat had already contacted this society through its members there. The society members, still in a state of shock after the closing of the society by the Vali, decided to send to Europe a six-member delegation, three Muslims and three Christians, to present the Beirutians' demands at this international forum, for they no longer believed that the government would implement the reforms out of goodwill. In a public fund-raising campaign to finance the delegation, 25,000 francs were quickly raised. When it came to forming the delegation, however, problems arose. The three Muslim delegates were initially to be Ahmad Mukhtar Bayhum, Salim 'Ali Salam and Ahmad Hasan Tabbara, and the three Christian delegates, Khalil Zayniyya, Dr Ayyub Thabit and Albert Sursuq.

Bayhum agreed willingly to attend and sailed to Egypt at the beginning of May. On 10 May the Society of the Lebanese Revival in Beirut convened and asked Zayniyya to go to Europe too, in order to present the Lebanese problem there. They also supplied him with a letter of accreditation addressed to Ghanim, the president of the Paris society. Two days later he sailed for Egypt. Salam was very hesitant, in the light of the fact that the congress was being held in a Christian state and was after all directed, to some extent, against the Ottoman authorities. Sheikh Tabbara also hesitated at first and then agreed, but later retracted, citing "reasons of health". (It should be recalled that his cousin Zakarya had been murdered on 12 May.) After another round of persuasion Salam and Tabbara finally left for Cairo at the end of May, together with Thabit, also a member of the Society of the Lebanese Revival and avowedly pro-French. They set out with a certificate from the leaders of all the Christian communities in Beirut, which seemed to them essential in the light of the fact that the opponents of the congress had accused them of not having the right to represent the Beirutians. Sursuq refused to join the delegation and did not participate in the congress "due to his brother's illness".[9]

In Cairo the delegates of the Reform Society of Beirut joined the two Decentralization Party delegates, 'Abd al-Hamid al-Zahrawi and Iskandar 'Ammun, and the whole group set out for Paris. Arriving in Paris at the beginning of June, Zayniyya went to the French foreign ministry and explained that the most important concern of the Reform Society was to improve the situation of the vilayet of Beirut and that they were very much in favour of foreign occupation, preferably French, or at least effective supervision by French advisers. He asked the opinion of the foreign ministry on the Syrian question and whether he could depend on the support of the French government for his demands. On a later visit Zayniyya also reported to the foreign ministry that the Reform Society's goal was to force the Ottoman government, through the creation of international pressure, to agree to the list of reforms suggested by the society. Zayniyya told the foreign ministry officials that he was prepared to modify the list according to their suggestions. On his third visit to the foreign ministry, on 11 June, a representative of the ministry gave him instructions regarding the matters of interest to France. Zayniyya promised to do his best to persuade his countrymen to forget their dream of Arab autonomy. On 21 June, in the middle of the congress, Zayniyya went to the foreign ministry once more, reported on the resolutions taken that day, and announced that he had succeeded, together with his friends, in preventing tendencies hostile to France at the congress, and also the raising of the "Arab question".

It seems that the other congress participants were aware of Zayniyya's initiatives. Several years later congress participant 'Abd al-Ghani al-'Uraysi, related that the members of the Reform Society of Beirut and the Society of the Lebanese

Revival had worked to persuade the French to pressure the Empire to annex Beirut to the Lebanon. The congress president, 'Abd al-Hamid al-Zahrawi, wrote to Rashid Rida after the congress that Zayniyya and Thabit had been interested only in the fate of Beirut, and that the relations between them and the Muslim members of the Reform Society delegation had not been particularly good. It seems that Charles Dabbas and Jamil Mardam (a member of al-Fatat) had also had contacts with the French foreign ministry before the congress.[10]

The Ottoman government did not remain passive in the face of the congress, which surely did not bring it good publicity. The Ottoman ambassador in Paris was ordered to try to get the congress cancelled, but his request to the French government was denied.[11] The CUP then began an intensive pan-imperial propaganda campaign against the congress. The Turkish newspapers in the capital attacked France for trying to intervene in the region. They threatened the congress organizers with harsh punishments, and tried to discredit them by undermining their authority to represent the Arabs. The organizers had "become Frenchified" a long time before and had already lost all their connection with Islam and Arabism, claimed the newspaper Tanin. Furthermore, the organizers of the congress were Syrians, whereas if they really were working for all the Arabs they should also include delegates from Yemen, Baghdad, Egypt, Tripolitania, Tunisia, Algeria and Morocco. A special attack was reserved for Khayrallah Khayrallah, described as an "extreme Francophile" who wanted a French protectorate—which was not necessarily very far from the truth.[12]

The protests did not come only from Istanbul. The CUP had a clear interest in proving that the Arab masses opposed the congress, and it is plausible that many of them did actually do so, as will be seen later. In a telegram of protest the Shi'ites of Jabal 'Amil asserted that the congress members were improperly claiming to represent the Arabs, and they argued that reforms should be requested only through the parliament and the provincial councils. The notables of Medina condemned both the Decentralization Party and the congress, whose organizers they described as traitors, for wanting to introduce a foreign influence into the country. Protest telegrams also arrived from Yemen and Iraq.[13]

However, the centre of opposition to the congress was Damascus. It began with ordinary protest letters. One of them claimed, for example, that two of the congress organizers were simply embittered against the government because it had not complied with their personal ambitions (this probably referred to Ghanim and Mutran), while four others were young people with no authority to play the role they were purporting to play. Vali 'Arif al-Mardini organized the True Reform Party (*Hizb al-Islah al-Haqiqi*), headed by Muhammad Fawzi Pasha al-'Azm and 'Abd al-Rahman al-Yusuf, who arranged conferences against the congress. Later they mobilized a delegation of congress opponents to work in Istanbul in cooperation with other opponents such as Sharif Ja'far, Sharif 'Ali Haydar and Yusuf Shatwan. The party argued that the congress participants wanted to bring about foreign control over the country, and the proof was that they were holding the congress in Paris. It also claimed that after the Empire's defeat in the Balkans it was wrong to add to its burden by demanding reforms. One member of the opposition delegation to Istanbul was Taha al-Mudawwar, editor of the Beirut newspaper *al-Ra'y al-'Amm*. On orders from the CUP, he wrote a sharp article attacking the congress and France, which he claimed wanted to exploit and control Syria. Why, he asked, had the organizers of the congress not organized it in a Muslim capital under the patronage of the Caliph? The CUP, however, was not prepared to rely only on authentic protests, and they ordered the government officials in the Arab countries to contribute to the protests. They also used underhanded ploys, such as convincing notables who did not speak Turkish to sign telegrams in Arabic and Turkish, when actually the two versions were different. When these telegrams were published in the newspapers, the notables protested that their signatures had been obtained by trickery. The Decentralization Party published a manifesto against the protest telegrams and the actions of the government against the congress.[14]

The opponents of the congress also included three men who had been, or later became, personally involved in the Arab movement. Because the congress was being held in Paris, the poet Ma'ruf al-Rusafi, one of the first members of the Literary Club, saw the participants as "lambs appealing to a wolf for help" and expressed his disappointment with the Arab movement in general. 'Aziz 'Ali al-Misri, a former member of *al-Qahtaniyya* and the future founder of *al-'Ahd*, then in Benghazi, also took exception to the holding of the congress in Paris, and he refused the congress members' request to support their demands on the grounds it was not right to do this while the Empire's armies were being defeated. He saw the participants' informing the French foreign minister about their resolutions as treason towards the East. A telegram from Sharif Husayn of

Mecca denounced the congress to the Sublime Porte as serving foreign interests and as treason towards the Ottoman fatherland.[15]

In response to the wave of protests and to present the congress to Europe, the intended president of the congress, 'Abd al-Hamid al-Zahrawi, gave an interview to the newspaper *Le Temps* on 10 June; the interviewer, an editor of the newspaper, was none other than Khayrallah Khayrallah. The reason for the congress, al-Zahrawi told Khayrallah, was the Arabs' desire to prevent their fate from being that of the European vilayets of the Empire, and to put an end to the discrimination that they suffered in the Empire. He declared that the congress was not being held on a religious basis, and the proof of this was that it had equal numbers of Muslim and Christian members. However, he added, the congress would not deal with the Arabs outside the Empire. The congress was being held in Europe because recent events in Beirut had proved that a free congress could not be held in Syria, and Paris had the largest Arab community in Europe. Congress members believed that a strong Ottoman society must be created, and this was possible only by means of reforms. If the government would not agree to this, warned al-Zahrawi, they would completely change their attitude towards it. The congress members represented the intelligentsia, he asserted; those who hated Europe were motivated only by their egotism, and the congress members looked upon them with sorrow and pity.[16]

On the eve of the congress opening all the participant delegations were already in Paris. They included the following delegates:

'Abd al-Hamid al-Zahrawi: Muslim, Decentralization Party delegate.
Iskandar 'Ammun: Christian, Decentralization Party delegate (also a member of the Society of the Lebanese Revival).
Salim 'Ali Salam: Muslim, Reform Society of Beirut delegate.
Ahmad Mukhtar Bayhum: Muslim, Reform Society of Beirut delegate.
Khalil Zayniyya: Christian, Reform Society of Beirut delegate (also a member of the Society of the Lebanese Revival).
Ahmad Hasan Tabbara: Muslim, Reform Society of Beirut delegate.
Ayyub Thabit: Christian, Reform Society of Beirut delegate (also a member of the Society of the Lebanese Revival).
Tawfiq al-Suwaydi: Muslim, Iraq delegate (member of *al-Fatat*).
Sulayman 'Anbar: Jew, Iraq delegate.
Muhammad Rustum Haydar: Muslim, Ba'albek delegate (member of *al-Fatat*).

Ibrahim Haydar: Muslim, Ba'albek delegate (member of *al-Fatat*).
Najib Diyab: Christian, Syrian Union Society of New York delegate.
Elias Maqsud: Christian, Syrian Union Society of New York delegate.
Na'um Mukarzal: Christian, Society of the Lebanese Revival of New York delegate.
'Abbas Bijani: Christian, Mexico delegate (member of the Society of the Lebanese Revival).
Shukri Ghanim: Christian, Paris delegate (member of the Society of the Lebanese Revival).
'Abd al-Ghani al-'Uraysi: Muslim, Paris delegate (member of *al-Fatat*).
Nadra Mutran: Christian, Paris delegate.
'Awni 'Abd al-Hadi: Muslim, Paris delegate (member of *al-Fatat*).
Charles Dabbas: Christian, Paris delegate (member of the Society of the Lebanese Revival).
Khayrallah Khayrallah: Christian, Paris delegate (member of the Society of the Lebanese Revival).
Jamil Mardam: Muslim, Paris delegate (member of *al-Fatat*).
Muhammad al-Mihmisani: Muslim, Paris delegate (member of *al-Fatat*).

Altogether there were 23 delegates, including 11 Muslims, 11 Christians and one Jew; 21 Syrians (in the extended sense of the word) and two Iraqis.[17]

In order that the resolutions of the congress be accepted unanimously, a committee of delegates was set up before the opening of the congress, to discuss the points to be raised and to eliminate in advance any that might arouse controversy. This committee was also assigned the task of formulating the resolutions to be adopted at the end of the congress.[18]

The congress was held at the auditorium of the French Geographical Society, an old colonialist organization that favoured expanding French influence. Some of its members were also members of the society "l'Asie Française", which had connections with the congress organizers. Programmes of the congress in French were sent to numerous invitees, statesmen and media representatives. "The First Arab-Syrian Congress" was printed at the head of each. Everything was ready for the opening.[19]

The congress was opened on 18 June at 2:30 pm in the presence of its delegates and about 150 observers. After giving the opening speech Nadra Mutran publicly announced the results of the elections for the administrative committee of the congress: President: 'Abd al-Hamid al-Zuhrawi; Vice-President: Shukri Ghanim; Deputies: Salim 'Ali Salam, Iskandar 'Ammun, Ahmad Hasan Tabbara, Nadra Mutran; Arabic secretaries: 'Abd al-Ghani al-'Uraysi, Muhammad al-Mihmisani, 'Awni 'Abd al-Hadi, Jamil Mardam; French secretary: Charles Dabbas.[20]

The next speech, by the congress president, "Our political culture", deprecated those who left all political matters to the ruler. The West had already liberated itself from the attitude of "We do not understand politics". He called upon the Easterners to emulate it, for it was the people's right to intervene in politics, to assist the government in improving the country's situation and to oppose it when it harmed the fatherland. It was the obligation of all the Arabs to work together with the Turks, the rulers of the Empire who had brought it to its present state, for the sake of the country. And this cooperation would be best carried out on the basis of the principle of decentralization. "Europe is not the devil, but rather the devil is bad administration and corrupt politics."[21]

At the second session on 20 June, again at 2:30 pm, 'Abd al-Ghani al-'Uraysi, spoke first, on the question "Do the Arabs have the right to be called a group (jama'a)?". According to the German experts in political science, in order to be called a group, unity of language and unity of race defined a group; according to the Italians, historical unity and unity of customs; and according to the French, unity of political aspirations. The Arabs had all of these, and therefore had the right to be called a group, a people and a nation. Yet the authorities related to the other nationalities of the Empire as conquerors to the conquered. In the senate, the Arabs, though they constituted 13 million of the Empire's subjects—more than half—had only five representatives. In the parliament, too, the Arabs were discriminated against, owing to the fact that the representatives were actually appointed and not elected. And how could the executive branch, the government be national if it did not represent all the sons of the fatherland? The Arabs were forcefully demanding to be given their fair share according to their numbers in the population. And as half the subjects of the Empire they were demanding half the loans that the Empire received from foreign states. They were also demanding that Arabic should become an official language in the Arab countries. They would pursue all legal methods to achieve this goal, but if the government should use force to quiet their demands, they would turn to other means.[22]

Following al-'Uraysi's speech Ahmad Mukhtar Bayhum contended that the government was trying to pacify the Arabs by giving out positions. Therefore any position offered by the authorities before the demanded reforms were implemented must be rejected. Charles Dabbas proposed that all the congress members should give their word of honour not to accept any position until the authorities agreed to the demands of the congress.[23]

Nadra Mutran, speaking on "Preserving national (*wataniyya*) life in the Ottoman Arab countries", dwelt on the connections of solidarity between the Muslim and the Christian Arabs and tried to prove that for the Arabs, race took precedence over religion. He explained the massacres of 1860 as a result of government instigation and the participation of the soldiers. He then defended the European states, claiming that it was not true that they wanted to occupy Syria or to divide it among themselves, but rather preferred that the Ottomans be able to administer the Empire by themselves, and thus contribute to the preservation of general peace. France's interests in Syria were purely economic. "Syria was created for the Syrians . . . and all we want is that the Ottoman Empire will grant the Syrians the reforms that the Syrians are requesting for Syria and the Arabs for the Arab countries."[24]

Mutran's speech aroused whispers and comments. Did he deny, asked one observer, that some states had ambitions in Syria? Syria should enter into a French protectorate, suggested another observer. The president objected that observers had no right to intervene and added that the topic did not conform at all to the focus of the congress. Zayniyya's prompt suggestion that the policies of other states not be discussed at further sessions was accepted.[25]

The next speaker, Najib Diyab, discussed "The hopes of the Syrian émigrés", which were to see the situation of their fatherland, which they had left against their will, improved. In the land of Uncle Sam they had tasted freedom and decentralization, and they sought these things for their fatherland as well. If this were realized, they would return to their land, just as the Israelites had returned from Egypt. They would bring back from the West what it had borrowed from the East, and restore the East's former superiority. They were willing to remain within the framework of the Empire if their rights were preserved, both Christian and Muslim; their property protected; their schools illuminated "with the electricity of Syrian nationalism (*wataniyya*)"; and their hearts burning "with love of the fatherland". The Lebanese considered Syria the mother of the Lebanon, and the Lebanon the heart of Syria, "and can the mother be distanced from her heart or can you remove her heart from her?". Their hope was to return to Syria when it had "a government of justice, of the people and for the people". His society, the speaker concluded, supported the demands for decentralization and for the appointment of foreign advisers according to the list of the Reform Society of Beirut.[26]

Tawfiq al-Suwaydi's speech in the name of the Arabs of Iraq made it clear that the Iraqis wanted reforms and the protection of their rights no less than the Syrians. They all sought to work together to preserve the fatherland and for the sake of the life of the Arab nation. The Iraqis, like the rest of their brothers, wanted decentralization, and he was announcing this in the name of all the intelligentsia of Iraq.[27]

After this short speech the controversy over accepting government positions before the reforms were realized arose again. Thabit suggested that the question be postponed for a later session, while Diyab insisted that it be discussed immediately. Bayhum repeated his position: that no one should accept positions until the requested reforms were implemented. Diyab demanded that the question should be put to a vote. Mutran announced that he wanted to add to the vote a demand that all Arab officials should resign from their positions if the demands of the congress were not met. This suggestion aroused much opposition. Bayhum pointed out that this would harm poor officials whose families were dependent on their income. Salam commented that it was precisely through the holding of offices that it would be possible to bring about the implementation of the reforms. Those who accepted appointments to office were selling their consciences and becoming opponents of reform, Bayhum responded. He suggested that the congress resolve "that the participants in the reform movement do not have the right to accept any position in the Ottoman government until the government accepts the fundamentals of the programme that the congress will decide upon". Salam declared once more that this resolution was too extreme and suggested the following amendment: "except according to the decision of the society the member belongs to." In response to an observer's query as to what punishment would await anyone who violated this resolution, Bayhum responded that this was a matter of conscience. At this point 'Ammun and Zayniyya allied with Salam's view that the acceptance of positions should be permitted with the authorization of the societies. While Bayhum insisted that the reforms must be implemented first, in the end his resolution was accepted with the addition of Salam's rider.[28]

Among those present in the conference hall was the Zionist activist Sami Hochberg. He prepared energetically for the third session of the congress, at which Tabbara was to speak about the immigration to Syria, a topic that obviously interested the Zionists. Before the congress began he had already warned the participants that if the congress accepted a resolution against the Jews, the Arabs would lose all possibility of assistance from the Jewish world and would set the Jews against them instead of with them. Hochberg tried especially to influence Tabbara, and he requisitioned from the Zionist Centre in Berlin 2,000 francs' credit to invite the principal congress members to a good dinner before the day of discussions about immigration.[29]

The third session of the congress opened on 21 June at 2:30 pm and Sheikh Ahmad Hasan Tabbara began his speech on "Migration to and from Syria". Statistics about the emigration from Syria were followed by his analysis of its causes. He contended that the emigration was against the emigrants' will. Born as Ottomans, the Arabs wanted to remain such, but they wanted reforms. They did not want to secede from the Empire, but it was marching towards ruin. The call for reforms emanated from Beirut and the entire Arab nation was responding to it. It would be wrong to retreat, because the life of the nation depended on reforms. It was imperative that the central government respond and grant reforms on the basis of participation in the government through decentralization for every vilayet. As for the immigration to Syria, Tabbara noted that Syria could hold four times as many residents, and organized immigration could be useful for the country.

A discussion followed Tabbara's speech and the speakers expressed their opposition to Turkish immigration to Syria. They demanded a resolution, but al-Zahrawi maintained that it was preferable to defer the resolution concerning the Turkish immigrants. Though there were those who protested, in the end a vote was not held. Khayrallah nevertheless felt the need to announce that he was against Turkish immigration and that only the immigration of the rich could benefit the country. At that moment Bayhum shouted: "Jewish immigration—yes! But Turkish immigration—no!" His statement was heard with astonishment by the observers, and there were some whispers, but no one spoke against him.[30]

Iskandar 'Ammun, speaking on "Reforms on the basis of decentralization", depicted the Ottoman nation as standing at the edge of a cliff. This situation had not come about by chance, but was a result of the centralized regime in the Empire. This regime put the rulership into the hands of a few individuals and kept it away from the rest the people, in spite of the fact that the Ottoman nation needed decentralization more than other nations because of the large number of nationalities in it. 'Ammun rejected the argument that the Arab revival was striving for secession from the Empire; the Arabs wanted a change of regime. But if the Turkish nation insisted on going to ruin, the Arabs would hesitate before accompanying it. The Arabs sought a regime in which the residents of each vilayet would administer their own internal affairs, and the general affairs of the Empire would be administered in a proportionally representative manner by the entire Ottoman nation. In a true Ottoman government, neither Turkish nor Arab, there would be equality for all, without distinction of race or religion, whether "Arab, Turk, Armenian, Kurd, Muslim, Christian, Jew or Druze". And if, in order to achieve this, there was a need for *shuhada'* (martyrs), then all the Arabs were prepared for this.[31]

In the discussion following, Dabbas, backed by Salam and Tabbara, supported the need for decentralization, but he argued that in order to succeed they needed the help of foreign advisers. 'Ammun noted that, unlike the Reform Society of Beirut, the Decentralization Party had not mentioned this matter in their platform because they did not want to oblige every vilayet to seek the assistance of foreign advisers, as this would affect the liberty of the vilayets.[32]

The next speaker was Na'um Mukarzal, on the topic of "The progress of the emigrants and their assistance in the reformist Arab revival". He called for a reformist revolution and urged those present to vigorous action on behalf of liberty and equality. Stressing that the Lebanese were already enjoying independence beyond the demands of decentralization, he noted that they were nevertheless cooperating with the other lovers of liberty and wanted their neighbours to have no less than they.[33]

'Abbas Bijani greeted the congress in the name of the Arabs of Mexico. Suddenly an observer sent to the session by the opponents of the congress got up and announced in French that holding the congress in Paris was contradictory to patriotism. Al-'Uraysi protested his speaking in French and Bayhum demanded that the opponent be silenced. Though the latter threatened (in French) that he would protest to the newspapers, Bayhum demanded again that he be silenced. Tawfiq Fa'id declared that whoever did not preserve his national (*wataniyya*) language could not be considered an Arab at all. A great uproar arose in the hall. If the opponent had read al-Zahrawi's interview to the press, said Khayrallah, he would understand why the congress was being held in Paris. The opponent shrugged his shoulders, said "All right, all right" and left the hall, palefaced.[34]

After this incident al-'Uraysi began reading the congress resolutions:

1. True reforms are vital for the Ottoman Empire and should be implemented rapidly.
2. It is crucial that the Arabs be guaranteed their political rights, and this by their active participation in the central administration of the Empire.
3. In each Arab vilayet a decentralized administration must be established to take care of its needs and customs.

Salam pointed out that this meant that each vilayet should make its own internal laws so that they would be appropriate for its local needs, and he added that the Reform Society of Beirut had demanded this in its list of reforms.

4. The vilayet of Beirut has presented its demands in a special list, which was unanimously approved on 31 January 1913, and which is based on two principles: Broadening the authority of the General Councils and the appointment of foreign advisers. The Congress requests the implementation of these two demands.

At this point one of the observers shouted out: "We do not want foreigners to intervene in our concerns". Salam responded that the Beirutians had decided on this unanimously, and that they were referring to advisers for a limited period, until it would be possible to manage without them. He added that people outside the vilayet had no right to intervene in the Beirutians' affairs just as they did not intervene in the affairs of other vilayets. Zayniyya followed him, saying that the Beirutians would not agree to the introduction of any modifications in their list, and those present must either approve it or reject it as one unit. The president, al-Zahrawi, intervened at this point and said that it was, on the contrary, permissible to hold a debate before approving a resolution. Then a doctor of jurisprudence from Cairo got up and asked if it was permissible for an Egyptian to participate in the discussion. Al-Zahrawi replied that it was not. The Egyptian asked: "But isn't Egypt an Ottoman Arab country?" The president replied: "We respect our Egyptian brothers and we respect their views . . . We realize that Egypt is an Ottoman Arab country, but since it has a separate administration in which the Ottomans' views are not taken into consideration, and since the Ottoman countries have an administration that does not consider the Egyptians' views, I am therefore requesting that this should be counted as a sufficient justification for keeping the discussion of internal Ottoman matters limited to those whose views can affect their situation." Al-'Uraysi continued:

5. The Arabic language must be recognized in the Ottoman parliament and the parliament must decide that it will be an official language in the Arab vilayets.

One of the observers commented that Arabic must also be the language of instruction, and al-Zahrawi replied that the term "official language" included this as well.

6. Military service will be done locally within the vilayets except in very exceptional circumstances.

Khayrallah asked who would decide when there was an especially vital necessity. Bayhum replied that the war minister would decide. Khayrallah then suggested that it might be worthwhile for the authority to be given to the parliament. The president asked him what would happen, then, at times when the parliament was not in session. At this point the discussion was joined by 'Ammun, who noted that since not all the races were represented in the government and it did not care about all of them, there was reason to consider Khayrallah's suggestion. Zayniyya concluded the discussion by saying that an especially vital necessity meant war or rebellion.

7. The Congress expresses the hope that the Ottoman government will grant the mutasarrifiyya of the Lebanon the means for improving its financial situation.

The president explained that in spite of the Lebanon's special status it was the government that allotted its funds, and at present it was suffering from a deficit in its balance of payments.

8. The Congress approves and expresses its sympathy with the demands of the Ottoman Armenians that are based on decentralization.

The president explained that the situation of the Armenians was similar to that of the Arabs, and the Arabs therefore wished them success as well.

9. These resolutions will be transmitted to the Ottoman government.

Khayrallah now wanted to know what steps would be taken if the congress resolutions were not accepted. Al-Zahrawi replied that this matter was beyond the limits of the article under discussion. Yet it was decided on that occasion to transmit the congress resolutions to the Ottoman ambassador in Paris.

10. The resolutions will also be transmitted to the governments friendly to the Ottoman Empire.

Mutran commented that the intention here was that these governments should put in a good word with the Ottoman government that would encourage it to carry out the reforms. Al-Zahrawi also thought that this might be useful.

11. The Congress cordially thanks the French government for its generous welcome to its guests.

Appendix to the Congress Resolutions

1. If the resolutions approved by the Congress will not be implemented, the members of the Arab reform societies will avoid accepting any positions whatsoever in the Ottoman government, except with special permission from the society they belong to.
2. These resolutions will be the political programme for the Ottoman Arabs and no candidate for election to the parliament should be assisted unless he commits himself in advance to support this programme and demand its implementation.
3. The Congress thanks the Arab émigrés for their nationalism (*wataniyyatihim*) in their support for it, and sends them its greetings through their delegates.[35]

In accordance with the resolution of the congress the list of resolutions was officially transmitted to the European powers. But there were a number of changes in the list that was transmitted to them that were not on the list authorized by the congress (emphases not in original):

3. It is important to establish in each *Syrian* and Arab vilayet a decentralized regime appropriate to its needs and aptitudes.
5. The Arabic language must be recognized in the Ottoman parliament and considered official in the *Syrian* and Arab countries.
6. Military service will be done locally within the *Syrian* and Arab vilayets except in cases of extreme necessity.

Appendix to the Preceding Resolutions

1. As long as the resolutions voted by the present congress are not properly executed, the members of the *Syrian* Arab reform societies will abstain from accepting any functions in the Ottoman Empire, except with special and express authorization from their respective societies.

2. These present resolutions constitute the political programme for the Ottoman *Syrians* and Arabs. No candidate for election to the parliament should be supported unless he engages himself in advance to defend this programme and demand its execution.[36]

On 23 June at 9:00 pm the closing session of the congress began. It was intended that this session would be held in French, and therefore French statesmen and journalists were present. The Archimandrite 'Atiyya of the Greek Orthodox Church in Paris joined the delegates on the dais. Mutran translated the president's greetings into French and Bayhum gave a speech summarizing the discussions of the congress and reporting its resolutions.[37] Charles Dabbas spoke on "The reformist revival in Syria", denouncing the behaviour of the CUP and outlining the history of the Reform Society of Beirut until its "tyrannical" closure by the authorities. He explained that the reforms the Arabs wanted would benefit both the Empire and the interests of the Powers, whom the Arabs wanted to mediate between them and their government on this matter. Dabbas added that at present the Ottoman authorities were faced with two alternatives: either to allow all the elements of the Empire to participate in its administration or to allow the inhabitants of each vilayet to administer their own internal affairs independently. If the government rejected these alternatives, then both the Empire and the Arabs would be lost. The reformists would continue their activities, he concluded, "and would fight with violence and force" until Syria was on the path that would lead it to a better future.[38]

Shukri Ghanim was the last speaker. "You, the Muslims of Syria, are our brothers in language, in ethnic origin and in nationalism, and the brothers of the Turks in religious belief," he declared. He called upon the Turks to understand that the reformists did not wish to bring about the Empire's ruin, but rather reforms that would preserve its integrity and independence. In conclusion he expressed the appreciation of all the Arabs for France, "which has always defended all liberal ideas".[39] At 10:00 pm the president of the congress closed the proceedings.

Fifty-eight letters and telegrams of support from all over the world, signed by 402 individuals and some organizations, arrived at the congress. The names of 43 members of the societies appeared, among them prominent activists such as Salah al-Din al-Qasimi, 'Abd al-Rahman al-Shahbander, Muhammad Kurd 'Ali, 'Arif al-Shihabi, 'Abd al-Wahhab al-Inklizi, Kamil al-Qassab, Lutfi al-Haffar, Salih Haydar, Nakhla Mutran, Rafiq

Rizq Sallum, Sayf al-Din al-Khatib, 'Asim Basisu, Jalal al-Bukhari, Isma'il al-Saffar, Hafiz al-Sa'id, Sayyid Talib al-Naqib, and Muzahim al-Amin al-Pachachi. There were also many supporters whose names did not appear again in the history of the Arab movements, as well as some who became known only many years later, such as the young Baghdadian Bakr Sidqi. Letters and telegrams sent by the societies included messages from the Reform Society of Beirut, the Society of the Lebanese Revival of New York, the Syrian Nationalist Society of Birmingham, the Canadian Syrian Club of Montreal, the Society of Young Zahla of Cleveland, the Syrian Reform Society of Winocka, Oklahoma, and others. In the letter of the last-mentioned society the following demand was made: "To request independent government for the three Syrian united vilayets (al-wilayat al-muttahida) and the mutasarrifiyya of Jerusalem, like the United States (al-wilayat al-muttahida) of America . . . and that the connections between Istanbul and Syria should be like the connections between Washington and the American states."[40]

During his visit on 21 June to the French foreign ministry, Zayniyya had already warned the French that some of the congress members wanted to begin contacts with the British by meeting in London with British Foreign Minister Edward Grey. In order to prevent this, Zayniyya suggested that the French foreign minister should meet with a delegation of the congress members, as such a meeting would undoubtedly leave a strong impression on them.[41] On 30 June a delegation of congress members, including al-Zahrawi, Ghanim, 'Ammun, Salam, Tabbara, Bayhum and Zayniyya, arrived at the foreign ministry. Thanking Foreign Minister Pichon in the name of the congress for hosting it, al-Zahrawi expressed his hope that just as France had always demonstrated its friendship, it would also assist, together with all of Europe, in the realization of the needed reforms. "The unity and brotherhood reigning between the Muslims and the Christians, on the one hand, and between the Syrians and the Lebanese, on the other hand, are the greatest proof of our progress and our ability to administer our affairs," he claimed, adding that this meant with the assistance of European advisers but under Ottoman sovereignty. Pichon replied that France did indeed feel friendship for the Empire and sought the good of the Syrians and expressed his admiration for the equanimity of the reformists, promising that France would agree to be Syria's advocate in Europe as a service for the Ottoman Empire and not against it.[42]

Immediately after leaving the foreign ministry, the members of the delegation (with the exception of Ghanim) turned to the Ottoman embassy in Paris. The Ottoman ambassador had already formulated his view—that he did not recognize the status of the reformists. He would be prepared to receive them because they were Ottoman subjects, but he would not recognize them as a representative group. Flattering the delegation on its arrival, he claimed that he too recognized the need to implement reforms, but also the need to act moderately. The delegation members handed him a copy of the congress resolutions to transmit to his government.[43]

Salam and the other Muslim delegates of the Reform Society of Beirut were suspicious of the activities of the Christian delegates. They heard rumours that the latter had gone to the French foreign ministry and requested the annexation of Beirut and the Lebanon to France. In order to iron out the difficulties another delegation went to the French foreign ministry in the beginning of July 1913, this time including Thabit, Zayniyya, Salam, Bayhum and Tabbara (actually, the entire delegation of the Reform Society), and they met there with de Margerie, who was responsible for the sub-department of European, African and Eastern affairs. Bayhum denied that the Syrians wanted Syria annexed to France. They had chosen Paris for their congress only because France was a place of liberty that loved those who sought liberty, but they were not prepared to exchange their state for another one. They wanted French assistance for reforms, but they did not want the French to be their rulers. France had no ambitions in Syria, de Margerie responded; it wanted only that the reformists should live in peace in their country. Upon Bayhum's request, de Margerie agreed to be quoted in public. No sooner had they left the building than Thabit and Zayniyya began raging in reaction to Bayhum's words. It was obvious that they were very dissatisfied with what had occurred. The officials of the French foreign ministry were also very disappointed with this declaration of Bayhum's.[44]

Chapter 23

THE PARIS AGREEMENT AND ITS CONSEQUENCES

The publicity surrounding the Paris Congress perplexed the authorities of the Empire. Even without the congress their situation was difficult. With the Balkan War then at its height, Enver's main concern was to recapture Edirne. A week before the congress was opened Grand Vizier Mahmud Shawkat was assassinated. Jamal, who was then Governor of Istanbul, reacted quickly to prevent the opposition from taking advantage of the situation and from then on the triumvirate of Enver, Tal'at and Jamal ruled the Empire. Troubled by the representation of the CUP at the Paris Congress as preventing any possibility of reform, the three decided to try to reach an agreement with the congress members—though they did not necessarily have any intention of keeping it. As a preliminary step the government announced its willingness to accept the reform demands and even announced that decentralist reforms were in preparation. It promised to send a draft of the new law on this matter to the Ottoman embassies abroad, for presentation to the European powers.[1]

As a preparatory step for direct negotiations with the congress members, the CUP leaders began contacts with the most prominent personality among the Arab reformists in Istanbul, 'Abd al-Karim Qasim al-Khalil, the president of the Literary Club. At this time al-Khalil was employed as the secretary of Sharif 'Ali Haydar, a loyal supporter of the CUP. 'Ali Haydar arranged a meeting between al-Khalil and Tal'at and Jamal, and after negotiations they reached an agreement containing 11 articles on reforms. Al-Khalil signed it in the name of the Arabs and Tal'at, in the name of the CUP.

Jamal related several years later that al-Khalil had been interested in the negotiations principally in order to guarantee government positions to his friends. He prepared a list of candidates for such positions, including Rafiq al-'Azm and 'Abd al-Hamid al-Zahrawi as candidates for the government, and 11 candidates for the senate, among them Rashid Rida and al-Zahrawi. Al-Khalil committed himself to work for the acceptance of the agreement by the congress members.[2]

It was then decided to send al-Khalil to Paris together with two senior members of the CUP, Hajji 'Adil and Midhat Shukri (secretary-general of the CUP, who was considered an expert in Arab affairs because he had served as a Vali in Iraq). The news that CUP people were going to meet with the congress members for negotiations spread quickly throughout the Arab vilayets. While in general the news aroused enthusiasm, not everyone was so optimistic; there were those who demonstrated greater caution in evaluating the situation—like Shafiq al-Mu'ayyad, for example, who told the French consul-general in Damascus that with the present CUP government there was no guarantee that he would not soon have to request political asylum at the consulate.[3]

Arriving in Paris on 25 June, al-Khalil gave al-Zahrawi and the other congress members a copy of the agreement he had signed with Tal'at to study. On 27 June Midhat Shukri also arrived in Paris alone; Hajji 'Adil did not come owing to illness. At this time a controversy broke out among the congress members. The Christians, led by Thabit and Zayniyya, had no trust in the Young Turks and absolutely refused to enter into negotiations with a CUP representative. The Muslims, on the other hand, entertaining suspicions about the plans of the Christian congress members who belonged to the Society of the Lebanese Revival, were willing to enter into negotiations with Midhat Shukri, if only to restrain the contacts between their Christian colleagues and foreign elements. The relations between the Muslims and the Christians became strained. (Zayniyya said about the Syrian Muslims: "They are more Muslim than Syrian.") However, after some changes in formulation were introduced into the articles of the agreement signed by al-Khalil and Tal'at, and two new articles were added—the second especially in order to satisfy the members of the delegation from the Reform Society of Beirut—a new agreement was signed by Midhat Shukri and the members of the Paris Congress:

1. Elementary and secondary education in the Arab countries will be in Arabic and higher education will be in the language of the majority.
2. All the leading officials except the Vali will be required to know Arabic. The other officials will be appointed by the vilayet. . . .
5. Soldiers will serve in nearby countries. . . .
6. The decisions of the local councils will always be valid.
7. It will be accepted as a principle that there will be at least three Arabs in the government . . .

8. At least five Arab Valis and ten Mutasarrifs will be appointed . . .
9. Arabs will be appointed to the senate in a ratio of two for every vilayet.
10. Foreign expert supervisors will be employed in departments requiring them in each vilayet . . .
12. It will be accepted as a principle that all official activities in Arab countries will be conducted in Arabic . . .
13. The jurisdiction of the General Councils will be expanded. Half the members of the Beirut General Council will be Muslims and half non-Muslims.

Midhat Shukri promised to try to persuade the CUP to accept the agreement and also promised to act "in other secret personal questions". He then returned with al-Khalil to Istanbul, while the delegates of the Decentralization Party and the Reform Society of Beirut remained in Paris to see how matters would develop.[4]

The signatories concurred that the agreement should remain secret until the CUP took appropriate steps and issued orders concerning the matter. The CUP members feared that the publication of the agreement would cause the other nationalities in the Empire to raise similar demands. But since there was general knowledge of it, the Reuter agency published a telegram announcing that the government had reached an agreement with the Arabs concerning the reforms, that 'Abd al-Hamid al-Zahrawi would be appointed Sheikh al-Islam and that Sharif 'Ali Haydar would be appointed president of the State Council. When the Reuter's telegram was published, Rafiq al-'Azm, the president of the Decentralization Party, believed that the government had offically decided to implement the agreement and that it was no longer necessary to keep it secret. He promptly not only sent a copy of it to the newspaper al-Muqattam but even a congratulatory telegram to the Grand Vizier. When al-Muqattam published the agreement on 12 July the CUP people were infuriated. It became clear that the rejoicing in the Decentralization Party was premature; the government had not yet decided anything and the Reuter's telegram had been entirely groundless. The CUP was now in a very uncomfortable position; not only were they angry about the breaching of confidentiality on the part of the Decentralization Party, but they were also under attack by those in Syria who had opposed the reforms at the request of the CUP and now felt that they had been deceived. The CUP therefore decided on a strategy of complete denial. The CUP newspaper Tanin announced that there had never been any such agreement and that Midhat Shukri had visited Paris only as a tourist. The General Centre of the CUP announced that the government did indeed intend to implement reforms in the Arab vilayets but that this had no connection with any agreement whatsoever.[5]

On 2 August 1913 the government actually did decide on a limited reform programme, and the interior minister sent a telegram about it to the Arab vilayets. Publication of the programme over the next few days in the Arab newspapers caused great disappointment among the reformists, for it was much less than what had been agreed upon in Paris and they considered its articles vague. They felt that they could no longer rely on the government, which apparently had no serious intention of implementing reforms.[6] The Sultan, as was customary, approved the government's decision, in an imperial edict on 16 August. Published in the Istanbul newspapers on 23 August, the edict caused the reformists additional disappointment; the government's programme was watered down further and some of its reforms no longer appeared at all.[7]

Al-Khalil, who then considered himself the liaison between the imperial authorities and the Arab nation, could not give up this position because of the "minor" problem of the government's retreat from the agreement signed with the congress members in Paris (and beforehand with him). After the publication of the government's decision by the interior minister he sent telegrams to the various Arab societies requesting that they send delegations to Istanbul to thank the government for its willingness to approach the Arabs. The reformists did not even bother to answer his telegrams. Next al-Khalil gathered together a large group of Arabs in the Literary Club for a speech about the government's willingness to implement reforms, and asked them to form a delegation to thank the government. Even in the formation of this delegation difficulties arose. In the end it included several CUP supporters, such as Sharif 'Ali Haydar and Sheikh 'Abd al-'Aziz Jawish, former Arab-Ottoman Brotherhood members Shukri al-Ayyubi and Shukri al-Husayni, and Literary Club members Ma'ruf al-Rusafi, Najib Shuqayr, Husayn Haydar and, of course, al-Khalil himself. When the delegation arrived at the Sublime Porte on 5 August, the Grand Vizier expressed his pleasure that the misunderstandings between the Arabs and the Turks had finally been eliminated. Thanking the Grand Vizier in the name of the delegation, al-Khalil expressed the hope that the promised reforms would be implemented quickly. He also requested the abolition of the military regime imposed on Beirut since the closing of its Reform Society, permission to reopen local newspapers closed by the authorities, and legalizing the import of Egyptian newspapers to the Empire.

That evening al-Khalil invited members of the government, senate and parliament, Arabs and Turks, to a party, among them senior members of the CUP such as Tal'at, Jamal and Enver. In another speech of thanks, al-Khalil again requested that the promised reforms be implemented soon, and expressed his happiness that the misunderstanding between the Arabs and the Turks had been eliminated. Tal'at gave a speech denying that there had ever been any such misunderstanding. He and his colleagues wanted to serve the Arabs faithfully; their previous opposition to decentralization had only stemmed from their fear that it would help the Balkan nations secede from the Empire. Now, since they had seceded anyway, there was no longer a need to oppose this idea.[8]

Afterwards al-Khalil sent a telegram to Paris, asking that a delegation of congress members supervise the implementation of the reforms in Istanbul. The three Muslim delegates of the Reform Society of Beirut were sent: Salam, Bayhum and Tabbara. Arriving in the capital on 15 August, the delegation was welcomed by a large crowd, mostly Arab students but also including some senior members of the CUP. Taken to the Literary Club, the delegation revealed that its purpose was to work for the official publication of the agreement that had been signed between the CUP and the congress members. On 23 August the delegation met with Sultan Muhammad Rashad, expressed the loyalty of the Arabs to the Ottoman crown, and requested that he take action to hasten the implementation of the reforms. They repeated this at a meeting with the crown prince, 'Izz al-Din, on 27 August. The prince promised that he would work to hasten the reforms.

That evening the CUP held a party for the congress delegation with the participation of all the government ministers and the prominent Arabs and Turks in Istanbul. Fethi, then secretary of the CUP, welcomed the delegation and expressed his hope that now a new era in the life of the nation and the Empire would begin. After al-Khalil had responded, expressing his happiness that the CUP had eliminated the tension between the Arabs and the Turks, Tabbara explained, in the name of the delegation, why the reforms had been demanded in the first place. Nevertheless, he declared, "The Arabs and the Turks are brothers . . . We grew up under the shadow of the Ottoman crescent, we want to live under its shadow, and we will die under its shadow. 'We' means the Arabs. And by 'Arabs' I mean every speaker of *dad*, and it does not matter if he is Muslim or non-Muslim. We do not want a substitute for our Empire . . ." But the Arabs must participate in the government, Tabbara stressed in conclusion. Promises were not enough; they had to be realized.⁹

Wrathful at the honoured reception the congress delegation had met in the capital, the opponents of reform in Syria sent angry letters to the CUP centre, claiming that they and not the reformists represented the views of the Syrian populace. The CUP saw such actions as a trend to encourage, in order to sow dissension among the Arabs and to discredit the reformists. By telegram they instructed the Vali of Damascus to send immediately to Istanbul the leaders of the reform opponents, Muhammad Fawzi Pasha al-'Azm, 'Abd al-Rahman al-Yusuf and others. The latter organized a delegation of reform opponents, among them Shakib Arslan, As'ad Shukayr and Muhammad Pasha al-Makhzumi, and they set out for Istanbul. The Beirut newspapers reacted with rage and protested a priori against any step the delegation might take in the capital. They also stressed the need to implement the reforms as soon as possible. Telegrams from Beirut requested the members of the congress delegation to continue their patriotic line, to demand the needed reforms, and not to be deterred by the intrigues that the anti-reformist delegation would carry out in Istanbul. They were also requested to reject any attempt by the opposing delegation to speak to or meet with them. The CUP indeed attempted to bring about a meeting between the two delegations, but the congress delegation, as requested, refused. An attempt by the CUP to persuade Rafiq al-'Azm to come to Istanbul also failed; the Decentralization Party did not see any point in it before the government officially approved the agreement signed by the congress members.¹⁰

The congress delegation in Istanbul soon realized that the authorities were only drawing matters out with constant postponements and organizing parties, and they did not intend to implement true reforms. The imperial edict of the Sultan, which was published on the day they visited him, also undoubtedly caused them disappointment. Full of bitterness, the delegation members decided to return to Beirut.¹¹ They arrived there on 2 September and were welcomed by a cheering crowd of 500 people and the band of the Ottoman College of Sheikh 'Abbas al-Azhari. From the port they proceeded in a great parade to the government palace, posters waving: "Long live the reforms" and "Reforms or death". At the government palace they were officially received by the Vali, and Sheikh Tabbara asked him to request his superiors to hasten the implementation of the reforms, according to the wish of the entire country. In order to pacify the crowd, the Vali was forced to send a telegram to Istanbul. The parade then marched to the club of the Reform Society, which had been closed by the previous Vali, and opened it; a series of speeches were given there as a crowd of thousands gathered. Rather than present its mission to Istanbul as a total failure, the delegation announced that its efforts had not been in vain—the central government had promised that reforms would eventually be implemented in the Arab provinces. But the Beirutians had had enough of government promises, and Reform Society member Iskandar 'Azar (one of those arrested in the April events) gave a speech publicly expressing the lack of confidence at the time in the government promises.[12]

Not only the Arabs of the Empire watched the contacts between the authorities and the reformists in Istanbul to see how matters would develop. Syrian and Lebanese émigrés in Cairo, Europe and America had similar hopes. When it gradually became clear that the government did not intend to implement the reforms and fulfil its promises on this matter, the first indications of protest arose. An unknown London group called the Central Society for Reform and Defence of the Syrian Interests (Comité central de Réforme et de Défense des Intérêts syriens) sent a memorandum at the end of August to the European powers and the important European newspapers concerning the sorry state of the Empire. The memorandum, signed by the society's secretary Gevget, reviewed the catastrophes which had recently befallen the Empire and described the great joy occasioned by the restoration of the constitution in 1908 and the subsequent disappointment caused by the behaviour of the CUP. It added that the Syrians now wanted reforms to be implemented, but did not believe that this could be accomplished without assistance from the European powers, and were therefore requesting the Powers to exert their influence towards this end. The memorandum was accompanied by a list of the Syrians' demands, according to the society:

1. Recognition of Arabic as an official language.
2. Participation of the natives in the service and rehabilitation of the country.
3. Modifying the military laws that had caused the emigration which had been continuing for many years.
4. Organization of the tax collection service and the abolition of certain vexatious taxes.

5. Absolute autonomy in everything connected with public works and public instruction.
6. Constituting a General Assembly to control the activities of the functionaries and cooperate with the governor-general in all administrative affairs, without the need to request instructions from Istanbul in every case.

The publication of the memorandum aroused a great outcry in Istanbul, and the Turkish newspapers attacked the Arabs for not remaining patient until the government implemented the reforms. In London the police searched for the group that had distributed the memorandum. Inspector Thomas McNamara of the Criminal Investigation Department combed the entire city and investigated the Syrian community there, but in the end he had to admit that he had not succeeded in finding any society of that name, and that the signer of the memorandum was not known among the Syrians living in London.[13]

In early October the Decentralization Party in Cairo finally lost patience with waiting for the reforms promised by the government and for the fulfilment of the Paris agreement. In a coordinated operation 42 identical telegrams were sent to Istanbul on 9 October from all parts of the Empire, from Egypt, Paris, London, the United States and Brazil, demanding the implementation of the reforms. On the same day the party published "A Manifesto to the Arab Nation from the Decentralization Party". It began with the announcement that the Arabs were indeed loyal to the imperial throne, but even their patience had a limit. Its analysis of the Empire led to the conclusion that the problem was the centralized regime; everything that needed to be done in the vilayets had to be authorized in the capital. The Arab intelligentsia had concluded that the vilayets must be given a measure of self-government and the authority to manage their administrative and educational affairs. This could be done with the kind of regime that existed in several European and American countries, known as "administrative decentralization". For this purpose the Decentralization Party had been founded, and for this purpose the Paris Congress had been held, representing most of the Arab societies. In order to prove to the government and to the world that the congress members were interested in reforms even if they would only be achieved gradually, the congress members had accepted the agreement that was offered them by the CUP delegate who had come to Paris, after introducing a small number of changes. The government had promised to carry out this agreement, but when an announcement concerning the reforms had been published a while later it had contradicted what was written in the agreement. Afterwards an imperial edict had been published, which was an additional retreat even from the government announcement. From all this it became abundantly clear that the government did not seriously intend to implement reforms.

The manifesto called upon the Arab societies in particular, and the Arab nation in general, to unite in supporting the party's demand for administrative decentralization, in order to save the nation and the fatherland from extinction. It stated that telegrams were streaming into Istanbul from the entire Empire and from the centres of Arab emigration abroad, to request reforms based on administrative decentralization, including one sent to the Grand Vizier by the party president, Rafiq al-'Azm. The manifesto ended with a summary of the basic demands of the Arabs:

1. Freedom of the nation in its representative bodies. Most important is the freedom to elect members of the general councils, members of the parliament, and the like . . .
2. Freedom in educational issues. Most important is that all education should be in the Arabic language and that its administration should be the responsibility of the local councils.
3. Freedom in matters of public works and economic affairs. All the activities in these areas should be in the hands of the local councils, except for what is connected to foreign policy or security matters . . .
4. The Arabic language will be recognized as official in all the Arab vilayets, and all government activities in these vilayets will be conducted in Arabic. No official will be employed in the Arab vilayets unless he is one of their residents and can speak and write Arabic well . . .[14]

'Abd al-Hamid al-Zahrawi, the congress president, remained during this time in Paris awaiting developments. The CUP people had tried during August to persuade him to come to Istanbul, but he refused. Some of the congress members had already planned in June to go to London to meet the British foreign minister, Edward Grey. When in July, after the congress, they wanted to carry out this plan, Zayniyya tried his best to persuade them not to, as it would offend their host country, France, and in the end they did not go. Al-Zahrawi even began contacts with the French foreign minister, mediated by Zayniyya and Thabit. Then, at the beginning of September, al-Zahrawi went to London for a six-day visit, at the invitation of 'Izzat Pasha al-'Abid. After his return to Paris he and Zayniyya chose to go back to Syria, while Thabit decided to remain in Paris on personal business (the next time Thabit saw Beirut was in 1920). Then, in October, Sharif 'Ali Haydar wrote to al-Zahrawi from Istanbul and asked him at the request of the authorities to come there. Al-Zahrawi refused, whereupon 'Ali Haydar sent a telegram through his secretary, al-Khalil, swearing on his grandfather's honour that no harm would come to him in the capital and even promising him membership in the senate. This time al-Zahrawi complied with the request and set out for Istanbul on 25 October.[15]

Arriving in Istanbul three days later, al-Zahrawi was greeted at the railway station by a large crowd, including notables, students and more than 70 Arab officers. The directorate of the Literary Club organized a caravan of 50 coaches to the club, where a reception was held for him. On 30 October al-Zahrawi began negotiations with Midhat Shukri and other representatives of the CUP. But after a week and a half he came to the conclusion that the CUP was only using delaying tactics and had no intention of implementing reforms. Interviewed by the editor of an Istanbul newspaper on 21 November, he claimed that not one of the CUP's fine promises had been carried out, and added that he intended to leave for Egypt. Asked if he feared that his leaving Istanbul would put an end to the dialogue with the government, he agreed, saying that he had even attempted to explain this to the government, but to no avail. And what was the reason for the delaying tactics of the government? Al-Zahrawi answered: "I think the reason is a controversy within the CUP. One group of its members supports our demands and wants to treat us well, while another group rejects our demands absolutely and wants to use force against us. We do not know which of the forces will prevail."

These words of al-Zahrawi led to some repercussions; there were even some Turks who claimed that the situation was genuinely serious and that reforms should be implemented. After al-Zahrawi had exerted a good deal of pressure, the authorities informed him that they had begun to implement the reforms by setting up two Arabic-language schools, one in Damascus and one in Beirut. Soldiers would serve in their own vilayets and Arabic would be an official language in the courts and government departments in the Arab vilayets. Al-Zahrawi was requested to assist in the selection of suitable Arabs for appointment to senior government positions and to the senate. Al-Zahrawi had by then come to the conclusion that there was no point in leaving the capital since the government would not care and might even be happy to get rid of him; he decided to stay and cooperate with the authorities, in the hope that he might after all succeed in bringing about the realization of the reforms. He even invited Rashid Rida and Rafiq al-'Azm to come to Istanbul to assist him. While Rida refused, believing that the CUP people were only waiting for them in order to eliminate them, Al-'Azm still believed that there was hope of brotherhood between the Arabs and the Turks and wanted to come—but in the end Rida succeeded in persuading him not to.[16]

Meanwhile the imperial authorities did not demonstrate great enthusiasm in implementing the reforms they had promised. With the Balkan War already over, they felt less pressured by the demands of the Arabs. They did, however, establish the secondary schools in Damascus and Beirut and give the responsibility for their administration to Rafiq al-Tamimi and Rustum Haydar (both members of al-Fatat, the latter also a participant in the Paris Congress). They also issued a government edict at the end of the year introducing changes in the Vilayets Law, requiring that the officials in the vilayets know the local language, use it in court processes, and publish the government announcements in it. They considered these changes sufficient to pacify the reformists.[17]

The authorities were more generous when it came to appointments to positions, seeing this as a means of buying the reformists. Positions as civilian inspectors of vilayets were promised to Shukri al-'Asali and 'Abd al-Wahhab al-Inklizi. The former, who had previously refused the offer to be Mutasarrif of Latakia at a time when the reformists had resigned from positions in protest against the non-implementation of the reforms, did not want to lose the opportunity again. To allay his discomfort in accepting before the reforms had been realized, he used his newspaper al-Qabas to announce that the government's beginning to employ Arab officials and to send Arabic-speaking officials to the Arab vilayets was credible evidence of its decision to implement the reforms based on decentralization. Al-'Asali then told the French consul-general in Damascus that he believed there had been a positive change in the attitude of the CUP and asked if he would advise him to accept the position. The consul-general quickly answered: "Certainly"; in a later statement, he explained: "I could not really answer otherwise. This was the answer that Shukri Bey awaited and desired. He seemed very satisfied." Al-'Asali and al-Inklizi had to wait for their appointments until the beginning of 1914, when the former was appointed first-grade civil inspector in Aleppo and the latter second-grade civil inspector in Bursa. Seeing this, Muhammad Kurd 'Ali hurried to Istanbul in early 1914 to demand reforms, in the unrealized hope that he too would get some good position.[18]

Then, on 4 January 1914, an imperial edict was issued announcing the senatorial appointments of 'Abd al-Hamid al-Zahrawi, Yusuf Sursuq and Muhammad Bayhum (the presidents of the Reform Society of Beirut) and four other Arabs.[19] The fact that al-Zahrawi, the president of the Paris Congress, accepted the appointment despite the explicit congress resolution not to take any positions until the reforms were implemented, shocked the Arab reformists. Though, as mentioned, a rider had been added to this congress resolution to the effect that positions could be accepted with special permission from one's society, al-Zahrawi did not bother to request the authorization of the Decentralization Party first. *Al-Fatat* therefore informed its members Sayf al-Din al-Khatib and Rafiq Rizq Sallum in Istanbul, both also among the leaders of the Literary Club, that they must work for the honouring of the congress resolution. These two and other young Arabs told al-Zahrawi that the reforms offered by the government were insufficient and that they considered him a traitor to the reforms. When al-Zahrawi replied that he had accepted the appointment to the senate only in order to be able to assist the government in implementing the reforms, and that if they insisted he would agree to resign, they answered that they were severing all connections with him; if he wanted to resign he should discuss the matter with his party.[20]

As a result, al-Zahrawi wrote the following letter to his friend Rashid Rida in Cairo, who was one of the leaders of the Decentralization Party:

> Your brother has been appointed, with the assistance and providence of Allah, as a member of the senate. Please inform me that you are pleased with my acceptance of the position. Allah is my witness that I agreed to accept it only in order to complete the work and you know, my brother, the pettiness of the men among us. Some of the hotheads are opposed, and the matter is given over to your wisdom and high-mindedness. Moreover, I believe that an expression of thanks to the Sublime Porte will assist in the completion of the work.

Several days later three Iraqi officers appeared at al-Zahrawi's home, headed by Jamil al-Madfa'i (later prime minister of Iraq), sent by 'Aziz 'Ali al-Misri, the leader of *al-'Ahd*. If he continued to support the CUP, they told him, they would kill him. Full of bitterness at the reward he had got from the Arabs for his activities on their behalf, al-Zahrawi wrote again to Rida. Heading his letter "completely confidential from everyone", he recounted to Rida what had happened to him from the time that the Paris Congress had ended until he had come to Istanbul and stated that he believed that the CUP people now "recognize their past mistakes and do not want to repeat them". He added: "I completely believe in their intentions and statements because of various proofs that have been shown to me." (He did not detail these proofs.) But the main part of the letter al-Zahrawi devoted to the political capabilities of the Arabs in Istanbul. He described the Arab merchants there as totally unfit for politics and matters of reform; the students as children "unsuited for politics"; and the officers too as having no experience in politics, so that it would be better if they did not intervene. For example: "'Aziz 'Ali [al-Misri] is embittered against the government at present and therefore wants to shake and ruin the state. He is angry about our union with the government and opposes it . . . He is making efforts to recruit some of these children and incite them against us." The retired Arab officials in the capital he likened to old women dissatisfied with everything, while those officials who had positions had no other interest except in keeping them. From all this, al-Zahrawi contended, one could see that it was impossible to rely on anyone. Continuing on to the Arabs outside the capital, he described those of Syria and Iraq as understanding nothing and not wanting to understand. Only the Arabs of the Arabian Peninsula were spared the lash of his tongue. (In this he adopted Rida's opinion—also that of al-Kawakibi—that the Arabs of the Arabian Peninsula were better.) Al-Zahrawi repeated his request that Rida express his opinion about his acceptance of the position, and that the party members should also discuss it, asking further that if they accepted his appointment they send a congratulatory telegram to the Sublime Porte.[21]

Rida responded with a sharp denunciation of al-Zahrawi's harsh remarks. (Al-Zahrawi told him later that this denunciation "broke his heart".) Nevertheless, Rida expressed the opinion that he should remain a senator and try to struggle from within. The Decentralization Party itself received a similar letter from al-Zahrawi, and after discussion the majority of the leadership decided to authorize al-Zahrawi's appointment to the senate after the fact, in the belief that it would not be advisable to deepen the crisis with the government at that time. A telegram informed al-Zahrawi that "Our Party has decided unanimously that you should accept membership in the senate, and the Party is relying on you to work with the government for the other Arab demands." But not all the party members were in favour of authorizing al-Zahrawi. Haqqi al-'Azm, the party's secretary, was strongly opposed, called al-Zahrawi derogatory names and even wrote to his acquaintances that the Decentralization Party was erasing al-Zahrawi's name from its membership list—which was not true.[22]

Not all the Arabs in the capital denounced al-Zahrawi's step. In a letter to a friend, the officer Salim al-Jaza'iri, another member of *al-'Ahd*, expressed an opinion differing from that of al-Misri:

> We are loyal to the CUP and there is no room to doubt their loyalty to us. It is true that we are not happy about the agreement they approved with al-Zahrawi and 'Abd al-Karim [al-Khalil] . . . but what can we do? Can we say that al-Zahrawi was mistaken and criticize him for this agreement? I am not of this opinion, since if al-Zahrawi had not reached an agreement with the government we would be in even worse straits.

Al-Zahrawi also received support from Ahmad Qadri of Damascus, who, contrary to the viewpoint of *al-Fatat*, to which he belonged, sent him a congratulatory telegram in the name of the young intelligentsia of Damascus, asking him to work for the realization of the national (*wataniyya*) demands, as expressed at the Paris Congress.[23]

The greatest of al-Zahrawi's supporters was 'Abd al-Karim Qasim al-Khalil. His standpoint did not please the Arab activists in Istanbul, and they held a conference at the Literary Club with the participation of hundreds of people, at which al-Khalil was asked to explain his stance towards the government and towards al-Zahrawi's appointment to the senate. Al-Khalil refused to discuss it in front of such a crowd, and a committee was selected, consisting of Najib Shuqayr, Sayf al-Din al-Khatib, As'ad Daghir, Jalal al-Bukhari, and Subhi Haydar, to discuss the issue with him. On 7 January the members of the committee met with al-Khalil in a closed session which lasted from 3:00 pm to 3:30 am, in which al-Khalil explained his standpoint: that al-Zahrawi acted wisely when he agreed to enter the senate since thus he could contribute more to the implementation of the reforms "and a bird in the hand is worth two in the bush". Al-Khalil also noted that there were great achievements for the Arabs in the secret agreement that was signed with the CUP, but that it would only be possible to implement it gradually so that ıer nationalities of the Empire would not raise similar ıds. He expressed his trust in the goodwill of the CUP, a.. ıdded that al-Zahrawi had accepted the position in order to prevent foreigners from taking advantage of the differences of opinion between the Arabs and the Turks to realize their ambitions in the Empire.

Though al-Khalil's justifications did not convince the members of the committee, they did not want to aggravate the crisis between the Arabs and the Turks. Thus they announced in the newspapers that at their meeting with al-Khalil it became clear that the implementation of the reforms "has not reached the desired stage and should not occasion joy". Nevertheless, in the then situation, and for the public good, they did not believe that it would be worthwhile to express a lack of confidence in al-Khalil; a four-member advisory committee should be chosen "that will strengthen him, and he will rely on them and consult with them" during his negotiations with the government. At this stage al-Khalil would remain the only representative of Arab youth confronting the government and the CUP, "because this is most useful for the public good".[24] In spite of this announcement, because of his activities for the attainment of understanding between the Arabs and the Turks, many activists continued to blame al-Khalil for the disintegration of the reform movement which occurred at that time.

Chapter 24

AL-'AHD

The Arab officers in the Ottoman army were not the last to enter into the politics of Arab-Turkish relations and the question of the future of the Arabs in the Ottoman Empire. At the beginning of the CUP's Turkification process three local officers in Baghdad, 'Ali Jawdat al-Ayyubi (1886-1969), Ja'far al-'Askari (1884-1936), and Nuri al-Sa'id (1888-1958), had already raised the idea of establishing a society that would strive for the rights of the Arabs. When Al-Ayyubi approached another Baghdadi officer, Yasin al-Hashimi (1882-1937), about the idea, al-Hashimi counselled caution. Al-Ayyubi responded to al-Hashimi's doubts about funds for financing the society with the suggestion that each of the members should give a monthly donation.[1] In the end the idea was shelved, but not for long. The planned society was established a few years later, with its centre in another city (Istanbul), but with a branch in Baghdad as well.

The founding of *al-Qahtaniyya* at the end of 1909 represented a landmark in the entry of Arab officers into political involvement. Among the founders was the officer Salim al-Jaza'iri of Damascus, with the somewhat hesitant assistance of 'Aziz 'Ali al-Misri. While the society was not limited to officers, a considerable number were involved. *Al-Qahtaniyya*'s goals were not revolutionary. The first revolutionary attempt was carried out in Istanbul towards the end of 1912 by 60 officers, mostly Baghdadi, who had apparently despaired of the future of the Empire in the light of its defeats in the Balkan War, and began planning to leave Istanbul to organize a revolt in Iraq. Upon the request of the Lebanese journalist Ibrahim Salim al-Najjar in the name of this group, conveyed by a junior official in the French embassy to an official in the British embassy, the British agreed to help these officers to be transferred to Iraq, but only on the condition that they would be transferred in groups of no more than ten. The officers refused out of fear that after the first ten had left the authorities would arrest all the others, and the idea was abandoned.[2]

The next revolutionary attempt was implemented in early 1913 under the leadership of Salim al-Jaza'iri, again with the cooperation of al-Najjar and again as a result of the Balkan War and the belief that the Ottoman Empire was about to disintegrate. At a secret conference headed by al-Jaza'iri, some 40 Arab officers serving in Chatalja and Gallipoli laid plans to return to Syria at the end of the war and begin a military movement that would work for the removal of the Turks. Their goal was to bring independence to Syria and to turn it into a principality under the rule of the Egyptian prince 'Umar Tusun. A manifesto in this spirit for distribution at the proper time was produced by the organizers. It seems that 'Abd al-Hamid al-Zahrawi, Rafiq al-'Azm and Rashid Rida were aware of this plan.

At the first stage of the plan al-Najjar and four officers, including al-Jaza'iri and Amin Lutfi al-Hafiz (both members of the Literary Club and former members of *al-Qahtaniyya*), left Istanbul on a French ship bound for Beirut on 27 January 1913, four days after the CUP coup d'état. Their goal was to test the atmosphere in the city and the readiness of the residents to assist a future uprising with men, arms and money. At the home of Salim 'Ali Salam, one of the leaders of the Reform Society of Beirut, one of the officers, a native of Beirut, told his audience:

> The health reasons I gave in order to explain my presence here were only a pretext intended to mask the true purpose of my voyage. I came here, in fact, to study the situation and the possibilities of a military action to liberate Syria. This mission was confided to me by my Arab comrades of the regiments stationed in Gallipoli, where the troops originating in our country are concentrated. The idea of Syrian independence, which we are preaching to our soldiers, has spread rapidly among them. When the moment comes, and if we can find the necessary support among you, we will act.

He informed them that the officers in Gallipoli had founded a society and already had a national anthem and a black, white and red flag. It was decided that the arrival of the new Vali in the city would serve as the excuse for the outbreak of the revolt.

Then this officer continued on to Damascus to examine the situation there as well, and al-Najjar was sent to ascertain the French government's viewpoint concerning this plan. The French consul-general told al-Najjar that he would not be able to help them; the Syrian question would be resolved in Paris, London and Berlin, and there was no point in their acting. Disappointed with this answer, the officers returned to Istanbul.[3] The plan was abandoned, and al-Jaza'iri returned to loyal service in the Ottoman army and in July 1913 participated in the liberation of Edirne from the Bulgarians. The leadership of the Arab officers now passed into the hands of his friend, the officer 'Aziz 'Ali al-Misri.

Al-Misri (1879-1965) was the descendant of Salim 'Arafat, a merchant who lived in Basra at the end of the eighteenth century. At the beginning of the reign of Sultan Mahmud II, Salim 'Arafat married the sister of his Circassian agent in the Caucasus, Hasan Bey, and moved to that region. By the time his grandson, Sheikh 'Ali, moved to Istanbul, following the Ottoman-Russian War of 1877-78, the family was already more Circassian than Arab. Sheikh 'Ali later moved to Egypt and became one of the notables of his quarter in Cairo. He soon began to be called 'Ali al-Misri to distinguish him from a Turkish neighbour whose name was also Sheikh 'Ali. His son, born in 1879, was named 'Abd al-'Aziz after the Sultan of the same name, and he became known as 'Abd al-'Aziz 'Ali al-Misri. Later, when he studied at the military academy in Istanbul and found out about the corruption during the reign of Sultan 'Abd al-'Aziz, al-Misri shortened his name to 'Aziz.

The young 'Abd al-'Aziz was the only surviving son of Sheikh 'Ali. He was six when his father died; when his mother died shortly afterwards, he went to live with his elder sister, who was married to the Cairo governor 'Ali Pasha Zulfikar. After completing his elementary and secondary education in Cairo he wanted to go to the military academy, but at his sister's insistence he studied law for a year. Rejected later as too short by the British-run military academy in Cairo, he turned to the military academy in Istanbul where he had heard of good German military instructors. He consulted first with Haqqi al-'Azm, telling him that he wanted military training in order to "drive out the British". The poet Ahmad Shawqi succeeded in persuading the sister to allow him to go, and in 1898 'Abd al-'Aziz left Cairo and entered the military academy in Istanbul.[4]

There 'Abd al-'Aziz, by now called 'Aziz 'Ali, was influenced by his German teachers, and his fondness for them continued to guide him until World War II. It is said that when he was still in the military academy he had already begun to spread Arabism among his friends and to call on the Arabs to unite in order to improve their situation. Another view contends that he was then working for the annexation of Egypt to the Empire. At any rate, during the period of his studies ideological differences broke out between him and one of his classmates, a young Turk named Enver; while 'Aziz 'Ali believed that Ottomanism was only a slogan and the nationalities of the Empire must be allowed to develop and grow, Enver favoured Turkification and the strengthening of the central regime over all the nationalities of the Empire.

Al-Misri graduated from the military academy in 1901 and from the Staff school in 1904, with the rank of Captain. Stationed in the Third Army in Macedonia, he fought against bands of Bulgarians, Greeks and Albanians. In 1906 al-Misri quarrelled with his commander at Uskub, 'Uthman Pasha, an incident which was of great significance for his later relations with the Turkish authorities; he insulted 'Uthman Pasha in public, in front of his soldiers, and in response 'Uthman Pasha ordered him to be imprisoned. In 1908 al-Misri was occupied with the elimination of rebel leaders in Bulgaria. When Sultan 'Abd al-Hamid, who had put a price of 1,000 liras on the head of each rebel leader, did not keep his promise, al-Misri's resentment against him increased. Thus, shortly before the 1908 revolution, al-Misri joined the CUP, some of whose senior members were his former classmates. Appointed commander of the Uskub region, he succeeded in turning the inhabitants into supporters of the revolution. General Shemsi Pasha, sent by 'Abd al-Hamid to put down the rebellion, was assassinated by one of al-Misri's men in Monastir on 7 July. After the restoration of the constitution, al-Misri was stationed in the Smyrna region. As a result of accusations levelled against him by members of the parliament over his heavy and brutal use of force to suppress local risings against the new regime, he was transferred to Rumelia.[5]

In October 1908 al-Misri went to Egypt where he invited Muhammad Farid and other members of the administrative committee of the Egyptian Nationalist Party (*al-Hizb al-Watani*) to join a secret society that he proposed to establish, the Society of the Young Arabs (*Jam'iyyat Shubban al-'Arab*). After a long debate they rejected his proposal, citing the "damage in spreading disunity between the elements of the Empire". The Egyptian nationalists had their own reasons for supporting the Empire and for not supporting—or even opposing—manifestations of Arab nationalism.[6]

Al-Misri returned to the Empire, and at the time of the suppression of the April 1909 counter-revolution he was charged with taking the Galata bridge and the nearby neighbourhoods. He next assisted Enver's forces in fighting the rebels in North Istanbul. Believing that he had influence in CUP circles, he sought to block the appointment of his old enemy, 'Uthman Pasha, to the position of commander of the Fifth Army in Damascus after the suppression of the counter-revolution. But when he told the war minister that he opposed the appointment

"by virtue of being an Arab", for the Arabs considered 'Uthman
Pasha an enemy, the minister expressed scepticism, suggesting
that the earlier dispute between them had given al-Misri personal
cause to hate 'Uthman Pasha. Al-Misri replied that the real reason 'Uthman Pasha had ordered him to be imprisoned at that
time was because he was an Arab, thus proving his hatred of the
Arabs. Since the minister remained unconvinced, al-Misri turned
to Dr Nazim, a senior member of the CUP, with the argument
that because the appointment of 'Uthman Pasha would offend
the Arabs, they would no longer be able to support the CUP as
they had so far. As their debate became hotter, al-Misri added:
"Is it not shameful that we hear your men calling black dogs
'Arabs'? Are all these things not enough for you? Do you also
have to send this enemy to our country?" He warned that the
ensuing division between Arabs and Turks would lead to dire
consequences. Al-Misri also turned to Jamal with the same arguments and complained that the Turks were insulting and humili-
ating the Arabs.[7]

The Ottoman security services began to keep an eye on al-
Misri as a result of these grievances, and when he took to visiting the Literary Club frequently (he was also involved in
al-Qahtaniyya), they decided that his presence in the capital was
undesirable. This was after the defeat of the Ottoman forces in
Yemen by Imam Yahya, and Al-Misri was sent there in 1910 as
chief of staff for 'Izzat Pasha. Because he helped the latter in
negotiations with the Imam (which ended on 9 October 1911
with an agreement according to which Yahya was given local
autonomy), his prestige rose considerably. While in Yemen he
was under the surveillance of Sulayman al-'Askari, one of the
commanders of the Teşkilât-i Mahsusa (the "Special Organization"), a secret service commanded by Enver. Al-'Askari
reported to the capital that "'Aziz 'Ali Bek is not loyal to Ottoman interests, but rather he is an Arab in the full sense of the
word and hates the Turks very much. His hatred of the Turks
does not stem from pure nationalist motives, but because the
Turks did not promote him to the high rank he aspires to."[8]

In late September 1911 Italy declared war on the Ottoman
Empire and invaded Libya. In November Ottoman officers were
sent to Libya to organize the Sanusi resistance movement
against the Italians, among them Enver, Mustafa Kemal, and
other senior officers of the CUP. When al-Misri also went to
Libya at the end of the year, he travelled through Egypt, where
he met with Khedive 'Abbas Hilmi. An Ottoman security service
agent reported that the Khedive tried to persuade him to work

for the annexation of Libya to Egypt, if possible—and if not, to enter into negotiations with the Italians in order to reach an agreement that the country would be given to them in return for extending Egypt's borders in Libya's direction. It seems that money was also offered to al-Misri in exchange for his consent to do this. In Libya al-Misri was appointed commander of the Benghazi sector. Relations between him and his chief of staff, Sulayman al-'Askari, at this stage were quite hostile. Enver, who was the supreme commander of the resistance movement against the Italians, was stationed in Derna, where the sector commander was Mustafa Kemal. Al-Misri could not tolerate Enver's being his commander—they had been in the same class at the academy—and he incited the Arab officers against Enver until a quarrel broke out between them and the Turkish officers. When al-Misri's equipment and ammunition ran out in April 1912 and he telegraphed Enver with a request for supplies, Enver refused. Al-Misri threatened to go to Derna at the head of the Sanusi forces in order to get the supplies by force, at which point Enver capitulated, but from then on relations between them were severed completely.

In October 1912 the Ottoman Empire signed a peace treaty with the Italians which ceded its sovereignty over Libya. Immediately afterwards the Balkan War broke out. The Ottoman officers in Libya decided to stay there to continue the struggle against the Italians independently. They planned to declare the independence of Tripolitania and Cyrenaica under the nominal leadership of Sayyid Ahmad al-Sanusi, and to put a number of officers in command of these regions to organize guerilla activities against the Italians. But when they discovered that the Empire's position in the Balkan War was deteriorating and that its lines of defence in Chatalja, a few dozens of miles west of the capital, were about to collapse, Enver immediately returned to Istanbul and from there sent an urgent message to the other officers to return to the capital in order to fight in the more crucial battles, in Macedonia and Western Thrace. Mustafa Kemal and most of the other Turkish officers returned to Istanbul immediately, leaving the continuation of the struggle against the Italians in the hands of al-Misri. Several of his later military achievements in battle against the Italians prevented them from advancing into the hinterland and won him great prestige in the Arab world.[9]

The Italians, who sought to end the Sanusis' resistance movement, requested the assistance of the Egyptian khedive, promising him in return to come to an understanding with him over the railway to Mariut. He was given the task of implementing part of the plan that he advised: that they try to enter into negotiations both with the Sanusis and with al-Misri, without either of them knowing about the contact with the other. The Khedive sent the Lebanese Hasan Hamada to al-Misri (a wise choice in the light of the fact that Hamada was a former fellow-member of al-Misri's in *al-Qahtaniyya*) with 600 Egyptian pounds and the advice that al-Misri leave Libya with his soldiers because there was no point in staying there after a peace treaty had been signed between the Empire and Italy. Hamada also suggested that if he was interested in Arab independence and the establishment of an Arab sultanate, it would be better to move to Beirut—then free of soldiers because of the Balkan War—and there declare Syria's independence with his soldiers. France and Britain would certainly assist him to become an independent amir. It was later claimed that al-Misri received no less than 15,000 pounds from the Italians in return for his agreement to retreat from Libya. At any rate, the servant who served him coffee informed the Ottoman security services about Hamada's visit.[10]

Shortly afterwards al-Misri quarrelled with Sayyid al-Sanusi, and in the end he did leave Libya. However, there were also other reasons for his departure. Before Enver returned to Istanbul he had left a large sum of money with al-Misri to use as payment for the Sanusi warriors. Al-Misri received additional sums of money from Egypt, apparently with the encouragement of the Khedive, who at first had been in favour of the resistance against the Italians. After the Khedive's contacts with the Italians and with al-Misri, the latter took most of the money that was left and sent it to his sister in Alexandria. Al-Sanusi, who saw that he was no longer receiving any money, wrote to Enver that he considered this a betrayal on the part of the Ottomans and he was therefore planning to reach an agreement with the Italians. Enver immediately sent al-Sanusi money, writing that he had also sent money previously but that al-Misri had used this money for private purposes. He promised al-Sanusi that when al-Misri returned to Istanbul he would be put on trial and executed.[11]

In June 1913 al-Misri decided to leave Libya. The local sheikhs, who considered him the leader of the resistance movement against the Italians, tried to persuade him to remain, but in vain. He travelled in the direction of Egypt with 800 of his soldiers, taking as much equipment as they could carry. When he reached Sollum at the beginning of July, he sent 650 of his soldiers to Smyrna by boat and continued on foot with the remainder in the direction of Alexandria. A force of tribesmen, sent by al-Sanusi to demand that al-Misri at least leave his men's arms, caught up with al-Misri near the Egyptian border. When al-Misri refused their demand, a bloody skirmish developed. The tribesmen fled, leaving behind 50 dead. Al-Misri lost one officer and 40 soldiers (by his account, four soldiers).[12]

When he returned to Istanbul and learned to his displeasure of 'Abd al-Karim al-Khalil's contacts with the Ottoman authorities, al-Misri decided to establish al-'Ahd (the Covenant), "so that it should be a covenant between its members and Allah for the service of the fatherland (watan)". According to his account, al-Misri also desired to establish a group that would constitute a counterweight to the contacts he had learned of between several Syrians and Lebanese and foreign states. He arranged a number of secret preparatory meetings with other Arab officers, not realizing that he was under the constant surveillance of the Ottoman security services. An Ottoman agent transmitted the following report concerning the first meeting:

> At 9:00 pm today, 23 September 1913, a meeting took place at the home of 'Aziz Bek [al-Misri] and . . . [missing in the original] were present, a total of eleven people. They began to formulate the basic articles of the [platform of the] party they had decided to establish, and they decided that the party would be secret and that it would work for the realization of the Arabs' hopes and their secession from the Ottoman Empire.

Another report said:

> The officer Nuri [al-Sa'id] explained to me that the purpose of these meetings was to found a military party that would strive for the independence of the Arab countries. This party is secret, and he will work to get me accepted to it.

A third report said:

> 'Aziz Bek and his partners swore not to reveal the articles of the party [platform], which will work for the independence of the Arab countries.[13]

The official opening conference of the society took place on 28 October 1913. Many of the members were officers, among them several who would figure prominently in the history of the Arab Middle East: Nuri al-Sa'id, the brothers Yasin and Taha al-Hashimi, Mawlud Mukhlis, Jamil al-Madfa'i, 'Ali Jawdat

al-Ayyubi, Salim al-Jaza'iri, Amin Lutfi al-Hafiz, 'Abdallah al-
Dulaymi, 'Ali al-Nashashibi, and others. Among the civilians
were 'Adil Arslan and Hamdi and Muzahim al-Pachachi. Al-
Misri, who had decided to broaden his society's base, found it
proper to introduce some Turkish officers as well, and even the
Albanian leader Darwish Hayma, but the mixed society did not
last long, and in the end the membership was limited to Arabs.[14]

"A person has nothing except what he toils for (*laysa lil-Insan
illa ma sa'a*)" was the slogan of the society and was also
stamped on its seal. Whoever joined placed his right hand on
the Qur'an and his left hand on a sword or pistol and swore loyalty to the society. As for the society's platform, it seems that
there were differences of opinion between al-Misri and the other
Arab officers. While the reports of the Ottoman spies did indeed
describe a general trend of desire to secede from the Empire and
to strive for the independence of the Arab countries, al-Misri
himself aspired towards a much more grandiose goal: an empire
that would include the Arabs, the Turks, the Albanians, and the
Bulgarians as well as Egypt, his birthplace, Sudan, Libya and
Tunisia. This empire, which would perhaps be called the Eastern
Mediterranean State, would be headed by the Ottoman Sultan as
nominal president, and its regime would be a decentralized one,
based on a federation. The new empire would be divided into
states each with its own parliament, and at the head there would
be a common parliament in Istanbul, the capital of the federal
empire. Each state would have its own government, except for
matters of education, security and foreign affairs, which would
be uniform for the entire empire. The official language of the
federal empire would be Turkish unless the states of the empire
decided on another language. In any case, each state would use
the local language as well. The future empire would have absolute religious tolerance. Al-Misri considered Austria-Hungary a
model for his empire. The Arab countries too would be separate
units in this federation, rather than being encompassed in one
large unit.

The other Arab officers were willing to accept al-Misri's programme in principle, but in a limited form that would include
only Arabs and Turks.' Thus the society's programme was
finally set out in the following form:

Art. 1: *Al-'Ahd* is a secret political society that was established in
    Istanbul, and its goal is to work for internal independence for the
    Arab countries, so that they will remain united with the Istanbul
    government, as Hungary is united with Austria.

Art. 2: The Society is pledged to the Islamic caliphate remaining as a consecrated trust in the hands of the Ottoman dynasty. [According to al-Misri the following should be added here: "On condition that they follow the regime of the English dynasty, that is, a government of the nation and the parliament."]

Art. 3: The Society will devote itself especially to the security of Istanbul against the ambitions of the European countries, since it sees Istanbul as the capital of the East, and the East cannot exist if one of the imperialist Western countries will sever Istanbul from it.

Art. 4: Since the Turks have constituted the front lines in guarding the East from the West for the past 600 years, the Arabs must now prepare themselves to be appropriate reserve forces for these front lines.

Art. 5: The members of al-'Ahd must invest the maximum effort in fostering and propagandizing for high virtues, since a nation cannot preserve its political and national (qawmi) existence if it is not equipped with high moral standards.

Al-Misri dictated the society's programme to Taha al-Hashimi, the society's secretary, and then printed it and gave a copy to Nuri al-Sa'id, who took upon himself the task of recruiting additional Arab officers to the society.[15]

Taha al-Hashimi (1888-1961) made the most important contribution to the opening of al-'Ahd branches outside the capital. In December 1913 he was appointed Chief of Staff of the Ottoman 7th Corps in Yemen. His journey from Istanbul to Yemen was rather indirect. At first he went to Beirut, where he set up a branch of the society headed by Sharif al-Sharif. From there he continued on to Damascus and set up a branch headed by Khalid al-Hakim. Then he proceeded to Mosul, where he gave 'Abdallah al-Dulaymi the task of setting up a local branch. At a conference al-Dulaymi held with the participation of Yasin al-Hashimi, Mawlud Mukhlis, Sharif al-Faruqi, and Dr Da'ud al-Jalabi, a discussion of the injustices of the Turks towards the Arabs and the necessity of spreading the Arab idea among army officers and civilians, was followed by the decision to set up a branch; Yasin al-Hashimi was chosen as its leader. Other Iraqi officers, such as 'Ali Jawdat al-Ayyubi and 'Abd al-Rahman Sharaf, joined, as well as a number of Syrian officers who were serving in Mosul, such as Hasan Fahmi and Sadiq al-Jundi. Contacts between the branch in Mosul and the centre in Istanbul were kept up by Jamil al-Madfa'i, who sent proclamations and manifestos from the centre to Mosul. The Mosul branch also had contacts with the Reform Society of Basra, and Sharaf was sent to Basra to coordinate activities between the branch and that society. The main activists in the Mosul branch were Yasin al-Hashimi, who was the commander of the 12th Corps there and a member of the town council of Mosul, and Mukhlis, an army instructor who also taught geography and history at the town secondary school. These two took advantage of their positions to spread Arab propaganda among the officers and the young.[16]

Al-'Ahd was not the only society in Mosul at that time. In 1914, shortly before the outbreak of the war, a number of civilians in Mosul founded a secret society which strove for Iraqi independence and propagandized against the Turks. It was called al-'Alam (the Flag) as a hint at the Arab flag, and also so that if it were discovered, the founders could tell the authorities that the society's name was al-'Ilm (knowledge), which is spelled the same way in Arabic. The president of the administrative committee of the society was Thabit 'Abd al-Nur, also a member of al-'Ahd, and other committee members included Ra'uf al-Shahwani and Ra'uf al-Ghulami. Although one of the leaders of the society was caught by the authorities, it nevertheless continued to operate on and off during World War I. In May 1919 it became the local branch of al-'Ahd al-'Iraqi, the Iraqi faction of al-'Ahd after the war.[17]

From Mosul Taha al-Hashimi went on to Baghdad, where he established a branch headed by Hamdi al-Pachachi. Among the members were the officers Tahsin 'Ali, Rashid al-Khawja, and 'Abd al-Hamid al-Shaliji, as well as the journalist Ibrahim Hilmi al-'Umar. The members prepared a pretentious programme for liberating the entire region from Ottoman rule, from Mosul in the north to the Persian Gulf in the south. They made contact with such leaders as the Sheikh of Kuwait and, by their own account at least, they received positive replies—except from the pro-Turkish Ibn Rashid. According to their programme the rebellion was to break out in Basra, where the authorities had always had trouble ruling. When military reinforcements were sent to Basra from Baghdad—weakening the army forces in Baghdad—a rebellion would break out in Baghdad as well, and thus they would be able to cut off all the military forces in the Basra region. The rebellion would then spread to Damascus as well, with the cooperation of the local al-'Ahd branch and the assistance of the Druzes and the tribes of central Syria. The Baghdad members intended to offer the leadership of the rebellion to Ibn Sa'ud. But then differences of opinion arose among them over the methods of implementing this programme, and it was suspended. It was decided that the rebellion would begin in the spring of 1915, but by then, of course, it was too late.[18]

Taha al-Hashimi continued from Baghdad on to Basra, where a branch was set up with only one member, Muzahim al-Amin al-Pachachi, who had fled to Basra from Baghdad. Other members of the society who came to Basra for various reasons later joined him. From Basra al-Hashimi went on to Yemen, the end of his long journey, arriving only in the middle of March 1914.[19]

In the meantime, in Istanbul, al-Misri continued trying to broaden the membership of the society by introducing Turkish officers. At the end of 1913 he held a meeting in his house with the participation of officers and civilians, among them many Turks, and described his ideas about federalism in the Empire. Those present expressed sympathy for these ideas, but suddenly one of them arose—Ahmad Agayev, a Turk from Azerbaijan who was one of the leaders of the pan-Turanians—and shouted: "You can be certain that these lowly people you call Arabs or Albanians are nothing. There is nothing except the Turkish race, which rules in Asia because it has more than five million people" (implying that the Chinese were also Turanians). The Albanian member of the society, Darwish Hayma, arose immediately and told Agayev that he was low and despicable. Al-Misri added that if he were not a guest in his home, he would kill him.[20] At this time al-Misri also sent Iraqi officers, led by society member Jamil al-Madfa'i, to threaten the life of 'Abd al-Hamid al-Zahrawi if he refused to stop his contacts with the CUP. Al-Misri considered al-Zahrawi and 'Abd al-Karim al-Khalil traitors because of their attempts to reach an agreement with the CUP people, whom he already considered the enemies of the Arabs.[21]

On 4 January 1914 Enver was appointed war minister, in place of al-Misri's friend 'Izzat Pasha. When Enver, to get al-Misri away from the capital, informed him that he was appointing him commander of the garrison in Ankara, it was too much for al-Misri. While he had only attained the rank of Lieutenant-Colonel, his former classmate as war minister was giving him orders and appointing him to a position under the command of an officer of equal rank (the governor of the town). On 20 January al-Misri sent the war ministry the following letter:

> I am leaving the Ottoman army effective from the present date. Yet I am still strongly attached to it because of my military past. Therefore, if war should break out or the fatherland should be in need of her sons, the war ministry may find me through the Ottoman commissariat in Egypt, my place of residence, to assign me a force which I will be appointed to command.

In reply Enver invited al-Misri for an interview. Another 300 Arab officers (not all society members) came to the war ministry with al-Misri to help him if it should be necessary. The discussion was friendly, but despite Enver's persuasion, al-Misri insisted on resigning. Dr Ibrahim Thabit, a Lebanese who was living in the capital, spread the news that many officers had come to protect al-Misri, citing this as proof that the army sympathized with al-Misri and that he could actually overthrow the government. Upon hearing this Enver, Tal'at and Jamal decided it was time to take further steps.[22]

On 24 January 1914 a special meeting was held in the war ministry, attended by Enver, Jamal, the Director of the General Security Service, 'Azmi Bek, and others. At the end of this meeting the following resolutions were among those decided upon:

1 — . . . b. To employ as spies Arabs who have connections with 'Aziz 'Ali [al-Misri] and his friends. c. To keep them [al-Misri and friends] under surveillance and to find out to what extent they are connected with foreign embassies, especially the French and British embassies. d. To fight against the Arab propagandists for secession from the Ottoman Empire. e. To set up a file for all the Arab leaders opposing CUP policies and to keep them under heavy surveillance. . . .

2 — To send the Arab officers in the capital to various parts of Turkey, and not to authorize the presence of an Arab commander in one centre with Arab officers assisting him. If there is no alternative to the presence of an Arab commander, it is obligatory that his staff officers should be Turks who are trusted by the CUP. No Arab officer with a rank higher than Lieutenant may be permitted in any circumstances to remain in the Arab countries.

3 — Turkish officers will be appointed to be commanders in the Arab countries. In order that this step will not arouse the Arabs, the Arab officers must be removed gradually from the Arab countries, by promoting them to a higher rank, which will serve as an excuse for their transfer from an Arab country to a Turkish country.

4 — To implement the policy of Turkification of all the non-Turkish races in the country by eliminating the nationalist societies that were founded in it . . .[23]

Immediately after the meeting Enver started to implement the resolutions. He removed more than 300 Arab officers to Anatolia, Thrace and Gallipoli, and, in order that they should not complain, he promoted them in rank. In addition he dismissed some 1,100 officers, claiming that they had failed in their tasks in the Balkan War, that they were not efficient and that they were too old.[24] Now it remained to take care of al-Misri himself. The

Ottoman security services had collected all their data on *al-'Ahd*, and it was decided to arrest him. But it was not in their interest to reveal publicly that the reason was his activities in *al-'Ahd*; publicizing the existence of an Arab society composed mainly of officers and striving for the autonomy of the Arab countries would certainly not help the CUP to suppress all such notions among the Arabs. After al-Misri's return from Libya rumours had circulated about inappropriate conduct on his part in Cyrenaica. Al-Misri had asked the previous war minister, 'Izzat Pasha, to conduct an enquiry and his name was cleared. (It may be assumed that the friendship between al-Misri and 'Izzat Pasha played some role in this conclusion.) The authorities now decided to renew the claim that al-Misri had embezzled state funds while he was in Libya as the justification for his arrest, as it was true in itself, even though they could have arrested him for this half a year earlier, before *al-'Ahd* had been founded.[25]

Al-Misri had just finished lunch at the Tokatlian Hotel on 9 February 1914 when he was surrounded by three agents of the secret police who told him that the Istanbul police inspector wanted to see him. Taken to the Istanbul police station, al-Misri was received by the police inspector after a five-hour wait and told that a warrant had been issued for his arrest. His pistol was taken away and he was put in the war ministry prison to await trial by a military court.[26]

His Arab friends soon began to appear at the police station to enquire about his arrest. The Director of the General Security Service received them politely and told them that al-Misri had not been arrested but only been asked to answer some questions about military matters and would be released in the evening. At midnight, when they saw that al-Misri had not been released, Jamil al-Madfa'i went to al-Zahrawi's home to inform him that the Arabs, both civilians and soldiers, were very angry, and to ask him to relay to the government "that our blood, the blood of the Arabs, must be preserved for the defence of the fatherland, and that it [the government] will not force us to spill this blood for the sake of individuals". When al-Zahrawi, who probably did not want to get involved with the officers again, tried to find out from Tal'at what had happened, he was told that Tal'at was not at home. After a meeting the next day held by al-Misri's friends to discuss what steps to take, a delegation of Literary Club members, led by Husayn Haydar, asked Jamal and Tal'at to intervene. The latter calmed them by saying that al-Misri was only being interrogated about military matters, and besides, the government had decided to appoint him Vali of Basra.

Al-Misri was actually not interrogated at all during the period of his detention in the war ministry prison, except for one occasion on which he was asked if he knew anything about a plan to incite the Arabs against the Ottoman Empire. After a few days he was permitted to receive visitors and his cell was full of well-wishers from then on. Thus one day, when Dr Ibrahim Thabit came to visit him, al-Misri was able to pass him a note on which was written: "Today a friend who is a senior member of the CUP visited me, revealed to me that there will be an attempt on my life tonight, and gave me a pistol to defend myself." Al-Misri's friends immediately gathered together at the home of Sulayman Faydi, then a representative of Basra in the parliament, to discuss the steps they should take to save al-Misri's life. Present at this meeting, in addition to Faydi, were Nuri al-Sa'id, Thabit 'Abd al-Nur, 'Abdallah al-Damluji, 'Adil Arslan, As'ad Daghir and Isma'il al-Saffar. At the suggestion of 'Abd al-Nur, a special car was prepared for an attempt to smuggle al-Misri out of the prison. But the plan was hopeless, and instead 'Abd al-Nur and two others were entrusted with the task of telling the foreign embassies in Istanbul and Marshal Liman von Sanders, the German inspector of the Ottoman army, of the plan to assassinate al-Misri and claim afterwards that he had committed suicide. The British ambassador and von Sanders did actually intervene afterwards on al-Misri's behalf. In addition, a special messenger was sent to Bucharest to telegraph from there to Sharif Husayn of Mecca and to Sayyid Talib of Basra with a request for help. As a consequence of the ensuing uproar, the plan to kill al-Misri was dropped.[27]

Al-Misri's arrest aroused outrage in Egypt, for he was considered a national hero there because of his victories over the Italians in Libya. The Egyptians' view was that Enver was taking advantage of his status as war minister to settle accounts with al-Misri out of personal animosity towards him, which stemmed from the time of their joint military service in Libya, and out of jealousy of his military achievements. This view was expressed in most of Egypt's newspapers and generated public opinion that was hostile to the Empire.

The Decentralization Party too took action on al-Misri's behalf, and on 26 March a conference of notables was held at the home of the Sheikh of al-Azhar Mosque to discuss ways of saving al-Misri's life. Among the speakers was Rashid Rida, who contended that even if al-Misri had committed a serious crime, he should be pardoned because of his activities on behalf of the constitutional government at the time of the repression of the counter-revolution in 1909, his work for the achievement of a treaty with the Imam of Yemen, and his actions against the Italians in Libya. Rida's suggestion that those present should send a telegram to the Sultan raising these points was not accepted, and instead a telegram was sent to the Grand Vizier expressing the stand of the Egyptian nation on the al-Misri affair. It elicited a laconic response from Enver: "The military court is absolutely independent and not the slightest influence is effective there!!" When it became known in mid-April that al-Misri had been condemned to death, the outrage in Egypt grew stronger. A number of Cairenes sent a telegram "in the name of four hundred thousand people" to British Foreign Minister Grey, requesting Britain to intervene to eliminate this injustice, which they attributed only to Enver's hatred, arguing that if the accusations that had been raised at his trial were true, al-Misri would not have been allowed to remain at liberty for seven months before being arrested. Other Egyptian notables appealed to Lord Kitchener to ask King George V to intervene. There were also Egyptians who turned to the Ottoman commissioner in Cairo, warning him that this affair would lead to serious consequences in the Empire's relations with Egypt and the Arab countries.[28]

Protests streamed into the capital from other places as well. Sharif Husayn of Mecca expressed his bitterness. Sayyid Talib of Basra announced that he would overthrow the government's forces in Basra with the assistance of Ibn Sa'ud. The signatories of a letter from Yemen protested against the scandalous treatment al-Misri had received. In Paris, 'Awni 'Abd al-Hadi gathered together a number of his friends, who sent protest telegrams to the Sublime Porte and even turned to the important newspapers in the city to protest to them as well.[29]

Al-Misri's trial began on 25 March 1914. The president of the military court was a general and another ten officers sat with him as judges. During the course of four sessions, twenty different accusations were levelled against al-Misri. The principal accusation was that he had embezzled 30,000 Turkish liras which he had received from Enver before the latter had left Libya. Asked to explain, Al-Misri claimed that he had never received such a large sum, that the money he had in his possession had been needed to cover debts left by Enver, and that what had been left had not been sufficient to cover expenses, so that he had been forced to collect taxes even within the army in order to pay for organizing its activities. Al-Misri was also accused of insulting Turkish officers and forcing them to return to Istanbul, of provoking al-Sanusi's hostility, and of freeing

Husayn Bisekri, an Italian spy, after the latter had been sentenced to death by a military court—he claimed that the man
had not been an Italian spy at all.

At the session held on 1 April the prosecution witnesses gave
the following testimony:

> Sulayman al-'Askari: 'Aziz 'Ali's way of thinking is opposed to Otto-
> man interests. While he was in Tripoli (Libya) he tried to spread the
> Arab idea among the local residents and to establish an independent
> Arab state that he would administer. He would have succeeded in his
> efforts if not for my opposition and that of a number of Turkish offi-
> cers.
> Ramzi al-Mahdawi: 'Aziz Bek held an important meeting with the
> Italians during the war, but I do not know what they talked about.
> Diya Efendi: 'Aziz Bek is an enemy of the Turks in general and of
> Enver Pasha in particular. He is a traitor to the Turkish Empire.
> Mulazim Nur al-Din: 'Aziz Bek reached an agreement with Imam
> Yahya to implement a joint programme whose aim was to annex
> Yemen to Egypt. While in Benghazi he strove to carry out that idea
> and to turn Benghazi and Yemen into one Arab state.

Here al-Misri responded that the idea was absolutely ridiculous
and he asked the judges how they thought he could have carried
this out.

> Rashid Efendi: 'Aziz Bek expressed happiness and satisfaction at
> what had happened to the Muslims in the Balkans. He slaughtered a
> number of Arabs in Benghazi and buried tens of others alive.

Here al-Misri explained the circumstances of the battle he had
waged against the tribesmen at the time he had left Libya.

At the court session that was held on 4 April two additional
prosecution witnesses gave their testimony:

> Almas (a Negro slave): I heard in Barqa that 'Aziz Bek had received
> no less than 15,000 pounds from the Italians for ceding them the
> country.
> Qasim (al-Misri's coffee server in Libya): The Egyptian khedive sent
> a man named Hasan Hamada to 'Aziz Bek to negotiate with him
> concerning the ceding of the country to the Italians.[30]

Al-Misri was sentenced to death.

At this stage Louis Mallet, the British ambassador in Istanbul,
entered the picture. As early as three days after al-Misri's arrest,
al-Misri's brother-in-law, the governor of Cairo, had beseeched
Lord Kitchener to ask the ambassador in Istanbul to act on al-
Misri's behalf. The governor had promised that he would

personally guarantee that if al-Misri were returned to Egypt he would not intervene any more in Libyan affairs. When the British ambassador in turn went to the Grand Vizier, he was met with the explanation that in fact al-Misri had not been arrested because of his activities in Libya, but because of his activities against the government since his return to Istanbul. The Grand Vizier ridiculed the Cairo governor's promise and said that al-Misri might not intervene in Libya any more, but he would almost certainly intervene in other Arab regions. The British ambassador, who had heard rumours about al-'Ahd's programmes in Iraq, was apprehensive about intervening too far in the affair, lest the impression be created that Britain had any part in al-'Ahd's activities. In late February and early March the ambassador continued his quiet, unofficial contacts with Tal'at and the Grand Vizier, in an attempt to convince them that the affair was creating a bad impression in Egypt, so that even if al-Misri was guilty it would be better to exile him to Egypt in exchange for a promise that he would never return to Istanbul, and thus end the affair. The ambassador stopped his contacts until the end of March, when he found out—before the trial was even completed—that it had been decided to sentence al-Misri to death. The ambassador once again warned the Grand Vizier of the consequences for public opinion in Britain and in Egypt were such a sentence to be executed. The Grand Vizier expressed his contempt for Egyptian public opinion and for the Egyptian government's promise that al-Misri would no longer be involved in Arab affairs, but he noted that if, on the other hand, Britain would guarantee it, this would be a different matter. When in early April—still before the end of the trial—the ambassador met with Tal'at again, the latter was able to tell him that al-Misri would be pardoned. The ambassador wanted to continue to work for al-Misri's complete release, but this Enver stubbornly opposed.[31]

On 14 April Tal'at told the British ambassador that it had been decided to commute al-Misri's death sentence to 15 years' imprisonment at hard labour, hinting that there was a chance that the sentence would be reduced further. On 15 April the war ministry made an official announcement that in the light of complaints that had been received against 'Abd al-'Aziz Bey, the former commander of Benghazi, he had been court-martialled and found guilty of the following: 1. The arbitrary freeing of Husayn Bisekri, who had been found guilty of spying. 2. Causing a clash between al-Sanusi's men and soldiers, as a result of which soldiers were killed and injured. 3. Retreating in opposition to orders in the battle of Shuwaymar and thus causing the death of officers and soldiers. 4. Taking 30,000 Turkish liras of government money and using them for his personal expenses. 5. Causing a rift between Ottoman subjects and the Muslim nation. For these crimes the court had decided to sentence him to death, but an imperial edict had commuted the sentence to the penalty of 15 years' imprisonment at hard labour. The British ambassador went once again to the Grand Vizier and asked him to work for al-Misri's complete release, which, he claimed, would end the accusations that public opinion was levelling at Enver.[32]

Not only foreign diplomatic circles intervened on behalf of al-Misri. Philip Graves, *The Times'* correspondent in Istanbul, published frequent articles on al-Misri's behalf in his paper, influencing public opinion in his favour. He also went to Jamal with a copy of a telegram he had sent to London with arguments on al-Misri's behalf, and added that he had a great many more things to say on this issue. Though Jamal "looked black", he promised to discuss the matter with Enver, who he said had already decided to pardon al-Misri in any case. Georges Rémond, a French journalist who had covered the war in Libya, went to Jamal as well, in an attempt to convince him of the absurdity of the claims against al-Misri and inform him of the damage that this sentence was causing to the Arab world's attitude towards the Empire—the evidence being the many protest telegrams that were arriving in the capital. At a party that Jamal and Enver attended at that time at the French ambassador's residence, many people approached the former, Rémond among them, with the request that he intervene on al-Misri's behalf. Jamal was apparently more aware of the public mood than Enver and wrote him the following note:

> Notwithstanding all the evidence which the court martial has accumulated against Asis Ali Bey, and the fact that sentence has been passed upon him, it is you whom public opinion condemns. Your condemnation in this way will do you a thousand times more harm than anything Asis Ali Bey will suffer from a few years in prison. Please try and get him the Imperial pardon and I will take good care that he leaves Constantinople, and never returns to Constantinople.[33]

On the next day, 20 April, Enver informed Jamal that he had requested and received a complete pardon for al-Misri from the Sultan. On 21 April al-Misri was released from prison, brought for an interview with Enver, and told to leave immediately for Egypt and to pledge never to intervene again in the affairs of the Ottoman Empire (an obligation that al-Misri apparently never

intended to keep). The next day he set sail for Alexandria on a
Romanian ship, arriving there on 26 April to a mass welcome.[34]

After al-Misri left Istanbul the al-'Ahd centre in the capital
was left without a leader to organize it and preserve its unity.
The Ottoman security services did not consider al-Misri's depor-
tation sufficient, and dealt the society additional blows. Society
members Rashid al-Khawja and 'Abd al-Latif al-Fallahi were
called to Istanbul from Iraq for interrogation. When they arrived
in Beirut on their way to the capital, they succeeded in escaping
with the assistance of the local police inspector. Nuri al-Sa'id
and 'Abdallah al-Damluji, warned that they were about to be
arrested, fled from Istanbul to Cairo on a French ship and
joined al-Misri. The authorities handed out a death sentence to
al-Sa'id in his absence for desertion from the army.

In Cairo al-Misri came to the decision that he must gain the
cooperation of Ibn Sa'ud of Najd, put him at the head of the
Arab movement and organize his army. This task was given to
Nuri al-Sa'id and 'Abdallah al-Damluji, who left Cairo for Basra
at the end of May 1914. Arriving in Basra in mid-June, they
received the patronage of Sayyid Talib. Ibn Sa'ud, to whom they
wrote about their mission, invited them to Riyad. At this point
Talib intervened and expressed his dissatisfaction, apparently
because he considered establishing such contacts as his preroga-
tive. Al-Sa'id gave in, but al-Damluji went on to Riyad, where
he remained in the service of Ibn Sa'ud during the following
years.

Al-Sa'id went south instead, to the Sultan of Masqat, who
invited him to come and help him organize his army. Al-Sa'id
wanted to recruit the Sultan to the Arab movement, but just as
he arrived in Masqat he heard about the assassination in Sara-
jevo and returned immediately to Basra, and from there went on
to Baghdad in disguise. In Baghdad he met with officers who
were members of the society and suggested that they instigate an
Arab rebellion. While al-Sa'id was certain that the Empire's
entry into the war was tantamount to suicide, in the end the
officers decided to wait and see how events would develop.
Al-Sa'id returned to Basra and wrote a detailed memorandum
concerning the intentions of the British in Iraq. It was sent by
Talib to Istanbul and gained al-Sa'id a pardon from the death
sentence that had been imposed on him. A few days after his
return to Basra al-Sa'id contracted a lung disease and was hospi-
talized in the American Hospital there, where he remained until
Basra was captured by the British. After the British occupation
al-Sa'id met with Percy Cox, the Chief Political Officer of the

British invasion force, to discuss the plans of the Arabs, on the
one hand, and the state of his health, on the other. Al-Sa'id's
request to return to Baghdad was denied by the British, for they
reasoned that because the Ottoman authorities knew him he
would not be able to work there as a spy. His suggestion of
touring the Euphrates and persuading officers and tribal chiefs to
oppose the Ottomans was also rejected. In early 1915 al-Sa'id
was tranferred to India.[35]

With the outbreak of World War I in Europe al-Misri began
contacts with the British authorities in Egypt. At the beginning
of August he told one of the British officials that Enver had
asked him to return to Istanbul and to organize a joint Arab-
Turkish action against the British. Al-Misri pointed out that he
had rejected this offer, and then he suggested to the British official that an Arab empire should be established under British
control, requesting for this purpose assistance to lead the Arab
tribes in Iraq and Syria against the Ottomans. The response of
the British Foreign Office was that al-Misri should be firmly
instructed to cease his activities with regard to Arab affairs and
to leave the Arabs alone. The task was entrusted to Captain
Russell of Military Intelligence. At a meeting with al-Misri, al-
Misri told him that he was the representative of a society centred
in Baghdad and that he had been given the task of investigating
the intentions of the British government with regard to the
establishment of an independent Arab state under British protection. Such a state would include all the Arabic-speaking areas
and its northern border would be Alexandretta-Mosul-the Persian border. Al-Misri said that his society was completely free of
religious leanings and did not aspire to an Arab caliphate; for
this reason it had not yet succeeded in recruiting "fanatics" like
Rashid Rida. His plans for rebellion were based on the Arab
forces in Baghdad, Najd and Syria, and he believed that the
Druzes and the Christians would join as well. He asked for British assistance, both money and arms (including fast-shooting
mountain guns) and promised in return that Britain would be
given favoured status by the future state. He added that this
assistance would guarantee Britain that it would never have to
withstand a rebellion in Persia or in India. The last assertion was
not particularly convincing, and the British officer noted that
Britain's involvement in such a programme might cause it more
harm than good. He added that Britain considered the present
time inappropriate for such a programme, and since al-Misri's
society could not act without Britain's goodwill, it would be better for him not to try to push Britain into action against its will,

lest he lose this goodwill. It was after this conversation that al-Misri told the members of *al-'Ahd* in the Empire—those that he succeeded in contacting—not to begin any hostile actions against the Ottomans that might help bring about the occupation of the region by a foreign power. They could begin such actions only after there was a guarantee that such a foreign takeover would not occur.[36]

Towards the end of October the British had already changed their attitude towards al-Misri, and Lieutenant-Colonel Clayton, the Director of Military and Political Intelligence, met him for a secret conversation. Clayton asked if the Arabs would join the Turks—if and when the Empire entered the war—in spite of their dislike for the Turks and their desire for autonomy. Al-Misri replied that at present the Arabs were not organized and would therefore join the strongest force, which in their opinion was the Empire. He added that the Turks had recently tried to win the sympathy of the Arabs by granting them positions, and had actually succeeded in this, at least to a degree. Al-Misri then turned to his plans for carrying out an organized rebellion in Iraq. He told Clayton that he would sell his property in Egypt, charter a ship and sail for Basra, where his friends were, and there he would be able to organize within a month a force of 15,000 men who would start a rebellion which other Arab leaders would later join. Britain would have to guarantee to provide money, rifles, ammunition and artillery. Al-Misri nevertheless opposed the possibility that Britain would also provide soldiers, lest this create the impression that Britain was interested in annexing Iraq. He also suggested that, together with the declaration of war against the Empire, Britain should carry out military operations in the Persian Gulf as well, as this would force the Empire to leave large military forces in Iraq, from which he hoped to get men for his plans. Al-Misri noted with sarcasm that it would have been worthwhile to begin preparations for these plans a few months earlier, but then the British were not even willing to listen. He concluded by saying that before starting to carry out this programme he would have to contact his friends in Iraq so that they could update him concerning the situation there. Clayton replied that in the then situation, when Britain had not yet declared war on the Empire, a programme of the type that al-Misri had suggested could not be implemented.[37]

By the middle of November, after Britain had invaded Iraq, the attitude of the British Foreign Office to al-Misri's plans was completely different. The British foreign minister told his representatives in Cairo that they could give al-Misri 2,000 pounds

sterling for organizational purposes, as well as all the additional
help he might require. Al-Misri, when he met with the British
representatives again, told them that he did not need money at
the moment, but had to contact his friends who were in Basra,
preferably Nuri al-Sa'id, but if he could not be located, then
Muzahim al-Amin al-Pachachi or 'Abdallah al-Damluji. He suggested that they should locate them through Sayyid Talib, asking
the British to tell them that "their friend in Egypt" wanted them
to prepare information "on all points" and go to Muhammara
with their ciphers. At this juncture a new obstacle appeared in
al-Misri's path. Iraq was within the domain of responsibility not
of the British Foreign Office, but of the India Office, which
asked the Foreign Office to delay al-Misri's departure for Basra
until they received the opinion of the British authorities in Basra
on the matter. The issue was brought to the attention of Percy
Cox in Basra, who replied that Talib and al-Damluji were
presently staying with Ibn Sa'ud. Al-Sa'id and al-Pachachi were
indeed in Basra, but the opinions of these "Young Arabs" were
not appropriate to the backward tribes of Iraq. Therefore the
plan was not practical and al-Misri should be prevented from
leaving Egypt. As a result of Cox's standpoint, which was supported by the Viceroy of India, the British foreign minister told
his representatives in Cairo that they should stop promoting al-
Misri's plans.[38]

   Al-Misri was not prepared to give up so easily. In early
December he spoke with Philip Graves, *The Times*' correspondent who had intervened on his behalf in Istanbul, and expressed
his opposition to the annexation of Iraq by the British. He suggested instead that the British should establish in Iraq a state
that would extend from the Persian Gulf to Armenia and Anatolia and assist the populace in organizing it in the modern manner. He explained that he was aware that the establishment of
such a state required a great deal of work and that it would
therefore be necessary for Britain to continue its military occupation of Iraq for a long time. He was also aware that the new
state would be dependent on British India economically and
financially. Nevertheless, the establishment of such a state was
preferable, in his opinion, to complete annexation. If the British
promised not to annex Iraq, al-Misri promised on his part that
he would go to Iraq and persuade the Arab officers in the Ottoman army to desert and the tribal chiefs not to resist the British,
by arousing Arab nationalist feelings against the Turks. Al-Misri
contended that without this assistance on his part the British
forces advancing to Baghdad would encounter stubborn

resistance on the part of the Arab and Kurdish soldiers in the Ottoman army, who would then remain loyal to the Empire in its war against the British invaders in spite of their complaints against the Ottoman authorities.[39]

These plans of al-Misri's were not adopted by the British. However, many exploits were ahead of him during the war, in the Arab revolt of Sharif Husayn of Mecca and after the war, until the revolution of the Free Officers in Egypt. *Al-'Ahd*, too, would write an important chapter in the history of the Fertile Crescent after World War I.

Chapter 25

THE ARAB REVOLUTIONARY SOCIETY

Haqqi al-'Azm, secretary of the Decentralization Party, decided during the early months of 1914 that it was necessary to act more aggressively towards the Ottoman authorities and not be satisfied with demands for reforms or decentralization. The relations between him and the rest of the Decentralization Party leadership cooled somewhat as a result of the affair of al-Zahrawi's appointment to the senate; the majority of the party's leaders had been prepared to authorize this appointment after the fact, while al-'Azm, strongly opposed, considered al-Zahrawi a traitor. When 'Aziz 'Ali al-Misri arrived in Cairo at the end of April 1914, full of rage about the attitude towards him in Istanbul in spite of his past services to the Empire, al-'Azm found him a suitable partner for the founding of the new Arab Revolutionary Society (al-Jam'iyya al-Thawriyya al-'Arabiyya). Its purpose was to struggle against the Turks and to incite the Arabs to revolt against them. At a meeting held at al-'Azm's home, it was decided that the establishment of the society should remain secret until the process of its founding and organization was completed. Among the few members of the society were Fu'ad al-Khatib, an Arabic teacher at the Gordon College in Khartoum who was vacationing in Cairo at the time, and Dr 'Izzat al-Jundi, both of whom were also members of the Decentralization Party. The al-Mihmisani brothers of Beirut also knew of the society's existence. Haqqi al-'Azm did not bother to reveal it to his cousin Rafiq al-'Azm, since the latter had already expressed his opposition to revolutionary societies of this nature.[1]

Immediately after its founding, the society distributed a proclamation condemning the Ottoman authorities for imprisoning al-Misri in spite of his 20-year army service, while Enver, who was no better than al-Misri but a Turk, had been promoted to war minister. They had sentenced al-Misri to death oblivious to the many protests, and the fact that he was saved in the end "was not due to the will of the Muslims and did not arise from honouring the feelings of the Arabs, whose wishes and feelings are not worth a piastre in the eyes of this miserable Empire, but

due to the will of another man who does not wear a tarbush . . .
This is the truth . . . If not for Britain 'Aziz would not have
been released from prison. But not all of our officers who will be
put in prison will be noticed by Britain, nor will the world hear
their voices." Attacking further the attitude of the Turks towards
the Arabs, the proclamation ended with an appeal to the Arab
officers:

> You, the officers . . . The enemy is not without but within . . . We
> must hold the opinion that we have no government over us, but we
> are among enemies and under the flag of a state that is not ours . . .
> If we kill three Valis in each vilayet, one after another, then anyone
> appointed Vali in our country will be terrified, and none of them will
> come to us, unless he decides to honour us, to grant our wishes and
> to act according to our interests. Where are the young people who
> will sacrifice themselves for their nation? Here are the Valis of Beirut
> and Damascus, both oppressors and robbers — why do you not kill
> them?[2]

One of the society's preferred methods of attacking the Ottoman Empire was accusing it of contempt for the Islamic religion.
In a letter to a friend in the Empire, al-Misri wrote: "In
conclusion, we instruct you to order brother . . . [missing in the
original] to find us a Qawm Jadid and a [Turkish] translation of
the Qur'an and other abominations of this sort, and to send
them to us at the earliest opportunity because we have a great
need of them . . ."[3] Qawm Jadid was a collection of speeches
given by Sheikh 'Ubaydallah, an extreme Turkish nationalist of
Afghan origin, in the Aya Sofia mosque in Istanbul. The book,
expressing the sheikh's opinions on matters of Islam and the status of the Turks, was considered by the Arabs to be one of the
most offensive at that time, and they frequently cited it to illus-
trate the hostile attitude of the Turks towards them. The translation of the Qur'an into Turkish—which in the end was not
carried out during the period under discussion—had been suggested time and again by the Turkish nationalists, arousing great
rage among the Arabs, who considered it an act of heresy.

The society's main and perhaps its only activity was the distribution of manifestos. Generally written by Haqqi al-'Azm, these
were sent through the French postal system to Mahmud al-
Mihmisani in Beirut for distribution within the Empire. For
security reasons they were called "the Baghdad merchandise" in
correspondence between the two. On at least one occasion
al-'Azm asked al-Mihmisani to send some of the manifestos he
had received from Egypt back to newspapers there, apparently in

order to give the impression that the source of these manifestos was a rebellious movement within the Empire. The Ottoman authorities discovered the source of the society's manifestos and asked their commissariat in Cairo to take action against al-'Azm. The Egyptian government rejected the request to put al-'Azm on trial for the crime of distributing revolutionary manifestos within the Empire, but at the same time one of its officials hinted to al-'Azm that he should remove every bit of suspicious evidence that he was the one responsible for their distribution, advice that the worried al-'Azm indeed followed, destroying all the manifestos in his possession at that time.[4] After a few weeks, however, the distribution of the manifestos began again.

A manifesto that the society distributed in thousands of copies to "the Arabs, the sons of Qahtan", and which had repercussions in Istanbul, turned to the Arabs with a call to awaken from their slumbers:

> When will you open your eyes . . . ? When will you understand the truth? When will you realize that your country has been sold to a stranger? . . . How long will you not understand that you have become a toy in the hands of those who have no other religion than killing the Arabs and despoiling their property? . . . Your country, in their opinion, is a mortgaged field which they inherited from their fathers, and its inhabitants are despised slaves to them.

The Arabs were called upon to emulate the Armenians, who had achieved administrative independence, and to stop being killed for the sake of the Turks in wars that were not theirs. The Turks were trying, the manifesto claimed, to create rifts between the Arab leaders. They had started quarrels between Yahya and al-Idrisi, between Ibn Sa'ud and Ibn Rashid, and between Sharif Husayn and 'Asir and Najd. They were sending governors whose task was to suppress the Arabs, such as 'Arif al-Mardini, Bakr Sami and Jawid Pasha. These governors were continuing in the path of Genghis Khan and Hulagu, and like them they wanted to destroy Arab culture. "What is the meaning of a life which passes in degradation and submissiveness, without honour and without property, and without the enjoyment of liberty and independence?" asked the manifesto. The alternative was:

> Arise, O Arabs! Draw the sword from its sheath, Qahtanians! Do not allow an oppressor and a tyrant who despises you to remain in your country! Cleanse your country of those who demonstrate hate for you, your race and your language . . . Be of one mind with the fellow members of your race and your fatherland in the Syrian and Iraqi

vilayets. Let your Muslims, your Christians and your Jews act together for the good of the nation and the land. You live in one country, you work one land and you speak one language. Therefore be one nation and work in complete agreement.

According to the manifesto, the government of the Empire was not an Islamic government:

How [could it be] if it destroys Islam, permits the shedding of the blood of the nation of Islam's prophet, and acts to destroy the language of Islam?! . . . Whoever wants proofs of this has in front of him the book *Qawm Jadid* by 'Ubaydallah, the stooge of the CUP.

The manifesto exhorted the Christians and the Jews to join the struggle: "Work together with your brothers, the Muslim Arabs! . . . They are your brothers in nationalism (*wataniyya*) and in race (*jinsiyya*)," and it concluded:

Know that a *fida'ic* society has been founded that will kill anyone who fights against the Arabs and opposes Arab reform. And this reform is not on a basis of decentralization . . . but on a basis of complete independence and the establishment of a decentralized Arab state, which will bring back our glory as of old, and every district within it will be ruled by a self-government, as is appropriate for it.[5]

In June 1914 another manifesto of the society arrived through foreign post offices and was distributed throughout Beirut. Packages of manifestos were put into the mailboxes of two of the foreign colleges in the city, arousing suspicion that the students there were involved in circulating them. An attempt to distribute these manifestos through the British postal system as well failed when a postal official turned over a package of 100 to the consul-general, who confiscated them. The manifesto protested the CUP's disavowal of the Paris agreement, describing this as "putting salt on a wound". CUP members were called liars and the Empire described as collapsing. The manifesto called upon the Arabs to follow the example of the many nations that had already succeeded in freeing themselves from the Turkish yoke, such as the Balkan nations, which were no better than the Arabs—on the contrary, the Arabs were more advanced. They had believed until now that the Turks would implement reforms, but no longer! The Arab movement "will not be halted by the plots of the politicians and they will shake the foundations of the Empire, until the Arab flag will wave in the country over all its inhabitants".[6]

A few days later 400 copies of another society manifesto appeared in Damascus. The Vali warned the manager of the Damascus post office not to allow the distribution of such manifestos, and permitted him to open every suspicious package that arrived. During August the manifesto was distributed in Beirut as well. It accused the Ottoman government of responsibility for all the military defeats of the Empire—"The Turks alone are the cause of all these disasters"—and accused it of selling parts of the Empire to foreigners:

> Do you know about Jawid, the Turks' broker, who has auctioned off your country in the markets of Europe? . . . Or do you know that the money for education that is collected in your country is used to send the sons of the Turks, the Armenians and the Jews to Europe, while your sons are deprived of this? . . . Have you seen how they caused your congress in Paris to fail, did not give a hoot for what they had promised you and made a joke of you? . . . Enough suffering! Arise and establish societies and bands to punish the aggressors and liberate yourselves from the oppressors.

How could the Ottoman government be an Islamic one, demanded the manifesto, when it allowed the Zionist invaders to buy the land of Jerusalem and Palestine? The practical conclusion, therefore, was that in the first stage the Arabs must refuse to pay taxes, using the money to buy arms with which to drive away the destroyers of their land.[7]

Haqqi al-'Azm, author of these manifestos, also expressed his feelings towards the Turks and the CUP government in a letter he sent at the beginning of World War I to his friend Jamil al-Rafi'i, an Arab activist from Tripoli who was living in Khartoum at the time. Al-'Azm denounced the Empire's entry into the war on the side of Germany and ridiculed the Turkish propaganda that promised to liberate Egypt, Libya, Tunisia, Algeria and Morocco. He found it very amusing that the CUP had suddenly remembered to renew its Islam and was talking about "the religion of Islam" and "the Islamic union". The letter ended with a prayer to Allah to protect the Arabs from the madness of the Turks and the CUP together.[8]

Part III

THE ARAB SOCIETIES: AN ANALYSIS

Chapter 26

IDEOLOGY

It has become accepted to draw a distinction among the nationalist movements of the modern Arab Middle East between particularist patriotic movements, called *wataniyya*—that is,
movements based on a specific territorial region, *watan* (fatherland), such as Lebanon and Syria—and the pan-Arab nationalist
movement, called *qawmiyya*, based on *qawm* (nation), in this
case the Arab nation. It is very doubtful whether the conceptual
division of *qawmiyya* versus *wataniyya* was really valid during
the period in which the nationalist movements were forming in
the Arab Middle East—the end of the nineteenth and beginning
of the twentieth centuries—without disavowing the very possibility of the existence of local nationalist movements versus a pan-
Arab movement. Moreover, the entire distinction between
nationalism versus patriotism (which underlies the Arabic translation of *qawmiyya* versus *wataniyya*) is actually a distinction of
European origin, and it is doubtful whether it can be applied to
the Arab Middle East in the period under discussion.

In the platforms of the societies, the declarations of their
members, and the like, the term most frequently used was *wataniyya*. It is repeated dozens of times, sometimes with the meaning of patriotism, sometimes with the meaning of nationalism,
and sometimes with other meanings. The term *qawmiyya* is very
rare, and when it appears its meaning is not necessarily nationalism. One might conclude from the frequency of the term *wataniyya* as opposed to the almost total absence of *qawmiyya* that it
was patriotism that reigned in the Arab Middle East of the late
nineteenth and early twentieth centuries. But this is not so. The
very fact that the term *wataniyya* appears almost exclusively, and
that it sometimes appears in a sense quite close to nationalism,
suggests that in this period the term had a different meaning for
the Arabs of the Middle East than patriotism in its European
sense. That is, behind the term *wataniyya*, among the Syrians,
for example, stood not only the Syrian fatherland (*watan*),
within certain distinct boundaries, but also the Syrian nation.

The distinction which should be used in the study of the nationalist movements in the Arab Middle East of this period is thus between Arabism (or pan-Arabism) and Lebanonism, Syrianism, and so forth, and not between nationalism and patriotism or *qawmiyya* versus *wataniyya*—terms of European origin whose current use in the Middle East began in a much later period.

ARABISM

Examination of the names of the 20-odd societies surveyed in the previous chapters, from the "Arab Revival" to those active at the outbreak of World War I, reveals that only in five of them does the word *'arabi* appear: *al-Nahda al-'Arabiyya* (whose name was later changed to *al-Nahda al-Suriyya*), *al-Ikha' al-'Arabi al-'Uthmani*, *Jam'iyyat al-Umma al-'Arabiyya al-Fatat* (whose name was later shortened to *al-Fatat*), *al-Jami'a al-'Arabiyya*, and *al-Jam'iyya al-Thawriyya al-'Arabiyya*. This finding in itself is not a proof of anything, but it provides enough evidence for a preliminary suggestion that Arabism was not the only idea, and perhaps not even the main idea, that stirred those Arabs who had had enough of the Ottoman rule.

It seems that the first figure in the modern age to call upon the Arabs as Arabs to secede from the Ottoman Empire was the exiled Maronite leader Yusuf Karam, who wrote to Amir 'Abd al-Qadir al-Jaza'iri at the time of the 1877-78 war between the Ottoman Empire and Russia about the rights of the Arab race and the necessity for the Arabs to attain independence. His alternative to association with the Ottoman Empire was the establishment of an Arab confederation, each unit of which would be headed by an independent amir.

Jamal al-Din al-Afghani and Muhammad 'Abduh cannot be included among the heralds of the Arab idea. Nevertheless they contributed, however indirectly, to the shaping of the technical framework for the Arab movement over the long term, through their call (especially al-Afghani's) for revolutionary activism that would be expressed in the struggle against European imperialism and also against tyrannical local rulers. It was 'Abd al-Rahman al-Kawakibi who took a clear step forward in the direction of the Arab idea in calling for a renewal of the world of Islam through a transfer of its centre of gravity to the Arabs. However, even al-Kawakibi cannot be considered an Arab nationalist; he did indeed awaken Arab consciousness with his ideas, but for him the Arabs were not the end but rather the means for attaining it. He presented 26 reasons why it was precisely the Arabs who were fit to gradually eliminate the weakness of the world of Islam. Al-Kawakibi's line of thought was continued within the younger generation by Muhibb al-Din al-Khatib, who, in accordance with what he had learned from his spiritual teacher Sheikh Tahir al-Jaza'iri, believed that the Arabs were the first to spread Islam at every time and place, and that "if any barrier is placed between Islam and Arabism, Arabism becomes like a body without a soul and Islam like a soul without a body".

The first true pan-Arab nationalist was apparently Najib 'Azuri, who publicly advocated the secession of all the Arabs from the Ottoman Empire and the establishment of a new pan-Arab empire, in which religion would be totally separated from the state. He saw it extending from the Tigris-Euphrates valley to the the Suez Canal and from the Mediterranean Sea to the Sea of 'Uman. The empire would be headed by an Arab sultan, but not a caliph. The caliph would rule only over the Hijaz and would be considered the religious caliph of all the Muslims. At the time that 'Azuri raised these ideas, he was alone in his opinions and had no influence on the Arab world.

The first Arab society in the twentieth century did not in any way call for the secession of the Arabs from the Ottoman Empire. When the Society of the Arab Revival began as a circle in Damascus in 1903, its members had indeed spread the Arab idea ('uruba) among the youth, but its aspirations did not go beyond the attainment of a decentralized regime with the rights of the Arabs in the government and the status of the Arabic language guaranteed. When the society was founded in Istanbul in 1906 its aim was "to make the intellectual Arab youth aware of their Arabism and to encourage them to cooperate in improving Ottoman society, whose righteousness was dependent on that of Arab society, from the Taurus mountains to Bab al-Mandib". The members of the society were motivated by thinking similar to that which motivated al-Kawakibi. They saw Arabism as "the noblest element in Islamic society", a foundation chosen "to carry the trust of Islam during the first period" because of its unique characteristics and which had been given the responsibility at present as well "for carrying the message of Islam and the renewal of its youth".[1]

Even these moderate ideas were not widespread among Arab intellectuals at the time of the Young Turk revolution in 1908. Tawfiq al-Suwaydi, one of the first members of *al-Fatat* and a prominent personality in Iraqi politics after World War I, attested that at the time of the restoration of the constitution he had only an "imaginary feeling" of Arabism.[2] The Arab-Ottoman Brotherhood, the first Arab society established, for rather dubious reasons, after the restoration of the constitution, tried, according to its programme, "to enhance the dignity of Arabism and the Arabs within the general Ottoman union, so that the Arabs, regardless of religion or aspiration, will benefit from constitutional equality expressed in the attainment of offices, positions and other legitimate rights". In other words, it intended primarily to deal with the "rights" of the Arabs, especially as concerned attaining "offices and positions". The vague expression "to enhance the dignity of Arabism", was to be repeated in various formulations in many of the programmes of future Arab societies.

Al-Fatat, the first secret Arab society after the restoration of the constitution, was also established to protect the rights of the Arabs. The first article of its programme, written in 1909, set out the society's goal: "to place the Arab nation in the ranks of living nations". In this formulation, no less vague than "to enhance the dignity of Arabism", there was no expression of any desire on the part of the Arabs to secede from the Ottoman Empire. And indeed Ahmad Qadri, one of the first members of the society, attested that at first it "did not harbour any hatred towards the Empire". Tawfiq al-Natur, another founding member, related that at the time the society was established the idea of Arabism had not been strong and all the Arabs had wanted was the same rights and the same duties within the Empire as the Turks. The motives of at least some of the members seem to have been similar to those of al-Kawakibi, and, later, some of the members of the Society of the Arab Revival. In 1913 the society's organ, *al-Mufid*, asserted that, unlike Turkish nationalism, there was no contradiction between Arab nationalism and Islam, but, on the contrary, "the salvation of the Muslim nation lies in the Arabs and their language". It defined an Arab as one who was tied to the Arab nation by "unity of language, ties of kinship and an Arab outlook".[3] Only the outbreak of World War I and the concrete fear for the fate of the Arab provinces of the Empire led the society to change its goals and strive for complete independence for the Arab countries.

Al-Qahtaniyya, founded for similar reasons to those that led to *al-Fatat*, strove to increase the Arabs' cultural, social and economic level and to arouse them to work out of solidarity and to demand their rights in the Empire. In other words, this society too considered it sufficient to demand equal rights for the Arabs, within the framework of remaining loyal Ottomans. The secret Green Flag society also strove for a vague and ill-defined goal of rescuing the Arab nation from the abyss into which it had fallen.

The Literary Club, on the other hand, had two goals, one overt: "To favour the intellectual progress of the students", and the other covert: "To train the thoughts [of the Arab youth] on the elements of nationalism ('*unsuriyya*) and independence". During the period after the Balkan War Arab consciousness increased, and 'Izzat al-Jundi, one of the members of the club's administrative committee, declared: "I am an Arab first and fore-most. The Muslim is an Arab and the Christian is an Arab . . . We are Arabs before we are Muslims and the Christian is an Arab before he is a Christian . . . and if we are Arabs before we are Muslims or Christians, then we should also be Arabs before we are Ottomans."[4] The failures of the Empire in Libya and the Balkans led to a reformulation of the club's principles, resolving that the only redress for Ottoman vulnerability if the Empire should be attacked was to strengthen the Arab element in the Empire and make it capable of defending itself. However, while the Literary Club showed some early signs of the impulse to rebel and throw off the Ottoman yoke, this wish was not yet crystallized nor expressed openly and clearly, and, most impor-tant, no alternative to the Empire was offered.

In 1911 the first attempt was made by 35 Arab members of the parliament, led by Sayyid Talib of Basra, to place an Arab religious authority at the head of the Arab countries. Yet their declaration to Sharif Husayn of Mecca — "We, the representa-tives of the Arabs in the parliament, recognize in Husayn the ruler of Mecca and we recognize, in the name of the countries which we represent, that he and only he is the religious leader of the Arab countries" — was only intended to give Husayn relig-ious authority, perhaps in the spirit of the appendix to al-Kawakibi's book *Umm al-Qura*.

The Paris Congress in 1913 was not worthy of being called "the First Arab Congress", as will be proved below. At any rate, a speech in the spirit of Arab nationalism was given there by *al-Fatat* member 'Abd al-Ghani al-'Uraysi, expressing his confi-dence in the right of the Arabs to be called a group, a people and a nation, because of their unity of language, race, history, customs and political aspirations. But even al-'Uraysi strove to improve the situation of the Arabs within the Empire and avoided speaking about the possibility of the Arabs seceding from it. Only at the end of his speech did he warn the imperial government that if it would not listen to the Arabs but would use force to quiet their demands, they would employ other—meaning illegal—means to resist it.

Sayyid Talib's attempt in late 1913 to organize a congress of all the important rulers of the north and centre of the Arabian Peninsula and the south of Iraq was another significant attempt to create a pan-Arab rapprochement. The congress was intended to discuss the problems and rights of the Arabs and to formulate guidelines for joint action with respect to the government. In the end it was not held because of the personal rivalries between these rulers. This was not the only time that such rivalries defeated attempts at Arab unity.

When he established *al-'Ahd*, 'Aziz 'Ali al-Misri aspired to an "Eastern Mediterranean State", an empire that would include the Arabs, the Turks, the Albanians, the Bulgarians and the Arab countries of Africa, from Sudan to Tunisia. In this empire, the Arab countries were to be included as separate and equal units within the framework of a decentralized federation under the symbolic presidency of the Ottoman Sultan. Al-Misri's vision was not accepted by his fellow members in the society; the first article of its programme defined its goal as working "for internal independence for the Arab countries, so that they will remain united with the Istanbul government, as Hungary is united with Austria". *Al-'Ahd* thus was also striving only for autonomy for the Arab countries, without secession from the Empire. The fifth article of the programme cited the need to preserve the political and national existence of the nation. However, not all the members of the society championed an Arab viewpoint, and some had Iraqi tendencies.

Al-Misri was also one of the founders of the Arab Revolutionary Society in mid-1914. Its name reflected an aspiration to the absolute liberation of the Arab countries from the yoke of the Ottoman Turks and the establishment of an Arab state. Its proclamations called upon the Arabs to acquire arms and to drive out the Turks, the destroyers of the land: "Enough suffering! Arise and establish societies and bands to punish the aggressors and liberate yourselves from the oppressors." "Arise, O Arabs! Draw the sword from its sheath, Qahtanians! Do not allow an oppressor and a tyrant who despises you to remain in your country! Cleanse your country of those who demonstrate hate for you, your race and your language." The society also offered an alternative to the Empire: "complete independence and the establishment of a decentralized Arab state . . . [such that] every district within it will be ruled by self-government, as is appropriate for it." This last clause reflected the fact that even this pan-Arab society was aware of the differences among the various Arab countries.

To work towards the realization of these plans al-Misri sent messengers to suggest to Ibn Sa'ud, the ruler of Najd, that he become the leader of the Arab movement. When World War I broke out al-Misri tried to interest the British in his programme for the establishment of an Arab empire that would include all the Arabic-speaking regions, with its northern border as Alexandretta-Mosul-the Persian border. He asked their assistance in leading the Arabs of Iraq and Syria against the Ottomans. The restoration of the Caliphate to the Arabs was not included in al-Misri's plans. The Decentralization Party also had contacts with the British during this period, concerning the possibility of liberating all the Arab countries from the Ottoman yoke, even at the price of the collapse of the Empire. Yet it seems that this activity was promoted by the true pan-Arabist of the time, Muhammad Rashid Rida.

Rida's pan-Arab nationalist activities during this period were focused on the secret society he had founded, the Society of the Arab Association. Its primary aims were to bring about union between the amirs of the Arabian Peninsula, to work for the development and defence of the Arab countries, and to create a connection between the Arab societies in Syria, Iraq and Istanbul within the framework of the struggle against the CUP. In the oath that he formulated for new members, Rida had already taken a step forward by speaking not only of the ill-defined term "Arab association" but also of "the founding of a new kingdom" for the Arabs. In a pamphlet he distributed later Rida called upon his readers to prepare to fight "so that you will be able to quickly answer the first call". Now he had become dissatisfied with the ideas of union and explained that the intention was to apply this eventually in practice and to fight for the independence of the Arabs, even against the European powers. He tried to realize these ideas by contacts with the rulers of the Arabian Peninsula and the Persian Gulf, in an attempt to convince them to join together in order to establish an independent Arab state. These attempts failed, just as other attempts to bring about some sort of agreement among these rulers had failed.

Rida's "General Organic Law of the Arab Empire", presented to the British in 1915, clearly defined how the future Arab empire should look: comprised of the Arabian Peninsula, the Provinces of Syria and Iraq and the territory between them, it would be decentralized, its official language, Arabic and its religion, Islam. Every province would be independent in its internal administration. The Caliph would come from the sharifs of Mecca. But while the headquarters of the Caliphate would be in Mecca, the headquarters of the Government and the Council of Representatives would be in Damascus. Even Rida, the pan-Arabist, recognized the differences between the Arabs in their various countries and saw that a strong foundation for the new empire must be set within a decentralized framework in which each country would have its independent internal administration. He differentiated at least between the Arabian Peninsula, Syria and Iraq, and it may also be assumed that, based on his experience with the rulers of the Arabian Peninsula, he did not see all of it as one province in the future empire.

The Christian pan-Arabist Najib 'Azuri sought a liberal constitutional monarchy under an Arab sultan for the future Arab empire. The Muslim pan-Arabist Rashid Rida thought that the Arab empire should be headed by a president who would be chosen by the Caliph every five years from among three candidates suggested by a council of representatives. This president would administer all the civilian and political affairs of the empire, with the assistance of a council of ministers, which would itself be chosen from among the members of the council of representatives.

The attitudes of these two pan-Arabists on the relation between religion and state in the future Arab empire are also noteworthy. Al-Kawakibi had already suggested that the rule of the Arab Caliph be limited to the Hijaz, that he should deal only with religious affairs, and that he should not intervene in the political and administrative affairs of the other Islamic countries. He was to be chosen by a council of advisers from all the Islamic countries, and it would be possible to abrogate the oath of loyalty to him if he were to act improperly. 'Azuri did not include the entire Arabian Peninsula in the independent Arab empire he envisioned, but left the region of the Hijaz as a separate independent state to be headed by the Caliph of all the Muslims. Because the Arab empire itself would be headed by a sultan, the problem of separation of religion and state in Islam would be solved; moreover, the interests of Islam would be separated from those of the Arabs. While 'Azuri's view can be explained by virtue of his being a Christian, Rida's approach, though no doubt can be cast on his Islamism, is surprisingly similar to that of 'Azuri. Rida's empire would be administered in practice by a president, while the Arab Caliph would administer only religious affairs and would be obliged to recognize the organic law of the empire and abide by it. He would indeed choose the president, but from among a group of candidates suggested by the Council of Representatives of the empire. The most outstanding expression of the separation of religion from state was embodied in Article 11 of Rida's General Organic Law: the headquarters of the Caliphate to be in Mecca and the headquarters of the Government and the Council of Representatives to be in Damascus.

A summary of the development of Arabism from the Young Turk revolution until the start of World War I yields the following picture. At the beginning of the period the societies that were founded felt the need to express the Arab idea, but did not offer any clear way of carrying it out. They did not suggest secession from the Ottoman Empire and they certainly did not have any well-defined alternative to the Empire. The Empire's defeats in Libya and the Balkans led to a change in the thinking of such societies as the Literary Club. But although talk of a need for the Arab to secede from the Empire began, no clear alternative was yet suggested. Rashid Rida, the first to offer such an alternative, was motivated by his wish to rehabilitate Islam through the Arabs. But his Society of the Arab Association, in practice at least, consisted only of him. Just before the war broke out others joined his viewpoint, such as the members of the Arab Revolutionary Society (which also had very few participants), but they were motivated by hatred of the Turks rather than Islamic ideas. Both Rida and the members of this society spoke of the establishment of a new, decentralized Arab empire, in which every part would have self-government.

The fact that even a pan-Arabist like Rida spoke of a decentralized Arab empire and not of a monolithic Arab state derived from his awareness of the differences between the inhabitants of the various Arab countries. In 1911 'Abd al-Karim al-Khalil spoke of the lack of cooperation among the Arabs themselves: "You see that the Iraqi knows very little about what is happening to the Syrian and the Hajizi does not feel the pain of the Yemenite."[5] A European orientalist expressed this in 1913 in sharper language: "The Arabs, Iraqis, inhabitants of the Arabian Peninsula and Syrians, are so different from one another in their social situation and their spiritual level that it is almost impossible to talk about cooperation or about common political ideas."[6] This variety inevitably led to the creation of a number of local national movements in the Arab Middle East in the period under discussion.

LEBANONISM

Mount Lebanon was the smallest territorial unit among the Arabic-speaking regions of the Ottoman Empire in which a nationalist movement arose. At the end of 1909 the British consul-general in Beirut said that "every Lebanese . . . is a 'Separatist' at heart, and would gladly join any disintegrating movement."[7] This pronouncement correctly described tendencies that had been apparent in the Lebanon for decades, reaching extremism after the Young Turk revolution had increased fears that the special status of Mount Lebanon would be harmed.

The general lines of the Lebanese struggle over the following years were determined by the Maronite lawyer Bulus Nujaym, who called for the extension of Mount Lebanon's borders and the restoration of the regions of Beirut, Tripoli, the Biqa' and Sidon (as they had been before the règlement organique of 1861). His justification for this and other demands was the existence of the Lebanese nation from the dawn of history and "the great role" that its glorious past imposed. Nujaym also spoke about political reform in the Lebanon and about the defence of its autonomy. A similar demand for administrative autonomy was raised by the Cedars of the Lebanon society, founded in 1910.

However, the main responsibility for the Lebanese struggle against the Ottoman Empire in the pre-World War I period was taken on by the Society of the Lebanese Revival, both within and outside the Lebanon. It began its activities by opposing the sending of Lebanese representatives to the Ottoman parliament, on the grounds that this harmed the special status of Mount Lebanon. Soon it was no longer satisfied with protecting this status and began to demand an increase in Mount Lebanon's autonomy and an extension of its borders, claiming that the Empire had no more rights over the Lebanon than the European powers that had signed its règlement organique. In 1910 a member Philippe al-Khazin tried to prove in a pamphlet that since the acceptance of the règlement organique the Lebanon had enjoyed autonomy in the areas of legislation, administration, justice, the army and finance, and had actually become an autonomous state. In the same year another member, Shahin al-Khazin, formulated the society's demands, among them "To organize the government in strict conformity with the règlement organique, with the faculty of legislating permanent laws" and "To restore to the Lebanon the territories that had been expropriated from it". Especially in the demand to allow the Lebanon powers of legislation, his list was actually not far from a bid to establish a truly independent Lebanon, under Ottoman suzerainty alone. The following year another member, Farid al-Khazin, stated this clearly: "The Powers have never recognized the Sublime Porte's right of *sovereignty* over the Lebanon, but only its *nominal suzerainty.*"

In a 1912 memorandum the society's Paris branch demanded that the Lebanon be granted extensive decentralization and the separation of authorities. It also demanded that the Lebanon be administered by an elected council with immunity and authority rather than by the governor of Mount Lebanon, who would have to be limited to supervisory tasks. The Paris branch, too, discussed the necessity for the return of the regions of the Biqa' and Ba'albek to Mount Lebanon, and it also demanded that the ports of Tripoli and Sidon or the port of Beirut be annexed to it. These demands were also raised by the society's Cairo branch, which insisted that the Lebanon be granted an effective autonomous government with the authority of legislation. In early 1913 the society's Beirut branch added another demand—absolute financial autonomy for Mount Lebanon.

The Empire's defeat in the Balkans led to the spread of these ideas outside the society's circles, to become the property of all the Lebanese. Some of them even turned to the French representative in Beirut at the end of 1912 to suggest taking advantage of the situation and declaring the Lebanon's independence, under the aegis of France. Christian aspirations in Syria, whether or not reforms would be implemented, were the subject of a memorandum that three members of the society who were also members of the Reform Society of Beirut wrote several months later, together with three additional members of the latter society. Presented to the French consul-general in Beirut, it included three alternatives, the last of which suggested "the annexation of Beirut to the Lebanon and the transfer of both to the practical control of France".

Although numerous delegates from the various branches of the Society of the Lebanese Revival participated in the Paris Congress, there was no overt Lebanese orientation there. Perhaps the reason for this was the Lebanese preference for solving the specific problems of Mount Lebanon through direct contacts with the French, separately from the general Syrian problem or the Arab problem. Yet the Lebanese did take care that there was a special article (No. 7) on Mount Lebanon among the congress resolutions: "The Congress expresses the hope that the Ottoman government will grant the mutasarrifiyya of the Lebanon the means for improving its financial situation."

Branches of the Society of the Lebanese Revival were also established in the New World, where there were large communities of Lebanese emigrants. The New York branch inscribed in its programme "rallying the Lebanese in the religion of nationalism" (Article 1), "extending the Lebanon's borders" (Article 5), and "placing a representative in Europe to represent the Lebanese and demand their rights" (Article 9). The significance of this last demand, in essence for a Lebanese embassy in Europe, lies in the fact that such an institution generally characterizes only an independent state. The ideology behind the demands of the Lebanese was expressed at that time by a Lebanese Arab newspaper published in Brazil: "The time has come . . . to put together a nation that will be recognized by the civilized world as the Lebanese nation."

With the outbreak of World War I there were Lebanese who were willing to realize their demands and dreams through an open revolt against the Ottomans. Although suggestions in this spirit were made to the representatives of the Allies in Beirut as well as by the society's Paris and New York branches, no Lebanese revolt broke out during World War I.

SYRIANISM

A larger unit than the sanjaq of Mount Lebanon was the vilayet of Beirut. The Reform Society founded in Beirut in late 1912 was interested solely in the problems of this vilayet, striving above all for the establishment of a supreme authority in the vilayet; in other words, decentralization so broad as to constitute virtual autonomy. Its demands included the right of the general council of the vilayet to decide on all the internal activities of the vilayet and the right to ask the Vali for explanations and to demand his dismissal. Whereas the first article of the list stated that army affairs would remain under the control of the central government, Article 15 of its list of demands—"Military service will be shortened to two years and will be performed in peacetime within the vilayet"—indicated that the demands actually went beyond extensive internal autonomy; the society actually thought that it had a say in army affairs as well, and it wanted the soldiers serving in the vilayet to be local men.

For some members of the society not even this was sufficient. A memorandum that six of the members presented to the French consul-general, as mentioned in the previous section on

Lebanonism, suggested as another alternative "full autonomy for the vilayet of Beirut, under the protection and practical control of France". Two of the authors of the memorandum, Ayyub Thabit and Khalil Zayniyya vigorously continued their activities on behalf of the vilayet of Beirut during the Paris Congress. Indeed, the vilayet of Beirut merited a special Article (No. 4) in the list of the congress resolutions, based on two principles: broadening the authority of the general councils and the appointment of foreign advisers; the congress requested the implementation of these two demands.[8] An attempt by one of the observers at the congress sessions to object to this resolution was angrily rejected by the society delegates with the argument that no one had the right to intervene in the affairs of their vilayet, just as they did not intervene in the affairs of other vilayets. Although the delegates were expressing an absolutely separatist tendency here, it must be pointed out that an examination of the history of the society does not reveal any ideological justifications of its activities, of a Beirutian nationalist movement—and it therefore seems that the society's demands were purely utilitarian and motivated by the wish to ameliorate the plight of the vilayet. The case was different with the movement that arose during this period on behalf of the largest unit in the Levant — Syria.

The first of the Syrian nationalists of modern times was Butrus al-Bustani, who in 1860 had already described Syria in his newspaper *Nafir Suriyya* as "our fatherland . . . and the population of Syria, whatever their creed, community, racial origin or groups, are the sons of our fatherland". He called upon the Syrians to abandon religious solidarity and to replace it with national identity; the two conditions which entitled the Syrians to be called a nation were living in the same country and speaking the same language.

The first practical attempt to realize the aspirations of the Syrians for independence began in Beirut and was crystallized in Damascus at the time of the Ottoman-Russian War in 1877-78. The initiators—all Muslim—of a scheme envisioning Syria's secession from the Empire and becoming an independent state that would extend over the regions that today are called Syria, Jordan, Lebanon and Israel, had not succeeded in discussing the nature of this independent state before the authorities discovered them. In parallel with this attempt, a group of Christians with similar goals was active in Beirut, within the framework of a secret society. This society reached the peak of its activities with the distribution in 1880 of proclamations addressed to "the sons of Syria", demanding autonomy for Syria and denouncing the oppressive Ottoman rule. The society indeed demanded "independence in which we will be partners with our brothers, the Lebanese", but it seems that it was willing to recognize Ottoman sovereignty, and in this it was more moderate than the Muslim group.

During the next 30 years there were no further initiatives of this type, apparently due to the intensification of the Hamidian authorities' surveillance. However, the Young Turk revolution of 1908 aroused anew the hopes of some Syrians that achieving at least some sort of autonomy was a real possibility. The first to express this in public were the Mutran brothers, through manifestos and proclamations distributed under the name of the Syrian Central Society. Their call for granting Syria self-government strong enough to protect it from any possible encroachment by the central government was motivated by their belief that such a government was the only means of reviving Syria. Although the opinions of the Mutrans did not meet widespread sympathy in Syria after the revolution, it seems that they were not alone in their views. At about the same time an anonymous pamphlet distributed in Beirut, entitled *La question sociale et scolaire en Syrie*, declared the existence of a Syrian national culture:

> We will toil and slave, we will exhaust every atom of our strength and energy, our youth and our spirit, we will sacrifice our very lifeblood if necessary, but our own culture will not die, and the sun's fair and burning rays will never shine upon the mighty ruins of our Syrian fatherland.[9]

Another step forward in the definition of Syrian ideology was taken by Lebanese Revival member Khayrallah Khayrallah, whose ideas were definitely not limited to the borders of the Lebanon. In 1912 he expressed his hope of seeing "one unified Syria" based on principles of democracy, secularism and decentralization. He envisioned this future state as a federation of districts, each based on a religious or ethnic unit, cooperating on the basis of a Syrian nationalism that would gradually come into being. The unity of Syria was also the idea behind the founding at that time of the Syrian Union Society in New York.

The Decentralization Party, established in Cairo in late 1912, ostensibly strove for the achievement of administrative decentralization for all the vilayets of the Ottoman Empire, Arab and non-Arab. Its platform called for a General Council at the centre of each vilayet, whose decisions were to be valid and binding and it was to be within its jurisdiction to supervise the vilayet's government and to investigate all the concerns of the local administration. The party thus demanded very extensive internal independence for the vilayets—but not only that. Like the Reform Society of Beirut, it called for the residents of each vilayet to perform their military service in their own vilayets so that its army would be ready to defend it during peacetime. This was already a demand for a certain degree of military independence for the vilayets.

It seems that all these far-reaching demands, apparently intended for all the vilayets of the Empire, were raised by the party on behalf of Syria. There are a number of proofs of this. The party was established because of the fear that Syria was about to fall into the hands of a European power, and in order to protect it from this danger the idea of decentralization was raised. All the members of the party were natives of Syria (in the wider sense of the term, as will be clarified below). All the branches of the party within the Empire were established only in Syria (again in the wider sense). Rafiq al-'Azm, the president of the party, had a short time before it was founded published an article in *al-Mu'ayyad* expressing the Syrians' loyalty to the Ottoman government but also their loyalty to the Syrian nation. Far more decisive was party member Shafiq al-Mu'ayyad, who at the beginning of 1913 expressed his belief that the three vilayets of Syria (Damascus, Aleppo and Beirut) should be turned into one unit, and a short while later pointed out most explicitly: "We demand reforms and decentralization only in order to preserve the whole of Syria."[10]

At a conference of the party leaders held in March 1913 it was decided that Syria must be turned into an independent principality ruled by a Muslim prince. Obviously the party lacked the means at this stage to realize its wish. But when World War I broke out the party decided that the appropriate moment had arrived, and in coordination with the Society of the Lebanese Revival an armed revolt against the Ottomans was planned, to begin in Zahla in the Lebanon. The revolt did not take place.

The Decentralization Party did not act publicly only on behalf of Syria, as for example the Syrian Central Society did, but it hid behind the cloak of decentralization, ostensibly for the entire Empire. In practice, it seems that the party was the largest group that worked on behalf of Syria during the period under discussion.

More moderate in its demands was the reform movement in Damascus; probably the very fact of its being a public movement within the Empire compelled it to act moderately. The list of reforms composed in Damascus called, like the one in Beirut, for the establishment of "an elected and independent administrative council . . . which will be free to take whatever steps seem necessary to protect the internal interests of the vilayet". In Tripoli as well it was decided to establish a society on the example of the one in Beirut, which would demand the granting of administrative autonomy to Syria. The more extreme groups in Aleppo, on the other hand, were not willing to be satisfied with autonomy, and in late 1912 and early 1913 they turned to foreign diplomats several times to suggest beginning a general revolt throughout Syria, driving out the Ottomans, and transferring the country to foreign rule. In Beirut, in early 1913, a representative of Syrian officers serving in Chatalja and in Gallipoli reported on the desire of these officers to return to Syria, carry out a revolt, and bring independence to Syria under the principality of 'Umar Tusun of the Khedivial family. This programme was surprisingly similar to that formulated previously by the Decentralization Party, and it seems that the party leaders were aware in some manner of the officers' plan.

In June 1913 the Paris Congress was held. The nature of the congress attested to its being Syrian, at least to a considerable extent, and indeed its original name was to be the Syrian Congress. (Changed as a result of the intervention of the Iraqi Tawfiq al-Suwaydi to the First Arab Congress, in the end it was also officially called the Arab-Syrian Congress.) At a preliminary conference before the congress, held with the participation of the Mutran brothers, the aim of the congress was perceived as the demand for administrative autonomy for Syria, and it was in this spirit that Nadra Mutran reviewed the topics of the discussions at the congress, in a letter to the French foreign minister. However, evidence for the Syrian character of the congress exists not only in the actions of the Mutran brothers, which were sometimes outside the bounds of what was agreed upon by the other participants. Twenty-one Syrians (in the wider sense) and only two Iraqis participated in the congress. The CUP newspaper *Tanin* asked sarcastically where the delegates of Yemen, Baghdad, Egypt, Tripolitania, Tunisia, Algeria and Morocco were at the congress which purported to represent all the Arabs.

Indeed, the name of Syria recurred over and over in the congress. Nadra Mutran, who was supposed to speak about "Preserving national life in the Ottoman Arab countries", spoke about Syria, which was "created for the Syrians". Najib Diyab spoke about his hope for the return of the Syrian émigrés to

Syria, on the condition that their rights in the Empire would be preserved, and that "their schools will be illuminated with the electricity of Syrian nationalism and their hearts will burn with love of the fatherland". Ahmad Tabbara spoke about the emigration from Syria and the immigration to it. Charles Dabbas threatened in his speech that the reformists would "fight with violence and force" until Syria was raised to the path which would lead it to a better future.

The congress resolutions presented to the European powers contained changes from the list approved by the participants. The later list made a clear distinction between the Syrians in particular and the Arabs in general, speaking of a decentralized regime to be granted to the Syrian and the Arab vilayets (Article 3); recognition of Arabic as an official language in the Syrian and the Arab countries (Article 5); local military service in the Syrian and the Arab vilayets (Article 6); and the congress resolutions as the political platform of the Syrians and the Arabs (Article 2 in the Appendix).

It seems that the clearest and most outstanding expression of the existence of Syrian nationalism in Syria before World War I was an anonymous placard distributed throughout Syria during that year:

> Awake, O Syrians! All the nations have been liberated and you remain sunk in your slavery. . . . There is no security for your property, your businesses are stagnating and your honour is being trampled. Your judges are avaricious, your shepherds are murderers. Unite in the name of liberty . . . Look through your windows at the happy Lebanon, only a short distance from you, whose inhabitants breathe the air of freedom. . . . Be zealous for your honour, Syrians. . . . Awake, O Syrians, in the name of the fatherland and in the name of the language, and unite. And there is no doubt that you will be crowned with success.[11]

The last question that must be asked with regard to the Syrian movement is: For which Syria were the Syrian nationalists striving? In 1866 Khalil al-Khuri spoke about the region from the Euphrates in the east to the Mediterranean Sea in the west and from the Arabian desert in the south to Anatolia in the north. Nadra Mutran began Syria's northern border from Cape Karatash, which was west(!) of the Gulf of Iskenderun, continued it along the west bank of the Jihan River to 'Aintab and from there to Birejik, Urfa, northwards to Diarbakr, southwards to a point west of the vilayet of Mosul and on to the Arabian desert. From there it continued west along the north of the vilayet of

the Hijaz until Aqaba and from there along a straight line to
Rafah. "Le Comte Cressaty de Damas" defined Syria as including the vilayet of Aleppo, the sanjaq of Dayr al-Zur, the vilayet
of Damascus, the vilayet of Beirut, the Lebanon and the mutasarrifiyya of Jerusalem.[12]
Undoubtedly these borders contradicted the nationalist aspirations of another local movement: the Lebanese movement. At a
March 1913 conference the Decentralization Party resolved to
work for Syria's independence, but also that it was necessary to
work for the annexation of Mount Lebanon to the future Syrian
principality. At the Paris Congress Najib Diyab claimed that the
Syrians considered Syria to be the mother of the Lebanon and
the Lebanon to be the heart of Syria: "Can the mother be distanced from her heart or can you remove her heart from her?"
Nadra Mutran, a Christian from Ba'albek, said this more forcefully in his book: "The Lebanon is an integral part of Syria . . .
the Lebanon has never been independent."[13] This controversy
between the two nationalist movements could remain latent
before World War I, as long as the aspirations of the Lebanese
and the Syrians seemed far from being realizable. At that time
the two movements could even participate in joint activities
against the common enemy—the Ottoman Turks. However,
immediately after the war the controversy broke out with all the
ideological vigour that lay behind it, and it has not died down to
this day.

IRAQISM

In Iraq before World War I, where the predominant loyalties
were to family or tribe, it is difficult to speak of an Iraqi movement. Nevertheless this period saw the seeds of a pan-Iraqi
vision extending beyond the borders of the three vilayets: Mosul,
Baghdad and Basra. The first of these was perhaps the pamphlet
"Iraq, Iraq", published by the Committee for the Defence of the
Interests of Iraq and distributed in Baghdad in 1910. Though
most of it was devoted to Baghdad's problems, it also touched
upon problems disturbing the other vilayets, and it presented the
other inhabitants of Iraq as no less weary of the then situation
than the people of Baghdad.
The main activities against the Ottoman authorities during
this period were carried out in Basra, under the leadership of
Sayyid Talib al-Naqib. In March 1913 he organized a meeting
with the Sheikhs of Kuwait and Muhammara and raised the

demand that Iraq be granted independence or at least self-government. In April, following the announcement of the new Vilayets Law, Talib demanded from the authorities full administrative autonomy for the vilayet. When the authorities did not accept this, he sent letters of incitement to Baghdad, calling upon the inhabitants to join a collective protest against the new law which was turning the inhabitants of Iraq into slaves of their Valis. The Reform Society that he founded published a list of its demands in August, among them the following:

> The Vali executes the decisions of the central government and of the General Council (5) . . . The General Council has broad authority to discuss anything that is for the benefit of the vilayet (7) . . . The General Council has the power to increase the gendarmerie and the police force and to set up guard stations (8) . . . The General Council is completely independent and has complete jurisdiction over the Vali (9) . . . The central government has the right to appoint the Vali, on the condition that he is an Iraqi (14) . . . Regular soldiers shall serve in their own vilayet in times of peace (23) . . .

This list of demands was more forceful that those of the Reform Society of Beirut and the Decentralization Party. It stressed that the decentralization demanded was both in the military sphere (as with the Reform Society of Beirut and the Decentralization Party) and in the police sphere. The supremacy of the General Council over the Vali was also emphasized. And above all, this list specified a demand not found in any other list of reforms—that the Vali must be an Iraqi.

Talib's activities were not limited to the borders of the vilayet of Basra. During the same month the society distributed a proclamation that was addressed to the Arab soldiers in Iraq and to the tribesmen, and called upon them, especially the former, to draw their swords and compel the government to implement decentralization. Talib also supported the National Scientific Club in Baghdad with financial assistance, and he sent Sulayman Faydi to Mosul with the task of spreading nationalist ideas. There is no doubt, however, that Talib's main interests were in Basra and were focused on his own status. When the war broke out he did not hesitate to suggest cooperation with the British in return for being appointed amir in Basra, under their aegis. After the war he already considered himself worthy of being king of Iraq.

The overt, declared aim of the National Scientific Club, founded in Baghdad at the end of 1912, was "to spread knowledge throughout Iraq", in order to strengthen the connections between the Arabs of the country and to awaken them. Rumours abounded that the club also had a secret political aim: to remove the Turks from Iraq and establish some form of self-government. During 1913 Baghdad joined the general trend spreading in the Arab vilayets of the Empire, demanding administrative decentralization.

It seems that if there was any real Iraqi movement before World War I, its leaders were the Iraqi officers in the Ottoman army. The first attempt at a revolt was carried out by a group of officers, mostly Baghdadi, who were staying in Istanbul in 1912 and wanted to return to Iraq and organize a revolt there. The attempt ended even before it began. In 1914 the members of the Baghdad branch of al-'Ahd, mostly officers, planned a general revolt from Mosul in the north to the Persian Gulf in the south. The question is whether this should be considered an attempt at an Iraqi revolt, for the initiators were interested in the rebellion spreading to Syria and even wanted to offer its leadership to Ibn Sa'ud. The plan of al-'Ahd leader 'Aziz 'Ali al-Misri for an organized revolt in Iraq (which he suggested to the British after the outbreak of the war) was also probably only the first stage of a supposed general revolt in all the Arab countries of the Empire. Later al-Misri suggested the establishment of an independent state in Iraq, under the aegis of the British, to extend from the Persian Gulf to Armenia and Anatolia. Perhaps this suggestion, which came after the British invasion of Iraq, was intended as an attempt to save Iraq from British annexation.

A genuine Iraqi society appears to have been the secret society al-'Alam, which was established in Mosul shortly before the outbreak of the war. It strove for the independence of Iraq and propagandized against the Turks.

THE ATTITUDE TOWARDS EGYPT

In exploring the ideology of the societies, their attitude towards Egypt is another question that demands attention. Since the Napoleonic invasion of Egypt in 1798, Egypt had been developing separately from the Ottoman Empire and this process was sharpened by the British conquest in 1882. A strong Egyptian nationalism had begun to develop, and the Arab idea did not have a foothold there during the period under discussion. While the members of many societies worked in Egypt and it was the centre of the Decentralization Party, all these people were Syrian émigrés and were considered by the Egyptians as foreigners, *dukhala'*, as defined by the Egyptian nationalist leader Mustafa Kamil. The Egyptians of that period did not consider themselves part of the Arab nation, and the question is how the society members considered them.

The Arab empire, according to Najib 'Azuri, extended from the Tigris-Euphrates valley to the Suez Canal. In other words, it did not include Egypt. 'Azuri claimed that "the Egyptians do not belong to the Arab race", but rather came from an African Berber family and their language before Islam did not resemble Arabic. He considered the Suez Canal and the Red Sea to be the natural border between Egypt and the future Arab empire. The Arab empire according to Rashid Rida also excluded Egypt. It can thus be seen that it was precisely the two pan-Arabists of the early twentieth century, 'Azuri before the 1908 revolution and Rida in the period from this revolution until World War I, who did not consider Egypt an Arab country or the Egyptians members of the Arab nation. The two men had something else in common: both vigorously opposed the Egyptian nationalists. 'Azuri called Mustafa Kamil a charlatan, and Rida called Egyptian nationalism an erroneous and false *wataniyya*. It seems that the Egyptian alternative offered by the (pro-Ottoman) Egyptian nationalists to the Arab ideas of 'Azuri and Rida, combined with the fact that Egypt was under a different government than the other Arab countries, led the pan-Arabists 'Azuri and Rida to the conclusion that Egypt did not merit inclusion in the future Arab empire.

'Abd al-Hamid al-Zahrawi, the president of the Paris Congress, was more moderate. However, even he, after agreeing to recognize Egypt as an Arab country and expressing his respect for the opinions of "our Egyptian brothers", refused to allow an Egyptian who was present at the congress discussions to express his opinion. He justified this refusal with the argument that "it [Egypt] has a separate administration in which the Ottomans' views are not taken into consideration", and "the Ottoman countries have an administration that does not consider the Egyptians' views"; discussion of internal Ottoman affairs was thus to be left to those whose views could affect their situation.

'Aziz 'Ali al-Misri, who, unlike all the other Arab activists of the period, was an Egyptian, understandably did consider Egypt part of "the Eastern Mediterranean State" he dreamed of founding. He could not ignore his homeland, then under British occupation he detested.

It seems that the only society that held a substantive discussion on the question of Egypt during this period was the

Literary Club. After lengthy sessions the members of the club reached the conclusion that the Arab nation could not relinquish Egypt, which was the largest, strongest, richest and most progressive of the Arab countries. In their view the importance of Egypt also derived from its location at the heart of the Arab countries (taking into account that west of it were Libya and the Maghrib countries). Nevertheless, the club members were apparently aware of the fact that the Egyptians themselves were not interested in the other Arab countries at all, and it is possible that 'Abd al-Karim al-Khalil's activity in Egypt in 1911, on behalf of his plan for the reform of Arab education, was an attempt to bring about joint activities between the Arabs of the Empire and those of Egypt, on an Arab topic.

Surprisingly, it was some of the Syrian particularists who aspired to the annexation of Syria to Egypt. However, they wanted it not because they identified with the Egyptians, but rather because of their desire to secede from the Ottoman Empire, even at the price of being under British occupation, which they considered an enlightened and progressive rule that allowed local participation in the administration of the country, as was the case in Egypt. Shukri al-'Asali of Damascus and Salim Thabit of Beirut even went to Cairo and tried to persuade the Egyptian nationalist leaders to support this viewpoint, but the latter, who clung to their separatist standpoint (and certainly were not interested in harming the Ottoman Empire, with which they sympathized), rejected this idea out of hand.

*

During the period from the Young Turk revolution until the outbreak of World War I three or four nationalist trends co-existed among the Arabs of the Ottoman Empire. One was Arabism, which began moderately and in an ill-defined manner, was pushed into extremism by the Turkification policy of the Young Turks, and finally reached a pan-Arabist ideology among certain individuals. Larger movements were Lebanonism, which stemmed from the desire of the Lebanese to preserve the special status of their mountain, and Syrianism, which dated back to the second half of the nineteenth century, but intensified as a result of the rapid decline of the Empire at the beginning of the twentieth century. Perhaps there were also buds of Iraqism in the period under discussion. As long as these movements had a common enemy—the Turks—they were able to engage in joint action, in spite of the ideological contrasts between them. The

Egyptians, who were outside of the Empire, therefore stood outside of this intricate complex.

Chapter 27

ATTITUDES TOWARDS THE EUROPEAN STATES

The beginnings of the separatist movements and of many of the Arab societies lay in part, and perhaps principally, in external causes. The Syrian independence movement grew out of the fear following the Ottoman-Russian War in 1877-78 that the Ottoman Empire would disintegrate and Syria would be occupied by a European power. The Secret Society of Beirut, established before this war, intensified its activities in its aftermath. The Arab-Ottoman Brotherhood and the Society of the Lebanese Revival were established in the wake of the 1908 revolution. The idea of *al-Fatat* also developed a short time after this revolution and as a result of it. *Al-Qahtaniyya* and the Literary Club were established after the repression of the counter-revolution in 1909 and the intensification of Turkification. In the wake of the occupation of Libya by Italy in 1911 and the defeat of the Empire in the Balkans in 1912-13, Rashid Rida increased his activities in his Society of the Arab Association, the Decentralization Party was founded, the Reform Society of Beirut was established and the Iraqi officers planned a rebellion, as did the Syrian officers under the leadership of Salim al-Jaza'iri.

It is thus clear that the establishment of societies and the attempts at revolt derived from a combination of two factors: not only Arab attitudes towards the Turks but also Arab attitudes towards Europe. Yet, while many Arabs were motivated by the fear that Europe would occupy the Arab countries, others sought the realization of this same eventuality.

Ambivalence towards the West and towards Europe was already present in the philosophy of Butrus al-Bustani. He maintained that the achievements of the West should not be ignored but rather that what Europe had taken a long time to attain should be adopted quickly by the Arabs, not in blind imitation but as was appropriate for the building of their new culture. Likewise, Rafiq al-'Azm, decades later, called upon the Arabs to imitate the West and Europe not only in such external manners as saying "pardon" and "merci", but to take the positive things from Europe—those which had led to its great

progress, which he defined as science and liberty. Yet, while
Muslims strove to attain Europe's level of progress through
these, it was incumbent upon them to remember that "the East
is for the Easterners". Pride in this, would lead to respect from
a Europe that would "shake your hand . . . as with a friend".
Al-'Azm also turned to the European states and asked them to
be aware of the revival in the world of Islam, where a danger
was felt from the European states, at the same time as it came
into close contact with European knowledge, acquiring it as well
as the principles that had led to the West's progress. He called
upon the Europeans to assist the Muslims as France had assisted
the Americans at the time of their War of Independence, and
upon the West to stop trying to subordinate the East.[1]

   In the eyes of the Society of the Arab Revival, the Ottoman
Empire had perpetrated a great evil upon the Muslim world by
ignoring the industrial and scientific renaissance of the West. The
West in consequence was progressing while the Muslims were
left behind. This belief in the technical powers of the Europeans
was expressed especially clearly in the demands of the Reform
Society of Beirut. Already at the time of its establishment the
society insisted on the principle of introducing foreign experts
and advisers to all the authorities of the local administration of
the vilayet. This demand was not accepted enthusiastically in all
places. Further north, in Tripoli, the local people dissociated
themselves from this and hoped that if such advisers and supervisors actually came to the vilayet, their authority would be very
limited. In a special article in al-Manar Rashid Rida denounced
the demand for foreign advisers, claiming that they would give
greater weight to the interests of their own countries, and were
being given too much authority. Rida rejected out of hand the
society's demand that the decisions of the Council of Advisers
should be final, claiming that only a ma'sum (infallible person)
deserved such a right. Rida based his principled opposition on
his experience with the administration in Egypt (which was
assisted by the British).[2]

   The desire expressed by the Beirut society for European assistance to realize reforms in the Arab vilayets of the Empire was
also among the reasons for holding the Paris Congress. By
removing the Arab-Syrian problem from the Ottoman to the
international arena, the congress organizers sought to put pressure on the government of the Empire and perhaps force it to
accept their demands. At the congress itself the president, 'Abd
al-Hamid al-Zahrawi, called upon the Easterners to emulate the
West and to adopt its liberty. Nadra Mutran used the platform

to persuade his listeners that the European states did not want to occupy or to divide Syria, but only for the Ottomans to be able to administer the Empire themselves and thus contribute to the general peace. Charles Dabbas contended, "There is no true reform without foreign advisers." When it was decided at the conclusion of the congress that its resolutions would be transmitted to the governments friendly to the Ottoman Empire, Nadra Mutran added the commentary that the intention was that these governments should put in a good word to the Ottoman government to persuade it to implement reforms. Afterwards, when the Paris agreement was signed, it stipulated that foreign expert supervisors would be employed in departments requiring them in all the vilayets.

In 1909 the Syrian Central Society called for the European powers to support the demand that Syria be granted self-government within the framework of the Empire. "The Central Society for Reform and Defence of the Syrian Interests", which strove—to the extent that it existed—for similar goals, also called for the European powers to use their influence for the granting of reforms to the Syrians.

The European powers had a special status with regard to Mount Lebanon, as they were the signatories of its règlement organique of 1861, which assured the special status of Mount Lebanon. Since then the residents of the Lebanon had turned to European powers whenever they feared that the Ottoman authorities were trying to harm its status. The members of the Society of the Lebanese Revival denied that the Empire had any greater rights over the Lebanon than did these Powers, so that it had no right to introduce changes in Mount Lebanon's status without their consent. The petitions to the European powers in this regard increased towards the end of the governor of the Lebanon's term of office in late 1912. In a petition to all the foreign ministers of the European powers, the members of the society in Cairo called upon them to protect the Lebanon by putting pressure on the authorities to grant reforms based on effective autonomy.

A proclamation evincing a positive attitude towards Europe also appeared in Baghdad in 1913, claiming that the Arabs had Europe's sympathy and that Europe was not aspiring to bring about the partition of Asiatic Turkey—though if this were to occur, then Europe would help the Arabs return to the glory of their ancestors. This proclamation was definitely exceptional and did not represent the general attitude in Iraq towards Europe. The demands of the Reform Society of Basra not only did not include the Beirutian demand for foreign advisers, but, on the contrary, declared, "No concessions to be made to foreigners in our country. It must be protected against foreign intrigues, and foreign influences must be prevented from infiltrating into the country." In a proclamation the society accused the imperial authorities of wanting to sell the lands of Iraq to foreigners and to make Sunday the day of rest in the Empire, as in Europe.

The revolutionary activism expressed in the struggle against European imperialism had been shaped much earlier by al-Afghani and 'Abduh. While he was in Egypt from 1871 to 1879, al-Afghani apprised his students of the danger in European inter-vention and the need for national unity in order to oppose it. In the newspaper *al-'Urwa al-Wuthqa* he and 'Abduh focused on propaganda against foreign occupation of Islamic countries, and especially against the British occupation of Egypt. Their loyal disciple Rashid Rida warned the Arabs of the ambitions of the European powers to gain control over parts of the Empire, not necessarily by means of war, but by occupation through peaceful means (*al-fath al-silmi*), using money and politics. Libya, he cautioned in 1914, had already been given to Italy; Britain was interested in annexing Egypt and Afghanistan and occupying Basra, Baghdad and the coasts of the Arabian Peninsula; France believed that Syria belonged to it; Germany was interested in the heart of Anatolia, up to Iraq; and Russia was interested in the north of Anatolia up to Istanbul.[3]

The failures of the Empire in Libya and in the Balkans led the members of the Literary Club to conclude that as the Arab countries were rich and thus gave rise to ambitions on the part of the Powers to subordinate them, and as the Ottoman govern-ment would be unable to protect the Arab countries in time of need if they were to be attacked by a powerful enemy, the only way to change the situation was by strengthening the Arab ele-ment in the Ottoman Empire and making it capable of defend-ing itself. *Al-'Ahd*'s programme stated that the society would devote itself especially to the security of Istanbul against the ambitions of the European countries, for if severed from its capi-tal the East could not exist. The programme also maintained that since the Turks had formed the front lines in guarding the East from the West for 600 years, it was now the turn of the Arabs to prepare themselves for this task.

The proclamations of the Arab Revolutionary Society likewise dwelt on the inability of the Empire to stand firm before Europe, accusing the Empire of being a collapsing state obliged to follow the dictates of Europe. They warned the Arabs that their country was being auctioned off in the markets of Europe by the rulers of the Empire. *Al-Fatat*, too, joined the anti-European front for a very short period after the outbreak of the war, deciding after the failure of its contacts with the British in Egypt that "in the event of European designs [on the Arab countries] appearing to materialise, the society shall be bound to work on the side of Turkey in order to resist foreign penetration of whatever kind or form". When it learned of the contacts between the British and Sharif Husayn of Mecca a few months later, the society reversed direction once again and demanded the establishment of an independent Arab state in return for cooperation with the British (the "Damascus Protocol").

ATTITUDES TOWARDS FRANCE

Najib 'Azuri characterized France as the champion of the oppressed and the unfortunate, the contributor of uncountable services to civilization, deserving of the gratitude of all Easterners regardless of race or religion. No other nation, in his opinion, had more rights and interests in the Ottoman Empire. 'Azuri tried many times to involve France in his plans for carrying out a rebellion in the Empire; his main goal was apparently to get large sums of money from the French ("600,000 francs . . . will be sufficient"). The French did not agree.

The view of France as a source of assistance was not unique to 'Azuri. In 1908 the Lebanese Bulus Nujaym wrote that the hopes of the Lebanese for the realization of their aspirations were dependent on the traditional protector of the Christians of the Lebanon for hundreds of years, France, which had always led the world in progress and liberty and had always been the patron of the oppressed. He called upon France "to understand its historical role and its own interests, and to give all its support to the valiant Lebanese".[4] France was the power that had intervened in favour of the Christians of the Lebanon and Syria during the 1860 massacres, and it was to France that the Lebanese turned first and foremost, in order to defend the special status of Mount Lebanon. The trust of the Lebanese in France was so far-reaching that at the end of 1912 some of them turned to its representative in Beirut and suggested working for the independence of the Lebanon under the aegis of France. Their suggestion was rejected.

The Society of the Lebanese Revival also took advantage of every possible opportunity to express its confidence in the

French and its loyalty to them. The Beirut branch of the society would send letters from time to time to the French foreign ministry with a request for French assistance in the realization of their demands. The president of the Paris branch of the society, Shukri Ghanim took advantage of contacts with the foreign ministry and various political circles to set up an interview with Premier Poincaré and two other members of the society in June 1912 in order to present their demands. At the end of 1913 the society transmitted to the French government 40 protest letters against the actions of the Ottoman authorities, signed (according to Paris branch secretary Khayrallah Khayrallah) by more than 300,000 Lebanese. In addition the society sent its own protests, greetings and other missives to the French authorities. The São Paulo branch of the society was also accustomed to send letters to the French premier and foreign minister to raise the demands of the Lebanon and request that it be protected.

Khayrallah Khayrallah expressed in an article his appreciation of French culture, language and literature, although not at the expense of their Syrian counterparts. It has been claimed that in late 1912 he called for the establishment of a greater France of which the Lebanon would be a part. At any rate, early in 1913 he went to the Levant as an emissary of the Paris branch of the society and there he distributed pro-French propaganda. He tried to convince the Syrians that France had no intention of occupying their land, which they feared following a declaration by Poincaré in late 1912. He tried to convince the French consul-general in Damascus of the seriousness of the British propaganda in Syria and the necessity of fighting it. In his attempt to convince Shukri al-'Asali, who was considered pro-British, of the more favourable attitude of France towards the Syrians, he pointed out: "I, a Syrian, am an editor of Le Temps, the largest journal in Paris. Nothing analogous could occur in London. Can you imagine the scandal that would be caused in England by the presence of a native in the editorial offices of The Times?" The French consul-general, who greatly valued Khayrallah's approach, asked his superiors to allot sums of money to Khayrallah for propaganda purposes. The Turks on their part were convinced that Khayrallah's entire trip to the Levant was funded by a secret fund of the French foreign ministry.[5]

A member of the society in Paris who called himself "le Comte Cressaty de Damas" dreamt of an independent Syria "which casts itself into the arms of France, like an infant dependent on his mother's kisses". He considered himself "a son of Syria, but also a son of France", and indeed spent half his life in

France speaking and lecturing in favour of its annexation of Syria.[6]

The members of the Society of the Lebanese Revival, who felt themselves related to France and its culture, spread propaganda in its favour in the many newspapers under their control. One of the most prominent pro-French journalists in the society, Rizq Allah Arqash, turned the papers *al-Ittihad al-'Uthmani*, *al-Ahwal*, and *al-Nasir* into partisans of France. The Turks claimed that *al-Ahwal* recieved various kinds of assistance from the French, that *al-Ittihad al-'Uthmani* received 1,000 francs a month from them, and *al-Nasir*, 5,000 francs a month. Other pro-French newspapers in the area were *al-Thabat*, published by Khalil Zayniyya, who was also a member of the society, and *Zahla al-Fatat* and *Dalil Hims*, published by Qustantin Yani, the head of the Homs branch of the Decentralization Party. In Cairo the editor-in-chief of the newspaper *al-Ahram*, Da'ud Barakat, a member of the Society of the Lebanese Revival, received, according to the Turks, 5,000 pounds from the French for the newspaper's expenses.[7]

When World War I broke out the Lebanese requested help to start a revolt against the Ottomans, from the French consul-general in Beirut, Georges Picot, among others. Picot mediated between them and the Greek government, but in the end the plan was not carried out because of the opposition of the French foreign minister. Shukri Ghanim, president of the Paris society, asked the French foreign minister to allow Georges Picot to remain in the Lebanon, in order that "his moral support" assist the local people. The New York society had similar requests. With all such requests rejected, a Lebanese revolt with French assistance never broke out.

At the end of 1912 there were differences of opinion regarding France within the Syrian community in Cairo. The proponents of France were primarily Christian émigrés, led by the Protestant Najib Shakur Pasha. A pro-French contingent in Syria itself was even willing to see it gain control of the country. The "foreign advisers" demanded by 'the Reform Society of Beirut were required to speak "Arabic, Turkish or French".[8] Six Christian members of the society did not consider even reforms implemented with French advice to be sufficient, and they brought a memorandum to the French consul-general detailing in order of preference the three possibilities they considered acceptable: the occupation of Syria by France; full autonomy for the vilayet of Beirut, under the protection and the practical control of France; and the annexation of Beirut to the Lebanon and the transfer of both to the practical control of France.

It is important to note that not only Christians were among the supporters of France during that period. The Mutawali Shi'ite leader Kamil al-As'ad approached the French consul-general in Beirut in the name of his 30,000 people for a French protectorate and assistance in eliminating Ottoman rule. A group of Muslim notables from Aleppo suggested to the French consul there that a revolt be initiated in all the Syrian centres, to drive out the Ottomans and transfer the country into the hands of French forces.

Before and during the Paris Congress—the reasons for holding the congress there were discussed in detail earlier—some of its participants worked for the strengthening of the ties between Syria and France. The justification offered by Shukri Ghanim, who had been involved in persuading the French government to allow the congress, was that this would raise France's prestige among the Muslims of North Africa, who would see that it was to France that the Syrians came in order to demand an improvement in their situation. In a conference that was held in Paris with the participation of the Mutran brothers two months before the opening of the congress, it was decided that if Syria were not given administrative autonomy, a French protectorate should be demanded. Khalil Zayniyya, a member of the Lebanese Revival and the Reform Society of Beirut who kept up a close relationship with the French foreign ministry, told them that the members of the Reform Society were interested in French occupation (although this was not true of all the members of the society). He even expressed his willingness to introduce changes into the list of reforms at the foreign ministry's suggestion, and they transmitted instructions to him on the congress topics that interested them. Congress Resolution 11 expressed the gratitude of the Arabs to France for hosting it, and a few days after the congress a delegation thanked the foreign minister once again and asked for the assistance of France in the realization of reforms. The foreign minister promised them that France would remain Syria's advocate in Europe.

There were also many contacts at the individual level between members of the societies and French diplomats. The al-Khazin family of Juniyya had connections going back several centuries with the French representatives in the Levant. The brothers Philippe and Farid al-Khazin were honorary dragomans in the French consulate-general in Beirut, and they gave its representatives essays they had written concerning the status of Mount Lebanon and the complaints of the Lebanese against the

Ottoman authorities. Nakhla Mutran of Ba'albek visited the French consul-general in Damascus in January 1913 and told him that he and his friends had decided that Ba'albek and the Biqa' must be annexed to the Lebanon and that they were requesting French protection over the area. He added that the Lebanese, Muslims and Christians, were united in these requests. Nakhla Mutran was also among the signers of a petition on this matter, which was transmitted to France in May 1913.

To justify the sympathizers with France, Nakhla's brother Nadra Mutran, also pro-French, cited Syria's obligation to France for its educational institutions and its intellectual education, as well as France's enterprises in public works and its defence of the Syrians in the face of Ottoman tyranny. He called France "our common mother", and tried during the war to persuade it that "France's presence in Syria is indispensable, not only in order to preserve naval equilibrium in the Mediterranean Sea, but also in order to assure tranquillity in its Muslim possessions in Africa". Nevertheless, he did not aspire to the complete annexation of Syria by France because of the cultural differences (such as the matter of polygamy), suggesting instead that a French protectorate should be established in Syria, headed by a high commissioner.[9]

Among the Muslims, the French had good relations with the family of 'Abd al-Qadir al-Jaza'iri's descendants and relatives, to whom they transmitted monthly payments. Among the recipients were the amirs Tahir al-Jaza'iri, a member of al-Fatat, and 'Umar al-Jaza'iri, who joined al-Fatat during the war. Shafiq al-Mu'ayyad expressed his ideas concerning Syria's future on frequent visits to the French delegations in Istanbul and in Syria. Shukri al-'Asali, apparently more pro-British than pro-French, nevertheless did not hesitate to turn to the French consul-general in Damascus, after Amir 'Umar al-Jaza'iri introduced them to each other. He requested French assistance in the implementation of reforms in Syria based on decentralization, and even suggested that France put pressure on the imperial authorities through the loan it was to give the Empire towards the end of 1913. When al-'Asali was to be appointed civil inspector at the end of 1913, it was the French consul-general that he consulted before accepting the position. The relationship of the journalist Muhammad Kurd 'Ali to the French was more complicated. At first he attacked France in his newspaper al-Muqtabas, but later he began to publish articles sympathetic to France. This reversal was apparently tied to a "recompense" he received from the French consul-general in Damascus. By the end of 1913 Kurd

'Ali was already writing that "in Syria, our aspiration is to satisfy France, as we do not want to see its decline."[10]

The request of Ibrahim Salim al-Najjar to a French representative in Istanbul in the name of the Baghdadi officers late in 1912 should also be mentioned among the practical initiatives to carry out a revolt within the Empire with assistance from the French, as should his request to the French representative in Beirut in the name of the Syrian officers early in 1913. The plan of the Decentralization Party, together with the Society of the Lebanese Revival, to carry out a revolt in the Lebanon at the outbreak of World War I was also supposed to have had the assistance of French military equipment and officers.

However, the Decentralization Party was not always pro-French. The apprehension among Syrian émigrés in Cairo that Syria might be occupied by France, which increased following Poincaré's declaration at the end of 1912 about French interests in Syria, in fact led to the founding of the party. Rafiq al-'Azm sharply denounced the Syrians who leaned towards France and were willing to give it a foothold in Syria, and he proclaimed that France had nothing to look for in Syria. At that time he, his brother 'Uthman and their cousin Haqqi considered France the enemy of Islam, because of its attitude towards the Algerians.

When the Arab-Syrian congress was held in Paris, its organizers and participants were attacked for this even by members of the Arab societies, among them Ma'ruf al-Rusafi, who described the participants as "lambs appealing to a wolf for help", and 'Aziz 'Ali al-Misri, who believed that the transmission of the congress resolutions to the French foreign minister was no less than treason towards the East. Indeed, not all the congress participants agreed with the pro-French orientation. Apprehensive about the tendencies on the part of some of the Christians, some of the Muslim participants organized a joint Muslim-Christian delegation to the French foreign ministry, this time to make it clear that the Syrians were not interested in the annexation of their country by France, where they had held the congress only because they knew that it was a place of liberty.

The one who sharply attacked France's intentions towards the Arab countries was Rashid Rida. After the Empire's defeat in the Balkans he attacked the foreigners who sought control over Syria and the coasts of the Arabian Peninsula, also specifying his belief that they would destroy the Ka'ba and take away the Black Stone and the relics of Muhammad to the Louvre. He warned that after the expected European occupation of Mecca and Medina, taverns would be set up there and prostitution would spread among Arab women. The fear of the occupation by France that increased with the outbreak of World War I was one of the causes of *al-Fatat*'s attempt to reach an understanding with the British, based on the establishment of an independent Arab state, on condition that Syria would not be occupied by France.

A reasonable explanation for Syrian hostility towards France during the period under discussion, especially among the Muslims, was given, surprisingly, by a Frenchman, who told the newspaper *Le Temps* that it derived from the fact that they compared the friendly and liberal attitude that the Muslims were enjoying under British rule in Egypt with the rigid attitude of the French towards the Muslims in Algeria. He expressed the opinion that a change in the attitude of the French towards the Muslims in Algeria would lead to a rise in France's prestige in the Levant.[11] Yet, despite this hostility among some of the Muslims in Syria, there were also Muslims who were sympathetic towards France, both Sunnis and Shi'ites, and even some Algerians.

ATTITUDES TOWARDS BRITAIN

According to Najib 'Azuri, Britain had no ambitions to occupy Syria and Mesopotamia, seeking only to gain control of the east bank of the Suez Canal and to prevent the Russians from advancing to the Dardanelles, to the Euphrates valley and to Syria. With the outbreak of World War I 'Azuri attempted without success to interest the British in Egypt in organizing a rebellion in Syria. The feeling that there was nothing to fear in Britain's intentions was indeed widespread among many circles of the Arab societies, and their members requested the services of the British representatives in the Ottoman Empire not a few times during the period under discussion.

When the Reform Society of Beirut was closed by the authorities in April 1913, the British consul-general in Beirut, at the behest of the society's leaders, facilitated the release of the members of the society who had been arrested. Sayyid Talib of Basra also maintained permanent contacts with the British consuls in Basra, Muhammara, and Bushir, within the framework of his various attempts to strengthen his position. He once helped them to carry out a secret reconnaissance in the neighbourhood of Faw, and another time he sought to help a group of British officers to tour the area of Qarmat 'Ali. In 1912 Talib travelled

to Egypt and to India and met with Lord Kitchener, Lord Hardinge, the Viceroy of India, and Arthur Henry McMahon, then
Secretary for Foreign Affairs in the Indian government. In a discussion with the consul in Basra early in 1914 Talib even suggested that the British should take it upon themselves to mediate
between him and the Ottoman authorities. (The British, of
course, did not even consider the possibility of intervening in the
raging cauldron of the relations between Talib and the authorities, as the consul made clear to him at once.) When World War
I broke out, Talib tried to convince the British of the benefit to
them of recognizing him as the sheikh or amir of Basra, under
their aegis. The British waived his services and preferred that he
go into exile in India.

Another leader who was assisted by the British was 'Aziz 'Ali
al-Misri, who was saved from execution in April 1914, primarily
through the intervention of the British ambassador in Istanbul
on his behalf, following the request of Lord Kitchener. The
Arab Revolutionary Society also acknowledged the importance
of the British intervention on behalf of al-Misri in a proclamation published a short time after his release.

The trust shown by some of the Syrians in the British and in
the fairness of their rule reached such proportions that at the end
of 1912 a fairly widespread movement began for the annexation
of Syria to Egypt under the Anglo-Egyptian government. Practical action towards this idea had already begun a year earlier,
when Shukri al-'Asali and Salim Thabit arrived in Cairo and
presented such a plan to various Egyptian politicians. The
names of Salim 'Ali Salam, who also visited Egypt and was
received by the Khedive, of the brothers Muhammad and
Ahmad Kurd 'Ali, the owners of al-Muqtabas, and of Dr 'Izzat
al-Jundi were also associated then with this plan. At the end of
1912 it was brought up once again, this time more forcefully.
The Muslim Syrian émigrés in Cairo not only supported the idea
but made plans to meet Lord Kitchener and to ask for a British
protectorate over Syria.

The Muslims of Beirut also leaned towards British occupation
or the annexation of Syria to Egypt, and even planned to send
their own delegation to Lord Kitchener to discuss the matter.
Students in the American schools in Beirut sent a message to
Cairo requesting British protection and the occupation of Syria
by the Anglo-Egyptian government. There were also rumours
that in a telegram sent to the British foreign minister the notables of Beirut asked for the immediate occupation of Beirut by
Britain. Many Beirutian families, such as the Sursuqs, the

Thabits, the Karams and the Tuwaynis, had important interests in Alexandria and in Cairo, which also contributed to this trend. A British officer who arrived in Beirut at the end of May 1912 was already asked on his first day by a local youth: "When are you British coming to free our country from the Turk? We will die rather than remain under the Turk, and the time of our deliverance is near. If England will, she can make our deliverance the more certain. Let her send her fleet here and the country will rise as one man to welcome her."[12]

The idea of the annexation of Syria to Egypt had many supporters in Damascus, even among some Christians. Their fellow countrymen in Cairo sent them letters describing their comfortable life under the tolerant and fair rule of the British. The Muslim Syrians, though they had become alienated from Ottoman rule, were apprehensive that French occupation might put them into an inferior position to the Christian Syrians, whom France had traditionally protected. They believed that British occupation, on the other hand, would grant them a Muslim prince, as in Egypt, and more honour for their religion. The most prominent of the pro-British activists in Damascus in 1912 were Shukri al-'Asali, 'Abd al-Wahhab al-Inklizi, and Muhammad Kurd 'Ali. In Aleppo some of the residents, mainly the Druzes, favoured Britain, and in early 1913 a group of Muslim notables requested the British consul that their country be placed under British rule with a regime similar to that in Egypt or in India. After an abortive effort to interest the French in the country's situation, the Aleppans went to the British consul again a month later with the request that the British government in Egypt extend its protection over their region. Similar leanings were expressed in the sanjaq of Jerusalem, whose residents had despaired of the possibility of reform; separatist tendencies were growing, with many preferring the annexation of the country to Egypt.[13]

Although the Society of the Lebanese Revival routinely sent its various letters and protests to the French government, this did not prevent it from turning to Britain occasionally as well. Philippe al-Khazin sent a copy of his pamphlet concerning the Lebanon to the Speaker of the British House of Commons. At the outbreak of World War I the president of the São Paulo branch of the society sent a letter to the British foreign minister, requesting the protection of the Allies for the Lebanese. At about the same time the Lebanese turned to the British consul-general in Beirut for military assistance in a rebellion against the Ottomans. The consul advised them against the plan since the war meant that the Allies had to worry about themselves, pre-cluding assistance to the Lebanese. The members of the New York branch of the society suggested a rebellion against the Ottomans to the British ambassador in Washington; there too the request was denied.

The outbreak of World War I led to a spate of appeals by the societies to the British authorities in Egypt, with suggestions of rebellion against the Ottomans. Rashid Rida complied with the British request to send emissaries to ask Ibn Saʿud, Imam Yihya, al-Idrisi, and a number of leaders in Syria how they would respond to the war breaking out in the Middle East. Contacts were made between the British and the Muslim heads of the Decentralization Party; an understanding was reached that the latter would transmit to the British their demands for the libera-tion of the Arab countries, and if these were accepted they would work to incite revolts within the Empire. The Turks believed that the contacts between the British and the party members had begun at the initiative of the owners of the news-paper al-Muqattam (Nimr and Sarruf), whom they accused of receiving large sums of money from the British.[14] A number of emissaries of the party actually embarked upon revolutionary agitation, but when the response of the British government did not satisfy the party members, the contacts ceased.

At the beginning of the war al-Fatat, which also sought to begin contacts with the British in Egypt and to reach an under-standing concerning the establishment of an independent Arab state, sent Kamil al-Qassab to Cairo—but his mission did not bring results. In August 1914 ʿAziz ʿAli al-Misri, suggesting to the British a rebellion in Iraq and Syria that would lead to the establishment of an independent Arab state under the aegis of Britain, requested British assistance in money and arms. Though he claimed that Britain would thus never face rebellion in Persia or in India, his plans were initially rejected, but by the end of October the British were already expressing willingness to accept them. Al-Misri then concentrated on his suggestion of a rebel-lion in Iraq, where Britain would assist with money, rifles, ammunition and artillery, but eventually the plan was dropped because of the opposition of the British government in India and its officials in Basra. Al-Misri did not give up, suggesting in December to a British journalist that Britain should assist in the establishment of an Iraqi state dependent upon British India, in return for which he, al-Misri, would go to Iraq to persuade the Arab officers in the Ottoman army to desert and the tribal chiefs not to oppose the British.

The welcoming attitude of the Muslim Syrians towards the British, as opposed to the hostility of at least some of them towards France, derived from the comparison they made between the British governments in Egypt and India, which were perceived positively, and the rigid attitude of the French to the Muslims of Tunisia and Algeria. Egypt, under the relatively liberal rule of the British, had become an attractive refuge for Syrian separatists, who fled there, while exiles from French North Africa arrived in Syria. Shukri al-Shurbaji, a young Arab officer who joined al-Fatat during the war, deserted at the Russian front and was handed over to the British, told Mark Sykes explicitly in 1916 that such comparisons had led most of the Syrian populace, excluding the Lebanese Christians, to prefer autonomy under the supervision of the British.[15]

But not everyone was partial to Britain. In the 1880s al-Afghani and 'Abduh were already combatting the British occupation of Egypt on the pages of al-'Urwa al-Wuthqa, arguing that the British government was very hostile to the Muslims and warning the Egyptians that the British aspired to enslave them. Thus they laid down the ideological line that guided some of the Egyptian nationalists afterwards. And not only the Egyptians were worried about Britain's intentions. Rashid Rida, who cooperated with the British at the outbreak of World War I, had attacked them fiercely in 1912 on the pages of al-Manar: "This covetous state is not satisfied with spreading its influence and its foothold in Iran, but is also paving the road to gain control over the Arab countries opposite it, such as Masqat and the rest of 'Uman, and further along the Arab coast until Kuwait and even Basra."[16]

Indeed, Britain's plans for the south of Iraq aroused the suspicions of the Iraqis. A pamphlet distributed by the Committee for the Defence of the Interests of Iraq expressed determined opposition to the concession given to the British maritime company Lynch for navigation between Baghdad and Basra. The authors considered that this concession constituted a danger of foreign penetration into their country. During 1913 the Iraqi press expressed its suspicions of the ambitions of the British in the region, and the newspaper al-Dustur, under the management of 'Abd al-Wahhab al-Tabataba'i, a member of the Reform Society of Basra, printed aggressive articles against them.[17]

There were also other reasons for opposing the British. Shukri Ghanim, pro-French, accused Britain of being a partner of the Ottoman authorities in preventing the development of the Lebanon, because this region of land tended towards France.[18] 'Aziz

'Ali Al-Misri, who was rejected by the British-run military academy in Cairo as being too short, explained to Haqqi al-'Azm that he was going to study instead at the military academy in Istanbul in order "to drive out the British". Despite his later contacts with the British and their intervention on his behalf during his trial, his personal attitude towards them, both during World War I and afterwards, until World War II, remained at best reserved, if not hostile.

ATTITUDES TOWARDS GERMANY

In general, the attitude of the members of the Arab societies to Germany in the decade preceding World War I was negative. Only a few individual exceptions are known: 'Abd al-Karim Qasim al-Khalil formed connections late in 1912 with a delegation of German officers who were to follow the French propaganda in Syria and to establish German intelligence agencies and propaganda centres there. In 1910 Ja'far al-'Askari was sent to Germany for military studies and later he even received the German Iron Cross. 'Aziz 'Ali al-Misri was influenced by his German teachers at the military academy in Istanbul and from then on was sympathetic to Germany, both during World War I and during World War II, when he tried to desert to the Germans. The societies' members requested the assistance of the Germans directly only during al-Misri's trial, when they asked Liman von Sanders to intervene on his behalf.

Najib 'Azuri suspected Germany of interest in gaining control over the entire region from the North Sea to the Persian Gulf and establishing a formidable German empire. He viewed the Germans as "the most colonizing nation in the world" and he believed that in their hands "Asia Minor will become an entirely German country within a few years." Suspicion of one of Germany's large projects in the Empire during this period, the Baghdad railway, was expressed in a pamphlet distributed by the Committee for the Defence of the Interests of Iraq, which warned of the danger of the infiltration of foreigners into the country. Distrust of Germany was also voiced among the Syrians living in Cairo, none of whom expressed a desire for their country to be occupied by Germany in discussions they held on its future. Haqqi al-'Azm, in his customary sharp style, later called the Germans the "savages" of the twentieth century. This hostility was also expressed by the members of the Reform Society of Beirut; they rejected the attempt of the German consul there to intervene during the crisis of the society's dissolution in April 1913, although they did not object to the intervention of the French and Russian consuls-general, and even sent a special delegation to the British one requesting his intervention in the affair.

The reason for this attitude is clear. The societies opposed the imperial authorities, some more and some less, and Germany (unlike Britain and France) was identified with them. The Germans considered themselves allies of the Turks and they scarcely concerned themselves with the Arabs in the Empire. In their contacts with the local Arab populace their behaviour was arrogant, which undoubtedly did nothing to increase sympathy for them on the part of the Arab intellectuals.[19]

ATTITUDES TOWARDS OTHER STATES

'Azuri was initially convinced that Italy would show sympathy for an Arab resistance movement since the Italians themselves had been subjugated for a long time. However, his attempts to persuade the Italians to give him arms for a revolt showed him that "Italy will not go with us".

In September 1911 Italy invaded Libya and conquered it, taking it from the Ottoman Empire. Among the Ottoman officers who went there to assist the Sanusi forces in the resistance movement against the Italians was 'Aziz 'Ali al-Misri. He did succeed in scoring a number of military achievements against the Italians, but he eventually left Libya after having contacts with them, at least indirectly; it was charged that he received 15,000 pounds from them. The fall of Libya to the Italians (together with the defeat of the Empire in the Balkans) had a great impact on the various Arab activists, and a number of societies were established as a result of these events, while the activities of other societies became more extreme. During the war between Italy and the Empire, Italy carried out naval activities in the Aegean Sea and also took action against the port of Beirut. This obviously mitigated against the sympathy of the populace for Italy. In an article in *al-Mufid* 'Abd al-Ghani al-'Uraysi denounced Italy as well as British and French imperialism in general.[20] The publication of a poem by Muhammad Kurd 'Ali in *al-Muqtabas* inciting his readers against all Europeans and the Italians in particular led to an attempt by the authorities to arrest him (he managed to escape), and to the arrest of his brother Ahmad.[21]

In Iraq, on the other hand, the defeat of the Empire by Italy aroused very little attention. Prayers were said for the success of the Empire and a number of impractical suggestions were raised for military service, but indifference prevailed among the populace.[22]

A number of states served the societies as models for the regime to aspire to. *Al-'Ahd* took Austria-Hungary as its model of a dual monarchy. The Decentralization Party cited Switzerland as a state with an efficient decentralized regime. 'Abd al-Rahman al-Kawakibi had already called upon the Arabs, Muslims and non-Muslims, to attain national union (*ittihad watani*) along the lines of the United States. The United States as the model was also adopted by Iskandar 'Ammun, the vice-president of the Decentralization Party.

*

In general the attitude of the societies to the European states may be characterized as pragmatic. In times of need they would turn even to states they were not in sympathy with, if they considered it necessary for the realization of their aims, with the exception of Germany, which they dissociated themselves from almost completely because of its identification with the imperial authorities. Nevertheless, there are clear characteristics that can be discerned in the attitudes of the societies towards the two European powers that were of central importance for them: France and Britain. The attitude of the inhabitants of the Levant—among them the members of the societies—evinced diametrically opposed stances regarding France: unambiguous sympathy, such as that expressed mainly by the Lebanese and the Society of the Lebanese Revival, but also by other Christian and Muslim groups throughout Syria; or hatred and fear of a French occupation of Syria. The attitude to Britain in the Levant, on the other hand, was not so extreme in either direction. There were no significant groups hostile to Britain, but, on the other hand, no groups that identified with it completely, as the Lebanese and the Society of the Lebanese Revival identified with France. Although at a certain point the idea of the annexation of Syria to Egypt was raised, this idea did not have a cultural or ideological basis, but rather was motivated by the desire to replace Ottoman rule with British rule, which was perceived to be better. The Syrians did not fear British ambitions for occupation as they did French ambitions, and were therefore able to approach the British at the outbreak of World War I to try to reach an understanding with them, perhaps also as a barrier to the intentions of France. In Iraq, on the other hand, suspicions were expressed about the ambitions of the British there, suspicions which sometimes were transformed into a state of hostility. This attitude towards France and Britain before World War I was a precursor to that of the post-war period. The occupation of Iraq and the Levant by Britain and France sharpened these feelings, as the fears or the hopes were realized. The British were hated by the Iraqis. The French were hated by the Syrians (who preferred the British), but they were favoured by the Christian Lebanese.

Chapter 28

THE SIZE OF THE SOCIETIES

There are two approaches to determine the size of the societies. The first is based on evaluations by various sources of varying levels of reliability. The second is based on a follow-up of the names of the activists in the societies. An "activist" is defined as anyone whose name appears, even if only once, in the documents or books on which the present research is based. While the second approach·is more trustworthy, its fault is that it admits the counting of only those members whom history has recorded on its pages. The following is a summary of the numerical data concerning the extent of the societies, compiled using the two approaches:

The Arab Revival: 37 activists.
The Ottoman Arab Brotherhood: According to the evaluation of the newspaper *al-Muqattam* there were 900 members in the Aleppo branch of the society.[1] A follow-up of names in the entire society reveals 23 activists.
The Syrian Central Society: 2 activists.
The Lebanese Revival: In 1914 *al-Manar* evaluated the number of members in all the Lebanese societies as in the thousands. In 1908 the British consul-general in Beirut believed that the society in the Lebanon numbered 4,000-5,000 members, headed by a committee of 25 members. In mid-1912 the French minister in Cairo estimated the number of members in the society in Cairo at eight or ten, and at the end of the year another French representative in Cairo transmitted a list of 14 names.[2] A follow-up of names of all the branches of the Society of the Lebanese Revival reveals 69 activists.
The Syrian Union Society (in New York): 4 activists.
Al-Fatat: In general, it is easier to determine, at least approximately, the number of members of the secret societies. The reason for this is that nearly everyone who was admitted to these societies was really an activist, and therefore his name appears sooner or later in the sources. For example, Muhibb al-Din al-Khatib was accepted by *al-Fatat* at the beginning of 1913 and was given the ordinal number 28.[3] From among the 27 members

who joined before him, the names of 20 are specifiable on the basis of the sources. A follow-up of names in the society until the end of 1914 reveals 37 activists.[4]

Al-Qahtaniyya: 21 activists.

The Literary Club: The newspaper *al-Ahram* wrote that there were more than 280 members in the club and about 500 additional people visited it.[5] A follow-up of names in the club reveals 51 activists.

The Society of the Arab Association: 4 activists.

The Green Flag: 12 activists.

The Decentralization Party: On the membership card of Mustafa Simisma for the party is listed the ordinal number 202. Simisma joined the party on 15 April 1914.[6] Since the party continued to grow for another half year, until the war broke out in the Middle East, it may be assumed that the number of registered members reached over 250. A follow-up of names in the party reveals 72 activists.[7]

The Reform Society of Beirut: The society officially consisted of 86 members, representatives of all the religions. A follow-up of names reveals 34 activists.

The Reform Society of Basra: 21 activists.

The National Scientific Club: 20 activists.

Al-'Ahd: 54 activists.[8]

Al-'Alam: 3 activists.

The Arab Revolutionary Society: 4 activists.

Many members participated simultaneously in more than one society, some of them even in societies with contradictory ideologies (see below). Therefore it is not possible simply to add up the number of members in the various societies for a combined total; one must subtract the overlapping membership.

The numbers in the following table refer to those activists whose names appear explicitly in at least one of the sources:

The Arab movement	The particularist movements
<u>The Arab societies</u> <u>The Arab Revival</u> The Arab-Ottoman Brotherhood *al-Fatat* *al-Qahtaniyya* The Literary Club The Green Flag *al-'Ahd* Total: 175 <u>The pan-Arab societies</u> The Society of the Arab Association The Arab Revolutionary Society Total: 8	The branches of the Lebanese Revival 69 The Reform Society of Beirut 34 <u>The Syrian societies</u> <u>The Syrian Central Society</u> The Syrian Union Society The Decentralization Party Total: 78 <u>The Iraqi societies</u> The Reform Society of Basra The National Scientific Club *al-'Alam* Total: 42
Total: 180	Total: 207
Total number of activists in the societies: 350	

It can be seen that those who became activists in the political societies during the period under discussion fall into four general blocs: those who joined societies with an Arab flavour (with a very small minority of pan-Arabists); those who set their sights on the interests of the Lebanon; those who set their sights on Syria's interests (with the society of Beirut standing, in a sense, between the last two blocs); and to a lesser degree those who set their sights on the interests of Iraq—or part of it.

The members of all the societies, numbering 350 men,[9] were a drop in the ocean among the Arabs of the Ottoman Empire, whether these numbered 5.3 million, according to low estimates, or 10.5 million, according to the high estimates. Nevertheless, they had a both a short-term and a long-term influence. The question of the impact of the societies on the population of the Arab provinces of the Empire will be discussed in a later chapter.

Chapter 29

COMPOSITION

The following data in percentages refer only to those society activists (according to the definition of "activist" given in the previous chapter) for whom the relevant details were available. Reference is made only to those societies with more than 10 members; a percentage analysis of the composition of societies with only a few members is meaningless.

ORIGINS

Origins of the activists of the Arab-oriented societies (in percentages):

	Arab Revival (Istan.& Dams.)	Arab-Ottom. Broth. (Istan.)	al-Fatat (Paris)	al-Qahtan. (Istan.)	Liter. Club (Istan.)	Green Flag (Istan.)	al-'Ahd (Istan.-centre)
Greater Syria							
Damascus	74	22	34	28	27	10	21
Hawran			3				
Homs	3	4	3	14	6		4
Hama	3						
Aleppo		4			2		
Latakia			3				
Tripoli					2		
Ba'albek		9	11	5	13		
Hasbaya	8		5	5	4		
Beirut		4	28	10	8		
Mt. Lebanon	6	9		18	8		6
Sidon	3	4	3		4		
Nablus			5		4		
Jerusalem		13		5	4	10	2
Haifa					2		
Gaza					2	20	
Total:	97	70	95	85	88	40	33
Iraq							
Basra		4					2
Baghdad		18	5	5	8	50	40
Mosul				5	2	10	23
Total:		22	5	10	10	60	65

(continuation)

	Arab Revival	Arab Broth.	*al-Fatat*	*al-Qahtan.*	Liter. Club	Green Flag	*al-'Ahd*
Other places							
Cairo				5	2		2
Libya		4					
Mecca		4					
Hudaida	3						

The Societies of the Arab Revival, *al-Fatat, al-Qahtaniyya* and the Literary Club were composed almost exclusively of members from Greater Syria. Most of the activists of the Society of the Arab-Ottoman Brotherhood were from Greater Syria, although there was a large minority from Iraq. In the Green Flag and *al-'Ahd* there were a majority of Iraqis with a large minority of members from Greater Syria. Among the members from Greater Syria in all the societies the largest number hailed from Damascus. The largest number of Iraqi society members came from Baghdad. Nevertheless, if Greater Syria and Iraq are divided into smaller units—vilayets or even towns—a substantial heterogeneity is found in nearly all the societies. Only in the Society of the Arab Revival did the members from one city (Damascus) constitute more than half of the activists in the society. The fact that all the societies of the Arab trend were founded in non-Arab cities (Istanbul and Paris), and were fairly heterogeneous from the viewpoint of the towns of origin of their activists, permits conjecture that the establishment of these societies as Arab-oriented ones was derived from the fact that their activists were searching for the greatest common denominator that could unite them despite their different origins—Arabism—for the purpose of joint activity in a foreign city.

Origins of the activists of the Lebanese/Syrian-oriented societies (in percentages):

	Lebanese Revival (The Lebanon & other Lebanese communities)	Reform Society of Beirut (Beirut)	Decentralization Party (centre in Cairo & branches in Greater Syria)
Damascus	1		20
Druze Mt.			2
Homs			6
Hama			3
Aleppo			2
Tripoli			4
Ba'albek			6
Hasbaya			2
Beirut	23	97	14
Mt. Lebanon	75	3	16
Sidon	1		3
Nablus			7
Tul Karm			2
Jenin			2
Jerusalem			3
Haifa			2
Jaffa			6

Origins of the activists of the Iraqi societies (in percentages):

	Reform Society of Basra (Basra)	National Scientific Club (Baghdad)
Kuwait	5	
Basra	76	5
Najaf		10
Middle Euphrates	5	5
Baghdad	9	80
Mosul	5	

It is not surprising that the activists of the particularist societies came from places the societies were working for. Most of the activists in the Lebanese Revival were from Mount Lebanon, with a large minority of members from Beirut, who wanted their city annexed to Mount Lebanon. The activists of the Reform Society of Beirut obviously came from Beirut while the activists of the Decentralization Party, which worked for all of Greater Syria, came from all parts of that area. The activists of the Reform Society of Basra were mainly from Basra, while most of the activists of the National Scientific Club were from Baghdad.

RELIGION

The religion of the activists of the Arab-oriented societies (in percentages):

	Arab Revival	Arab Broth.	al-Fatat	al-Qahtan.	Liter. Club	Green Flag	al-'Ahd	Total*
Muslims	97	95	97	90	91	100	94	96
Christians	3	5	3	10	9		6	4

*With overlap between societies subtracted and the activists of the small societies added.

The numbers speak for themselves. The Arab movement in the period under discussion was led almost exclusively by Muslims. The Christians were on the fringes of the movement.

The religion of the activists in the Lebanese Revival (in percentages): Christians — 96, Druzes — 4.

The religion of the activists in the Reform Society of Beirut (in percentages):[1] Muslims — 50, Christians — 44, Jews — 6.

The religion of the activists of the Syrian-oriented societies (the Decentralization Party and the small societies, in percentages): Muslims — 69, Christians — 28, Jews — 3.

The religion of the activists of the Iraqi societies (in percentages):

	Reform Society of Basra	National Scientific Club	Total*
Muslims	100	95	95
Christians		5	5

*With overlap between societies subtracted and the activists of al-'Alam added.

That the Lebanese movement was led almost entirely by Christians, the Syrian movement by a Muslim majority with a large Christian minority, and the Iraqi movement, to the extent that it could be labelled as such, almost entirely by Muslims, corresponds to the general breakdown of religions in the Lebanon and in Iraq: an absolute majority of Christians (with a Druze minority) in Mount Lebanon and a Muslim population in Iraq. As for Syria, however, it seems that the Christian minority in the Syrian societies was much larger than the Christian minority in the Syrian population (slightly over ten per cent within Syria itself). The explanation for this may be found in the extensive participation of Beirut and Mount Lebanon residents in the Decentralization Party, for reasons which will be discussed later.

The following division into percentages is between younger and older activists, where younger activists are defined as those under the age of 30 at the time they joined the society.[2]

The age of the activists in the Arab-oriented societies (in percentages):

	Arab Revival	al-Fatat	Arab Broth.	al-Qahtan.	Liter. Club	Green Flag	al-'Ahd
			Socs. in Istanbul in the constitution period				
Younger	89	90	21	50	68	100	76
Older	11	10	79	50	32		24

The Society of the Arab Revival, which was established before the promulgation of the constitution, and al-Fatat, founded in Paris, had an absolute majority of young people, for these societies were composed mainly of students. On the other hand, among the societies in Istanbul during the constitutional period, there is an evident process in the proportion of younger to older activists, beginning with the Arab-Ottoman Brotherhood, which was composed mainly of adults, continuing with al-Qahtaniyya, which was evenly divided, and ending with the societies to which the young people gave the tone. One can therefore speak of two generations of Arab nationalists, such that, after the moderate and fruitless activities of the first generation, the second generation took upon itself the responsibility for nationalist activism and gave it a more radical flavour. On the eve of World War I the Arab movement was already, by and large, a movement of the young.

The age of the activists of the particularist societies (in percentages):

	Lebanese Revival	Reform S. of Beirut	Decentral. Party	Reform S. of Basra	National Scien. Club
Younger	26	29	44	36	87
Older	74	71	56	64	13

Regardless of which particularism they aspired to, activists in the particularist societies were in the main mature. The exception was the National Scientific Club, which was established on a similar basis to the Literary Club in Istanbul and with a similar composition in terms of age, as well as religion, class, occupation and education, although it limited its activities to matters concerning Iraq.

CLASS[3]

The class of the activists of the Arab-oriented societies (in percentages):

	Arab Revival	Arab Broth.	al-Fatat	al-Qahtan.	Liter. Club	Green Flag	al-'Ahd	Total*
Upper	70	96	73	74	87	27	44	70
Middle	30	4	21	26	13	55	28	22
Lower			6			18	28	8
			Excluding the officers	Upper Middle Lower		50 50	56 44	78 21 1

*With overlap between societies subtracted and the activists of the small societies added.

The class of the activists of the particularist societies (in percentages):

	Lebanese Revival	Reform S. of Beirut	Decentral. Party	Reform S. of Basra	National Scien. Club	Total*
Upper	64	95	64	80	67	70
Middle	36	5	34	13	22	27
Lower			2	7	11	3

*With overlap between societies subtracted and the activists of the small societies added.

The salient phenomenon here is that the participants in the political societies were generally from the upper class, with a minority from the middle class and an almost negligible minority from the lower class. Most of the participants from the middle or lower classes were army officers. From this it may be concluded that the members of these two classes considered attaining the rank of officer as the only way to go beyond the limitations of their class and gain equality with the upper class from the standpoint of political involvement and importance. Subtracting the officers from the total shows that the civilians who participated both in the Arab movement and in the various particularist movements were almost exclusively from the upper class. The apparent explanation is that the members of the upper class had the luxury of being able to engage in politics, while those of the lower class (and to a certain extent also the middle class) were preoccupied with providing for their daily existence. The members of the upper class could also afford higher education abroad, which also led to political involvement, as will be shown below.

Among the upper class were prominent families with a number of members in the societies. The record was held by the al-'Azm/al-Mu'ayyad al-'Azm family of Damascus and Hama, and the Shi'ite Haydar family of Ba'albek, each with eight members in the societies. They were followed by the al-Shihabi family of Hasbaya and Damascus and the 'Abd al-Hadi family of Nablus and Jenin, each with five members in the societies. There were four participants from each of the following families: the Mardams of Damascus, the al-Jundis of Damascus and Homs, the al-Husaynis of Jerusalem and Gaza, the al-Khazins of Mount Lebanon, the al-Sulhs of Beirut and the al-Suwaydis of Baghdad. Many members of these families were among the Arab leaders in their various states after World War I as well. Nevertheless, it should be noted that the participation of many of the family members in the societies does not mean that these families can be considered pro-Arab movement or pro-particularist movements per se. For example, Muhammad Fawzi Pasha al-'Azm, who was one of the senior members of the al-'Azm family before the war, and perhaps the most senior member, was a leader of the opposition to the reform and decentralization movements and was staunchly pro-Ottoman.

OCCUPATION

The following data in percentages refer to the occupations of the activists at the time of joining the societies.
The occupation of the activists in the Arab-oriented societies (in percentages):

	Arab Revival	al-Fatat	Arab Broth.	al-Qahtan.	Liter. Club	Green Flag	al-'Ahd
			Socs. in Istanbul in the constitution period				
Officer	4	6	6	35	12	46	78
Student	75	63	12	18	50	36	7
Journalist	13	6		6	2		5
Physician					2	18	2
Lawyer		6		6	2		
Merchant			6		2		
Landowner		3	6		2		2
Cleric	4						
Educator		3	6		2		2
Parliament			29	12	12		2
Gover./Admin.	4	10	35	23	14		2
Judicial system		3					

The societies of the Arab Revival, *al-Fatat* and the Literary Club were dominated by students. On the other hand, the majority of the participants in the Arab-Ottoman Brotherhood, the first society established in Istanbul after the promulgation of the constitution, were government and administrative officials and members of parliament. The relative strength of the latter two groups was less in the second society established in Istanbul, *al-Qahtaniyya*, less yet in the third society, the Literary Club, and disappeared almost completely in the fourth and fifth societies, the Green Flag and *al-'Ahd*. There was a parallel increase in the relative strength of students in the societies that were established in Istanbul after the promulgation of the constitution. They were a minority in the Arab-Ottoman Brotherhood, somewhat more in *al-Qahtaniyya*, and half the activists in the Literary Club. In the Green Flag there were already fewer students, and in *al-'Ahd* they became a small minority. The place of the students was then taken by a new factor: the officers. The latter entered Arab politics in Istanbul significantly when joining *al-Qahtaniyya*, the first secret society established there, were more than half the activists in the second secret society, the Green

Flag, and were the absolute majority of the activists in the third secret society, *al-'Ahd*.

The removal of government and administrative officials and members of parliament from Arab politics in the capital, and the takeover of activities first by the students and then by the officers, angered the members of the first group. Thus 'Abd al-Hamid al-Zahrawi called the Arab students in Istanbul children "unsuited for politics and it is not suited for them"; the officers he described as inexperienced in politics, so that it would be better for them not to intervene.[4] It should be recalled, in any case, that eventually the students as well were pushed aside and the tone set from then on by the officers. The latter, who entered politics in *al-Qahtaniyya* and became the leading factor in *al-'Ahd*, had apparently despaired of the inability of the civilians to improve the situation, and felt that they had to take matters into their own hands. In order to accomplish this, they even planned a number of rebellions (although these attempts sometimes had a local flavour, Syrian or Iraqi), and thus the first seeds were sown for a phenomenon that was to repeat itself many times in the Arab Middle East after World War I — officers as organizers of coups d'état.

The occupation of the activists of the Lebanese/Syrian-oriented societies (in percentages):

	Lebanese Revival	Reform Society of Beirut	Decentralization Party
Officer			2
Student		5	12
Journalist	50	26	31
Physician	17	5	8
Lawyer	9	11	6
Merchant	3	21	4
Banker		11	
Landowner	3	11	2
Cleric	3		8
Educator	3	5	
Writer	6		2
Parliament			2
Gover./Admin.		5	21
Judicial system	6		2

The two prominent elements in the Arab-oriented societies, the students and the officers, are almost entirely absent here. On the other hand, it can be seen that the majority of the members of the Lebanese/Syrian-oriented societies were in journalism. There were also doctors, lawyers, merchants, bankers, landowners, and government or administrative officials. The difference in the composition of the two orientations is highly significant. The students and the officers, who lived within a framework that provided for their daily existence (the students, supported by their upper-class families or by others during their studies), had time for ideological discussions about the Arab situation. On the other hand, the orientation of the activists in the Lebanese/ Syrian societies, most of whom were men of free professions, was pragmatic, for they had to cope continually, not with the ideological degradation caused by the behaviour of the Turks, but with the practical difficulties they created. These people were naturally interested in the local movements, which were intended to find specific solutions for local problems.

The occupation of the activists of the Iraqi societies (in percentages):

	Reform Society of Basra	National Scientific Club
Officer	30	38
Student		22
Journalist	10	11
Lawyer	5	
Merchant	5	
Landowner	30	11
Educator		6
Writer		6
Parliament	15	
Gover./Admin.		6
Judicial system	5	

The fact that the prominent elements in the Reform Society of Basra were landowners, officers and members of parliament derived from the special nature of the society and the power of Sayyid Talib in that town. The society consisted from the first of landowners with local interests, like Talib himself. Talib then invited Arab officers to join in order to increase his power, and through his unlimited influence in the town he was also able to send parliamentary representatives to the capital. The National Scientific Club was made up of officers and students and, to a lesser extent, journalists and landowners. This composition was quite similar to that of the Literary Club in Istanbul, yet since all the participants here were Iraqi, the Iraqi character of the club was dominant, and it did not have an Arab character, as did the club in Istanbul.

The relative absence of Muslim clerics and professional ideologues—people like the Islamic thinker Rashid Rida—is salient both in the Arab movement and in the particularist movements. The clerics preferred to support the Ottoman Empire, the last independent Muslim empire. Rida, who attained his pan-Arabism through Islamic ideology, was relatively isolated in his viewpoint. While most of the officers and the students did support the Arab movement, they did not go as far as pan-Arabism. The merchants, physicians, journalists, landowners, and other "practical" men were mostly particularists.

EDUCATION[5]

The education of the activists in the Arab-oriented societies (in percentages):

	Arab Revival	Arab Broth.	al-Fatat	al-Qahtan.	Liter. Club	Green Flag	al-'Ahd
Higher	70	59	80	53	78	64	23
Military	4	8	3	23	10	36	71
Religious	7	8	3	12	5		2
Other	19	25	14	12	7		4

The majority of the members of these societies had higher education. In all the societies except al-'Ahd the university-educated constituted more than half the activists, with al-Fatat holding the record. Members with a military education constituted a large minority in al-Qahtaniyya, a larger minority in the Green Flag, and an absolute majority in al-'Ahd. The fact that in nearly all the societies the university-educated were the absolute majority is explained by their being members of the upper class, who could afford to travel to Istanbul or Paris and acquire this education. The members of the societies were conscious of this factor; the president of the Paris Congress said in an interview on the eve of the congress: "I express the opinion of the educated stratum."[6]

The education of the activists of the particularist societies (in percentages):

	Lebanese Revival	Reform S. of Beirut	Decentral. Party	Reform S. of Basra	National Scien. Club
Higher	55	56	23	5	30
Military				28	40
Religious	4	15	8		5
Other	41	29	69	67	25

In the particularist societies the outstanding fact is that many of their activists lacked higher education. In the two reform societies close to 70 per cent of the activists were in this category. Indeed, the activists of these two societies were, as mentioned above, practical people and not ideologues, primarily concerned about the material interests of their country and of their immediate environs. Nevertheless, it should be noted that in all the societies except for the Reform Society of Basra the highly educated still constituted a considerable proportion of the activists, and in the Lebanese Revival and the Decentralization Party they were more than half. Another outstanding fact is that in the Lebanese/Syrian societies there were no activists whose education was attained exclusively in military academies (the only officer in the Decentralization Party had also studied medicine). There were also relatively few men with an advanced religious education, either in the Arab-movement societies or in the local-movements societies. Such people tended to prefer remaining loyal to the Muslim empire, and they were not interested in participating in movements that were not based on the religion of Islam.

*

Based on the data presented above, profiles can be drawn of the "typical" members of the various kinds of societies. The Arab activist emerges as a young, upper-class Muslim student from Damascus, such as Shukri al-Quwwatli, or a young Muslim officer of any class from Baghdad, such as Nuri al-Sa'id. Philippe al-Khazin typifies the Lebanese activist: a mature upper-class Christian journalist from Mount Lebanon. The Syrian activist frequently was a mature, upper-class Muslim independent professional from Damascus, such as 'Abd al-Rahman al-Shahbandar. 'Abd al-Latif Mandil was representative of one type of Iraqi activist: a mature, upper-class Muslim landowner from Basra; while the young Baghdadi Muslim officer (any class) was typified by Tahsin al-'Askari. It is noteworthy that the young Muslim Iraqi officers belonged to both the Arab and the Iraqi trends. Those in Istanbul who joined the *al-'Ahd* centre adhered to an Arab ideology, while those who were in the Iraqi societies, or in Iraqi *al-'Ahd* branches (especially the Baghdad branch), focused on Iraq and intended to begin their revolt plans there.

On the eve of World War I the importance of the student factor vanished entirely, even in the Arab movement. The student members of the societies had already completed their higher studies in Istanbul or in Paris and returned to their countries as members of the free professions—doctors, lawyers, and the like. Together with the officers and led by them, they now constituted the backbone of the nationalist movements in the Arab Middle East, and it was they who led the nationalist movements and the struggle against foreign rule after the war.

Chapter 30

THE INFLUENCE OF THE SOCIETIES

THE POPULAR ATTITUDE TOWARDS THE ARAB MOVEMENT

Because most of the societies of the Arab trend were secret in nature, they were also limited in extent. These two factors—secrecy and limited extent—necessarily meant that they had very little influence on the Arab masses in the Ottoman Empire. The societies in this category, established during the period from 1908 to 1914, were *al-Fatat, al-Qahtaniyya,* the Green Flag, the Black Hand, and *al-'Ahd.* The sole influential activity of *al-Fatat* during this period was organizing the Paris Congress, which went in directions that the society did not approve of and that did not suit its ideology. The officers of *al-'Ahd* did have various plans for carrying out rebellions in the Empire, but not only were they not realized during the period under discussion; they did not even become known to the masses. The Ottoman authorities for their part tried to damage this society as much as possible, and thus to decrease its power even more.

The two pan-Arab societies of the period, the Society of the Arab Association and the Arab Revolutionary Society, with only a few members, had even less influence than the other societies. Rashid Rida, who intended from the first to turn only to the rulers and not to the masses, failed even in this intention because of the rivalries that existed among the rulers of the Arabian Peninsula. The Arab Revolutionary Society was established too close to the outbreak of World War I to be able to effect the creation of pan-Arab feeling among the Levantine Arabs, and its activities were limited to distributing proclamations.

The success of the first overt society, the Arab-Ottoman Brotherhood, was also not especially great. It was established immediately after the Young Turk revolution, when the masses were hoping for a new Golden Age for the Empire, for an era of constitutional regime where justice and equality would reign. The society itself did not propose a clear programme to adhere to. Given that there were those who believed that it had been established with the encouragement of the Sultan in order to assist him against the CUP, it is not surprising that Arabs sent many protests against it to Istanbul. Against the backdrop of the desire for Arab-Turkish brotherhood that prevailed after the revolution, the society was attacked for being "Arab" by such personalities as Rashid Rida and Rafiq al-'Azm, who led their own societies a few years later.

The Literary Club, on the other hand, had a greater influence. It had close to 300 members and 500 additional people visited it. However, most of these people were aware only of its overt activities, which did not differ from those of an ordinary literary club. The secret, more radical activities on behalf of the Arab idea were known only to a limited circle, and from this aspect the club's influence did not go beyond that of societies which were officially secret.

The lack of sympathy on the part of the Arab masses for the Arab idea, proposed in one way or another by each of the societies named above, stemmed not only from a lack of communication with the societies or from the fear of reprisals by the authorities. Mostly Muslims, the Arabs considered the Ottoman Sultan their caliph and believed that their religion obligated them to be loyal to the Muslim Empire to the end. Many of them considered the Arab nationalist tendency to be *bid'a* and deviation from religion. And many feared that the alternative to the Ottoman Empire would be the occupation of their countries by foreign, Christian powers.

EGYPT'S ATTITUDE TOWARDS THE ARAB MOVEMENT

In general, the Egyptians did not consider themselves part of the Arab nation during the period under discussion, and they did not show any active interest in the fate of the Arab countries within the Ottoman Empire. The Egyptian nationalists were interested in Egypt, and their nationalism was territorial rather than being based on ethnic origin and language. They were acquainted with the other Arab countries through the Syrian and Lebanese émigrés in Egypt, but their feeling towards them was hostility, for the émigrés were intellectual and ambitious and had become dominant in their new country in trade, in the British administration and even in cultural life. They were rivals of the local Egyptians in the struggle to attain official positions. They were also more pro-British than the local people, describing the British occupation in their newspapers as advantageous for Egypt. The Egyptian nationalist leader Mustafa Kamil called them "*dukhala'*" (foreigners); "*khawarij*" who did not display the loyalty to the Ottoman Empire that he deemed proper. The Syrians and Lebanese in Egypt became a separate unit that was not politically involved with the local populace and was generally also unpopular.[1]

The exception was 'Aziz 'Ali al-Misri, but his Arab activism stemmed from the unique circumstances of his life. When he returned to Egypt a short time after the promulgation of the constitution in 1908, his suggestion to the Egyptian nationalist Muhammad Farid and his colleagues in the leadership of al-Hizb al-Watani to join a secret society that would work on behalf of the Arabs was rejected. The attempt of Shukri al-'Asali and Salim Thabit in 1911 to bring about the annexation of Syria to Egypt was likewise rejected. This time the opponent was Lutfi al-Sayyid, the leader of Hizb al-Umma. Muhammad Farid was also opposed to the Decentralization Party, founded in Cairo at the end of 1912 and composed only of Syrians, for he believed that it was striving for the annexation of Syria to Egypt with the goal of establishing a new Arab kingdom, and he claimed that it was motivated by ambitious people and driven by foreign influences.[2]

The principal confrontation between the Egyptian nationalists and the Arab movement occurred at the time of the establishment of the Society of the Arab Association by the pan-Arabist Rashid Rida. The Egyptian 'Ali Yusuf, owner of the newspaper al-Mu'ayyad, was also a member of this society, but it seems that this fact derived more from the latter's friendly relations with Rida than his belief in the chances that Rida's ideology would be realized. Rida's opposition to Egyptian nationalism, together with his opinions and activities against the Ottoman Empire, which the Egyptian nationalists favoured, brought their wrath down upon Rida. Their newspaper al-'Alam attacked him, under the inspiration of Muhammad Farid and its editor-in-chief, 'Abd al-'Aziz Jawish. He was accused of establishing a society striving for the secession of the Arab countries from the Ottoman Empire, to be ruled by an Arab caliph under the aegis of Britain. The newspaper also claimed that the school Rida founded was intended to create propagandists not for Islam but for the struggle against the Turks. Jawish accused him of working for the destruction of Ottoman unity (al-jami'a al-'uthmaniyya) and fighting against Allah and his messenger, while sowing seeds of hatred for the Empire which had given Islam strength and enhanced the glory of the Muslims.[3]

The only instance of widespread activity among the Egyptians on behalf of an Arab activist was the trial of 'Aziz 'Ali al-Misri, which generated much excitement in Egypt and many expressions of support for him. Many petitions on his behalf were sent to the imperial authorities and to European representatives, and there was an atmosphere of rupture between Egypt and the Empire. However, this support was not for al-Misri as an Arab activist, but rather as an Egyptian national hero in the wake of his victories against the Italians in Libya.

THE POPULAR ATTITUDE TOWARDS THE PARIS CONGRESS

While the Arab masses in the Ottoman Empire were indifferent to or even in disagreement with the Arab movement during the period under discussion, they evinced a more ambivalent approach to the Paris Congress, which was on the border between being an expression of the Arab movement and the Syrian movement. Their responses to this congress ranged from wholehearted support on the one hand to determined opposition on the other. Many letters and telegrams of support were sent to the congress, and the vast majority of the signers (359 out of 402) were not activists in the Arab or the particularist societies. Rather, they came from all ranks of the nation, although mainly intellectuals, and from all the Arab provinces of the Fertile Crescent, although primarily from Syrian towns or Syrian émigré communities.

On the other hand, a determined opposition movement to the congress had also begun. Sheikh 'Abd al-'Aziz Jawish contended that the congress would cause a split in the Islamic community. Others claimed that the congress participants wanted to bring about foreign control over the country, and there were those who argued that after the defeat of the Empire in the Balkans was the wrong time to make things more difficult by demanding reforms. In Damascus a special conference was held at the home of 'Abd al-Rahman al-Yusuf, with the participation of Sheikh As'ad Shuqayr, Muhammad Fawzi Pasha al-'Azm and Muhammad Pasha al-Makhzumi, to denounce the congress. In cooperation with the Vali, 'Arif al-Mardini, they started a propaganda campaign against the congress and sent protest telegrams to Istanbul in the name of the populace. Petitions against the congress were distributed in Damascus, Beirut, Acre, Haifa, Nazareth and Tiberias.

The CUP supporters in Damascus sent identical telegrams to the capital: "The advocates of the idea of reform in Syria are a group of deserters from the exalted government, and all Syrians negate their words and wash their hands of them." In order to organize the activities against the congress, they established the True Reform Party (*Hizb al-Islah al-Haqiqi*), headed by Muhammad Fawzi Pasha al-'Azm, and a delegation of its leaders later set out for Istanbul in order to pose a counterweight to the congress members. Protests against the congress also came from Jabal 'Amil in the Lebanon, from Iraq, from Medina, from Yemen and from other places. Among the opponents of the congress were personalities such as 'Aziz 'Ali al-Misri and Sharif Husayn, in both cases because they were afraid that it would serve foreign interests. The congress members called their opponents "clockwork machines in the factory of the rulers". Indeed, there is no doubt that some of the opposition to the congress was directed by the authorities, but nevertheless some of it was authentic and motivated by the factors detailed above. Many of the opponents were religious functionaries, which strengthens the assumption that their opposition to Arabism, or to the congress, came first and foremost out of religious motivations of loyalty to the Muslim Empire and to the Caliph-Sultan.[4]

POPULAR ATTITUDES TOWARDS THE LOCAL MOVEMENTS

While the attitude of the Arab populace towards the Arab movement was indifferent or hostile, and its attitude towards the Paris Congress split between support and opposition, in the Lebanon, Syria and Iraq the inhabitants showed more sympathy towards the movements that were working on behalf of their countries.

When revolutionary proclamations appeared in Beirut at the end of 1880, the city notables hurried to deliver a petition to the Vali expressing their loyalty to the Sultan and denounced any revolutionary movement. The ideas raised in these proclamations were too advanced for their time and the local populace did not think at all in the terms of the members of the Secret Society of Beirut. Such was also the fate of the manifestos distributed after the 1908 revolution by the Syrian Central Society. The demand of the Mutran brothers that Syria be granted self-government was denounced by the Damascus notables as well as by such figures as Shukri Ghanim, Rafiq al-'Azm and Haqqi al-'Azm, who came to support the very same idea a few years later. At this time all of them believed that such a demand sabotaged the integrity of the Empire and the loyalty to the Ottoman idea.

Four years later local attitudes to the ideas of decentralization and self-government had changed completely. The Turkification policy of the Ottoman authorities harmed the local populace directly. The decision of the Ottoman government that only Turkish or French be used for customs forms, court proceedings and similar matters created a very concrete obstacle for the inhabitants of the Arab provinces who did not know Turkish. The defeats of the Empire in Libya and later in the Balkans demonstrated to the local people the inability of the Empire to protect them. And CUP policy, perceived by the Arabs as anti-religious, detracted from the glory of the Caliph in their eyes and led to a weakening of the religious identification with the central government. The populace was now willing to look for alternatives that would provide practical solutions. While the Arab movement with its vague ideas did not offer such a solution, the local movements did.

Although caution may be required in approaching such declarations as Khayrallah Khayrallah's claim at the end of 1913 that 300,000 Lebanese inside and outside of the Lebanon backed the demands of the Society of the Lebanese Revival, its ideas had broad support among the Lebanese, who took part in activities on behalf of these ideas, although not necessarily within the framework of the society. The decentralization movement also enjoyed support in Syria, although it is doubtful whether all the members of the Decentralization Party there were aware of the radical plans formulated by some of the party leaders. The opponents of the movement came from the same pro-CUP circles that opposed the Paris Congress. Sheikh 'Abd al-'Aziz Jawish, of Tunisian origin and pan-Islamic opinions, demanded in the Beirutian pro-CUP newspaper al-Ra'y al-'Amm: "And what then does the idea of a decentralized government mean if not to prepare the Ottoman Empire for final liquidation?"[5]

But most of the support of the local populace was granted to the two most pragmatic societies, the Reform Societies of Beirut and Basra. The demands of the Reform Society of Beirut, meant to make the vilayet semi-independent, came to improve the situation of all strata of the population. The intention was concrete benefit for the officials, the merchants, the artisans and the teachers, all of whom would have found the replacement of Turkish by Arabic as an official language a most significant improvement. The demand to reduce the length of military service and lower the indemnity for release from military service (badal) was certainly accepted by all. Thus the society, which was composed of members of the upper class, also enjoyed the support of the other classes, and this was expressed when the authorities closed the society in April 1913. A civil insurrection began which encompassed virtually all the inhabitants of the city—a unique event in the pre-war period. Shops were closed, the masses rioted in the streets, and most of the newspapers cooperated with the reformists. A protest petition to the prime minister and the interior minister bore over 1,300 signatures of "property owners, merchants, bankers, doctors, lawyers, journalists, publishers, etc.".

The events in Beirut also led to a wave of identification throughout the Arab countries. Protest activities were carried out in Damascus, and telegrams streamed in from Basra and from the Syrian-Lebanese community in Egypt. Although the reform movement was officially suppressed by the authorities, the enthusiasm that greeted the delegation of reformists returning from the Paris Congress in September 1913 pointed to its continued support within the population.

The Reform Society of Basra's list of demands was even more far-reaching than that of Beirut's society. The Reform Society of Basra could allow itself to go so far because of Sayyid Talib's almost unlimited power in the town. Talib had the support of the Arab officers who served in the town, and many of them were members of the society. He also had the support of others, such as the Sheikhs of Kuwait and Muhammara and local notables, some of whom backed him out of common interests while others did so out of fear. Recruiting numerous signers for his petitions was easy and routine for him, and on the eve of the assassination of Farid Bek he told the British consul in Basra that he had 30,000 armed men at his disposal to repel any possible invasion by 'Ujaymi. Even if one treats this boastfulness sceptically, it is a fact that Talib was the strong man of southern Iraq until the beginning of World War I and that the movement he led was more popular than the legal authorities in the region.

Hostility towards the Ottoman authorities also motivated important families in Baghdad, such as the al-Suwaydis, to support the National Scientific Club established there. Such families, together with local officers and students, constituted the circle of the club's supporters. It seems that the club's influence did not significantly penetrate the popular strata in the region, as they were steeped in ignorance and showed no interest in politics or ideology.

*

To sum up, the Arab-movement societies did not enjoy support among the Arab population they were working for. In some cases this population was totally unaware of the existence of the societies and it did not hurry to back the societies it did know about. The societies lacked a well-defined, crystallized ideology that could attract the masses, speaking primarily in general terms about justice and equality for the Arabs, and enhancing the glory of the Arab nation. The pan-Arab societies, which did propose an alternative to the Empire, were so small that they were practically unnoticed. On the other hand, the local movements enjoyed at least relative success among the Arabs of the Lebanon, Syria and Iraq, because they offered clear solutions to the local people that seemed realistic enough to be a practical alternative to the sorry situation in which they felt bogged down in the Ottoman Empire.

Examination of the influence of the societies on the history of the Middle East in the first quarter of the twentieth century shows that it was the societies of the Arab trend that set the tone during World War I, and some of their activists who served in the Arab revolt of Sharif Husayn of Mecca. However, these men, who were the leaders of Syria and Iraq after the war, had already become, during the war and the Arab revolt, particularist activists who were interested first and foremost in the good of their native lands. The clearest example of this was the Arab society *al-'Ahd*, which split at the end of the war into two particularist societies, *al-'Ahd al-'Iraqi* and *al-'Ahd al-Suri*. The Arab officers became Iraqi officers and Syrian officers when the liberation of their countries from the Turkish yoke became imminent.

The heritage of the Arab societies left an influence that extended far beyond the period under discussion. In the eyes of the Arab writers and historians who wrote about Arab nationalism all these societies—without justification—represented the first stage of this nationalism. Many leaders of the independent Arab states prided themselves on having been members of these societies at the beginning of their political career. When Nuri al-Sa'id wanted to establish in the early 1930s a party that would support his views, he called it *al-'Ahd*.[6] When the Free Officers in Egypt deposed Najib, the position of President of Egypt was offered to 'Aziz 'Ali al-Misri, whom they considered their spiritual father because of his continuing activities on behalf of the Arab cause, which began with the leadership of *al-'Ahd*.[7]

Chapter 31

METHODS OF ACTION

Although a widely-held distinction is commonly drawn between societies that acted openly and secret societies, a more accurate distinction would be between the societies that officially defined themselves as open while actually carrying out secret activities and societies that defined themselves as secret. In other words, the differences lay more in self-definition than in the nature of their practical activities.

Among the societies that may be included in the first category was the Arab-Ottoman Brotherhood, accused by the Turks of secret activity against the government. Even if this was untrue, the fact that its leaders were spies and former functionaries of the Hamidian regime gave rise to suspicion that it was connected with reactionary elements that were striving for the downfall of the constitution and participated in the counter-revolution of 1909. The Lebanese Revival, which was not officially a secret society, in practice maintained continuous secret contacts with outside elements, with the intention of fostering their intervention in the affairs of the Lebanon, even including capturing it from the Empire. The Literary Club also carried out secret activities on behalf of the Arab idea, under the name "The Arab Youth Society", and had a secret action plan known only to a limited circle of its members. The Decentralization Party's constitution overtly disclaimed secrecy, and publicly called for broad decentralization. In practice, however, its leaders formulated a radical plan for Syrian independence, and did not hesitate to cooperate with the French and the British in order to carry out their plans for driving the Turks out of Syria. The Reform Society of Beirut ostensibly worked only for reforms, yet at least some of its members had contacts with foreign elements for purposes similar to those of the Lebanese Revival. The Reform Society of Basra certainly attained the most spectacular achievements in harassing the authorities, and its leader carried out the only successful assassination in the period under discussion. The National Scientific Club, officially considered a literary club, was also suspected of secret political activity to drive the Turks out of Iraq. The Arab Revolutionary Society's activists had not themselves decided whether the society would be open or secret, but its proclamations were certainly not considered legitimate by the imperial authorities.

The second category, of officially secret societies, included: *al-Fatat, al-Qahtaniyya*, the Society of the Arab Association, the Green Flag, the Black Hand, *al-'Ahd* and *al-'Alam*.

PRESERVING SECRECY

The first element in preserving the secrecy of the societies was strict selection from among those who wanted to join them. Only those deemed appropriate, able to keep secrets, were accepted. *Al-Fatat*'s security measures were the most strict from this standpoint. Every new candidate had to be recommended by a current member, and in most cases even this was not sufficient, and another member of the society was appointed to investigate him. After the investigation the candidate was given basic information about the society, but in such a way that retreat was still possible without affecting the secrecy of the society. Even after the member was already sworn into the society, he would only know the two members who had sworn him in (one of them the person who had recommended him), and he would receive the society's instructions through them. The programme of the society would only be revealed after a trial period of three months. Letters from the society's centre would reach the members from the address "The Desert" (*al-badiya*), without their knowing who the senders or the members of the centre were. And as an additional security measure for preserving secrecy, each member had a personal number.

Al-Fatat's shortening of its full name, *al-Jam'iyya al-'Arabiyya al-Fatat*, in order that the name would not attest to the character of the society, was another of its security measures. (A similar security measure was taken by the Iraqi society *al-'Alam*, whose name could be read as "the flag", which the members intended as the real name of the society, or "knowledge", which would not reveal the real revolutionary character of the society.) In their letters the *al-Fatat* members referred to the society by the code name "*Ata'*". They also used a cipher for their correspondence, constructed in such a way that they could remember it without committing it to writing.[1]

In contrast to *al-Fatat*, *al-Qahtaniyya* instructed each of its members to admit another one to the society without prior authorization from the centre. This step, intended to broaden the ranks of the society, carried the risk of severely damaging its secret character and of exposure to the authorities, if an agent succeeded in infiltrating the society in this way (as actually happened to *al-'Ahd*). The security measures of this society were to transmit messages only orally, and sophisticated methods of identifying members. When two of the members met, one would press the hand of the other with his finger and then put his right palm on his left arm with the index and the middle fingers spread out and the other fingers folded. He would then utter the first letter of the word "*HiLAL*" (crescent) — "*H*". The second member would respond with "*L*", the first would continue with "*A*" and the second would conclude with "*L*". In meetings demanding a lesser degree of secrecy they would spell out the name "*ABU BaKR*".[2]

The members of *al-'Ahd* had fictitious names as a security measure. Thus, for example, member Muhammad Sharif al-Faruqi was called "'Umar Efendi". The importance of secrecy in the eyes of *al-'Ahd*'s leaders may be inferred from the following story told by Literary Club member Sayf al-Din al-Khatib:

> Salim al-Jaza'iri entered the club with 'Aziz 'Ali [al-Misri] and said publicly: "They say that I founded a society here intended for Arab officers." I said to him: "Your bosom friend 'Izzat al-Jundi was seen with a ciphered letter that could not be read without a key, and this aroused everyone's suspicion, since 'Izzat al-Jundi always accompanies you." Salim said: "There is no such society, and if there were I would admit 'Izzat al-Jundi to it. [And he added:] There are many rotten people in the Literary Club. Therefore twenty are better than fifty and fifty are better than two hundred." And [with this] he ended the argument.

'Izzat al-Jundi, at any rate, was not a member of *al-'Ahd* (perhaps because he tended to go around in the streets with ciphered letters).[3]

The activities of the ostensibly open Decentralization Party also took place secretly within the Empire. Thus, the party leaders' instructions to 'Awni 'Abd al-Hadi, one of its prominent activists in Palestine, were: "Each branch will remain secret until the government recognizes the party officially." Because of their fear of the authorities' reaction, all contacts between the party centre in Cairo and the branches within the Empire were maintained cautiously and secretly. 'Abd Al-Hadi, for example, was asked not to sign his letters to the centre with his own name but to write his membership card number instead. The centre's letters to him were addressed to "Husayn". In mid-1914 the party members decided to make the security measures stricter; Haqqi al-'Azm wrote to the head of the Beirut branch: "I decided to write a key for a cipher, and I will send you a copy of it soon, so that you can send telegrams and letters when necessary using its secret words."[4]

The use of code words was also customary in the Arab Revolutionary Society, which called its proclamations "the Baghdad merchandise".[5] This "merchandise" was sent to the Empire via the foreign postal systems, generally the French or British ones that were among the capitulations to the European states in the Empire. Through such post offices in Beirut, Jaffa, Alexandria, and elsewhere, the members of the Decentralization Party in Cairo were able to correspond with their branches within the Empire without surveillance by the Ottoman authorities. It was through these post offices that the party sent its platform for distribution within the Empire in spite of the ban that the Ottoman authorities had imposed on it. Another way to deceive the authorities was to insert an envelope addressed to the party centre into another envelope addressed to Sheikh Haqqi Khalaf, an official of a Cairo mosque, who was not known to be connected with the party. When there was no alternative, letters were also sent to the party through the Ottoman post office in Beirut, where Mahmud al-Mihmisani, the head of the party's local branch, worked as an official.[6]

MOBILIZING PUBLIC OPINION

The societies, especially those that also had overt activities, were aware of the necessity to spread their message publicly if they were to have real significance. The two elements for them to address were Europe, on the one hand, and the masses of Arabs in the Ottoman Empire, on the other. Najib 'Azuri had already understood this when he distributed two manifestos at the end of 1904 and the beginning of 1905, one addressed "to the enlightened and humane nations of Europe and North America" and the other "to all the inhabitants of the Arab fatherland who are oppressed by the Turks".

The means for mobilizing sympathetic public opinion among the Arab populace were varied. The Literary Club used the facilities it had as a club, as well as occasionally staging plays meant to present the heritage of Arab history to the spectators, including "Salah al-Din al-Ayyubi", "Imru' al-Qays" and "The Arabs". The club also distributed handbills which were ordered in Egypt and from the printing house of the newspaper *al-Mufid* in Beirut. These handbills sometimes arrived at the club inside newspapers sent to the editors of its periodical.

The Decentralization Party also distributed handbills, printing them in Egypt and sending them to the Empire; the party member responsible for the distribution was the secretary, Haqqi al-'Azm. This means of disseminating opinion was accepted by most of the societies, and even a "strong man" like Sayyid Talib considered it necessary to distribute handbills among the Arab soldiers in Iraq to obtain their support for his views. But the record for such distribution was apparently held by the Arab Revolutionary Society, which had no other activities. It carefully prepared its proclamations so that they would touch the emotions of the readers. For example, 'Aziz 'Ali al-Misri asked one of his acquaintances within the Empire to send him a copy of *Qawm Jadid*, considered by the Arabs to be one of the books most offensive to them in the period under discussion. Shortly afterwards the society published a proclamation citing this book as a proof that the imperial government was striving to destroy Islam.

One of the most important means of disseminating the societies' various ideas was the press. Most societies used newspapers or periodicals, whether official or unofficial, as organs to spread their ideas. While some of these publications had only a limited circulation and many of the inhabitants of the region were illiterate, the problem was solved by the literate people standing up in the middle of cafés and reading the newspapers aloud. Another phenomenon to be noted was the large number of newspapers supporting the Society of the Lebanese Revival and the Decentralization Party. Half of the activists in the Society of the Lebanese Revival and about a third of those in the Decentralization Party were journalists. These members assumed control of many newspapers and thus created a situation in which these publications supported their societies and spread their propaganda much more extensively than their relative size warranted.[7]

Another method of persuasion was giving public speeches. In general, the use of this method was limited because of the danger of immediate reaction on the part of the authorities. When Muhibb al-Din al-Khatib and 'Abd al-'Aziz al-'Atiqi, who had been sent by the Decentralization Party to the Persian Gulf and Iraq at the outbreak of World War I, were arrested by the British there, instructions for speeches were found among their effects: 1) Mocking the government; 2) cursing the Christians; 3) giving a helping hand to religious superstitions.[8] These notes are especially interesting in the light of the fact that Rashid Rida was one of the initiators of this mission and, as a "*salafist*", surely opposed religious superstitions. It may therefore be concluded that, in order to incite the populace to rebel against the government, cold and cynical use was made even of such means as the spreading of superstitions.

An additional method for attaining influence was to put pressure on the Arab members of the parliament. The Society of the Arab-Ottoman Brotherhood already understood the usefulness of this, and tried to form an Arab parliamentary party. Article 9 of the Decentralization Party's constitution imposed a mandate upon its members in the parliament to strive to the best of their ability to implement the party's programme there. Article 18 read: "The Administrative Committees of the branches . . . must strive for the election to the parliament of talented representatives who support the party's principle." The second Article of the Appendix to the resolutions of the Paris Congress stipulated that no candidate for election to the parliament be assisted without committing himself in advance to support the congress programme and to demand its implementation. When the general mobilization began in the Empire on the eve of the war, the members of the Decentralization Party's branch in Beirut tried to influence the Arab representatives in the parliament directly through a telegram demanding their resignation if they did not succeed in bringing about the postponement or abolition of the implementation of the mobilization law.

Another element that the societies tried to mobilize for their activities was the moneyed class, which was not always enthusiastic about cooperating. (Although most of the society activists were from the upper class, they nevertheless constituted a minority within that class.) As mentioned, Sayyid Talib had his own methods of mobilizing the rich to support his goals, but he was not the only one who addressed this class with threats. An anonymous manifesto distributed in Syria in 1913 included the following:

> This is a call to our notables and wealthy people in particular, from one end of the land of the Caliphs to the other, to assist this blessed movement with their money and their souls. In this way they will capture the hearts of their sons and forestall their becoming their enemies and learning from the Armenians how to force the wealthy to assist in these advantageous matters and to come to the aid of their country and nation, if not with a revolver—then with dynamite.[9]

ASSASSINATIONS

The societies' plans for assassinating their opponents and enemies greatly exceeded the number of assassinations they actually
attempted to carry out, not to mention those they carried out
successfully. The Black Hand society was established with the
express purpose of assassinating Arabs who cooperated with the
CUP out of a desire to strengthen their personal position and
influence—but it did not actually carry out any murders.

The representative of the Syrian officers, who arrived in Beirut
immediately after the January 1913 coup d'état returning the
CUP to power, told city notables that the officers stationed in
Chatalja and Gallipoli intended, in addition to their planned
activities for Syrian independence, to assassinate Enver and
Mahmud Shawkat. He added that two teams of assassins, each
with three Arab non-commissioned officers, had already been
organized for this purpose.[10] (The plan was never carried out.)

In July 1914 Haqqi al-'Azm wrote to Mahmud al-Mihmisani,
asking: "What do you think of the arrival of Tal'at and Jawid
[CUP leaders] in Syria next month? . . . It seems to me that a
strongly-worded proclamation must be distributed immediately,
calling upon the Arab nation to welcome these two 'heroes' with
dynamite and lead, as they deserve." In a proclamation distributed by the Arab Revolutionary Society a short time after it was
established, it sought to persuade its readers that "if we kill three
Valis in each vilayet, one after another, then anyone appointed
Vali in our country will be terrified". It appealed to the Arab
youth, declaring: "Here are the Valis of Beirut and Damascus,
both oppressors and robbers — why do you not kill them?"
Another proclamation announced the establishment of a *fida'ic*
society "that will kill anyone who fights against the Arabs and
opposes Arab reform".[11]

All these strong expressions lacked action. Only Sayyid Talib
succeeded in carrying out assassinations during this period; on 20
June 1913, after sunset, his men assassinated Farid Bek, the military commandant of Basra, and Badi' Nuri, the Mutasarrif of
the Muntafik. No other assassinations of senior Ottoman functionaries were carried out by members of the societies.

PLANS FOR REVOLT

The peak of activity for an underground society aspiring to bring
about independence is implementing a revolt against the

authorities. The society members and other Arab elements had many plans for revolt during this period, though none was carried out. The plans were, in chronological order:

Late 1911—Early 1912: Shukri al-'Asali and Salim Thabit plan for the annexation of Syria to Egypt.

December 1912: Aleppo notables suggest to French consul a simultaneous revolt in all Syrian centres, in order to drive out the Ottomans and transfer the country to French forces.

Late 1912: Baghdadi officers in Istanbul conspire to arrange their transfer to Iraq in order to organize a revolt there.

January-March 1913: Syrian officers in Chatalja and Gallipoli plan a return to Syria to organize a military revolt there against the Ottomans.

March 1913: The Decentralization Party resolves to turn Syria into an independent principality ruled by a Muslim prince.

April 1913: Aleppo notables suggest to British consul that a popular movement be organized there with British assistance to bring about the extension of British government protection from Egypt to their region.

April 1913: Sayyid Talib threatens revolt after the publication of the new Vilayets Law.

1914: Al-'Ahd's Baghdad branch plans to liberate the entire area from Mosul in the north to the Persian Gulf in the south from the Ottoman yoke.

August 1914: 'Aziz 'Ali al-Misri proposes a revolt with British assistance against the Ottomans in Iraq and Syria, and conceives the establishment of an Arab empire under British protection.

August 1914: The Decentralization Party plans a revolt meant to break out in Zahla in the Lebanon, with French assistance.

August-December 1914: The Lebanese plot an open revolt against the Ottomans with British, French or Greek assistance.

October-November 1914: The Decentralization Party contrives to send emissaries to incite rebellions throughout the Empire, in exchange for the liberation of the Arab countries and a British commitment not to occupy them.

October-November 1914: Al-Fatat suggests to the British through Kamil al-Qassab cooperation on the basis of the establishment of an independent Arab state.

October-November 1914: 'Aziz 'Ali al-Misri makes plans for a revolt in Iraq with British assistance.

November 1914: The Society of the Lebanese Revival of New

York proposes that a revolt be organized in the Lebanon against the Ottomans, with British and French assistance.

This summary reveals that, with the exception of al-'Asali and Thabit's plan, no revolt was proposed before the defeat of the Empire in the Balkans at the end of 1912. Only as a result of this defeat did various elements begin to consider revolt a possibility. Even then, only a few plans were formulated; it was only in August 1914, after the outbreak of World War I in Europe, that the societies began to plan one revolt after another.

An examination of the societies' methods of activity reveals that they brought about an actual turning point in the history of the Arab Middle East; activists and ideologists went from speech to action, in an attempt to realize in practice what they believed in theory.

Chapter 32

CONNECTIONS BETWEEN THE SOCIETIES

The network of connections between the societies existed on two levels. The first was individual: connections through people who were members of more than one society. The second was organizational: various official connections that existed between the societies.

Of the 350 activists in the period under discussion, 74 participated in more than one society. The record for multiple participation was held by three activists, each of whom participated in no less than five societies before the war: 'Abd al-Karim Qasim al-Khalil (the Arab Revival, the Arab-Ottoman Brotherhood, al-Qahtaniyya, the Literary Club and the Decentralization Party), 'Arif al-Shihabi (the Arab Revival, al-Fatat, al-Qahtaniyya, the Literary Club and the Decentralization Party) and Haqqi al-'Azm (the Arab-Ottoman Brotherhood, al-Qahtaniyya, the Literary Club, the Decentralization Party and the Arab Revolutionary Society). Seven activists participated in four societies: Tawfiq al-Basat, 'Izzat al-Jundi, Jurji Haddad, 'Abd al-Hamid al-Zahrawi, Shukri al-'Asali, 'Aziz 'Ali al-Misri and Ibrahim Salim al-Najjar.

Inspection of the data according to the ideological plane of the societies reveals a more interesting finding. Many of the members of the societies of the Arab Revival, the Arab-Ottoman Brotherhood, al-Fatat, al-Qahtaniyya and the Literary Club, all Arab societies, participated in the Decentralization Party, a Syrian society. Many members of the Lebanese Revival, a Lebanese society, participated in the Decentralization Party as well. Many members of the Lebanese Revival also participated in the Reform Society of Beirut. Similarly, many members of the National Scientific Club, an Iraqi society, participated in the Arab-oriented al-'Ahd. In other words, not only did members not hesitate to participate simultaneously in several societies, but they even joined societies with different and sometimes contradictory ideologies. It appears that the activists were attempting to investigate all possible available solutions to respond to the sorry situation of their people and countries at the end of the Ottoman Empire's rule.

The societies, aware of each other's existence—and this is true of the secret societies as well—were interested in cooperation, to varying degrees. The Lebanese Revival maintained connections both with the Decentralization Party (through the society's branch in Cairo, whose president, Iskandar 'Ammun, was vice-president of the Decentralization Party) and with the Reform Society of Beirut (through the society's branch in Beirut). Activists of the Lebanese Revival joined the Decentralization Party and the Reform Society of Beirut with the intention of modifying the ideology of these societies in the direction of their own as far as possible. There are those who claim that the Reform Society of Beirut's demand for foreign advisers and supervisors resulted from the influence of members who were part of the Lebanese Revival. When World War I broke out the Lebanese Revival began to cooperate with the Decentralization Party, with the goal of starting an armed revolt in the Lebanon.[1]

Al-Fatat encouraged its members to join other societies as well for maximum awareness of current events. When three prominent activists of the Literary Club, Sayf al-Din al-Khatib, Rafiq Rizq Sallum and Yusuf Mukhaybar Sulayman Haydar, joined the *al-Fatat*, there was some coordination between the activities of the society and of the club. Nevertheless, the society refused to accept 'Abd al-Karim Qasim al-Khalil, the club president, as a member because of his "tendency to love publicity". The ties between *al-Fatat* and the Decentralization Party began through the agency of Muhibb al-Din al-Khatib, a member of both societies. The latter also persuaded the leaders of the party to accept the invitation by the initiators of the Paris Congress (members of *al-Fatat*) to participate in it. When *al-Fatat*'s centre moved to Beirut, the connections between it and the party were managed by the brothers Muhammad and Mahmud al-Mihmisani, who were members of both societies. On the outbreak of World War I, *al-Fatat* sent Muhammad al-Mihmisani to Cairo to hold discussions with the party leaders concerning the Arabs' attitude towards the war. Two months later society member Kamil al-Qassab was also sent to Cairo in order to renew contacts with the Decentralization Party members, to find out about the nature of their contacts with the British and to inform them that the activists in Syria would not accept less than complete independence.[2]

Al-Qahtaniyya attempted to spread its ideas among the members of the Literary Club, and many of its members joined the club. The club, for its part, maintained connections with the members of the Decentralization Party and the Reform Society of Beirut. Liaison with the party was through the club president, 'Abd al-Karim al-Khalil, while liaison with the Reform Society of Beirut was through Sayf al-Din al-Khatib. On the other hand, the club quarrelled with the Green Flag society, which resisted the club's attempts (eventually successful) to gain control over its periodical.[3]

The Decentralization Party was, as mentioned, in contact with the Lebanese Revival through the members of the society's Cairo branch, which eventually led to joint planning of the revolt that was meant to break out in Zahla in the Lebanon with French assistance. Soon after the establishment of the Reform Society of Beirut, the party sent it a copy of its platform and even tried to persuade the society to unite with it. To this end 'Abd al-Karim al-Khalil, a member of the party, was sent to Beirut, where he opened negotiations on unification with the society members. The latter rejected his appeal to establish a united front against the authorities, apparently because they considered their reform plans an internal affair of their own vilayet that would not be helped by the intervention of outside factors. The Decentralization Party nonetheless continued to try to help the Reform Society as much as possible. Thus, when the society was closed by the Vali of Beirut, the party president, Rafiq al-'Azm, sent a telegram to Grand Vizier Mahmud Shawkat demanding the dismissal of the Vali, and another telegram to the Vali himself, demanding that the decree be rescinded. The party secretary, Haqqi al-'Azm, sent similar telegrams to the foreign ministers of the European powers and to the large European newspapers. The connections between the reformists of Beirut and the Decentralization Party actually became stronger after the closure, for they were then too weak to forgo the support of the party, as they had done a short while earlier.[4]

It seems that Sayyid Talib's contacts with the leaders of the Decentralization Party began even before the party was established, when he visited Cairo at the end of 1912 and discussed with them the need to establish such a party. After he established the Reform Society of Basra, the society was coordinated with the Decentralization Party. However, the society's main connections were to the National Scientific Club in Baghdad. Talib sent the club large sums of money through Sulayman Faydi, enabling it to open a large library and evening school. In return Talib was granted the honorary presidency of the club. When acting president Muzahim al-Pachachi was pursued by the authorities, he fled to Basra for Talib's protection. Talib did not confine his activities to connections with the club in Baghdad, and in July 1913 he sent Faydi to Mosul on a mission to spread nationalist ideas.[5]

When 'Aziz 'Ali al-Misri was exiled from Istanbul to Cairo, he had contacts with the Decentralization Party members there in order to achieve cooperation between *al-'Ahd* and the party. The discussions were conducted slowly because each side considered itself to be the stronger player and so worthy of dominating their joint activities. According to Da'ud Barakat, a member of the supreme committee of the party, the two sides reached an understanding just before the Empire entered World War I, but no ensuing practical activity is known.[6] The Mosul branch of *al-'Ahd* had connections with the Reform Society of Basra through *al-'Ahd* member 'Abd al-Rahman Sharaf, who was sent to Basra to coordinate the branch's activities with the Reform Society.[7]

The relationships among the societies reveal a ramified network of connections, some quite strong, among societies of different and even contradictory ideologies. This cooperation stemmed from a shared goal: the struggle against the common enemy, the Turks, and the CUP in particular. However, sometimes these connections were influenced by another motivation: the desire of the societies of one trend to influence the ideology of societies of another trend.

Chapter 33

THE IMAGE OF THE LEADERSHIP

Some of the societies had a collective leadership, while others were led by a single leader. The Arab-Ottoman Brotherhood was headed by a four-member administrative committee: a notable, a merchant, a government official and an army officer. It appears that the society thus represented the sectors of the population it wished to address. The founders of the society had decided against having a president,[1] apparently because too many of its members considered themselves fit for the position. (It should be remembered that all the founders of the society were from wealthy and prestigious families, and most were also senior functionaries in the Hamidian regime.)

According to the constitution of the Decentralization Party, its supreme committee was to consist of 20 members, from among whom a president, a vice-president, a secretary, two assistant secretaries and a treasurer would be elected. In practice the committee consisted of 16 members, and those who were elected for these offices remained in their positions during the entire existence of the party. Decisions were eventually made within a very narrow circle of people, which did not even include all the members of the supreme committee; in general this circle included Rafiq and Haqqi al-'Azm, Rashid Rida, Iskandar 'Ammun, Da'ud Barakat and Muhibb al-Din al-Khatib.

The Reform Society of Beirut also had a collective leadership. The society was officially headed by a committee of 25 members, but in practice it was run by three Muslims (Salim 'Ali Salam, Ahmad Mukhtar Bayhum and Sheikh Ahmad Hasan Tabbara) and three Christians (Pietro Tarrad, Dr Ayyub Thabit and Khalil Zayniyya). Their authority was only moral and they had, of course, no means of imposing their opinions on the populace of the city. A survey of the history of this society, especially of the events of April 1913, when the society was dissolved by the Vali, shows that its leaders did indeed succeed in establishing their leadership among the inhabitants of the city.[2]

The structure of the Reform Society of Basra was different. One leader, Sayyid Talib al-Naqib, had absolute authority over the members of the society, not because he had moral authority but because he knew how to use various means, forceful when necessary, to impose his views. His supporters in the town followed him because of their identity of interests, or out of fear. Talib founded the society in order to strengthen his personal power, and he closed it when he had no more use for it.

A figure of authority was Salim al-Jaza'iri, the leader of the officers within *al-Qahtaniyya*. He was an officer with typically military manners, who was never involved in disciplinary offences (unlike 'Aziz 'Ali al-Misri, for example). Al-Jaza'iri's military career did not prevent him from simultaneously writing a book on logic and inventing pocket compasses intended for various types of drawing. He spoke Arabic, Turkish, French and Zawawa (an African language), and he also knew a little German, English, Armenian and Russian. In his autobiography he related: "I was born very sensitive and with a nervous temperament, but my body can withstand all sorts of hardship." He insisted that all of his orders be carried out to the letter and that the activities of the society took place in an orderly manner, for he believed that only activities run in an orderly way (*nizam*) would succeed. Khalil Hamada, al-Jaza'iri's partner in founding the society, did not succeed to the same extent among the civilian members of the society, and there were those who doubted the wisdom of the lines of action he chose.[3]

Al-Fatat was collectively led. The members of the leadership were not uniform in their views, and the differences of opinion among them, centred on their attitudes to the Empire, came to the surface at the outbreak of World War I, when it was necessary to decide whether to support or oppose it. Muhammad al-Mihmisani returned quickly to Beirut from a mission in Cairo to join the Ottoman army. 'Abd al-Ghani al-'Uraysi, on the other hand, was among those who, in early 1915, suggested starting a revolt against the Ottomans. It seems that the members of the society were aware of the difficulties that stemmed from the lack of an accepted leader.[4]

The secret society, the Green Flag, was also without a single leader, although the dominant figure in it was Da'ud al-Dabbuni. A sworn enemy of the Turks, al-Dabbuni was disappointed with the society's lack of radical activity, and established the Black Hand society to promote such activity. But in this society as well he failed to establish his leadership, and the controversies that broke out over the methods of implementing its plans led to its dissolution before it was a year old.

The leader of *al-'Ahd*, 'Aziz 'Ali al-Misri, was an exception as an Egyptian among the officers in the society, most of whom

were Iraqis, with a minority of Syrians. However, it seems that
this was not the only reason that he failed to establish his
authority over the other members of the society and was forced
to submit to their ideology. His fellow members were not interested in his grandiose plans for an "Eastern Mediterranean
State" that would include the Arabs, the Turks, the Albanians,
and the Bulgarians, as well as Egypt, Sudan, Libya and Tunisia.
They wanted to work for the Arabs, and it was eventually
decided that the society would strive for a dual Turko-Arab
monarchy only. *Al-'Ahd*, which al-Misri sought to see open to
all the nationalities of the Empire, became open only to Arabs
and Turks. But his fellow members did not like him encouraging Turkish officers to join the society either, and eventually it
became open only to Arabs. Then al-Misri wanted the society
to cooperate with Ibn Sa'ud of Najd and even sent emissaries to
him, but eventually in this matter as well he was forced to go in
the direction outlined by most of his peers in the society: cooperation with Sharif Husayn of Mecca, whom he did not trust.[5]

It seems that the controversies between al-Misri and the other
members of the society were also based on unstable personal
relations. Al-Misri was a loner and at the same time very ambitious. Most of the other members of the society were equally
ambitious. This undoubtedly led to tensions in the society and
to an unwillingness to submit to the view of an accepted leader.
Al-Misri's rivals for the senior position in the society were the
Iraqi officers who constituted 65 per cent of its members. When
al-Misri was exiled from Istanbul, there was a leadership vacuum
in the society for some time. Without an accepted leader to
organize it and preserve its unity, the centre in Istanbul was liquidated. However, the vacuum was soon filled by the Iraqi officers, and the branches in Iraq and in Syria became more
important. Yasin al-Hashimi became the dominant personality
in the society from then until after World War I, while al-Misri
was pushed aside. Decades later he still held this against the
Iraqi officers. He had relatively better relations with the Syrian
officers, such as Salim al-Jaza'iri and Amin Lutfi al-Hafiz, perhaps because they too considered themselves a minority among
the Iraqis in the society.[6]

The leadership controversies were not confined to the officers'
circles. When 'Abd al-Karim Qasim al-Khalil established the
Literary Club, there was opposition to his presidency on the part
of 'Abd al-Qadir al-Jaza'iri, 'Izzat al-Jundi and Ahmad Qadri,
based, it seems, on both personal hostility and lack of confidence in his qualifications for the office. Only with the

intervention of 'Abd al-Hamid al-Zahrawi and Husayn Haydar
were the rival factions reconciled, and a neutral candidate, neither a supporter nor an opponent of al-Khalil, chosen as a compromise president of the club. Representatives of both factions
were chosen for its first administrative committee. Qadri moved
to Paris but continued to bear a grudge against al-Khalil, and it
is possible that it was he who prevented al-Khalil from being
accepted as a member of *al-Fatat* ("because of his tendency to
love publicity"). Although within the year most of his other
opponents had left the capital as well, and al-Khalil was finally
chosen as president, not all the members accepted this. The
members of the al-Sulh family (Rida, Riyad, and Sami participated in the club) suggested—under the influence of Mukhtar al-
Sulh, the escort of the Ottoman crown prince—that the club be
under the honorary presidency of the crown prince. This suggestion was not accepted, but when al-Khalil supported al-
Zahrawi's acceptance of an appointment to the senate in
opposition to the resolutions of the Paris Congress, his position
as president of the club was undermined even further. At a well-
attended meeting held to discuss the matter, al-Khalil was asked
to provide explanations, and it was made clear that, if he
refused, the club members would bring a no-confidence motion
against him. Al-Khalil was eventually limited by a four-member
advisory committee which he was obliged to consult when nego-
tiating with the authorities. Even this solution did not satisfy
some opponents, who continued to attack him sharply and to
blame him for the disintegration of the reform movement in late
1913 and early 1914. Muhammad Kurd 'Ali later wrote that al-
Khalil was a liar and added that he was "quite stupid, neglecting
his papers . . .".[7]

The problem of most of the societies which suffered from lack
of authoritative leadership was that members heeded their leaders only as long as the latter followed their members' views. As
soon as the leaders deviated from the accepted line, for various
reasons, they lost authority and all their prestige could not help
them.

The outstanding example of this was the case of al-Khalil's
ally during this period, 'Abd al-Hamid al-Zahrawi (1871-1916).
Al-Zahrawi began his political activity during the 1890s, when
he published the secret newspaper *al-Munir* in Homs, which
supported the Young Turks and their struggle against the Sultan.
Moving to Istanbul in 1895, he opened a shop which soon
became more a centre for ideas of freedom than for selling merchandise. Many of the shop's customers were Arabs, some of

whom had already begun to debate the possibilities for rescuing their countries from the sorry situation of the Empire. One of them was the owner of the newspaper *Ma'lumat*, who persuaded al-Zahrawi to become its editor. In this position al-Zahrawi began writing articles about the difficult situation the Arabs were in, and thus he incurred the hostility of the authorities. When he and a few others visited the British embassy to congratulate the ambassador following one of Britain's victories in the Boer War, the authorities took advantage of this to exile him to Damascus. In a 1901 article he attacked the four schools (*madhahib*) of Sunni Islam, arousing the rage of the Damascus conservatives, who had him arrested. At the time of his arrest he was carrying a copy of an even more damaging article in which he claimed that Sultan 'Abd al-Hamid was not fit for the caliphate. He tried to swallow the article, but the police inspector caught him and seized the article. As a result al-Zahrawi was sent to Istanbul, where he would have been imprisoned but for the intervention of Abu al-Huda, an Arab who was close to the Sultan. He was allowed to return to Homs, where he was placed under police supervision.

In 1902 al-Zahrawi escaped to Egypt and worked there as a journalist on the newspapers *al-Mu'ayyad* and *al-Jarida*. After the 1908 revolution he was chosen as Hama's representative in the parliament and he joined the opposition to the CUP. He participated in the Society of the Arab-Ottoman Brotherhood and later became a senior member of *al-Qahtaniyya*. When he intervened on behalf of al-Khalil in 1910 during the struggle for the leadership of the Literary Club, it was the beginning of a close relationship between these two personalities. In late 1911 he was one of the founders of the Party of Liberty and Union, and he brought about al-Khalil's appointment as its secretary-general. During this period al-Zahrawi was one of the leaders of the struggle for Arab rights, as well as one of the leaders of the opposition in Istanbul. However, he attained the peak of his importance in 1913, when he was sent by the Decentralization Party to be the president of the Paris Congress. At this time he was considered by the various Arab activists as the central figure in the struggle for their rights. Yet he lost this position in a trice when he agreed to accept the CUP's offer of the position of senator. The Arab activists now considered him a traitor, and they had the same attitude towards al-Khalil, who supported him.[8]

When the motives that led the leaders of the societies to enter political activity are examined, a common denominator can be found in at least some of them. Ahmad Qadri, one of the first members of *al-Fatat*, began his political activity as a result of the humiliation he felt a few days after the promulgation of the constitution, hearing a Turkish officer denouncing the Arab officials who had assisted 'Abd al-Hamid's deposed regime while ignoring the Turkish officials who had done the same. 'Aziz 'Ali al-Misri began his activity against the CUP after some of its senior members refused to listen to his request not to appoint to a high-level position the Turkish commander who had imprisoned him several years earlier; he interpreted, or preferred to interpret, this as an offence against the Arabs. While he was serving in Libya his conflict with the CUP intensified, and the quick promotion enjoyed by his fellow classmate, Enver Pasha, while al-Misri himself remained a lieutenant-colonel, only increased his anger.

However, the best example of entering into politics because of personal anger is perhaps Mawlud Mukhlis (1884-1951), one of the senior members of *al-'Ahd* in Mosul and a leader of the society after World War I. Expelled as a youth from the military academy in Baghdad after a minor quarrel among a number of students, Mukhlis fled the army because of this and went to Istanbul to fight for his rights. Due to the pressure by a senior Arab army officer he was reinstated in the academy, but academy officials, displeased with this intervention, put him in prison a short while afterwards under the accusation of speaking against 'Abd al-Hamid. They then began transferring him from one prison to another until he succeeded in escaping from one of them. After much wandering, during which he was robbed by bedouins and compelled to work as a relief labourer on the Hijazi railway, he reached Ibn Rashid in Najd, where he remained for 13 months. Ibn Rashid's attempts to persuade the authorities to reinstate Mukhlis in the military academy in Baghdad failed. Some time later a new military academy was opened in Damascus which Mukhlis thought that he would be able to enter, but he again became involved in a quarrel and was rejected. The same senior Arab army officer who had intervened on his behalf at the beginning of his career now intervened once again and he was accepted by the military academy in Monastir. But two years later a report from Baghdad concerning his expulsion from the military academy in Baghdad arrived in Istanbul, and the war ministry decided to expel him from Monastir as well. Sent as a private to the Balkans, he met 'Aziz 'Ali al-Misri there for the first time. (Only after the 1908 revolution was Mukhlis allowed to complete his studies at the military academy, and he graduated four years later than his other original classmates.)[9] For Mawlud Mukhlis, like many other leaders of the societies, personal anger against the imperial authorities preceded the development of a nationalist ideology and political activity.

The members of the societies influenced the shaping of the image of the Arab leadership after World War I as well. Members of the pre-war societies, both those of the Arab trend and those that were locally-oriented, held senior positions in the leadership of the post-war Arab states. While members of the former societies who did not adjust to separate states (such as the pan-Arabist Rashid Rida) did not attain such positions, those able to adjust became, along with the members of the particularist societies, presidents, prime ministers and ministers. *Al-Fatat* and the Lebanese Revival members became presidents and prime ministers in Syria, Lebanon and Transjordan. The Iraqi members of *al-'Ahd* became prime ministers in Iraq. A study of the Iraqi-born members of *al-'Ahd* before World War I shows that while three of 34 activists died a short while after the war, of the remaining 31, seven eventually held the position of prime minister of Iraq, three became ministers of defence in Iraq, one became foreign minister of Iraq, one became interior minister of Iraq, one became president of the Iraqi parliament, one attained the position of mutasarrif, and another three attained senior positions in the Syrian army during Faysal's reign in Syria in 1919-20. Of the seven prime ministers, Nuri al-Sa'id held this office 14 times, Jamil al-Madfa'i seven times, 'Ali Jawdat al-Ayyubi three times, Yasin al-Hashimi and Hamdi al-Pachachi twice each, and Taha al-Hashimi and Muzahim al-Pachachi once each. Altogether these seven prime ministers headed 30 of the 59 governments formed in Iraq from 1920 to 1958.[10]

It would be an error to assume that the members of the societies only led the establishment in the Arab Middle East after World War I. This was indeed true of the majority, but there were some exceptions. Bakr Sidqi, who led the first military coup d'état in the independent Arab states, had only signed a letter of support for the Paris Congress, but his partner in this coup d'état, 'Abd al-Latif Nuri, had been a member of *al-'Ahd* before the war. 'Aziz 'Ali al-Misri was involved in the circles of the Free Officers in Egypt on the eve of the 1952 revolution, and when necessary he hid Jamal 'Abd al-Nasir and his comrades from the police.

Conclusion and Epilogue

During the period from the Young Turk revolution in 1908 until the outbreak of World War I in 1914, about 20 societies were established within and outside the Ottoman Empire, their members Arabs and their goal finding solutions for the situation of the Arabs in the Empire. The necessity to find such solutions became most acute in the light of the disintegration of the Empire during this period, on the one hand, and the Turkification policy employed by the Young Turks towards the Arabs, on the other. Some of the societies defined themselves as secret and some as open, although the latter also engaged in secret activities. The societies were divided into several nationalist trends: Arabism, which began as moderate and ideologically vague, was pushed to extremism by the Turkification policy, and finally reached pan-Arab ideology among a few individuals. Broader movements were Lebanonism, whose origin was the desire of the Lebanese to preserve the special status of their mountain, and Syrianism, which already existed during the latter half of the nineteenth century, but which gained in strength in the wake of the Empire's rapid decline in the early twentieth century. One may also speak of budding Iraqism during this period. The Egyptians, outside the Empire with their own independent nationalism, were also outside this entire system of societies.

The societies with Arab tendencies did not gain the backing of the populace for which they worked. This populace was totally unaware of the existence of some of the societies and did not hasten to support those it was aware of. During this period these societies did not have a crystallized and defined ideology that could attract the masses. The pan-Arab societies, which did have such an ideology, were so small that they were practically unnoticed. On the other hand, the local movements attained at least relative success among the Arabs of the Lebanon, Syria and Iraq, because they had specific solutions to offer the local people, solutions which seemed sufficiently realistic that the populace could imagine them a practical alternative to their plight in the Ottoman Empire.

There was a ramifying, and at times very close, network of connections among the societies, even those of different and contradictory trends. This cooperation stemmed from the common cause of all the trends: the struggle against the common enemy, the Turks, and especially the CUP. The evolution in the societies' methods of action reveals a real turning point in the history of the Arab Middle East, as the activists and the ideologists went from speech to action in an attempt to realize in practice the ideologies they believed in.

*

When World War I broke out some of the societies disappeared from the political scene and others began contacts with the Allies in order to arrange cooperative action to liberate the Arab countries from the yoke of the Ottoman Empire. *Al-Fatat* and *al-'Ahd* combined efforts in early 1915 and formulated a joint list of demands (the "Damascus Protocol"), in which they demanded the independence of the Arab countries, from southern Anatolia in the north to the Indian Ocean in the south and from the Mediterranean Sea in the west to the Persian border in the east, in return for their cooperation with Britain in its war against the Empire. This protocol was delivered to Sharif Husayn of Mecca and constituted the basis for a letter he sent in July 1915 to Arthur Henry McMahon, the British high commissioner in Egypt, the first of a series of letters known as the McMahon-Husayn correspondence, which eventually led to the outbreak of Husayn's Arab revolt against the Ottoman Empire.

At the beginning of the war Jamal Pasha, the Ottoman navy minister, who had been appointed commander of the Fourth Army in Syria and became the omnipotent ruler throughout the Levant, discovered documents belonging to the French consulates in Beirut and Damascus that had not been destroyed by the consuls-general before they left their offices. The documents incriminated many of the members of the societies, and in mid-1915 Jamal Pasha began an extensive wave of arrests among the members of the societies, culminating in a long series of executions in August 1915 and in May 1916. This harsh blow did not end the activities of the societies, and new members joined in place of those who had been executed. With the outbreak of Sharif Husayn's Arab revolt in Mecca in June 1916, it was joined by a number of the societies' members, including some who had fled from Syria, a small number of deserters from the Ottoman army, and a majority of army officers who had been captured by the British and preferred enlisting in the revolt army to remaining in the prisoner-of-war camps. However, the members of the societies who participated in the revolt constituted a minority of those who took part in it and a minority of the ranks of the societies.

After the war ended with the defeat of the Empire and the occupation of the Arab countries by the British Army, the members of the societies took the senior positions in leading the Arab countries towards independence. The members of *al-Fatat*, which expanded greatly after the war, in practice administered the short-lived Syrian state ruled by Faysal, Husayn's third son. The fall of Syria to the French in July 1920 symbolized the end of the society. The officers of *al-'Ahd* were divided after the war into two societies, *al-'Ahd al-Suri*, which was insignificant, and *al-'Ahd al-'Iraqi*. Though the officers of the latter obtained most of the senior positions in Faysal's Syrian army, their interests lay in the direction of Iraq, where the British were in control. The officers started harassing the British from the direction of the Syrian-Iraqi border, activity which constituted a preface to the Iraqi revolt of 1920.

Eventually the Arab states were established separate from one another, and thus the ideology of the particularist societies was actually realized. The members of the pre-war societies, both of the Arab and the local trends, obtained the most senior positions in these states, for the majority of even the first group adapted to the new situation of separate states. The members of *al-'Ahd*, *al-Fatat*, and the Lebanese Revival became presidents, prime ministers and ministers in Syria, Iraq, Transjordan and Lebanon.

The heritage of the societies outlasted the era of their existence. Arab writers and historians recounted their stories, some accurately and some portraying them as the first stage of mere Arab nationalism. For many of the leaders of the Arab states, having been members of these societies at the beginning of their political careers became a matter of pride.

Notes

PART I

Chapter 1

1 For al-Bustani's biography see Henry Harris Jessup, *Fifty-Three Years in Syria* (New York, 1910), vol.2, pp.483-485. K.T. Khairallah, *La Syrie* (Paris, 1912), pp.49-51. George Antonius, *The Arab Awakening: The Story of the Arab National Movement* (London, [1938] rep.1945), pp.47-51. Albert Hourani, *Arabic Thought in the Liberal Age 1798-1939* (London, [1962] 1970), pp.99ff. For a brief summary of his thought see Butrus Abu-Manneh, "The Christians between Ottomanism and Syrian Nationalism: The Ideas of Butrus al-Bustani", *IJMES*, 11:3 (1980), pp.287-304.
2 The encyclopaedia was completed after his death by his sons and his cousin Sulayman al-Bustani and includes 11 volumes.
3 *Nafir Suriyya* 25 Oct.1860, cited in Abu-Manneh, p.293.
4 *Al-Jinan* vol.1 (1870), p.386, cited in *ibid*, p.296.
5 *Al-Jinan* vol.1 (1870), pp.645, 673, 706, cited in *ibid*.
6 *Al-Jinan* vol.1 (1870), p.642, cited in *ibid*, pp.296-297.
7 *Al-Jinan* vol.2 (1871), pp.573-574, 789; vol.4 (1873), p.362, cited in *ibid*, p.299.
8 See Hourani, *Arabic Thought*, p.100.
9 The borders of this 'Syria', as formulated at about the same time by the Lebanese Khalil al-Khuri (1836-1907), included the area from the Euphrates in the east to the Mediterranean Sea in the west and from the Arabian desert in the south to Anatolia in the north. *Hadiqat al-Akhbar* 19 May 1866, cited in Moshe Ma'oz, "Attempts at Creating a Political Community in Modern Syria", *MEJ*, 26:4 (1972), p.391. It may be assumed that this 'Greater Syria' was the 'Syria' meant by Butrus al-Bustani.
10 'Isa Mikha'il Saba, *Al-Shaykh Ibrahim al-Yaziji 1847-1906* (Cairo, 1955), pp.49-51, 71-74, cited in C.E. Dawn, *From Ottomanism to Arabism: Essays on the Origins of Arab Nationalism* (Urbana, 1973), p.132.

Chapter 2

1 FO 78/1389: d20, J.H. Skene (Aleppo) to Istanbul 31 July 1858, cited in Zeine N. Zeine, "Unpublished Documents Concerning

Independence Movements in the Arab Provinces of the Ottoman Empire" in *Actes du premier congrès international des études balqaniques et sud-est européenes*, 4 (1969), p.694.

2 Ahmad 'Abbas al-Azhari (1852-1927) was to play an important role 35 years later in the Reform Society of Beirut.

3 A detailed description of the Syrian independence movement may be found in 'Adil al-Sulh, *Sutur min al-Risala: Ta'rikh Haraka Istiqlaliyya Qamat fil-Mashriq al-'Arabi Sanat 1877* (Beirut, 1966), especially pp.92-101, 124-127. 'Adil al-Sulh was the grandson of Ahmad al-Sulh, and therefore his book is a primary source about this movement.

4 MAE, CPC Damas 11: d7, Alfred Rousseau (Damascus) to William-Henri Waddington (Paris) 30 July 1878, enclosing the two placards.

5 MAE, CPC Beyrouth 22: d19, Delaporte (Beirut) to Waddington 9 Oct.1879. Another echo of this movement is found in Muhammad Jamil Bayhum, *Al-'Arab wal-Turk fil-Sira' bayna al-Sharq wal-Gharb* (Beirut, 1957), pp.148-149. Bayhum relates that his cousin told him that his father Husayn Bayhum, who was the president of the Syrian Scientific Society after the death of its founder Muhammad Arslan, had contacts with Sharif 'Abd al-Muttalib of Mecca. According to him, this Sharif was involved in a revolutionary movement against the Ottoman Empire, in coordination with 'Abd al-Qadir al-Jaza'iri in Damascus and probably with French support. 'Adil al-Sulh too claims that the Syrian Scientific Society (*al-Jam'iyya al-'Ilmiyya al-Suriyya*), which was founded in 1868 and was ostensibly a literary society, worked secretly on the political level, aspiring to stimulate a national (*watani*) feeling among the Syrians. Al-Sulh, p.36.

6 Yusuf Karam (1823-1889) rebelled in 1866 against Da'ud Pasha, the governor-general of Mount Lebanon, and after several battles was compelled to go into exile in Europe.

7 *Ibid*, pp.104-106.

8 *Ibid*, p.111, citing Sam'an Khazin, *Yusuf Bek Karam fil-Manfa* (Tripoli, 1950), p.347.

9 *Ibid*, p.113-114, citing Khazin, p.364.

10 *Ibid*, p.123, citing Khazin, p.354-355.

Chapter 3

1 The data about the Secret Society of Beirut are derived from two kinds of sources: documents available in the archives of the British Foreign Office and the French Foreign Ministry, and the books of Antonius, pp.79-88, and Zeine N. Zeine, *The Emergence of Arab Nationalism* (New York, [1958] 3rd ed.1973), pp.51-59. Antonius was the son-in-law of Faris Nimr, a member of this society, and

from him he obtained his knowledge about it. Zeine, too, learnt about the society from Faris Nimr, who when interviewed was its last surviving member. While one can find many details about the society in Antonius' book, one has to be cautious with his conclusions about the society's importance and its position as the first Arab national society (Antonius, pp.79, 85). Zeine already understood that the society had been more Lebanese-Syrian than Arab and that the idea of Arab nationalism had not even crossed the minds of its founders.

2 For his biography see Philippe de Tarrazi, *Ta'rikh al-Sahafa al-'Arabiyya* (Beirut, 1913-14), vol.1, pt.1, pp.115-116. On his influence on the Syrian youth see Faris Nimr in *al-Muqtataf* 36:3 (1910), p.258.

3 Zeine, *Emergence*, p.52.

4 Thus according to Zeine's version, *ibid*. Antonius, p.79, reduces the number of the members of the founding nucleus to five and claims that at its height the society numbered 22 men.

5 Faris Nimr (1856-1951) and Ya'qub Sarruf (1852-1927) studied and taught in the Syrian-Protestant College of Beirut. Together with Shahin Makaryus (1853-1910) they founded the periodical *al-Muqtataf* in 1876 in Beirut. The three left for Cairo in 1885 and founded the newspaper *al-Muqattam* there a year later. Ibrahim al-Yaziji, too, emigrated to Egypt.

6 Zeine, *Emergence*, pp.52-53.

7 *Ibid*, pp.52-53, 55. Antonius, pp.79-80.

8 MAE, CPC Beyrouth 23: d15, Joseph-Adam Sienkiewicz (Beirut) to Louis-Charles de Freycinet (Paris) 2 June 1880. The French diplomat noted that these placards appeared because of the hostility that existed between the Arabs and the Turks and the Arab aspirations for autonomy that arose after the war between the Ottoman Empire and Russia and the Empire's partial dismemberment following it. He added that at a public meeting in Damascus one Muslim said without encountering the slightest protest: "Anyone who will use a Turkish word to indicate 'bread' will be beaten to death."

9 FO 195/1306: t, John Dickson (Beirut) to George J. Goschen (Istanbul) 28 June 1880. d47, same to same 3 July 1880. Dickson enclosed with his report a copy of one of the placards which appeared on the second occasion and an original placard of those which appeared on the third occasion. Zeine notes that this placard, which is available in the PRO, is in the handwriting of Faris Nimr. See Zeine, "Unpublished Documents", p.695.

10 FO 195/1306: d47, Dickson to Goschen 3 July 1880. Dickson instructed one of his dragomans to investigate this and the latter suggested that perhaps Midhat Pasha was their initiator, intending by this to extract from the Sublime Porte unlimited authority in the vilayet. *Ibid*: memo, John Abcarius (Beirut) 3 July 1880.

11 A copy of the placard is enclosed with FO 195/1368: d2, Dickson

to Frederick R. St. John (Istanbul) 14 Jan.1881.
12 *Ibid*: d1, Dickson to Goschen 3 Jan.1881. ds 2 and 3, Dickson to St. John 14 and 17 Jan.1881.
13 This question is resolved in Shimon Shamir, "Midhat Pasha and Anti-Turkish Agitation in Syria", *MEJ*, 10:2 (1974), pp.115-141.
14 *Ibid*, p.131.
15 FO 424/91: d31, Layard (Istanbul) to Salisbury (London) 20 Oct.1879; d24, same to same 28 Oct.1879, both cited in Shamir, pp.122, 130, respectively.
16 FO 195/1306: d47, Dickson to Goschen 3 July 1880 and memo of Abcarius 3 July 1880.
17 The reports (*jurnals*) of 'Abd al-Hamid's spies were examined by Shamir. See Shamir, pp.120-121.
18 FO 195/1306: d13, Sampson Jago (Damascus) to Goschen 3 Aug.1880. The vice-consul pointed out in this despatch that the population virtually did not notice these placards.
19 FO 78/3130: d53, Dickson to Goschen 13 Aug.1880; d14, Jago to Goschen 16 Aug.1880, both cited in Max L. Gross, *Ottoman Rule in the Province of Damascus 1860-1909* (Ph.D. Dissertation, Georgetown University, 1979), p.313.
20 FO 195/1306: d2, Dickson to St. John 14 Jan.1881. The French consul in Damascus reported at the same time that the police arrested a local woman who had posted on the walls of the government palace a placard calling for a rebellion. See MAE, CPC Damas 12: Maurice-Ernest Flesch (Damascus) to Jules Barthélemy Saint Hillaire (Paris) 23 Jan.1881.
21 Zeine, *Emergence*, p.54.
22 FO 195/1370: d21, Trevor J.C. Plowden (Baghdad) to Granville (London) 20 May 1881. Plowden enclosed with his despatch the handbill of *Jam'iyyat Hifz Huquq al-Milla al-'Arabiyya*, dated 17 Rabi' al-Thani 1298h (19 Mar.1881), and noted that it seemed to him that it had been printed in London. Copies of the handbill appeared also in Alexandria, Khartoum and Algeria. See Jacob M. Landau, "An Arab Anti-Turk Handbill, 1881", *Turcica*, 9:1 (1977), p.215.

Chapter 4

1 There are many publications about the life and thought of al-Afghani and 'Abduh. Particularly comprehensive are Charles C. Adams, *Islam and Modernization in Egypt: A Study of the Modern Reform Movement Inaugurated by Muhammad 'Abduh* (New York, [1933] 1968). Nikki Keddie, *Sayyid Jamal al-Din "al-Afghani"* (Berkeley, 1972). It is not within the scope of this chapter to deal with al-Afghani's pan-Islam or with 'Abduh's reform in Islam.
2 In *al-'Urwa al-Wuthqa* (Beirut ed., 1970), p.109 he said:

"li-annana bayanna anna la jinsiyya lil-muslimin illa fi dinihim" (we explained that there was no nationalism[?] for the Muslims but in their religion).

3 On al-Afghani's and 'Abduh's plan to assassinate Isma'il see Earl of Cromer, *Modern Egypt* (London, 1908), vol.2, p.181 and also *al-Manar* 11 (1908), p.98. On their plan to remove Tawfiq see *ibid*, p.199. On 'Abduh's opinion about the right to depose a ruler see Muhammad 'Abduh, *Al-Islam wal-Nasraniyya ma'a al-'Ilm wal-Madaniyya* (Cairo, 1367h), p.84. The article "The Nation and the rule of the Tyrant" is in *al-'Urwa al-Wuthqa*, pp.145-146.

4 Al-Afghani's article was partially translated from Persian to French: Mehdi Hendessi, "Pages peu connues de Djemal al-Din al-Afghani", *Orient*, 6 (1958), pp.123-128. See also Nikki R. Keddie, "Pan-Islam as Proto-Nationalism", *Journal of Modern History*, 41:1 (1969), pp.17-28.

5 *Al-'Urwa al-Wuthqa*, p.50.

6 Muhammad Rashid Rida, *Ta'rikh al-Ustadh al-Imam al-Shaykh Muhammad 'Abduh* (Cairo, 1931), vol.2, pp.194-195.

7 Adams, pp.9-10. Ahmad Amin, *Zu'ama' al-Islah fil-'Asr al-Hadith* (Cairo, 1965), pp.81-82, 305.

8 *Al-'Urwa al-Wuthqa*, pp.369, 411, respectively.

9 Ahmad Shafiq Pasha, *Mudhakirrati fi Nisf Qarn* (Cairo, 1934), vol.1, p.290. *Al-'Urwa al-Wuthqa*, p.321.

Chapter 5

1 A concise book about the life and thought of al-Kawakibi is Sami al-Dahhan, *'Abd al-Rahman al-Kawakibi 1854-1902* (Cairo, 1964). See also Amin, pp.249-279.

2 Al-Kawakibi's life was narrated according to al-Dahhan, pp.18-31, 67-68. On al-Kawakibi's connections with the Khedive see *ibid*, p.29 and Elie Kedourie, "The Politics of Political Literature: Kawakibi, Azoury and Jung" in Elie Kedourie (ed.), *Arabic Political Memoirs and Other Studies* (London, 1974), pp.109-111. Eight years after al-Kawakibi's death, the British Ambassador in Istanbul reported on a complaint, made by pro-Turkish leaders from Egypt and addressed to the Sultan, against the attempts of Khedive 'Abbas Hilmi to establish an Arab sultanate. Among his emissaries they mentioned 'Abd al-Rahman al-Kawakibi, who, according to them, was sent to Mecca for that purpose. See FO 371/1007: d433, Gerard Lowther (Istanbul) to Grey (London) 28 July 1910.

3 So Ibrahim Salim al-Najjar related in the periodical *al-Hadith* (1951), p.118, cited in al-Dahhan, p.37.

4 Al-Rahhala K ['Abd al-Rahman al-Kawakibi], *Taba'i' al-Istibdad wa-Masari' al-Isti'bad* (Cairo ed., 1931), p.2. In this book al-Kawakibi imitated the book *Della Tirannide* by the Italian writer

Vitorio Alfieri (1749-1803), who had also developed strong anti-tyrannical ideas. Al-Kawakibi adapted these ideas to the Eastern community and the Islamic thought. See Amin, p.254, al-Dahhan, p.44 and Sylvia G. Haim (ed.), *Arab Nationalism: An Anthology* (Berkeley, [1962] 1976), p.25.

5 *Taba'i' al-Istibdad*, pp.12-24.
6 *Ibid*, pp.28-31.
7 *Ibid*, pp.61-63, 92.
8 *Ibid*, pp.84-85, 97-100.
9 *Ibid*, pp.109-111.
10 *Ibid*, pp.125-130.
11 *Ibid*, p.131.
12 Al-Sayyid al-Furati ['Abd al-Rahman al-Kawakibi], *Umm al-Qura* (Cairo ed., 1931), pp.3-8.
13 *Ibid*, pp.10-12.
14 *Ibid*, p.23.
15 *Ibid*, pp.25-26.
16 *Ibid*, p.27.
17 *Ibid*, p.28.
18 *Ibid*, pp.32-34.
19 *Ibid*, pp.35-36.
20 *Ibid*, p.46.
21 *Ibid*, p.51.
22 *Ibid*, p.60.
23 *Ibid*, pp.136-149.
24 *Ibid*, pp.143-147.
25 *Ibid*, pp.168-169.
26 *Ibid*, pp.169-185.
27 *Ibid*, pp.192-197.
28 *Ibid*, pp.197-209.
29 *Ibid*, p.217.
30 MAE, NS Egypte 14: d55, George Cogordan (Cairo) to Théophile Delcassé (Paris) 12 Apr.1902. It was already noted by Kedourie, *Arabic Political Memoirs*, pp.110-111.

Chapter 6

1 An extensive article on 'Azuri's activities, based on archival material, is the above mentioned article of Kedouri in his *Arabic Political Memoirs*, pp.111-121.
2 According to a French report 'Azuri was about 25 in 1898. His presumed year of birth is therefore 1873. This is probably the only existing indication of 'Azuri's year of birth. See MAE, NS Turquie 109: d14, Ferdinand Wiet (Jerusalem) to Delcassé 8 Feb.1905.
3 MAE, NS Turquie 131: d39, Jules-Auguste Boppe (Jerusalem) to Delcassé 30 June 1904. MAE, NS Turquie 109: d14, Wiet to

Delcassé 8 Feb.1905. MAE, NS Turquie 177: d165, Boppe (Istanbul) to MAE 29 Sept.1905. On the accusations against the governor of the sanjaq of Jerusalem and his dragoman see Nagib Azoury, *Le Réveil de la Nation Arabe dans l'Asie Turque* (Paris, 1905), pp.28-30. 'Azuri's death sentence is cited in *L'Indépendance Arabe* 7-8 (Oct.-Nov.1907), p.97.

4 On Jung and the military and administrative roles played by him in Saigon and Tonkin see MAE, NS Turquie 118: Directeur du Cabinet de la Préfecture de police (Paris) to Prime Minister and MAE 2 Dec.1912. Jung's two primary publications concerning the Arab question were *Les Puissances devant la révolte arabe: La Crise mondiale de demain* (Paris, 1906) and *La Révolte Arabe* (Paris, 1924-25), 2 vols.

5 An original copy of the first manifesto may be found in ISA 67/25 and MAE, NS Turquie 177. An original copy of the second manifesto may be found in French in MAE, NS Turquie 109 and 177, and in Arabic in MAE, NS Turquie 109 and ISA 67/25. Both manifestos in French are cited in Jung, *Puissances*, pp.22-29.

6 FO 195/2187: d5, A.F. Townshend (Adana) 1 Feb.1905, cited in Kedourie, *Arabic Political Memoirs*, p.115. MAE, NS Turquie 109: d14, Wiet to Delcassé 8 Feb.1905. MAE, NS Turquie 177: d18, René Péan (Beirut) to Delcassé 14 Feb.1905. ISA 67/25: ds 608 and 699, von Rössler (Jaffa) to von Bieberstein (Istanbul) 25 May and 15 June 1905. Eight years later Hafiz al-Sa'id was the president of the Jaffa branch of the Decentralization Party.

7 Azoury, pp. iii, v, viii.

8 The chapter on Russia *ibid*, pp.51-81. On Britain *ibid*, pp.83-100. On France *ibid*, pp.101-130 (the citations from pp.101-102, 108). On Germany and Austria *ibid*, pp.131-142 (the citations from p.136). On Italy *ibid*, pp.143-147. On the United States *ibid*, pp.149-156.

9 *Ibid*, p.183.

10 *Ibid*, pp.210-214.

11 *Ibid*, p.239.

12 *Ibid*, pp.242-244.

13 See the society's programme *ibid*, pp.245-247. On Egypt, *ibid*, p.246.

14 *Ibid*, pp.247-248, 256-257.

15 MAE, NS Turquie 177: ls, 'Azuri to Christian 8 and 22 Jan.1906.

16 *L'Indépendance Arabe* 1 (Apr.1907), p.1.

17 *Ibid* 13-14 (Apr.-May 1908), p.195, 3 (June 1907), p.38, respectively.

18 *Ibid* 1 (Apr.1907), p.9.

19 MAE, NS Turquie 179: d29, Paul Chevandier de Valdrome (Cairo) to Stéphen Pichon (Paris) 29 Jan.1908.

20 *L'Indépendance Arabe* 16-17-18 (July-Aug.-Sept.1908), p.2.

21 CZA L2/26i: Central Zionist Office (Cologne) to Arthur Ruppin (Jaffa) 15 Sept.1908. CZA Z2/632: Ruppin to President of Zionist

Actions Committee (Cologne) 29 Feb.1908. MAE, NS Turquie 132: d17, Georges-Félix Gueyraud (Jerusalem) to Pichon 8 Oct.1908.
22 Kedourie, *Arabic Political Memoirs*, p.119. Hourani, *Arabic Thought*, p.278.
23 Jung, *Révolte*, vol.1, pp.38-40.
24 MAE, NS Turquie 117: 'Azuri (Port Said) to Jung 17 Nov.1912.
25 Jung, *Révolte*, vol.1, p.49.
26 *Ibid*, pp.56-57, 60-61.
27 *Ibid*, pp.67-68.
28 *Ibid*, pp.81-82.
29 *Ibid*, pp.108-109.
30 His letter may be found in MAE, Guerre 852 and is cited in Kedourie, *Arabic Political Memoirs*, p.120.
31 FO 371/2147: memo by Percy Loraine (Paris) 15 Dec.1914, enclosed with 1, Granville (Paris) to George R. Clerk (London) 16 Dec.1914.
32 Jung, *Révolte*, vol.1, p.119.
33 MAE, Guerre 874: Jung (Paris) to President of the Republic 20 Aug.1914.

Chapter 7

1 The two main sources on the Society of the Arab Revival are: Salih Hirfi, ".Mudhakkirat Muhibb al-Din al-Khatib", *al-Thaqafa* [Algeria], 6 (Jan.1972), pp.86-97; 7 (Mar.1972), pp.82-90; 8-9 (Apr.-May 1972), pp.92-99; 10 (Sept.1972), pp.63-69; 11 (Nov.1972), pp.97-103; 12 (Jan.1973) pp.91-97. The article is based on the manuscript of the memoirs of Muhibb al-Din al-Khatib, founder of the Society of the Arab Revival. Muhibb al-Din al-Khatib (ed.), *Al-Duktur Salah al-Din al-Qasimi 1305-1334: Atharuhu — Safahat min Ta'rikh al-Nahda al-'Arabiyya fi Awa'il al-Qarn al-'Ishrin* (Cairo, 1959). The book is a collection of the articles of Salah al-Din al-Qasimi, who was the society's first secretary in Damascus.
2 On Sheikh Tahir al-Jaza'iri see 'Adnan al-Khatib, *Al-Shaykh Tahir al-Jaza'iri: Ra'id al-Nahda al-'Ilmiyya fi Bilad al-Sha'm* (Cairo, 1971).
3 *Ibid*, pp.24, 44. Mustafa al-Shihabi, *Al-Qawmiyya al-'Arabiyya: Ta'rikhuha wa-Qiwamuha wa-Maramiha — Muhadarat* (Cairo, [1959] 2nd ed.1961), pp.49-51. M. Burj, "Tahir wa-Salim al-Jaza'iriyyan: Ra'ida al-Nahda al-Haditha fil-Mashriq", *al-Thaqafa* [Algeria], 6 (Jan.1972), pp.33-37.
4 Al-Shihabi, p.51.
5 Hirfi, "Mudhakkirat" 6, pp.87-95. Al-Khatib, *al-Shaykh Tahir*, p.42. Al-Shihabi, pp.52-54.
6 Hirfi, "Mudhakkirat" 6, pp.95-97. Al-Shihabi, p.54.

7 Hirfi, "Mudhakkirat" 7, pp.82-88. *Salah al-Din al-Qasimi*, pp.4-5. Al-Shihabi, pp.54-55.
8 Hirfi, "Mudhakkirat" 7, pp.88-90; 8-9, pp.92-94.
9 Al-Khatib, *al-Shaykh Tahir*, pp.44-45, 47.
10 Hirfi, "Mudhakkirat" 8-9, pp.93-99. *Salah al-Din al-Qasimi*, pp.5-6.
11 *Ibid*, pp. ix-x, 6-7. Zafir al-Qasimi, *Maktab 'Anbar* (Beirut, 1964), p.100.
12 *Salah al-Din al-Qasimi*, pp.11-12. Hirfi, "Mudhakkirat" 12, pp.91-92, 94-95.
13 *Salah al-Din al-Qasimi*, pp.8-7, 13-16.
14 *Ibid*, p.xi.
15 FO 424/226 [No.107]: r, 'Ali Rida Pasha (Muhafiz and Commandant of Medina) to Interior Minister and War Minister 11 Jan.1911, enclosed with d99, Lowther to Grey 13 Feb.1911.

Chapter 8

1 The word council, *shura*, meant Council of Representatives, i.e., parliament.
2 *Al-Manar* 9:12 13 Feb.1907, p.951; 12:1 21 Feb.1909, p.13.
3 *Majmu'at Athar Rafiq Bek al-'Azm* (Cairo, [1925]), p.v. The book is a collection of Rafiq al-'Azm's articles.
4 *Al-Manar* 9:12 13 Feb.1907, p.952.
5 *Ibid*, 12:1 21 Feb.1909, p.13; 12:9 14 Oct.1909, p.706. *Rafiq al-'Azm*, pp. v-vi. Tarrazi, vol.2, pt.2, p.188.
6 *Al-Manar* 12:1 21 Oct.1909, p.13. *Rafiq al-'Azm*, p.vi.
7 Hirfi, "Mudhakkirat" 10, pp.67-69; 11, pp.97-101.
8 *Rafiq al-'Azm*, p.vi. Hirfi, "Mudhakkirat" 11, p.101.

Chapter 9

1 A detailed description of the Young Turks' history may be found in Ernest Ramsaur, *The Young Turks: Prelude to the Revolution of 1908* (New York, [1957] 1970) and Feroz Ahmad, *The Young Turks: The Committee of Union and Progress in Turkish Politics 1908-1914* (London, 1969).
2 Jessup, vol.2, p.786. The author, a Protestant missionary, lived in Syria at that time.
3 Philip P. Graves, *Briton and Turk* (London, 1941), p.101. The author, a *Times* journalist, stayed in Istanbul during the revolution.
4 G.F. Abbott, *Turkey in Transition* (London, 1909), p.105.
5 For diplomatic reports of the rejoicing in the Arab provinces following the restoration of the constitution see: FO 371/545: ds 449, 467 and 488, Lowther (Istanbul) to Grey 4, 11 and 18 Aug.1908.

FO 195/2277: ds 51 and 54, Henry A. Cumberbatch (Beirut) to Lowther 1 and 8 Aug.1908. MAE, NS Turquie 111: d65, Charles-Augustin Fouques Duparc (Beirut) to MAE (Paris) 21 Aug.1908. FO 195/2277: d28, George P. Devey (Damascus) to George H. Barclay (Istanbul) 28 July 1908. ds 29, 33, 35 and 51, Devey to Lowther 3, 12 and 22 Aug. and 1 Oct.1908. d35, Henry Z. Longworth (Aleppo) to Lowther 20 Aug.1908. MAE, NS Egypt 15: d266, François Dejean (Cairo) to Pichon 29 July 1908, etc.

6 *Al-Manar* 11:6 28 July 1908, pp.417, 423.

7 Al-Shihabi, p.63.

8 There are differences of opinion regarding the numbers of Turks and Arabs in the Ottoman Empire in the period under discussion: Antonius, p.104, claims that there were 7.5 million Turks and 10.5 million Arabs, while Ahmad, p.156, claims that in 1914 there were 12.5 million Turks and 5.3 million Arabs.

9 On Ziya Gökalp and the development of his ideology see Uriel Heyd, *Foundations of Turkish Nationalism: The Life and Teachings of Ziya Gökalp* (London, 1950). On the pan-Turanian movement see *The Rise of the Turks — The Pan Turanian Movement* (Feb.1919). Jacob M. Landau, *Pan-Turkism in Turkey* (London, 1981).

10 Ahmad 'Izzat al-A'zami, *Al-Qadiyya al-'Arabiyya: Asbabuha, Muqaddimatuha, Tatawwuratuha wa-Nata'ijuha* (Baghdad, 1931-34), vol.6, p.90.

11 Ahad A'da' al-Jam'iyyat al-'Arabiyya [As'ad Daghir], *Thawrat al-'Arab: Muqaddimatuha, Asbabuha, Nata'ijuha* (Cairo, 1916), p.159.

12 *Ibid*, pp.52-53.

13 *Al-Manar* 12:12 11 Jan.1910, p.926. On the complaints of the Arabs regarding the attitude towards the Arabic language see: *ibid*, pp.916-927; 12:7 16 Aug.1909, pp.508-510. *Al-Muqtabas* 4:2 Feb.-Mar.1909, pp.109-112; 5:8 1910, pp.513-515. FO 195/2342: d18, Wilkie Young (Damascus) to Lowther 12 July 1910. MAE, NS Turquie 180: d270, André Ribot (Cairo) to Pichon 23 Oct.1909.

14 Nasif Abi Zayd, *Ta'rikh al-'Asr al-Damawi* (Damascus, 1919), pp.115-117.

PART II

Chapter 10

1 FO 195/2277: d65, Devey (Damascus) to Lowther (Istanbul) 24 Nov.1908. FO 371/768: d105, Lowther to Grey 17 Feb.1909. FO 371/1000: d515, Lowther to Grey 27 July 1910. MAE, NS Turquie 118: d154, Joseph-Fernand Couget (Beirut) to Raymond Poincaré

(Paris) 3 Dec.1912.
2 MAE, NS Turquie 112: d17, Fouques Duparc (Beirut) to MAE 19 Feb.1909. MG, 7N2145: note 420-9/11, "sur M. Mautran, Président du Comité Franco-Syrien à Paris" (Paris) 31 Jan.1915.
3 CZA Z3/48: Richard Lichtheim (Istanbul) to Central Zionist Office (Berlin) 28 Apr.1914.
4 FO 371/1000: d515, Lowther to Grey 27 July 1910. Amin Sa'id, *Al-Thawra al-'Arabiyya al-Kubra* (Cairo, [1934]), vol.1, p.53. Al-A'zami, vol.3, p.73. Ahmad Qadri, *Mudhakkirati 'an al-Thawra al-'Arabiyya al-Kubra* (Damascus, 1956), pp.10, 19.
5 MAE, NS Egypte 15: d282, Jules-Albert Defrance (Cairo) to Pichon 20 June 1912. Muhammad 'Izzat Darwaza, *Nash'at al-Haraka al-'Arabiyya al-Haditha* (Sidon, Beirut, [1971]), p.414. Al-A'zami, vol.3, pp.72-73.
6 FO 882/24: *Who's Who in Damascus — 1919* (Damascus) 14 May 1919, p.2. ISA 2/15: Brunton (General Staff Intelligence) to Acting Civil Secretary 13 Aug.1921.
7 Philip Hendrick Stoddard, *The Ottoman Government and the Arabs 1911-1918: A Preliminary Study of the Teşkilât-i Mahsusa* (Ph.D. Dissertation, Princeton University, 1963), pp.146, 222.
8 Sa'id, *al-Thawra*, vol.1, p.53. Al-A'zami, vol.3, p.73.
9 *Al-Mufid* 24 May 1913, cited in Tawfiq 'Ali Baru, *Al-'Arab wal-Turk fil-'Ahd al-Dusturi al-'Uthmani 1908-1914* (Cairo, 1960), p.507. Khayr al-Din al-Zirikli, *Al-A'lam* (Beirut, 3rd ed.1969), vol.6, p.325.
10 Amin Sa'id, *Asrar al-Thawra al-'Arabiyya al-Kubra wa-Ma'sat al-Sharif Husayn* (Beirut, [1960]), p.28. Al-Qa'id al-'Amm lil-Jaysh al-Rabi' [Jamal Pasha], *Idahat 'an al-Masa'il al-Siyasiyya Allati Jarat Tadqiquha bi-Diwan al-Harb al-'Urfi al-Mutashakkil bi-'Aleyh* (Istanbul, 1916), p.8. Al-A'zami, vol.2, pp.98-99. Qadri, pp.8-9. K.T. Khairallah, *Le Problème du Levant: Les Régions Arabes Libérées* (Paris, 1919), p.26. *RMM* 6:10 Oct.1908, p.241.
11 The articles cited here are a combination of the two similar French versions in *RMM* 6:10 Oct.1908, p.241 and 6:11 Nov.1908, pp.517-518, and the Arab version in Abi Zayd, pp.89-91. Another version (not completely different) is cited in two later books: Muhammad al-Mahdi al-Basir, *Ta'rikh al-Qadiyya al-'Iraqiyya* (Baghdad, 1923), pp.16-17 and Sa'id, *al-Thawra*, vol.1, pp.7-8.
12 *RMM* 6:10 Oct.1908, pp.241-242; 6:11 Nov.1908, p.518. Al-Basir, p.16. Sa'id, *al-Thawra*, vol.1, p.7. Tarrazi, vol.2, pt.2, p.362.
13 *Idahat*, p.9. *Al-Muqattam* 6046 17 Feb.1909, cited in Taj El-Sir Ahmet Harran, "The Young Turks and the Arabs: The Role of Arab Societies in the Turkish-Arab Relations in the Period 1908-1914" in *Türk-Arap İlişkileri: Geçmişte, Bugün ve Gelecekte* (Ankara, 1980), p.187, *AB* no.90 (Cairo) 24 May 1918, p.165.
14 Baru, p.111. Qadri, p.10. Al-Shihabi, p.68. Sa'id, *al-Thawra*, vol.1, p.8. Idem, *Asrar*, p.28. *Al-Muqattam* 6041 3 Feb.1909, cited in Harran, "Young Turks 1908-1914", p.188. *AB* no.90 (Cairo) 24

May 1918, p.165.
15 *Rafiq al-'Azm*, p.130.
16 *Al-Manar* 11:12 22 Jan.1909, pp.936-937. In another place Rida said: "I and all the Ottoman Arabs whom I know in Egypt and Syria opposed the society's establishment, and when I visited Syria I kept the people far from it." *Ibid* 13:10 2 Nov.1910, p.748.
17 Nadra Moutran, *La Syrie de demain* (Paris, 1916), p.210.
18 *Al-Hilal* 17:7 1 Apr.1909, p.415.
19 *Idahat*, pp.9-10. Qadri, p.10. *Tanin* 254 18 May 1909 and 256 20 May 1909, cited in Harran, "Young Turks 1908-1914", pp.187, 189.
20 FO 371/761: d799, Lowther to Grey 29 Sept.1909. FO 371/780: d709, same to same 1 Sept.1909, enclosing French version of the law. An Arabic version of the law may be found in *al-Muqtabas* 6:7 1911, pp.459-470.

Chapter 11

1 MAE, NS Turquie 112: d17, Fouques Duparc (Beirut) to MAE 19 Feb.1909. MAE, NS Turquie 121: Le Chef du Secrétariat particulier au nom du Préfet de Police (Paris) to MAE 29 May 1913.
2 There is no connection between this society and a society of similar name that was founded in 1917 in Paris by Shukri Ghanim.
3 The manifesto and proclamation of 25 Dec.1908 may be found in MAE, NS Turquie 111 and FO 371/561.
4 *Cd'O* 8 15 Jan.1909, p.229. MAE, NS Turquie 112: d17, Fouques Duparc to MAE 19 Feb.1909.
5 *Ibid*. *Al-Ahram* 18 and 21 Jan.1909, cited in Baru, p.92.
6 FO 195/2311 and FO 618/3: d7, Devey (Damascus) to Lowther (Istanbul) 21 Jan.1909.
7 MAE, NS Turquie 112: d17, Fouques Duparc to MAE 19 Feb.1909.
8 Ahmad, pp.33-36.
9 Both manifestos are enclosed with MAE, NS Turquie 6: d79, Fouques Duparc to MAE 23 June 1909.
10 MAE, NS Turquie 151: d17, Gustav-Joseph Rouet (Baghdad) to MAE 1 Apr.1909. MAE, NS Turquie 180: d32, Sous-Directeur du Levant (Paris) to Beirut 29 Apr.1909.

Chapter 12

1 FO 371/545: d488, Lowther (Istanbul) to Grey 18 Aug.1908. FO 371/561: d84, Cumberbatch (Beirut) to Lowther 19 Nov.1908. Cumberbatch reported that he had received 195 petitions bearing 30,000 signatures against sending representatives from the Lebanon

to the parliament.

2 M. Jouplain [Bulus Nujaym], *La Question du Liban: Etude d'Histoire Diplomatique et de Droit International* (Paris, 1908), pp.576-585, 597-598.

3 MAE, NS Turquie 111: d, Fouques Duparc (Beirut) to Jean Antoine Constans (Istanbul) 15 Sept.1908. ds 79 and 80, Fouques Duparc to MAE 20 and 21 Sept.1908. Khairallah, *Syrie*, pp.131-134. Georges Samné, *Le Liban Autonome (de 1861 à nos jours)* (Paris, 1919), p.8. Abi Zayd, pp.87-89.

4 On the al-Khazin family being the initiators of the society see *Idahat*, p.30, 'Aziz Bek, *Suriya wa-Lubnan fil-Harb al-'Alamiyya: Al-Istikhbarat wal-Jasusiyya fil-Dawla al-'Uthmaniyya* (Beirut, 1933), p.277 and Abi Zayd, p.102.

5 MAE, NS Turquie 111: d84, Fouques Duparc to MAE 27 Sept.1908. FO 424/217 [No.48]: d77, Cumberbatch to Lowther 30 Oct.1908. FO 424/218 [No.14]: d2, same to same 7 Jan.1909. Cumberbatch estimated the number of the society's members during that period at 4,000-5,000 men. The Society of the Lebanese Revival was called in French in that period "l'Union Libanaise" and sometimes "l'Alliance Libanaise" or "Ligue Libanaise". Later, it was officially named "Comité Libanais de Beyrouth".

6 MAE, NS Turquie 112: René Ristelhueber (Beirut) to Pichon 21 Dec.1909. Ristelhueber described the society's members as so extremist that they endangered the goal they were defending, since their demands would lead them to collision with the Ottoman government.

7 The pamphlet may be found in MAE, NS Turquie 113.

8 *Ibid*: d7, Ristelhueber to Pichon 11 Feb.1910.

9 Philippe al-Khazin's letter, dated 15 Feb.1910, may be found in FO 371/1006. The Ambassador's response is in *ibid*: ds 154 and 214, Lowther to Grey 15 Mar. and 9 Apr.1910.

10 *Cd'O* 1 July 1910, p.34.

11 Farid al-Khazin's list of complaints is enclosed with MAE, NS Turquie 115: d102, Couget (Beirut) to Cruppy (Paris) 5 June 1911. The petition of the Lebanese and its French translation by Farid al-Khazin may also be found there.

12 The society's letter to the consuls-general in Beirut, dated 6 May 1912, and the list of the society's demands, dated 29 Apr.1912, may be found in MAE, NS Turquie 116. See also Khairallah, *Problème*, p.64.

13 MG, 7N2145: Commission de Controle Postale de Marseille. Note No.4 26 Apr.1917, enclosing an article by Ibrahim Salim al-Najjar 19[?] Apr.1917.

14 MAE, NS Turquie 177: d131, Robert Coulondre (Beirut) to Poincaré 11 Oct.1912.

15 The residents of Dayr al-Qamar, for example, decided in December 1912 to demand the annexation of Beirut, Tripoli and the Biqa' to Mount Lebanon. In the village of Dabya a meeting was to be held

in the same month at which the notables of the Lebanon intended
to demand that the government annex Beirut, Tyre and Sidon to
the Lebanon. See *ha-Herut* 5:67 9 Dec.1912; 5:79 23 Dec.1912,
and also MAE, NS Turquie 118: d159, Couget to MAE 16
Dec.1912.

16 *Cd'O* 103 1 Jan.1913, p.46; 105 1 Feb.1913, pp.120-121.

17 MAE, NS Turquie 119: 1, Comité Libanais de Beyrouth to Poincaré 12 Jan.1913.

18 *Ibid*: 1, Bishara al-Khuri to Jonnart (Paris) 27 Feb.1913.

19 Bishara al-Khuri's proposal is in MAE, NS Turquie 121: 1, Bishara
al-Khuri to Shukri Ghanim (Paris) 7 May 1913. The list of reforms
is in *ha-Herut* 5:191 12 May 1913.

20 *Idahat*, pp.31-32. 'Aziz Bek, *Suriya*, pp.199-204, 207.

21 The members of the other societies were aware of this. See 'Abd
al-Ghani al-'Uraysi in *Idahat*, p.32 and al-A'zami, vol.4, pp.75-76.

22 FO 195/2460/3421: d56, Cumberbatch to Louis Mallet (Istanbul) 5
Aug.1914. MAE, Guerre 867: t147, Defrance (Cairo) to MAE 5
Nov.1914. t213, Gabriel-Pierre Deville (Athens) to MAE 3
Dec.1914. t126, Delcassé (Paris) to Deville 6 Dec.1914. FO
371/2147: t388, Francis Elliot (Athens) to FO 7 Dec.1914. t1173,
FO to Francis Bertie (Paris) 9 Dec.1914. t550, Bertie to FO 10
Dec.1914. d273, Elliot to Grey 14 Dec.1914. t1243, FO to Bertie
17 Dec.1914. t315, FO to Elliot 30 Dec.1914. MAE, Guerre 867:
memos, British Embassy (Paris) 18 and 31 Dec.1914. t53-53bis,
Delcassé to French Ambassador (London) 8 Jan.1915.

23 MAE, NS Turquie 112: *Les Pyramides* 24 Nov.1909. MAE, NS
Turquie 116: t31, Defrance to MAE 7 June 1912. MAE, Syrie-
Liban 1: d96, Defrance to Pichon 23 Mar.1918.

24 The list of demands may be found in MAE, NS Turquie 116, as
well as the certificate given by the society to Da'ud 'Ammun on 5
May 1912.

25 MAE, NS Turquie 117: note, Gaillard (Cairo) 19 Nov.1912. d508,
Defrance to Poincaré 25 Nov.1912. The telegram, signed by Iskandar 'Ammun, dated 20 Nov.1912 and addressed to the French,
British and German foreign ministers, may be found in *ibid*, FO
371/1521 and GFM 10/405, respectively.

26 MAE, NS Turquie 118: d546, Defrance to Poincaré 16 Dec.1912.
The telegram, signed by Iskandar 'Ammun, dated 15 Dec.1912 and
addressed to the French ambassador, may be found in *ibid*. The
same telegram to the British ambassador may be found in FO
371/1522 annexed to d1072, Lowther to Grey 15 Dec.1912.

27 *Idahat*, p.92. 'Aziz Bek, *Suriya*, p.278.

28 MAE, NS Turquie 116: Da'ud 'Ammun to MAE 14 May 1912.
The negative response of the French foreign ministry's officials to
'Ammun's appeal is attached to that letter.

29 On Shukri Ghanim's career see Christopher M. Andrew and A.S.
Kanya-Forstner, *The Climax of French Imperial Expansion
1914-1924* (Stanford, 1981), p.47.

30 Khairallah, *Problème*, p.65. *Idahat*, p.31. 'Aziz Bek, *Suriya*, p.278. The authorization of Ghanim and Khayrallah, dated 1 June 1912, may be found in MAE, NS Turquie 116.
31 *Ibid*: note, "Affaires du Liban" 11 June 1912. Georges-Louis Degrand, "Note au Ministre" (Paris) 18 June 1912. Shukri Ghanim to Director 28 June 1912.
32 *Ibid*: note 6 July 1912. *Cd'O* 92 15 July 1912, p.78. The memo was also sent to the British Foreign Minister. See FO 371/1491: Comité Libanais de Paris to FO 26 June 1912. d283, Bertie to Grey 28 June 1912. 127467/12, FO to Comité Libanais de Paris July 1912.
33 The memo may be found in MAE, NS Turquie 116 and FO 371/1491.
34 Khairallah, *Syrie*, pp.16, 65-68, 106, 142. Khayrallah was being cited as calling at the end of 1912 for the establishment of a greater France, the Lebanon being a part of it. See John P. Spagnolo, *France and Ottoman Lebanon 1861-1914* (London, 1977), p.291.
35 MAE, NS Turquie 117: ls, Shukri Ghanim to Poincaré 21 and 26 Nov.1912. *Cd'O* 103 1 Jan.1913, p.46.
36 MAE, NS Turquie 117: note (Paris) 20 Nov.1912. MAE, NS Turquie 118: note 6 Dec.1912. MAE, NS Turquie 119: d8, Paul-Antoine Ottavi (Damascus) to Jonnart 27 Jan.1913. *Idahat*, p.31. 'Aziz Bek, *Suriya*, p.199.
37 The protest enclosed with l, Shukri Ghanim and Khayrallah Khayrallah to Pichon 27 June 1913 may be found in MAE, NS Turquie 122. A copy addressed to the British Foreign Minister is enclosed with FO 371/1828: d348, Lancelot D. Carnegie (Paris) to Grey 28 June 1913.
38 The society's protest and an accompanying letter dated 4 July 1913 are enclosed with *ibid*: d361, Carnegie to Grey 5 July 1913. See also *Cd'O* 116 16 July 1913, pp.21-22.
39 K.T. Khairallah, *La Question du Liban* (Paris, 1915), pp.73-74.
40 MAE, Guerre 867: l, Shukri Ghanim to Delcassé 14 Sept.1914.
41 MG, 7N2145: Commission de Controle Postale de Marseille. Note No.4 26 Apr.1917, enclosing an article by Ibrahim Salim al-Najjar 19[?] Apr.1917. AN, 423AP 8: Ibrahim Salim al-Najjar, "Les Colonies Syriennes à l'étranger" (Paris) 23 Oct.1916. Khairallah, *Problème*, p.65. *Idahat*, p.31.
42 *Al-Manar* 17:8 24 July 1914, pp.618-623.
43 The memo is enclosed with MAE, Guerre 867: d614, Jean Adrian Jusserand (Washington) to Delcassé 3 Nov.1914. FO 371/2146: d358, Cecil Spring Rice (Washington) to Grey 2 Nov.1914.
44 *Al-Muqtataf* 44:1 1 Jan.1914, pp.45, 49. CZA Z3/116: *Al-Muqtabas* (daily) 27 July 1913. *Al-Mufid* 21 July 1913, cited in Baru, p.504. Al-Lajna al-'Ulya li-Hizb al-Lamarkaziyya bi-Misr [Muhibb al-Din al-Khatib], *Al-Mu'tamar al-'Arabi al-Awwal* (Cairo, 1913), p.120. Tarrazi, vol.2, pt.2, pp.408-409.
45 *Al-Manar* 17:8 24 July 1914, pp.624-625.

46 MAE, NS Turquie 118: 1, Asad Bishara to Poincaré 24 Dec.1912.
47 *Abu al-Hawl* 7:153 1 Feb.1913.
48 MAE, Guerre 867: 1, Joseph Lutayf and Salim 'Aql to Delcassé 1 Dec.1914. FO 371/2417: 1, Joseph Lutayf and Salim 'Aql to Grey 1 Dec.1914.

Chapter 13

1 There are those who claim that *al-Qahtaniyya* was the first secret society. It will be clarified here that the idea of *al-Fatat* preceded that of *al-Qahtaniyya*.
2 Qadri, pp.6-7. Ahmad Qadri was one of the prominent members of the society until 1920. See also Khayriyya Qasimiyya (ed.), *'Awni 'Abd al-Hadi: Awraq Khassa* (Beirut, 1974), p.9.
3 Qadri, p.11. Al-Shihabi, pp.72-73. Mustafa al-Shihabi was a member of *al-Fatat* too.
4 The fact that the society's name had originally been *Jam'iyyat al-Natiqin bil-Dad* was related by Tawfiq al-Natur in an interview to Zeine. See Zeine, *Emergence*, p.83. The name *Jam'iyyat al-Umma al-'Arabiyya al-Fatat* is mentioned by al-Shihabi, p.73. Qadri, p.12 discusses the shortening of the name to *al-Fatat*.
5 Darwaza, *Nash'a*, pp.485-488.
6 Qadri, p.283. Tawfiq al-Natur is cited in Zeine, *Emergence*, p.84.
7 Muhammad 'Izzat Darwaza, *Hawla al-Haraka al-'Arabiyya al-Haditha* (Sidon, 1950-53), vol.1, p.29. Idem, *Nash'a*, pp.502-504. Qadri, pp.12-13. Al-Shihabi, pp.73-74. Sa'id, *al-Thawra*, vol.1, p.9. The society's oath is cited in Qadri, p.13.
8 Darwaza, *Nash'a*, pp.481-482, 484. Qadri, pp.12-13, 29. Al-Shihabi, p.72. Rafiq Rizq Sallum is cited in *Idahat*, p.49. On *al-Mufid* being the society's organ see L/P&S/10/586: Arabian Report N.S. No.XI 27 Sept.1916.
9 L, 'Abd al-Ghani al-'Uraysi (Paris) to Muhibb al-Din al-Khatib (Cairo) 2 Jan.1913, cited in Sulayman Musa, "Jam'iyyat al-'Arabiyya al-Fatat", *al-'Arabi*, 151 (1971), p.54.
10 Qadri, pp.12, 14-15. Darwaza, *Nash'a*, p.503. *Idahat*, p.49. Hirfi, "Mudhakkirat" 12, p.97.
11 Qadri, pp.20-21.
12 Darwaza, *Nash'a*, p.503. Qadri, pp.13, 29. Musa, "Jam'iyya", pp.54-55. Al-A'zami, vol.4, pp.98-99.
13 Darwaza, *Hawla*, vol.1, p.31. Sa'id, *al-Thawra*, vol.1, p.10. Musa, "Jam'iyya", p.55. Idem, *Al-Haraka al-'Arabiyya: Sirat al-Marhala al-Ula lil-Nahda al-'Arabiyya al-Haditha 1908-1924* (Beirut, 1970), pp.136-137. 174, Haqqi al-'Azm (Cairo) to Mahmud al-Mihmisani (Beirut) 3 July 1914, cited in *Idahat*, pp.73-74 and *JB* 409 27 Aug.1915. See also L/P&S/10/586: Arabian Report N.S. No.XI 27 Sept.1916.

14 Al-Shihabi, p.106. *Thawrat al-'Arab*, p.129. Sa'id, *Asrar*, p.38. Musa, *al-Haraka*, p.159. Idem, "Jam'iyya", p.55.
15 Darwaza, *Nash'a*, p.503. Al-A'zami, vol.4, pp.99-100. Qadri, p.37. Sa'id, *al-Thawra*, vol.1, pp.107-108. Idem, *Asrar*, pp.38-39. On Kamil al-Qassab's mission see also MAE, Guerre 871: d362, Defrance (Cairo) to Aristide Briand (Paris) 25 Nov.1915. FO 371/2141: t251, Milne Cheetham (Cairo) to Grey 9 Nov.1914 and minute by Kitchener. FO 882/17: Osmond Warlond, report on Arab Committees (Cairo) July[?] 1918.
16 Antonius, p.153. Qadri, p.38.

Chapter 14

1 *AB* no.90 (Cairo) 24 May 1918, p.165.
2 *Idahat*, p.16. Al-Basir, p.18. Sa'id, *al-Thawra*, vol.1, p.10. Al-A'zami, vol.3, p.31. Muhammad Tahir al-'Umari, *Ta'rikh Muqaddarat al-'Iraq al-Siyasiyya* (Baghdad, 1924-25), vol.1, p.168. Antonius, p.110. See also James Jankowski, "Ottomanism and Arabism in Egypt 1860-1914", *MW*, 70:3-4 (1980), p.259.
3 Salih Hirfi, "Al-Jaza'ir wa-Dawruha fil-Nahda al-'Arabiyya al-Haditha fil-Mashriq", *al-Thaqafa* [Algeria], 26 (Apr.-May 1975), pp.33-34. Burj, pp.38-40. Al-Khatib, *al-Shaykh Tahir*, pp.79-81. Al-A'zami, vol.3, pp.32-33.
4 *Idahat* pp.16, 18. Al-A'zami, vol.3, pp.31, 33, 35. Al-Shihabi, p.69. Sa'id, *al-Thawra*, vol.1, p.10. Sulayman Faydi, *Fi Ghamrat al-Nidal* (Baghdad, 1952), p.85. Antonius, p.110.
5 *AB* no.90 (Cairo) 24 May 1918, pp.165-166. FO 882/24: note, "The AHD Committee or Committee of the Covenant" by Arab Bureau (Cairo) Apr.1919. Al-Shihabi, p.69. Sa'id, *al-Thawra*, vol.1, p.10. Burj, pp.41-42. Antonius, p.110 argues that the society strove to turn the Ottoman Empire into a dual monarchy, following the example of Austria-Hungary. Antonius does not give any proof for this claim, and since the rest of the above mentioned sources (among them al-Shihabi, whose brother 'Arif was a member of *al-Qahtaniyya*) disagree with it, it seems that Antonius' claim can be disqualified. In fact, the idea of a dual monarchy, following the example of Austria-Hungary, was *al-'Ahd*'s.
6 *Idahat*, pp.16-17. Al-A'zami, vol.3, pp.33-34. Sa'id, *al-Thawra*, vol.1, p.10. Hirfi, "al-Jaza'ir", p.33. L/P&S/10/586: Summary no.2 of the Arab Bureau, by David G. Hogarth (Cairo) 12 June 1916.
7 On the society's branches see *AB* no.90 (Cairo) 24 May 1918, p.165. Antonius, p.111. Al-Basir, p.18. Al-Shihabi, p.70. On the society's newspaper see Salim Taha al-Tikriti, "Al-Sayyid 'Abd al-Hamid al-Zahrawi", *Afkar*, 16 (1967), p.32. Tarrazi, vol.2, pt.2, p.362. On the end of the society see *Idahat*, p.17. Darwaza,

Nash'a, p.461. *Al-Manar*, 13:6 7 July 1910, p.470. Antonius, p.111 claims that the society was dissolved after one of its members had betrayed it. There is no other source that confirms this claim.

8 MAE, NS Turquie 117: d146, Coulondre (Beirut) to Poincaré 12 November 1912. Ahmad Lutfi al-Sayyid, *Qissat Hayati* (Cairo, 1962), p.137.

Chapter 15

1 Al-A'zami, vol.3, pp.7-8. As'ad Daghir, *Mudhakkirati 'ala Hamish al-Qadiyya al-'Arabiyya* (Cairo, n.d.[1959?]), p.70. *Al-Manar*, 13:6 7 July 1910, p.469.

2 Al-A'zami, vol.3, pp.8-9. Darwaza, *Nash'a*, p.354. Sa'id, *al-Thawra*, vol.1, p.8. *Idahat*, p.10. Baru, p.312. *Al-Manar*, 13:6 7 July 1910, p.469; 14:8 24 Aug.1911, p.636; 28:6 27 Aug.1927, p.470.

3 Qadri, p.11.

4 Al-A'zami, vol.3, pp.9-11, 13. *Al-Manar*, 13:6 7 July 1910, p.470 (Rashid Rida, who attended this event, gives a somewhat different version). *Idahat*, pp.10-11. Al-Shihabi, p.70. Baru, p.310.

5 Daghir, *Mudhakkirati*, p.35. Darwaza, *Nash'a*, p.354. Al-Shihabi, p.71. *Idahat*, p.11. Al-A'zami, vol.3, p.3. *Al-Ahram* 5 May 1910 and 13 July 1911, cited in Baru, p.313. L/P&S/10/586: Arabian Report N.S. No.XI 27 Sept.1916.

6 *RMM* 10:2 Feb.1910, p.248.

7 *Idahat*, pp.12-13.

8 Al-A'zami, vol.3, p.28. Al-Shihabi, p.70, too, relates that while the club's open activity was on the educational and cultural level, it also had secret activity on the nationalist level.

9 Al-A'zami, vol.3, pp.11-12. Al-Shihabi, p.70. *Idahat*, p.12. Darwaza, *Hawla*, vol.1, p.24. Idem, *Nash'a*, p.355. *Al-Ahram* 9769 5 May 1910, cited in Baru, pp.317-318. *Al-Muqtabas* (daily) 1399 24 Jan.1914; *Lisan al-Hal* 6623 1 May 1911, cited in Harran, "Young Turks 1908-1914", p.193. On the complaints that the club's members were neglecting their studies see *Al-Ahram* 9769 5 May 1910 and 9770 6 May 1910, cited in *ibid*.

10 Tawfiq al-Suwaydi, *Mudhakkirati: Nisf Qarn min Ta'rikh al-'Iraq wal-Qadiyya al-'Arabiyya* (Beirut, 1969), p.24. See also Musa, *al-Haraka*, pp.135-136.

11 Daghir, *Mudhakkirati*, p.70.

12 *Ha-Herut* 2:77 29 Mar.1910. *Al-Ahram* 9730 17 Mar.1910; *Lisan al-Hal* 6247 15 Mar.1911 and 6277 18 Mar.1910, all cited in Harran, "Young Turks 1908-1914", pp.193-194. FO 195/2342: d31, Cumberbatch (Beirut) to Lowther (Istanbul) 16 June 1910. 'Abdallah ibn al-Husayn, *Mudhakkirati* (Jerusalem, 1945), p.44. Sati' al-Husri, *Muhadarat fi Nushu' al-Fikra al-Qawmiyya* (Beirut, [1951]

4th rep.1959), p.199. Muhammad Kurd 'Ali, *Al-Mudhakkirat* (Damascus, 1948), vol.1, p.147.
13 Al-A'zami, vol.3, pp.14-28. *Al-Manar*, 14:8 24 Aug.1911, pp.636-637.
14 *Al-Muqtabas* 7:12 1913, p.893.
15 Daghir, *Mudhakkirati*, p.70.
16 MAE, NS Turquie 119: d7, Defrance (Cairo) to Poincaré 6 Jan.1913. t11, Defrance to MAE 13 Feb.1913. d59, Defrance to Jonnart 13 Feb.1913. MAE, NS Turquie 120: d57, Couget (Beirut) to MAE 10 Mar.1913. *Idahat*, p.15.
17 *Thawrat al-'Arab*, pp.99-102. Daghir, *Mudhakkirati*, p.67-68. Al-'Umari, vol.1, p.175. *Fatat al-'Arab* 1470 26 Jan.1914 and 1473 29 Jan.1914, cited in Harran, "Young Turks 1908-1914", p.196. For a detailed description of this affair see the chapter about the Paris agreement and its consequences.
18 *Thawrat al-'Arab*, p.68. Daghir, *Mudhakkirati*, p.35. Abi Zayd, p.92. *Al-Manar* 19:2 15 July 1916, p.68. Tal'at's speech is according to the version of Al-A'zami, vol.3, p.30.
19 Daghir, *Mudhakkirati*, p.69.
20 Djemal Pasha, *Memories of a Turkish Statesman 1913-1919* (New York, [1922] rep.1973), p.63.
21 Al-A'zami, vol.3, pp.37-38. Tarrazi, vol.2, pt.2, p.394. Darwaza, *Hawla*, vol.1, p.24. Idem, *Nash'a*, p.356. Rafiq Rizq Sallum and Sayf al-Din al-Khatib are cited in *Idahat*, pp.14-15.
22 Daghir, *Mudhakkirati*, p.46.
23 *Thawrat al-'Arab*, p.129. Al-Shihabi, pp.106-107. Al-A'zami, vol.3, p.90. *Idahat*, p.16.
24 Darwaza, *Nash'a*, p.357. Abi Zayd, p.92. Al-A'zami, vol.3, p.30. *AB* no.90 (Cairo) 24 May 1918, p.166.

Chapter 16

1 The life and thought of Rashid Rida are described extensively in Shakib Arslan, *Al-Sayyid Rashid Rida aw Ikha' Arba'in Sana* (Damascus, 1937); Ahmad al-Sharbasi, *Rashid Rida Sahib al-Manar: 'Asruhu wa-Hayatuhu wa-Masadir Thaqafatuhu* (Cairo, 1970); and also in Adams, pp.177-204 and Hourani, *Arabic Thought*, pp.222-244. It is not within the scope of this chapter to deal with Rashid Rida's Islamic thought, following Muhammad 'Abduh's teachings, or with his *Salafiyya* methods.
2 Arslan, pp.35-36, 51, 99-101, 128-130. Al-Sharbasi, pp.102-103, 110-111, 120-121, 136-137, 145-147. Adams, pp.177-181.
3 Hourani, *Arabic Thought*, pp.299-300. Marcel Colombe, "Islam et nationalisme arabe a la veille de la première guerre mondiale", *Revue Historique*, 223:1 (1960), p.92. Muhammad Rashid Rida, *Al-Khilafa aw al-Imama al-'Uzma* (Cairo, [1923]), p.123.

4 *Ibid*, p.88.
5 *Al-Manar* 14:3 30 Mar.1911, p.199. Adams, p.184. Hourani, *Arabic Thought*, p.301. See also Henri Laoust, *Essai sur les doctrines sociales et politiques de Taki-D-Din Ahmad B. Taimiya* (Cairo, 1939), p.566.
6 *Al-Manar* 20:1 30 July 1917, pp.33-34. See also J. Jomier, "Les Raisons de l'adhésion du Sayyed Rashid Rida au nationalisme arabe", *Bulletin de l'Institut d'Egypte*, 53-54 (1971-72/1972-73), p.54.
7 *Al-Manar* 11:12 22 Jan.1909, p.904.
8 *Ibid* 12:12 11 Jan.1910, pp.956-958; 13:2 11 Mar.1910, pp.145-149; 13:3 10 Apr.1910, p.230; 13:6 7 July 1910, pp.465-468, 471; 13:10 2 Nov.1910, pp.750-752; 14:1 30 Jan.1911, pp.43-46; 19:2 15 July 1916, pp.76-77. FO 371/1011: ds 466 and 717, Lowther (Istanbul) to Grey 6 July and 9 Oct.1910. Adams, pp.196-197.
9 *Al-Manar* 14:1 30 Jan.1911, pp.52-54, 59-62; 14:2 1 Mar.1911, pp.115-120, 128-134; 14:3 30 Mar.1911, pp.191-193; 14:6 27 June 1911, p.480; 14:10 22 Oct.1911, pp.785-800; 14:11 21 Nov.1911, pp.801-821; 15:3 19 Mar.1912, p.226; 17:6 24 May 1914, pp.461-468; 18:4 14 May 1915, pp.314-315. PRO 30/57/36: "Report respecting Secret Societies" (Secret Service Bureau, Cairo) 22 June 1911, enclosed with d68, Cheetham (Cairo) to Grey 30 June 1911. Adams, pp.197-198.
10 Sa'id, *al-Thawra*, vol.1, p.49. *Rafiq al-'Azm*, p.vii.
11 *Al-Manar* 21:4 28 June 1919, p.203.
12 Sa'id, *al-Thawra*, vol.1, p.49-50.
13 *Al-Manar* 15:11 9 Nov.1912, p.838; 16:2 6 Feb.1913, p.145; 16:4 7 Apr.1913, pp.316-317.
14 *Ibid* 24:8 13 Aug.1923, p.607; 28:1 3 Mar.1927, pp.4-5; 28:6 27 Aug.1927, p.470. Sa'id, *al-Thawra*, vol.1, p.50. *Idahat*, p.76.
15 So says Rida in *Rafiq al-'Azm*, p.vii.
16 The pamphlet was also distributed by Rashid Rida when he was on hajj in Mecca in 1916 and a copy of it then fell into the hands of the French. Its translation is enclosed with MAE, Guerre 1687: d440, Defrance (Cairo) to Briand 29 Oct.1916.
17 The call was first published in *al-Ahram* 26 Sept.1914, and again in *al-Manar* 17:12 18 Nov.1914, pp.956-958.
18 Sa'id, *Asrar*, pp.37-38.
19 "General Organic Law of the Arab Empire" by Rashid Rida, enclosed with FO 882/15: note, Ronald Storrs (Cairo) to Gilbert F.Clayton (Cairo) 5 Dec.1915.

Chapter 17

1 Al-A'zami, vol.3, pp.35-36.
2 *Ibid*, p.36. Faydi, p.85. Sa'id, *al-Thawra*, vol.1, p.11. Darwaza,

Nash'a, p.479.
3 Sa'id, *al-Thawra*, vol.1, p.11. Al-A'zami, vol.3, p.36. Faydi, p.85. Darwaza, *Nash'a*, pp.478-479.
4 Al-A'zami, vol.3, pp.37-38. Darwaza, *Nash'a*, pp.479-480. Tarrazi, vol.2, pt.2, p.394.
5 Al-A'zami, vol.3, pp.37-39. Faydi, p.86.

Chapter 18

1 MAE, NS Turquie 117: ds 477 and 481, Maurice-Nicolas Fouchet (Cairo) to Poincaré 31 Oct. and 5 Nov.1912. t92, Defrance (Cairo) to MAE 16 Nov.1912. MAE, NS Turquie 118: d524, Defrance to Poincaré 4 Dec.1912. FO 371/1522: t85, Kitchener to Grey 8 Dec.1912.
2 MAE, NS Turquie 118: *al-Mu'ayyad* 2 Dec.1912.
3 Poincare's speech is cited in many sources, e.g. *Le Temps* 24 Dec.1912; *Cd'O* 103 1 Jan.1913, p.1; and Raymond Poincaré, *Au Service de la France* (Paris, 1926), vol.2, pp.411-412.
4 *Al-Manar* 17:5 25 Apr.1914, pp.395-396. Al-A'zami, vol.3, pp.41-42. Sa'id, *al-Thawra*, vol.1, p.14.
5 MAE, NS Turquie 120: d109, Defrance to Jonnart 14 Mar.1913. PRO 30/57/44: *al-Muqattam* 18 Jan.1913, enclosed with Intelligence Department, WO (Cairo) 20 Jan.1913.
6 *Thawrat al-'Arab*, pp.57-62. Sa'id, *al-Thawra*, vol.1, pp.14-18.
7 MAE, NS Turquie 119: d71, Defrance to Jonnart 21 Feb.1913. CZA Z3/752: S. Hasamsony (Cairo) to Central Zionist Office (Berlin) 21 Feb.1913.
8 *Al-Manar* 16:3 8 Mar.1913, pp.226-231. The platform and manifesto in French may be found in MAE, NS Turquie 119.
9 *Al-Manar* 16:5 7 May 1913, pp.344-351.
10 *Ibid* 17:4 27 Mar.1914, pp.306-307, 310.
11 L, Haqqi al-'Azm (Cairo) to Mahmud al-Mihmisani (Beirut) 16 Apr.1914, cited in *Idahat*, pp.65-66. CZA L2/26iii: J. Thon (Jaffa) to Central Zionist Office (Berlin) 8 Apr.1913. Qasimiyya, p.10. Darwaza, *Nash'a*, pp.371-372.
12 L, Haqqi al-'Azm to 'Abd al-Hafiz Mahmud al-Hasan 15 June 1914, cited in *Idahat*, pp.69-70.
13 L, Rafiq al-'Azm (Cairo) to Salih Haydar (Ba'albek) 23 July 1914, cited in *ibid*, p.71.
14 Al-A'zami, vol.3, p.45. Qasimiyya, pp.9-10.
15 L, Haqqi al-'Azm 25 Aug.1913, cited in Musa, *al-Haraka*, p.63. *Al-Manar* 17:3 25 Feb.1914, p.237.
16 'Aziz Bek, *Suriya*, pp.258-259. After Kamil Pasha had been deposed from his position as Grand Vizier, following the coup d'état of January 1913, he came to Egypt and was in contact there with the members of the Decentralization Party. See Martin

Hartmann, *Reisebriefe aus Syrien* (Berlin, 1913), p.93. On the agreement between Sadiq Bey and Rafiq al-'Azm see also in *Idahat*, p.45.

17 *Ibid*, pp.45-48.

18 MAE, NS Turquie 119: d31, Louis-Maurice Bompard (Istanbul) to Poincaré 15 Jan.1913.

19 MAE, NS Turquie 120: d85, Couget (Beirut) to Pichon 22 Apr.1913.

20 MAE, NS Turquie 121: d49, Ottavi (Damascus) to Pichon 18 May 1913.

21 *Ha-Herut* 5:189 9 May 1913.

22 MAE, NS Turquie 120: d123, Defrance to Jonnart 21 Mar.1913. t17, Defrance to MAE 22 Mar.1913. d131, Defrance to Pichon 28 Mar.1913. d15, Georges-Maurice Paléologue (Paris) to Ottavi 25 Mar.1913, cited in *JB* 622 6 May 1916. The list of the resolutions adopted at this meeting was delivered to the Ottoman Agency in Cairo by one of its spies who attended the meeting. See 'Aziz Bek, *Suriya*, pp.262-263.

23 CZA Z3 115: *al-Muqattam* 3 Mar.1913.

24 Rafiq al-'Azm's telegrams to the Grand Vizier and the Vali of Beirut, dated 13 Apr.1913, may be found in MAE, NS Turquie 120. Haqqi al-'Azm's telegram to the French Foreign Minister, dated 13 Apr.1913, which was published also in *Le Temps* 15 Apr.1913, may also be found there.

25 *Al-Mu'tamar al-'Arabi*, pp.5-8.

26 GFM 10:405: d70[?], Consul in Cairo to Theobald von Bethmann Hollweg 7[?] May 1913. MAE, NS Turquie 121: d223, Defrance to Pichon 23 May 1913. *Times* 3 May 1913. *Idahat*, p.58. *Al-Manar* 16:5 7 May 1913, p.394; 17:3 25 Feb.1914, p.238. The speeches given at this meeting were reported in *ha-Herut* 5:192 13 May 1913.

27 L, Haqqi al-'Azm to 'Awni 'Abd al-Hadi (Nablus) 29 Sept.1913, cited in Qasimiyya, p.9.

28 The "Manifesto to the Arab Nation from the Decentralization Party" is cited in *al-Manar* 16:11 30 Oct.1913, pp.849-859. For the detailed contents of the manifesto see the chapter below on the Paris agreement and its consequences.

29 *Al-Manar* 17:3 25 Feb.1914, p.236; 17:5 25 Apr.1914, p.399. *Thawrat al-'Arab*, p.135. Al-A'zami, vol.4, p.18.

30 L, Haqqi al-'Azm to Mahmud al-Mihmisani 16 Apr.1914, cited in *Idahat*, p.21.

31 L, Haqqi al-'Azm to Muhammad al-Mihmisani (Beirut) 16 Apr.1914, cited in *ibid*, p.89. CZA L2/94ib: l, Haqqi al-'Azm to Nisim Malul (Jaffa) 29 Apr.1914.

32 L74, Haqqi al-'Azm to Mahmud al-Mihmisani 3 July 1914, cited in *Idahat*, p.86 and *JB* 409 27 Aug.1915. 131, same to same n.d. [June 1914], cited in *Idahat*, pp.68-69 and *JB* 414 2 Sept.1915. 175 to Muhammad al-Mihmisani n.d. [July 1914], cited in *Idahat*, p.67 and *JB* 410 28 Aug.1915. For security reasons Haqqi al-'Azm was

signing his letters by the name H. al-Misri (Haqqi the Egyptian).
33 L32, Haqqi al-'Azm to Mahmud al-Mihmisani 24 July 1914, cited
    in *Idahat*, pp.83-84 and *JB* 412 31 Aug.1915.
34 So said 'Abd al-Ghani al-'Uraysi, who was a member in the Decen-
    tralization Party. *Idahat*, pp.91, 94.
35 According to *Idahat*, pp.92-94, this letter was addressed to Kamil
    Hashim, and according to *Idahat*'s French version — Le Com-
    mandement de la IVe Armée Ottoman, *La Vérité sur la question
    syrienne* (Istanbul, 1916), p.125, it was addressed to Sayyid Shukri.
    The letter is signed by 'A.R. (al-'Azm Rafiq?).
36 FO 371/2140: t264, Cheetham (Cairo) to Grey 13 Nov.1914. Sa'id,
    al-Thawra, vol.1, pp.128-129. *Idahat*, p.94. 'Aziz Bek, *Suriya*,
    p.358.
37 FO 371/2140: ts 223 and 228, Cheetham to Grey 26 and 28
    Oct.1914. MAE, Guerre 868: d44, Defrance to Delcassé 4
    Feb.1915. 'Aziz Bek, *Suriya*, p.358. Sa'id, *Asrar* pp.37-38. Idem,
    al-Thawra, vol.1, p.129.
38 FO 371/2140: t228, Cheetham to Grey 28 Oct.1914. L/P&S/11/95:
    t, SSI to Viceroy 31 Oct.1914. t, Arthur Henry McMahon (Cairo)
    to FSI (Delhi) 9 Feb.1915. t, Percy Z. Cox (Basra) to FSI 13
    Feb.1914. t, Viceroy to IO 16 February 1915. l, Cox to McMahon
    18 Mar.1915. t1377-B, Cox to FSI (Simla) 11 July 1915.
39 FO 371/2140: t347, Grey to Cheetham 14 Nov.1914, and Reuters'
    announcement. Sa'id, *al-Thawra*, vol.1, p.129.

Chapter 19

1 MAE, NS Turquie 117: note, Gaillard[?] (Cairo) 16 Nov.1912.
   MAE, NS Turquie 118: d154, Couget (Beirut) to Poincaré 3
   Dec.1912. d159, Couget to MAE 16 Dec.1912. FO 195/2446: d88,
   Peter J.C. Mc Gregor (Jerusalem) to Lowther (Istanbul) 8
   Nov.1912. ds 76, 78 and 79, Cumberbatch (Beirut) to Lowther 14
   and 21 Nov. and 4 Dec.1912. FO 371/1521: d485, Bertie (Paris) to
   Grey 18 Nov.1912. FO 371/1522: d1072, Lowther to Grey 15
   Dec.1912. *BD*, vol.10, pt.2, p.824.
2 MAE, NS Turquie 119: d1, Couget to Poincaré 2 Jan.1913. Kamal
   S. Salibi, "Beirut Under the Young Turks as Depicted in the Political Memoirs of Salim 'Ali Salam (1868-1938)" in Jacques Berque
   and Dominique Chevallier (eds.), *Les Arabes par leurs archives
   (XVIe-XXe siècles)* (Paris, 1976), pp.204-205. This article includes
   excerpts from the manuscript of Salim 'Ali Salam's memoirs. The
   above narrative is based on pp.9-10 of the manuscript. See also
   al-Muqattam 7227 4 Jan.1913, cited in Zeine, *Emergence*, p.89.
   Cd'O 104 16 Jan.1913, p.50. Adham Bek's telegram is cited in
   al-A'zami, vol.3, p.47 and in an almost identical version in Muhammad Kurd 'Ali, *Kitab Khitat al-Sha'm* (Damascus, 1925), vol.3,

p.129.

3 MAE, NS Turquie 118: d166, Couget to Poincaré 26 Dec.1913. This despatch also includes Bayhum's article and a preliminary list of the major reforms demanded by the society. FO 371/2446: d87, Cumberbatch to Lowther 31 Dec.1912. 'Aziz Bek, *Al-Istikhbarat wal-Jasusiyya fi Lubnan wa-Suriya wa-Filastin khilala al-Harb al-'Alamiyya* (Beirut, 1937), pp.22-23.

4 MAE, NS Turquie 119: ds 1, 8 and 19, Couget to Poincaré 2, 10 and 28 Jan.1913. FO 195/2451/484: d8, Cumberbatch to Lowther 24 Jan.1913. MG, 7N2145: Ayyub Thabit (New York) 14 Oct.1918. 'Aziz Bek, *al-Istikhbarat*, pp.24-26. Al-A'zami, vol.3, p.47. Kurd 'Ali, *Khitat*, vol.3, p.129. *Ha-Herut* 5:98 14 Jan.1913. Hartmann, *Reisebriefe*, p.39. Khairallah, *Problème*, p.39. Al-Azhari's speech is cited in *L'Asie Française* May 1913, p.224.

5 MAE, NS Turquie 119: d20, Couget to MAE 29 Jan.1913. FO 195/2451/340: d12, Cumberbatch to Lowther 30 Jan.1913. *Times* 28 Jan.1913. Hartmann, *Reisebriefe*, pp.39-40. *Al-Mu'tamar al-'Arabi*, p.136. Al-A'zami, vol.3, pp.47, 50.

6 An Arabic version of the list of reforms is cited in *al-Manar* 16:4 7 Apr.1913, pp.275-279; *Thawrat al-'Arab*, pp.62-67; Sa'id, *al-Thawra*, vol.1, pp.19-23. A French version may be found in MAE, NS Turquie 119 and FO 195/2451/484.

7 On the authorities' view see *Idahat*, p.35, where the author raises the suspicion that the members of the Lebanese Revival, who were also members of this society, were those who led to this demand. For Rida's opinion see *al-Manar* 16:4 7 Apr.1913, pp.280, 312-314.

8 Salibi, "Beirut", p.207, citing p.22 of Salim 'Ali Salam's manuscript.

9 MAE, NS Turquie 120: d61, Couget to Jonnart 10 Mar.1913. *Cd'O* 108 15 Mar.1913, p.283.

10 FO 195/2451/484: d28, Cumberbatch to Lowther 27 Mar.1913. Hartmann, *Reisebriefe*, p.23. CZA Z3/115: *Al-Ra'y al-'Amm* 12 Mar.1913. *Ha-Herut* 5:159 26 Mar.1913. *Le Temps* 12 Apr.1913. *L'Asie Française* May 1913, p.225.

11 MAE, NS Turquie 120: d63, Couget to Jonnart 18 Mar.1913, enclosing the memo signed by the six, dated 12 Mar.1913.

12 MAE, NS Turquie 120: ds 62 and 64, Couget to Jonnart 17 and 20 Mar.1913. FO 195/2451/484: d28, Cumberbatch to Lowther 27 Mar.1913. Salibi, "Beirut", pp.207-208, citing pp.23-24 of Salim 'Ali Salam's manuscript. *Al-Ahram* 3 Apr.1913, cited in Baru, p.472. On the new Vilayets Law and its contents see the next chapter.

13 The chain of events of the week from 8 to 15 Apr.1913 is very complicated and based on the following sources: MAE, NS Turquie 120: d75, Couget to Pichon 11 Apr.1913. ts 26 and 27, Couget to MAE 12 and 14 Apr.1913. d77, Couget to Pichon 15 Apr.1913. FO 195/2451/484: ds 31 and 34, Cumberbatch to Lowther 10 and 17 Apr.1913. FO 424/238 [Nos.36 and 42]: ts 190 and 191, Lowther to Grey 13 and 14 Apr.1913. GFM 10/405: t214, Hans

von Wangenheim (Istanbul) to A.A. 12 Apr.1914. t943, Consul in Beirut to Bethmann Hollweg (Berlin) 12[?] Apr.1913. MG, 7N2145: Ayyub Thabit 14 Oct.1918. *Le Temps* 15 Apr.1913. *Times* 14 and 16 Apr.1913. *Cd'O* 111 1 May 1913, pp.418-420; 112 16 May 1913, pp.467-468. *Ha-Herut* 5:173 13 Apr.1913; 5:174 14 Apr.1913; 5:176 16 Apr.1913; 5:178 18 Apr.1913; 5:187 7 May 1913. *Al-Mu'ayyad* 16 Apr.1913, cited in Baru, pp.473-475. *Al-Muqattam* 16 Apr.1913, cited in Zeine, *Emergence*, p.91. Djemal Pasha, p.57. Khairallah, *Problème*, pp.39-40. Hartmann, *Reisebriefe*, p.96. Salibi, "Beirut", p.208, citing p.26 of Salim 'Ali Salam's manuscript. *Idahat*, p.37. 'Aziz Bek, *al-Istikhbarat*, pp.27-31. Al-A'zami, vol.3, p.52.

14 The telegrams of the Decentralization Party may be found in MAE, Turquie 120, in *Le Temps* 15 Apr.1913, and in *al-Ahram* 14 and 15 Apr.1913 (cited in Baru, pp.477, 529). On a strong response in particular from the Syrian community in Alexandria see MAE, Turquie 120: d173, Defrance (Cairo) to Pichon 23 Apr.1913. The telegram of the congress members is cited in *Le Temps* 14 Apr.1913 and *Cd'O* 111 1 May 1913, pp.418. It was also published in *al-Mu'ayyad* 17 Apr.1913, cited in Baru, p.477.

15 FO 195/2451/484: d36, Cumberbatch to Lowther 18 Apr.1913.

16 MAE, NS Turquie 121: d92, Couget to Pichon 2 May 1913. GFM 10/405: t1160, Consul in Beirut to Bethmann Hollweg 5 May 1913. The society's telegram to the Paris Congress is cited in *al-Mu'tamar al-'Arabi*, p.151.

17 *JB* 1 17 May 1913. MAE, NS Turquie 121: d104, Couget to Pichon 16 May 1913. FO 371/1775: P.T.H. Beamish (Commander of 'Proserpine') to Senior Naval Office, Syrian Coast 14 May 1913. *Al-Manar* 16:6 5 June 1913, pp.475-476.

18 FO 371/1822: d46, Cumberbatch to Lowther 27 May 1913. Hugo Grothe, *Die asiatische Türkei und die deutsche Interessen* (Halle, 1913), p.34. Salibi, "Beirut", pp.208-209, citing p.28 of Salim 'Ali Salam's manuscript.

19 FO 195/2451/484: d59, Evelin C.D. Rawlins (Beirut) to Charles M. Marling (Istanbul) 10 July 1913.

20 MAE, NS Turquie 119: d6, Ottavi (Damascus) to Jonnart 24 Jan.1913. *Al-Mufid* 15 and 22 Jan.1913, cited in Baru, pp.456-459.

21 MAE, NS Turquie 120: d40, Ottavi to Pichon 25 Apr.1913. FO 371/1775: J.S. Luard (Commander of 'Black Prince') to C-in-C, Mediterranean Station 16 Apr.1913. Djemal Pasha, p.57. Darwaza, *Nash'a*, p.414. Baru, p.479.

22 FO 424/237 [No.10]: d78, Raphael A. Fontana (Aleppo) to Lowther 14 Dec.1912. MAE, NS Turquie 118: d60, François-Georges Laporte (Aleppo) to MAE 28 Dec.1912. MAE, NS Turquie 9: d7, Laporte to Jonnart 2 Feb.1913. FO 424/238 [No.40]: d17, Fontana to Lowther 25 Mar.1913. MAE, NS Turquie 120: d19, Laporte to Jonnart 8 Apr.1913. FO 195/2453/1966: d24, Fontana to Lowther 21 Apr.1913. Hartmann, *Reisebriefe*,

p.91.
23 *Ibid*, p.47.
24 MAE, NS Turquie 119: d8, Couget to Poincaré 10 Jan.1913. Hartmann, *Reisebriefe*, p.65.
25 MAE, NS Turquie 135: d13, Gueyraud (Jerusalem) to MAE 31
   Jan.1913. FO 195/2451/484: d35, Mc Gregor to Lowther 12
   Apr.1913. GFM 10/405: t208, Wangenheim to A.A. 9 Apr.1913.
26 FO 195/2451/484: d27, William Hough (Jaffa) to Mc Gregor 12
   Apr.1913.

Chapter 20

1 L/P&S/10/535: memo, "History of Sayid Talib and his Family" by
  Henry Dobbs (Basra) 19 July 1916. memo on Sayyid Talib by
  Francis E. Crow (Basra) 3 Jan.1915. *Personalities — 'Iraq* (Lon-
  don, Oct.1919), p.93. *AB* no.17 (Cairo) 30 Aug.1916, pp.183-184.
  MAE, NS Turquie 151: d63, Rouet (Baghdad) to MAE 29
  Dec.1908. Al-Basir, pp.38-40.
2 L/P&S/10/535: memo, Dobbs 19 July 1916. FO 882/13: note,
  Philip P. Graves (Cairo) 5 Dec.1914. FO 195/2275: d88, Crow to
  Lowther (Istanbul) 14 Dec.1908. *Personalities — 'Iraq*, p.93. *AB*
  no. 17 (Cairo) 30 Aug.1916, p.184.
3 L/P&S/10/535: memo, Crow 3 Jan.1915. Faydi, p.134. Faydi was
  Talib's right-hand man and his memoirs are a primary source for
  Talib's history. Al-Basir, pp.44-45.
4 Faydi, pp.87-88. Al-A'zami, vol.4, pp.93-94. *Thawrat al-'Arab*,
  p.78. Khairallah, *Problème*, pp.32-33.
5 FO 195/2369: d49, William D.W. Matthews (Basra) to Lowther 9
  Sept.1911. FO 371/1246: d736, Lowther to Grey 18 Oct.1911. FO
  371/1487: d9, same to same 3 Jan.1912. L/P&S/10/617: "Extracts
  from Baghdad Residency Diaries, July 1911—July 1914" by Dobbs
  19 July 1916. Faydi, p.97.
6 L/P&S/10/617: "Note on the Muntafik" (Basra) 4 Mar.1917.
  L/P&S/10/535: memo, Dobbs 19 July 1916. FO 424/228 [No.95]:
  d39, Matthews to Marling (Istanbul) 28 July 1911. MAE, NS Turquie 152: d76, Ferdinand Wiet (Baghdad) to MAE 28 July 1911.
  FO 371/1236: d42, Wilkie Young (Aleppo) to Lowther 28
  Nov.1911. *Personalities — 'Iraq*, pp.93, 103-104. *RMM*, vol.17
  Feb.-Mar.1912, p.223.
7 FO 195/2389: d24, Crow to Lowther 20 Apr.1912. FO 371/1521:
  ds 47 and 52, same to same 1 Oct. and 29 Nov.1912.
  L/P&S/10/617: "Note on the Muntafik" (Basra) 4 Mar.1917.
  Faydi, p.101.
8 L/P&S/10/535: l, Talib (Bellary, India) to Viceroy 24 Nov.1915.
  memo, Dobbs 19 July 1916. *Pesonalities — 'Iraq*, p.93. *AB* no.17
  (Cairo) 30 Aug.1916, pp.184-185.

9   FO 424/237 [No.104]: d6, Crow to Lowther 1 Feb.1913. [No.100]:
    t5, same to same 22 Feb.1913. [No.171]: d236, Lowther to Grey 24
    Mar.1913. d11, Crow to Lowther 24 Feb.1913. MAE, NS Tur-
    quie 152: d21, Wiet to MAE 15 Mar.1913.
10 *Personalities* — *'Iraq*, pp.70-71, 92, 120. Faydi, p.130. Al-Basir,
    p.40-41. 'Abdallah al-Fayad, *Al-Thawra al-'Iraqiyya al-Kubra
    Sanat 1920* (Baghdad, 1963), pp.75-76.
11 Faydi, pp.130-131.
12 L/P&S/10/617: "Extracts from Baghdad Residency Diaries, July
    1911—July 1914" by Dobbs 19 July 1916. FO 424/238 [No.37]:
    d16, Crow to Lowther 15 Mar.1913.
13 FO 371/1822: d21, Crow to Lowther 26 Apr.1913.
14 A summary of the law can be found in FO 371/2137: "Turkey
    Annual Report 1913" by Henry Beaumont (Istanbul) 4 Dec.1914,
    pp.24-25; and in Baru, pp.481-488.
15 FO 424/238 [No.337]: d22, Crow to Lowther 29 Apr.1913. MAE,
    NS Turquie 152: d39, Wiet to MAE 1 May 1913. FO 371/1801:
    d26, Crow to Lowther 8 May 1913. L/P&S/10/617: "Extracts from
    Baghdad Residency Diaries, July 1911—July 1914" by Dobbs 19
    July 1916. Baru, pp.494-495.
16 The episode of the assassination of Farid Bek and Badi' Nuri is a
    very complicated one and the sources dealing with it sometimes
    contradict one another. This description is based on the following
    sources: FO 371/1799: d34, Crow to Lowther 31 May 1913. FO
    371/1801: d26, same to same 8 May 1913. FO 424/238 [No.399]:
    t284, Lowther to Grey 17 June 1913. [No.416]: t288, Lowther to
    Grey 19 June 1913. [No.426]: d30, Crow to Lowther 18 May 1913.
    [No.438]: t291, Lowther to Grey 22 June 1913. FO 424/239
    [No.146]: d39, Crow to Lowther 20 June 1913. [No.174]: d40,
    same to same 27 June 1913. [No.206]: d41, Crow to Marling 5 July
    1913. [No.290]: d43, same to same 19 July 1913. L/P&S/10/617:
    "Extracts from Baghdad Residency Diaries, July 1911—July 1914"
    by Dobbs 19 July 1916. L/P&S/11/57: d18, A.E. Wood (Com-
    mander of 'Alert') to C-in-C, East Indies 7 May 1913.
    L/P&S/11/64: Wood to C-in-C, East Indies 6 July 1913. MAE, NS
    Turquie 152: d46, Philippe Dozon (Baghdad) to Pichon 28 June
    1913. ds 52, 53 and 55, same to same 3, 9 and 14 Aug.1913.
    Faydi, pp.105-115. Al-Basir, pp.43-44. Baru, p.495. Talib's tele-
    gram to the Paris Congress, dated 19 June 1913, is cited in
    Al-Mu'tamar al-'Arabi, pp.195-196.
17 FO 424/239 [No.206]: d41, Crow to Marling 5 July 1913.
    L/P&S/11/64: r250/75, Wood to C-in-C, East Indies 12 July 1913.
    FO 195/2451/153: d44, Crow to Marling 19 July 1913.
18 An original placard of the list of reforms is enclosed with FO
    195/2451/423: d51, Crow to Marling 28 Aug.1913.
19 An original placard is enclosed with *ibid*: d52, Crow to Marling 30
    Aug.1913. See also L/P&S/10/535: memo, Dobbs 19 July 1916.
    Personalities — *'Iraq*, p.94.

20 FO 195/2451/423: d55, Crow to Marling 9 Oct.1913.
21 MAE, NS Turquie 123: d102, Ottavi (Damascus) to Pichon 21
    Nov.1913. FO 195/2457/350: d193, Mallet (Istanbul) to Grey 18
    Mar.1914. Jung, *Révolte*, vol.1, p.76. Shafiq Pasha, vol.3,
    pp.78-79.
22 FO 195/2451/423: d71, Crow to Mallet 22 Dec.1913.
23 Faydi, pp.131-132. Al-Basir, pp.46-47. Al-A'zami, vol.4, pp.96-97.
    Sa'id, *al-Thawra*, vol.1, p.24. FO 195/2457/350: d9, Crow to Mal-
    let 4 Feb.1914. L/P&S/10/535: memo, Dobbs 19 July 1916. *Per-
    sonalities — 'Iraq*, p.94. *AB* no.17 (Cairo) 30 Aug.1916, p.186.
24 L/P&S/10/617: "Extracts from Baghdad Residency Diaries, July
    1911—July 1914" by Dobbs 19 July 1916. FO 195/2457/350: d9,
    Crow to Mallet 4 Feb.1914. Faydi, pp.140-141, 143. *Al-Ahram* 13
    Feb.1914, cited in Baru, p.598.
25 FO 195/1457/350 and 602/21: d29, Crow to Mallet 9 May 1914.
    FO 371/2135: "Summary of Events in Turkish Iraq for June-July
    1914" by Norman Scott (Baghdad) 15 Aug.1914. L/P&S/10/535: l,
    Talib (Bellary, India) to Viceroy 24 Nov.1915. On the agreement
    with Ibn Sa'ud see H.V.F. Winstone, *The Illicit Adventure: The
    Story of Political and Military Intelligence in the Middle East from
    1898 to 1926* (London, 1982), pp.146, 148.
26 FO 424/253 [Nos.5, 16, 17 and 25]: ts 399, 413, 414 and 422, Mal-
    let to Grey 2, 6 and 9 July 1914, respectively. L/P&S/10/535:
    memo, Dobbs 19 July 1916. *Personalities — 'Iraq*, p.94.
27 FO 371/2140: ts 941, 942 and 1019, Mallet to Grey 7 and 21
    Oct.1914. t655, Grey to Mallet 10 Oct.1914. L/P&S/10/535:
    tS992, FSI to Consul in Muhammara 28 Oct.1914. t, Viceroy to
    SSI 30 Oct.1914. l, Talib to Cox 10 Dec.1914. l, Cox (Basra) to
    Talib 12 Jan.1915 (including passport). l, Talib (Bellary, India) to
    Viceroy 24 Nov.1915. L/P&S/11/88: t46-B, Cox to FSI 13
    Jan.1915. Winstone, pp.145, 148-149.

Chapter 21

1 L/P&S/10/839: Mesopotamian Police, "Abstract of Intelligence",
   vol.2, no.1 (Baghdad) 3 Jan.1920.
2 *Al-Raqib* 1:12 8 Apr.1909, cited in al-Fayad, p.52.
3 L/P&S/10/188: d736/37, John Lorimer (Baghdad) 22 Aug.1910.
4 Several Baghdad newspapers suspected that the author of the booklet was an Egyptian journalist who was in conflict with the Vali.
   See *ibid*. MAE, NS Turquie 151: d40, Wiet (Baghdad) to MAE 21
   Aug.1910. An original booklet may be found in FO 371/1013.
5 FO 371/1243: "Summary of Events in Turkish Iraq during the
   Month of December 1910" by Lorimer 7 Jan.1911.
6 *Al-Muqtabas* 7:12 1913, p.950. Ghassan R. Atiyyah, *Iraq
   1908-1921: A Socio-Political Study* (Beirut, 1973), p.56.

7 Al-Basir, pp.37, 41. Faydi, p.116. Sa'id, *al-Thawra*, vol.1, p.24.
   'Abd al-Razzaq al-Hasani, *Al-'Iraq fi Dawray al-Ihtilal wal-Intidab* (Sidon, 1935), vol.1, p.52.
8 *Al-Muqtabas* 7:12 1913, p.951. *Al-Muqattam* 5 Apr.1913, cited in Zeine, *Emergence*, p.94. Faydi, p.116.
9 *Al-Muqtabas* 7:12 1913, pp.950-951.
10 FO 371/1796: "Summary of Events in Turkish Iraq for December 1912" 25 Feb.1913. See also Faydi, p.116.
11 MAE, NS Turquie 152: d27, Wiet to MAE 28 Mar.1913. *Al-Mufid* 14 Apr.1913, cited in Baru, pp.493-494. Darwaza, *Nash'a*, p.408. Bayhum, p.162.
12 Philip Willard Ireland, *'Iraq: A Study of Political Development* ([London, 1937] rep. New York, 1970), pp.235-236. MAE, NS Turquie 9: d, Dozon (Baghdad) to Pichon 21 June 1913. Darwaza, *Nash'a*, p.415.
13 MAE, NS Turquie 123: d54, Dozon to Pichon 9 Aug.1913. MAE, NS Turquie 152: d58, same to same 22 Aug.1913.
14 L/P&S/10/617: "Extracts from Baghdad Residency Diaries, July 1911—July 1914" by Dobbs 19 July 1916. L/P&S/10/839: Mesopotamian Police, "Abstract of Intelligence", vol.2, no.1 (Baghdad) 3 Jan.1920. Ireland, pp.236-237. Faydi, p.116. Al-Basir, p.41. Sa'id, *al-Thawra*, vol.1, p.25. 'Abd al-Razzaq al-Hasani, *Ta'rikh al-Sahafa al-'Iraqiyya* (Baghdad, 1957), p.60.
15 MAE, NS Turquie 152: ds 46 and 53, Gérant du Consulat (Mosul) to MAE 21 July and 15 Sept.1911. FO 371/1487: d9, Lowther (Istanbul) to Grey 3 Jan.1912.
16 FO 195/2452/988: d10, Henry C. Hony (Mosul) to Lowther 23 Apr.1913. *Ha-Herut* 5:229 26 June 1913.
17 Faydi, pp.118-119, 122-125. Al-'Umari, vol.3, p.45.

Chapter 22

1 *Al-Mu'tamar al-'Arabi*, p.4. 'Aziz Bek, *Suriya*, pp.274-275. Al-Suwaydi, pp.25-26. FO 195/2451/484: d40, Cumberbatch (Beirut) to Lowther (Istanbul) 14 May 1913.
2 *Al-Mu'tamar al-'Arabi*, pp.5-8.
3 MAE, NS Turquie 120: note, Directeur du Cabinet du Préfet au nom du Préfet de Police (Paris) to MAE 17 Apr.1913. MAE, NS Turquie 121: Chef du Secrétariat particulier au nom du Préfet de Police (Paris) to MAE 29 May 1913. *Le Temps* 18 Apr.1913.
4 *Al-Mu'tamar al-'Arabi*, pp.9-11. MAE, NS Turquie 121: d97, Couget (Beirut) to Pichon 6 May 1913. d30, Laporte (Aleppo) to Pichon 29 May 1913. Both enclose a French translation of the manifesto of the congress committee.
5 *Ibid*: note, "Réunion du Comité de l'Asie Française du 5 Mai 1913 — La Question syrienne".

6 MAE, NS Turquie 122: l, Nadra Mutran (Paris) to Pichon 1 June 1913.
7 MAE, NS Turquie 120: note, Gauthier (Paris) 27 Mar.1913. MAE, NS Turquie 121: l, Shukri Ghanim (Antibes) 29 May 1913. MAE, NS Turquie 122: "Note confidentielle pour son excellence Monsieur Pichon, Ministre des Affaires Etrangères" by Shukri Ghanim 17 June 1913.
8 *Ibid*: Degrand, "Note pour le Directeur a.s. du Congrès arabe" 12 June 1913.
9 MAE, NS Turquie 121: ds 92 and 112, Couget to Pichon 16 and 26 May 1913. MAE, NS Turquie 122: d122, same to same 10 June 1913, enclosing the certificate, signed by the two archbishops of Beirut, the Greek Orthodox metropolitan and the Syrian Catholic patriarch. An original certificate may also be found in FO 371/1775. FO 195/2451/484: d47, Cumberbatch to Lowther 30 May 1913. FO 424/238 [No.442]: d49, same to same 6 June 1913. *BD*, vol.10, pt.2, p.825. Salibi, "Beirut", p.209. *Ha-Herut* 5:191 12 May 1913. Qadri, p.15.
10 MAE, NS Turquie 122: notes on Zénié 2 and 6 June 1913. note, "Le Congrès syrien-arabe de Paris" 11 June 1913. note, Ristelhueber, "Le Congrès Syrien de Paris — Visite de M. Zénié" (Paris) 21 June 1913. 'Abd al-Ghani al-'Uraysi is cited in *Idahat*, pp. 37, 59. 'Abd al-Hamid al-Zahrawi is cited in *al-Manar* 19:3 29 Aug.1916, p.176. On the contact of Dabbas and Mardam with the French Foreign Ministry see 'Aziz Bek, *Suriya*, pp.274-276.
11 MAE, NS Turquie 121: d, Ottavi (Damascus) to Pichon 22 May 1913. t243, Bompard (Istanbul) to MAE 30 May 1913. *Al-Mu'tamar al-'Arabi*, p.215. 'Aziz Bek, *Suriya*, p.275.
12 MAE, NS Turquie 121: ds 424 and 459, Bompard to MAE 20 and 27 May 1913. MAE, NS Turquie 122: d508, same to same 10 June 1913. *Times* 14 May 1913. Al-A'zami, vol.3, p.75. *Thawrat al-'Arab*, pp.75-77.
13 *Le Matin* 28 June 1913. *Le Temps* 29 June 1913. MAE, NS Turquie 122: d499, Boppe (Istanbul) to MAE 10 June 1913. *Ha-Herut* 5:226 23 June 1913.
14 MAE, NS Turquie 121: d105, Couget to Pichon 19 May 1913. d, Ottavi to Pichon 22 May 1913. d459, Bompard to MAE 27 May 1913. d67, Ottavi to Bompard 30 May 1913. MAE, NS Turquie 122: Coulondre (Beirut) to Pichon 20 June 1913. Grothe, p.33. *Al-Manar* 16:8 2 Aug.1913, p.635. *Al-Mufid* 24 May and 6 June 1913, cited in Baru, pp.508-509. *Ha-Herut* 5:214 8 June 1913; 5:215 9 June 1913. Al-A'zami, vol.3, pp.71-74. Qadri, p.19. Darwaza, *Nash'a*, p.441. *Al-Mu'tamar al-'Arabi*, pp.11-12. The manifesto of the Decentralization Party is cited in *ibid*, pp.215-221.
15 On Ma'ruf al-Rusafi see Wamidh J.O. Nadhmi, *The Political, Intellectual and Social Roots of the Iraqi Independence Movement, 1920* (Ph.D. Dissertation, Durham University, 1974), p.56. On 'Aziz 'Ali al-Misri see Shafiq Pasha, vol.3, p.83. On Sharif Husayn

16 *Le Temps* 10 June 1913. Khairallah, *Problème*, pp.48-52. *Al-Mu'tamar al-'Arabi*, pp.17-21.

17 *Ibid*, pp.14-16. In most of the books it is written that the number of participants in the congress was 24. This fact is incorrect and is based on *ibid*, p.16, where it was indicated that 'Abd al-Karim al-Khalil was Istanbul's representative in the congress. Yet the truth is that al-Khalil arrived in Paris only after the congress had ended (see below).

18 CZA Z3/114: Hochberg (Paris) to Jacobson (Berlin) 10 June 1913.

19 An original programme may be found in MAE, NS Turquie 122.

20 *Al-Mu'tamar al-'Arabi*, pp.25-27. MAE, NS Turquie 122: r, Préfecture de Police (Paris) 19 June 1913.

21 Speech of 'Abd al-Hamid al-Zahrawi in *al-Mu'tamar al-'Arabi*, pp.28-39.

22 Speech of 'Abd al-Ghani al-'Uraysi in *ibid*, pp.42-50.

23 *Ibid*, pp.50-52.

24 Speech of Nadra Mutran in *ibid*, pp.54-64.

25 *Ibid*, p.64. MAE, NS Turquie 122: r, Préfecture de Police (Paris) 21 June 1913.

26 Speech of Najib Diyab in *al-Mu'tamar al-'Arabi*, pp.66-74.

27 Speech of Tawfiq al-Suwaydi in *ibid*, pp.75-76.

28 *Ibid*, pp.76-80.

29 CZA Z3/114: Hochberg to Jacobson 10 and 16 June 1913.

30 Speech of Ahmad Hasan Tabbara in *al-Mu'tamar al-'Arabi*, pp.83-93. MAE, NS Turquie 122: r, Préfecture de Police (Paris) 22 June 1913. CZA Z3/114: Hochberg to Jacobson 24 June 1913.

31 Speech of Iskandar 'Ammun in *al-Mu'tamar al-'Arabi*, pp.98-104.

32 *Ibid*, pp.104-106.

33 Speech of Na'um Mukarzal in *ibid*, pp.107-110.

34 *Ibid*, pp.111-112.

35 *Ibid*, pp.113-120.

36 An original copy of the list of resolutions in French, which was delivered to the French Foreign Minister, may be found in MAE, NS Turquie 122. The same to the British Chargé d'Affaires in Paris may be found in FO 371/1827 and is cited in *BD*, vol.10, pt.2, p.826. The same version of the list is also cited in *Cd'O* 115 1 July 1913, pp.14-15.

37 *Al-Mu'tamar al-'Arabi*, pp.122-134. A copy of Bayhum's speech may be found in MAE, NS Turquie 122. See also *ibid*: r, Préfecture de Police (Paris) 24 June 1913.

38 Speech of Charles Dabbas in *al-Mu'tamar al-'Arabi*, pp.135-139.

39 Speech of Shukri Ghanim in *ibid*, pp.140-146. MAE, NS Turquie 122: r, Préfecture de Police (Paris) 24 June 1913.

40 *Al-Mu'tamar al-'Arabi*, pp.150-210. In the calculation of the number of signatories, the illegible signatures were taken into account. On the other hand, those who had signed twice were excluded from the account. (E.g. in letter no.3 Ahmad Kurd 'Ali's signature

appears twice. *Ibid*, p.154).

41 MAE, NS Turquie 122: note, Ristelhueber, "Le Congrès Syrien de
Paris — Visite de M. Zénié" 21 June 1913.

42 *Al-Mu'tamar al-'Arabi*, pp.147-148. *Le Temps* 1 July 1913.

43 *Al-Mu'tamar al-'Arabi*, p.149. *Le Temps* 29 June 1913. See also
FO 424/238 [No.478]: d346, Carnegie (Paris) to Grey 26 June 1913.

44 Salibi, "Beirut", p.210, citing p.30 of Salim 'Ali Salam's manuscript.
See also *Idahat*, p.60. Al-A'zami, vol.4, pp.84-85.

Chapter 23

1 *Times* 3 July 1913.

2 The Turkish text of the agreement is cited in *al-Manar* 16:8 2
Aug.1913, pp.638-639. An Arabic translation may be found in
Sati' al-Husri, *Al-Bilad al-'Arabiyya wal-Dawla al-'Uthmaniyya*
(Beirut, 2nd rep.1960), pp.134-135, and idem, *Muhadarat*,
pp.221-223. See also *al-Manar* 16:8 2 Aug.1913, p.636. Djemal
Pasha, p.59. *Idahat*, p.60.

3 MAE, NS Turquie 122: d81, Ottavi (Damascus) to Boppe (Istanbul) 25 June 1913. MAE, NS Turquie 186: t314, Boppe to MAE 6
July 1913. *Ha-Herut* 5:234 2 July 1913.

4 MAE, NS Turquie 123: note, Ristelhueber, "Visite de M. Zénié —
Les Suites du Congrès syrien" 11 July 1913. MG, 7N2145: Ayyub
Thabit (New York) 14 Oct.1918. CZA Z3/114: Hochberg (Paris)
to Jacobson 25 and 26 June 1913. Jacobson (Paris) to Zionist
Actions Committee 29 June 1913. *Al-Manar* 16:8 2 Aug.1913,
p.636. Al-A'zami, vol.3, p.78, vol.4, p.91. An Arabic version of
the agreement may be found in *al-Manar* 16:8 2 Aug.1913,
pp.639-640.

5 *Ibid*, p.637. Reuters' telegram was also published in *ha-Herut*
5:250 21 July 1913. The agreement was published in *al-Muqattam*
7,388 15 July 1913. *Tanin* is cited in *al-Ahram* 15 Aug.1913 (cited
in Baru, p.536). See also *al-Muqtabas* (daily) 30 Aug.1913 in CZA
Z3/116.

6 The text of the Interior Minister's announcement is cited in *al-
Manar* 16:9 1 Sept.1913, pp.718-719. A French translation may be
found in MAE, NS Turquie 123. See also FO 195/2451/484: d65,
Beirut to Marling (Istanbul) 6 Aug.1913.

7 The text of the edict is cited in *al-Manar* 16:9 1 Sept.1913, p.720.
See also FO 424/240 [No.13]: d818, Marling to Grey 25 Sept.1913.

8 *Al-Manar* 16:10 30 Sept.1913, p.798. *Ha-Herut* 5:278 24 Aug.
1913. Al-A'zami, vol.3, pp.85-88. *Thawrat al-'Arab*, pp.82-84.
Daghir, *Mudhakkirati*, pp.61-63. Al-Husri, *al-Bilad al-'Arabiyya*,
p.136.

9 *Al-Manar* 16:10 30 Sept.1913, p.798. *Ha-Herut* 5:283 29 Aug.
1913; 5:298 16 Sept.1913. Al-A'zami, vol.3, pp.89-92. *Thawrat*

al-'Arab, pp.85-90. Daghir, *Mudhakkirati*, pp.63-65. Al-'Umari, vol.1, p.174. Salibi, "Beirut", p.210, citing p.34 of Salim 'Ali Salam's manuscript.

10 MAE, NS Turquie 123: ds 152 and 158, Coulondre (Beirut) to Pichon 19 and 28 Aug.1913. *Al-Manar* 16:10 30 Sept.1913, p.799. *Ha-Herut* 5:277 22 Aug.1913. *Thawrat al-'Arab*, p.90.

11 *Ibid*, pp.91-92. Daghir, *Mudhakkirati*, pp.65-66. Al-A'zami, vol.3, p.94. See also FO 424/240 [No.13]: d818, Marling to Grey 25 Sept.1913.

12 MAE, NS Turquie 123: d162, Coulondre to Pichon 6 Sept.1913. note, Ristelhueber, "Visite de M. Zénié" 11 Sept.1913. FO 195/2451/484: Rawlins (Beirut) to Marling 3 Sept.1913. CZA Z3/116: press report, Thon (Jaffa) to Zionist Actions Committee 21 Sept.1913.

13 FO 371/1775: 138936/13, Eyre C. Crowe (FO) to Under Secretary of State (Home Office) 23 Sept.1913. r, Thomas McNamara (Criminal Investigation Department, Metropolitan Police) 23 Sept.1913, enclosed with 1243,138, Home Office to Under Secretary of State (FO) 7 Oct.1913. A copy of the memo, dated 22 Aug.1913 and addressed to the British Foreign Minister, may be found in *ibid*. Same memo to the French Foreign Minister may be found in MAE, NS Turquie 123. The memo was also published in *L'Echo de Paris* 26 Aug.1913 and *Cd'O* 121 1 Oct.1913, pp.330-332.

14 The manifesto was also published in *al-Manar* 16:11 30 Oct.1913, pp.849-859. See also MAE, NS Turquie 9: d97, Ottavi to Pichon 10 Nov.1913.

15 MAE, NS Turquie 123: notes, Ristelhueber, "Visite de M. Zénié" 11 July, 5 and 11 Sept.1913. note, Ristelhueber, "a.s. des délégues Syriens" 24 Sept.1913. note, Ristelhueber 14 Oct.1914. d915, Ristelhueber to Istanbul 25 Oct.1913. *Ha-Herut* 5:277 22 Aug.1913. *Al-Manar* 16:10 30 Sept.1913, p.799. *Al-Mustaqbal* 20 14 July 1916. Al-A'zami, vol.4, p.3.

16 CZA Z3/47: Lichtheim (Istanbul) to Jacobson (Berlin) 29 Oct.1913. *Al-Manar* 17:3 25 Feb.1914, p.235; 19:3 29 Aug.1916, p.174. *Rafiq al-'Azm*, p.xi. *Thawrat al-'Arab*, pp.92-94. Daghir, *Mudhakkirati*, p.66. Al-A'zami, vol.4, pp.7-8.

17 *Al-Ahram* 27 and 29 Sept.1913, cited in Baru, p.548. Qadri, p.20.

18 MAE, NS Turquie 9: d97, Ottavi to Pichon 10 Nov.1913. MAE, NS Turquie 124: d15, Ottavi to Gaston Doumergue (Paris) 19 Feb.1914. CZA Z3/116: press report, Thon to Zionist Actions Committee 10 Nov.1913.

19 FO 195/2457/316: d3, Cumberbatch to Mallet (Istanbul) 16 Jan.1914. MAE, NS Turquie 124: d7, Couget (Beirut) to Doumergue 13 Jan.1914. d45, Boppe to MAE 28 Jan.1914. *Cd'O* 130 16 Feb.1914, p.163. *Al-Ahram* 21 and 30 Jan.1914, cited in Baru, p.548. *Thawrat al-'Arab*, p.99. Daghir, *Mudhakkirati*, p.67. Al-A'zami, vol.4, pp.10-11.

20 Qadri, p.21. *Thawrat al-'Arab*, pp.99-100. Daghir, *Mudhakkirati*,

p.67.
21 The first letter from al-Zahrawi to Rida, dated 6 Jan.1914, is cited
in *al-Manar* 19:3 29 Aug.1916, p.174. His second letter, dated 13
Jan.1914, is cited in *ibid*, pp.175-180 and Al-A'zami, vol.4,
pp.19-30. On the threats of the officers against al-Zahrawi see 'Aziz
Bek, *al-Istikhbarat*, p.12.
22 *Al-Manar* 17:3 25 Feb.1916, p.236; 19:3 29 Aug.1916, pp.175, 182.
Al-A'zami, vol.4, pp.14, 18-19. The party's telegram is cited in *Idahat*, p.61.
23 Salim al-Jaza'iri's letter, dated 15 Jan.1914, is cited in *Thawrat
al-'Arab*, pp.127-128. See also Qadri, pp.57-58.
24 *Thawrat al-'Arab*, pp.100-102. Daghir, *Mudhakkirati*, p.67-68.

Chapter 24

1 'Ali Jawdat, *Dhikrayat 'Ali Jawdat 1900-1958* (Beirut, 1967),
pp.25-26. All four officers were later to become prime ministers of
Iraq.
2 MG, 6N197: note, Ibrahim Salim al-Najjar, "L'armée arabe" n.d.
[1917].
3 MAE, NS Turquie 120: d105, Defrance (Cairo) to Jonnart 13
Mar.1913. ds 309 and 328, Bompard (Istanbul) to MAE 13 and 19
Apr.1913. d84, Couget (Beirut) to Pichon 21 Apr.1913. d, Couget
to Bompard 31 Mar.1913. MAE, NS Turquie 121: d92, Couget to
Pichon 2 May 1913. MAE, NS Turquie 186: d142, Defrance to
Doumergue 26 Mar.1914. AN, 423AP 8: Ibrahim Salim al-Najjar,
"Les Colonies Syriennes à l'étranger" (Paris) 23 Oct.1916.
4 "'Aziz al-Misri Yatahaddathu ila al-Ahram", *al-Ahram* 21 July
1959, pp.3, 9. Muhammad Subayh, *Batal La Nansahu: 'Aziz al-
Misri wa-'Asruhu* (Beirut, Sidon, [1971]), pp.13, 18, 21. Al-Basir,
pp.22-23. *AB* no.28 (Cairo) 1 Nov.1916, p.404. Ronald Storrs,
Orientations (London, 1937), p.209. Majid Khadduri, "'Aziz 'Ali
Misri and the Arab Nationalist Movement" in Albert Hourani
(ed.), *St Antony's Papers No.17 — Middle Eastern Affairs No.4*
(London, 1965), pp.146-147.
5 "'Aziz al-Misri", p.3. Subayh, *Batal*, pp.30-31, 49. Al-Basir, p.14.
'Aziz Bek, *Suriya*, p.22. Al-'Umari, vol.1, pp.368, 371. Djemal
Pasha, p.60. Antonius, p.118. Khadduri, pp.146-147. Stoddard,
Ottoman Government, p.167.
6 Muhammad Subayh, *Mawaqif Hasima fi Ta'rikh al-Qawmiyya
al-'Arabiyya*, vol.2: *Al-Yaqza khilala al-Qarnayn al-Tasi' 'Ashar
wal-'Ishrin al-Miladi* (Cairo, 1964), p.257, citing Muhammad
Farid's diary 27 July 1913.
7 'Aziz Bek, *Suriya*, pp.23-25. Al-'Umari, vol.1, p.368. Subayh,
Batal, p.34. Djemal Pasha, pp.61-62.
8 'Aziz Bek, *Suriya*, pp.25-26. Subayh, *Batal*, p.50. Idem, *al-Yaqza*,

p.257. Al-'Umari, vol.1, p.368. *Times* 24 Apr.1914. *BD*, vol.10, pt.2, p.833. Antonius, p.119. Khadduri, pp.142-143.

9 MAE, NS Turquie 186: d87, Defrance to Doumergue 19 Feb.1914. Stoddard, *Ottoman Government*, pp.86-91, 146. Djemal Pasha, p.62. *Times* 24 Apr.1914. *Cd'O* 94-95 15 Aug. and 1 Sept.1912, p.186. 'Aziz Bek, *Suriya*, p.27. Subayh, *Batal*, pp.48-49. Al-'Umari, vol.1, p.369.

10 FO 371/2131: t153, Mallet (Istanbul) to Grey 9 Mar.1914. *BD*, vol.10, pt.2, p.834. *Thawrat al-'Arab*, p.106. Subayh, *al-Yaqza*, pp.256-257, citing Muhammad Farid's diary 27 July 1913.

11 FO 371/2131: t249, Mallet to Grey 12 Apr.1914. *BD*, vol.10, pt.2, p.836. FO 407/180 [No.79]: t, Kitchener (Cairo) to Grey 27 Mar.1914. Stoddard, *Ottoman Government*, pp.92, 209. Stoddard is based on interviews with one of the senior officers of the Teşkilât-i Mahsusa and with Salih Pasha Harb, who was the acting military commandant at Mersa Matruh on behalf of the British. Salih Pasha mentioned also a report sent by Sayyid Ahmad al-Sanusi to Enver, as well as testimonies of spies who had traced the money in Alexandria. Stoddard interviewed al-Misri several times. The latter described his being accused of embezzlement as "another of Enver's plots" against him, but he resolutely refused to explain why he eventually had left Libya.

12 FO 371/1772: ts 77 and 78 Kitchener to Grey 22 and 23 June 1913. t82, Cheetham (Cairo) to Grey 10 July 1913. *L'Echo Egyptien* 28 Apr.1914. Graves, p.185. Stoddard, *Ottoman Government*, pp.92-93. Subayh, *al-Yaqza*, p.257.

13 'Aziz Bek, *Suriya*, p.28. Shafiq Pasha, vol.3, p.82. Baru, p.561. Baru interviewed al-Misri.

14 Sa'id *al-Thawra*, vol.1, p.46. Darwaza, *Hawla*, vol.1, p.33. Al-A'zami, vol.4, p.55. Baru, p.561. Khadduri, pp.149-150. Khadduri interviewed al-Misri.

15 Al-Basir, p.33. Baru, pp.557-561 (based on an interview with al-Misri). "'Aziz al-Misri", p.3. Ahmad Shuman, "'Aziz al-Misri Abu al-Thawra al-Misriyya", *al-Jarida* 18 Aug.1955, p.8. Subayh, *Batal*, p.87. Qadri, p.14. Al-A'zami, vol.4, p.54. Shafiq Pasha, vol.3, p.82. Taha al-Hashimi, *Mudhakkirat Taha al-Hashimi 1919-1943* (Beirut, 1967), p.6. Khadduri, pp.149-150. The society's programme is cited in al-Basir, pp.33-34; Sa'id, *al-Thawra*, vol.1, pp.46-47; Al-A'zami, vol.4, pp.53-54; 'Aziz Bek, *Suriya*, pp.28-29 (all the versions are almost identical). Austria-Hungary was chosen as a model probably because it was geographically close to the Ottoman Empire and therefore familiar to the Arab officers, and because it resembled the Empire in being a multi-national and multi-lingual state. It is interesting to note that a day after the establishment of the society, the British ambassador in Istanbul wrote: "Many Young Turks now hold the view that the Ottoman Empire should be formed into a 'Turco-Arabia' on the lines of Austro-Hungary, with the Sultan-Caliph as the Crown

link." See FO 371/1848: d904, Mallet to Grey 29 Oct.1913.

16 Sami 'Abd al-Hafiz al-Qaysi, *Yasin al-Hashimi wa-Dawruhu fil-Siyasa al-'Iraqiyya bayna 'Amay 1922-1936* (Basra, 1975), vol.1, pp.36, 38-40. Al-'Umari, vol.2, p.231, vol.3, pp.45-46. Al-Hashimi, p.6. Jawdat, p.30. 'Abd al-Razzaq al-Hasani, *Al-Thawra al-'Iraqiyya al-Kubra* (Sidon, [1952] 2nd ed.1965), p.47.

17 Al-'Umari, vol.3, pp.26, 46. Jawdat, p.105. Nadhmi, p.75.

18 Norman N.E. Bray, *Shifting Sands* (London, 1934), pp.45-47, 59-60. Atiyyah, p.61. Sa'id, *al-Thawra*, vol.1, p.47. al-Basir, p.38. The plan is mentioned also in FO 371/2131: t, Mallet to Kitchener 21 Feb.1914. FO 424/251 [No.184]: d117, Mallet to Grey 24 Feb.1914. *BD*, vol.10, pt.2, pp.833-834.

19 Al-Hashimi, p.6. Sa'id, *al-Thawra*, vol.1, p.47.

20 Baru, p.561. Daghir, *Mudhakkirati*, p.36.

21 'Aziz Bek, *al-Istikhbarat*, p.12. Djemal Pasha, p.60.

22 Daghir, *Mudhakkirati*, pp.49-50. *Thawrat al-'Arab*, p.108. Baru, p.562. *L'Echo Egyptien* 28 Apr.1914. Djemal Pasha, p.63.

23 The above is according to the version cited by 'Aziz Bek, *al-Istikhbarat*, pp.9-10, who probably attended this meeting. A similar version, although less detailed, is cited in al-A'zami, vol.4, pp.56-57. Sa'id, *al-Thawra*, vol.1, p.47 brings another similar version, with several modifications.

24 Liman von Sanders, *Fünf Jahre Türkei* (Berlin, 1920), pp.17-18. Daghir, *Mudhakkirati*, p.50.

25 'Aziz Bek, *Suriya*, p.29. 'Aziz Bek was in charge of collecting intelligence material on al-'Ahd and al-Misri. *L'Echo Egyptien* 28 Apr.1914.

26 *Ibid. Thawrat al-'Arab*, pp.103-104. Daghir, *Mudhakkirati*, p.50. Khadduri, p.144. Antonius, p.118. MAE, NS Turquie 186: d87, Defrance to Doumergue 19 Feb.1914.

27 Daghir, *Mudhakkirati*, pp.50-51. *Thawrat al-'Arab*, pp.104, 106. Faydi, pp.150-151. Al-A'zami, vol.4, p.62. Al-'Umari, vol.1, p.377. MAE, NS Turquie 186: d121, Defrance to Doumergue 6 Mar.1914. *L'Echo Egyptien* 28 Apr.1914. *Times* 24 Apr.1914. Djemal Pasha, p.63. Liman von Sanders, pp.18-19.

28 MAE, NS Turquie 186: ds 86, 87 and 121, Defrance to Doumergue 19 Feb. and 6 Mar.1914. FO 141/492: t58, Kitchener to Grey 4 Apr.1914. FO 371/2131: Appeal from Cairo to Grey 16 Apr.1914. *BD*, vol.10, pt.2, pp.831, 837. *Times* 16 Feb., 8, 11, 13, 14 and 18 Apr.1914. Graves, p.185.

29 Daghir, *Mudhakkirati*, p.51. Qasimiyya, p.11. *Times* 18 Apr.1914.

30 *Thawrat al-'Arab*, pp.105-106 (its author cites the official protocol of the trial). Al-A'zami, vol.4, p.60. *L'Echo Egyptien* 28 Apr.1914. *Times* 17 and 24 Apr.1914. Djemal Pasha, p.63. Antonius, p.120.

31 FO 371/2131: t, Mallet to Kitchener 12 Feb.1914. t, Kitchener to Mallet 12 Feb.1914. t, Mallet to Kitchener 13 Feb.1914. t, Kitchener to Mallet 14 Feb.1914. ts, Mallet to Kitchener 21 and 25 Feb.1914. ts 117 and 153, Mallet to Grey 21 Feb. and 9 Mar.1914.

t 135, Grey to Mallet 16 Mar.1914. ts 189, 191 and 209, Mallet to Grey 26, 27 Mar. and 1 Apr.1914. d249, same to same 12 Apr.1914. FO 424/251 [No.184]: d117, same to same 24 Feb.1914. *BD*, vol.10, pt.2, pp.833-836. MAE, NS Turquie 186: d163, Boppe (Istanbul) to MAE 10 Mar.1914.

32 FO 371/2131: ts 235 and 243, Mallet to Grey 14 and 17 Apr.1914. *BD*, vol.10, pt.2, p.837. MAE, NS Turquie 186: d174, Defrance to Doumergue 14 Apr.1914. d246, Bompard to MAE 21 Apr.1914. *Times* 15 and 16 Apr.1914. *Al-Hilal* 22:8 1 May 1914, p.627.

33 MAE, NS Turquie 186: d246, Bompard to MAE 21 Apr.1914. Djemal Pasha, p.64. Graves, p.185. Faydi, p.151.

34 FO 371/2131: ts 246 and 251, Mallet to Grey 18 and 20 Apr.1914. *BD*, vol.10, pt.2, p.837. MAE, NS Turquie 186: d199, Defrance to Doumergue 28 Apr.1914. *Times* 20, 22, 23, 24 and 27 Apr.1914. *L'Echo Egyptien* 28 Apr.1914. Djemal Pasha, p.64.

35 MG, 7N2141: note 76, L'Officier Interprète attaché à la Mission Militaire Française d'Egypte, "Noury Ben Said" (Aqaba) 20 June 1918. MG, 6N197: note, Ibrahim Salim al-Najjar, "L'armée arabe" n.d. [1917]. FO 371/2140: t, Viceroy to SSI 8 Dec.1914. L/P&S/11/88: t74-B, Cox (Basra) to FSI 17 Jan.1915. Lord Birdwood, *Nuri as-Said: A Study in Arab Leadership* (London, 1959), pp.18-19, 22-24. Nadhmi, p.125. Elie Kedourie, *England and the Middle East: The Destruction of the Ottoman Empire 1914-1921* (London, [1956] 1978), p.59. Al-A'zami, vol.4, p.65. Al-'Umari, vol.1, pp.176, 380. Subayh, *Batal*, pp.74-75. Musa, *al-Haraka*, p.162.

36 FO 371/1968: t76, Cheetham (Cairo) to Grey 9 Aug.1914. L/P&S/10/464: t87, FO to Cheetham 11 Aug.1914. FO 371/2140: "Precis of Conversation with Abd El Aziz El Masri on 16 August, 1914" by R.E.M. Russell (Cairo) 17 Aug.1914, enclosed with d143, Cheetham to Grey 24 Aug.1914. Antonius, p.155.

37 FO 371/2140: "Conversation with Aziz Bey El Masri" by Clayton (Cairo) 30 Oct.1914, enclosed with d177, Cheetham to Grey 15 Nov.1914. Daghir, *Mudhakkirati*, p.75.

38 FO 371/2140: t347, Grey to Cheetham 14 Nov.1914. t274, Cheetham to Grey 16 Nov.1914. t, SSI to Viceroy 27 Nov.1914. t, Viceroy to SSI 8 Dec.1914. t432, Grey to Cheetham 18 Dec.1914. FO 882/2: t550, Clayton to Reginald Wingate (Khartoum) 21 Nov.1914. L/P&S/11/88: t, SSI to Viceroy 19 Nov.1914. tDS-102, FSI (Delhi) to Cox 28 Nov.1914. t82-B, Cox to FSI 3 Dec.1914. PRO 30/57/45: t331E, John Maxwell (Cairo) to Kitchener 27 Nov.1914.

39 FO 371/2140: r, Graves (Cairo) 6 Dec.1914, enclosed with d203, Cheetham to Grey 13 Dec.1914.

Chapter 25

1 L74, Haqqi al-'Azm (Cairo) to Mahmud al-Mihmisani (Beirut) 3 July 1914, cited in *JB*, 409 27 Aug.1915. Sa'id, *al-Thawra*, vol.1, p.48. Al-A'zami, vol.4, pp.105-106 (Al-A'zami is wrong in claiming that al-Misri was not a member of this society). Qadri, p.30. Al-'Umari, vol.1, p.168. *Idahat*, p.21.

2 *Ibid*, pp.22-24.

3 *Ibid*, p.21. Excerpt of this letter, in al-Misri's handwriting, may be found in *ibid*, photo no.5.

4 L, Haqqi al-'Azm to Mahmud al-Mihmisani 16 Apr.1914, cited in *Idahat*, p.66. 131, same to same n.d., cited in *Idahat*, p.69 and *JB* 414 2 Sept.1915. 174, same to same 3 July 1914, cited in *Idahat*, p.86 and *JB* 409 27 Aug.1915. Qadri, p.30.

5 The manifesto is cited in *Idahat*, pp.24-29; Al-A'zami, vol.4, pp.108-117; Abi Zayd, pp.93-96.

6 The manifesto is cited in *Idahat*, pp.98-99, and paraphrased in FO 371/2136 and MAE, NS Turquie 124. See also FO 371/2136: d41, Cumberbatch (Beirut) to Mallet 25 June 1914. MAE, NS Turquie 124: d, François Georges-Picot (Beirut) to René Viviani (Paris) 24 June 1914.

7 The manifesto is cited in *Idahat*, pp.62-64, and translated in FO 618/3 and FO 195/2457/350. See also *ibid*: d22, Devey (Damascus) to Mallet 29 June 1914. FO 195/2460/3421: d56, Cumberbatch to Mallet 5 Aug.1914.

8 The letter is enclosed with FO 371/1972: d175, Cheetham (Cairo) to Grey 10 Nov.1914.

PART III

Chapter 26

1 Muhibb al-Din al-Khatib, the founder of the society, points out explicitly in his memoirs that in that period "it did not cross our minds to be separated from the Ottoman Empire". Hirfi, "Mudhakkirat" 12, p.92.

2 Al-Suwaydi, p.20 (. . . *la amliku min al-'uruba illa shu'uran wahmiyyan*).

3 *Al-Mufid* 1409 23 Oct.1913; 1412 27 Oct.1913; 1435 15 Dec.1913, all cited in Rashid I. Khalidi, "The Press as a Source for Modern Arab Political History: 'Abd al-Ghani al-'Uraysi and al-Mufid", *Arab Studies Quarterly*, 3:1 (1981), pp.31, 40.

4 *Al-Ahram* 22 Apr.1913, cited in Baru, p.315.

5 Al-A'zami, vol.3, p.16.

6 Grothe, p.26.

7 FO 371/781: d72, Cumberbatch (Beirut) to Marling (Istanbul) 5 Nov.1909.
8 The delegates of the society took care also that their vilayet would be mentioned in the Paris agreement.
9 The pamphlet is cited in Hans Kohn, *A History of Nationalism in the East* (New York, [1929] rep.1969), p.271.
10 Rafiq al-'Azm is cited in *al-Mu'ayyad* 2 Dec.1912. Shafiq al-Mu'ayyad is cited in MAE, NS Turquie 121: d249, Ottavi (Damascus) to Pichon 18 May 1913. 'Abdallah Sufayr Pasha, who was not a member of the party but was well aware of its activity, defined its aims as follows: "To tell the truth . . . the program of the said party is but an adoption and an enlargement of the Lebanese règlement organique to the vilayets of Syria." See FO 371/2147: note, 'Abdallah Sufayr (Cairo) 19 Nov.1914, enclosed with d180, Cheetham (Cairo) to Grey 23 Nov.1914.
11 The placard, signed by Jim[?], may be found in CZA Z3/115.
12 Ma'oz, p.391. Moutran, p.71. Le Comte Cressaty (de Damas), *La Syrie française* (Paris, 1915), p.34.
13 Moutran, pp.97-98.

Chapter 27

1 *Rafiq al-'Azm*, pp.63-65, pt.2, pp.77-87.
2 *Al-Manar* 16:4 7 Apr.1913, pp.280, 312-314.
3 *Ibid* 17:4 27 Mar.1914, p.306; 17:5 25 Apr.1914, p.395.
4 Jouplain, pp.585, 598.
5 See chapter 12 notes 34 and 36.
6 Le Comte Cressaty (de Damas), *La Question syrienne et la France* (Paris, 1920), pp.4, 6.
7 'Aziz Bek, *Suriya*, pp.201-204, 207. *Idahat*, p.94.
8 Al-A'zami, vol.4, p.76 and Sa'id, *al-Thawra*, vol.1, p.24 claim quite justly that the Christian members of the Reform Society of Beirut, some of whom were also members of the Society of the Lebanese Revival, were those who initiated the demand of the Reform Society for foreign advisers, with the intention that the latter would be French.
9 On Nakhla Mutran see MAE, NS Turquie 119: d3, Ottavi (Damascus) to Poincaré 15 Jan.1913. MG, 7N2145: Ayyub Thabit (New York) 14 Oct.1918. *Idahat*, p.33. Yusuf al-Hakim, *Bayrut wa-Lubnan fi 'Ahd Al 'Uthman* (Beirut, 1964), p.41. On Nadra Mutran see Moutran, pp. v, 45, 131, 214-215.
10 On the Jaza'iri family see *Idahat*, pp.105-106. On Shukri al-'Asali see MAE, NS Turquie 9: d97, Ottavi to Pichon 10 Nov.1913. MAE, NS Turquie 119: d9, Ottavi to Jonnart 28 Jan.1913. MAE, NS Turquie 123: d79, Ottavi to Pichon 19 Sept.1913. On Muhammad Kurd 'Ali see MAE, NS Turquie 120: d33, Ottavi to Pichon 7

Apr.1913. MAE, NS Turquie 123: 1, Muhammad Kurd 'Ali (Rome) 18 Dec.1913. MAE, NS Turquie 124: d15, Ottavi to Doumergue 19 Feb.1913. Kurd 'Ali denies in his memoirs (vol.1, pp.99-100) that he made his newspaper pro-French following a French request.

11 FO 371/1794: d79, Bertie (Paris) to Grey 12 Feb.1913, citing a certain Mr Besnard.

12 On the idea of annexing Syria to Egypt see documents mentioned in chapters 14, 18 and 19, and also MAE, NS Turquie 116: d247, Bompard (Istanbul) to MAE 30 Apr.1912. MAE, NS Turquie 117: d146, Coulondre (Beirut) to Poincaré 30 Nov.1912. note, Gaillard (Cairo) 19 Nov.1912. Bray, p.20.

13 MAE, NS Turquie 117: d68, Ottavi to Poincaré 23 Nov.1912. MAE, NS Turquie 118: d154, Couget (Beirut) to Poincaré 3 Dec.1912. Bray, p.43. On the tendencies in Aleppo and Palestine see chapter 19.

14 On the role of the owners of al-Muqattam see Idahat, p.95 and 'Aziz Bek, Suriya, p.358.

15 L/P&S/10/586: Arabian Report N.S. No.XI 27 Sept.1916. See also FO 371/1775: "Notes on the situation on the Syrian Coast and in the neighbourhood of Alexandretta" by A. Berkeley Milne 16 July 1913. FO 424/226 [No.107]: d99, Lowther (Istanbul) to Grey 13 Feb.1911.

16 Al-Manar 15:7 14 July 1912, p.558.

17 Ha-Herut 5:190 11 May 1913. FO 371/1841: d1822, Cox to McMahon (Simla) 7 June 1913.

18 FO 371/1522: d541, Bertie to Grey 28 Dec.1912.

19 FO 371/1775: "Notes on the situation on the Syrian Coast and in the neighbourhood of Alexandretta" by Berkeley Milne 16 July 1913. Bray, p.51.

20 Al-Mufid 795 1 Oct.1911, cited in Khalidi, "Press", p.38.

21 FO 195/2427: d21, Devey (Damascus) to Lowther 18 Apr.1912. See also MAE, NS Turquie 116: d167, Defrance (Cairo) to Poincaré 11 June 1912.

22 Stephen Hemsley Longrigg, Iraq 1900-1950: A Political, Social and Economic History (Beirut, [1953] 3rd imp.1968), p.42.

Chapter 28

1 Al-Muqattam 6046 17 Feb.1909, cited in Harran, "Young Turks 1908-1914", p.187.

2 Al-Manar 17:8 24 July 1914, p.617. FO 424/217 [No.48]: d77, Cumberbatch (Beirut) to Lowther 30 Oct.1908. MAE, NS Turquie 116: t44, Defrance (Cairo) to MAE 7 June 1912. MAE, NS Turquie 117: note, Gaillard (Cairo) 19 Nov.1912.

3 Darwaza, Nash'a, p.484.

4 Of the imaginary estimations of *al-Fatat*'s membership before World War I it is worth mentioning a letter of Osmond Warlond, who determined it to be 150,000 in 1913. See FO 882/17: 1, Warlond to Clayton 17 July 1918. George Kirk stated it to be 2,000. See George E. Kirk, *A Short History of the Middle East* (New York, 1965), p.121. Antonius fixed it at 200. See Antonius, p.112. Prof. Dawn published an article in 1962 with the object of determining the size and composition of the Arab societies: C. Ernest Dawn, "The Rise of Arabism in Syria", *MEJ*, 16 (1962), pp.145-168 (pp.148-179 in his collection of essays). The problem is that Dawn derived his list of names from only three books: Darwaza, *Hawla*, Sa'id, *al-Thawra*, and Hartmann, *Reisebriefe* (*ibid*, p.152 note 7). The result is that the numbers he presented are incorrect. It is also noteworthy that many of the *al-Fatat*'s members who were natives of Syria before the war, whom Dawn listed (*ibid*, p.174), entered the society only during the war, such as 'Abd al-Wahhab Muyassir, Bahjat al-Shihabi and others. Dawn made this mistake because he followed Darwaza, *Hawla*, vol.1, pp.30-31, who indeed listed 61 names, but explicitly noted that he was referring to the society's members from its establishment until the end of World War I. (Sixty members in this time period was indicated also by al-Shihabi, p.73). Dawn's assumption (p.158 in his collection of essays), that the number of members who joined the society during the war years was so small that it could be ignored, is baseless. The number of *al-Fatat*'s members in fact tripled during the war.

5 *Al-Ahram* 5 May 1910; 13 July 1911, cited in Baru, p.313. Darwaza, *Nash'a*, p.354, cites 800 members. Antonius, p.109, claims that there were thousands of members in the club.

6 A photograph of Simisma's membership card may be found in *Idahat*, photo no.27.

7 Jung, *Révolte*, vol.1, p.61, gives the imaginary number of 10,000 members.

8 Of the imaginary estimations given of the number of *al-'Ahd*'s members before the war it is worth mentioning Lawrence's assertion that all the officers who were natives of Mesopotamia participated in the society. See T.E. Lawrence, *Seven Pillars of Wisdom* (New York, 1938), p.46. Daghir, *Mudhakkirati*, p.36, told of thousands of members. Bayhum, p.160 and Jung, *Révolte*, vol.1, p.32, fixed the number at 4,000. Sa'id, *al-Thawra*, vol.1, p.47, decreased it to 315 members.

9 Prof. Dawn claimed (p.152 in his collection of essays) that the number of activists before World War I was only 126 (with 30 of them in doubt). This number, which is frequently cited, is totally meaningless, as proven above, and is the consequence both of the limited number of sources from which Dawn derived the activists' names and of his supposition that "a complete list of the pre-1914 members of the Ottoman Decentralization Society, *al-Fatat*, and

al-'Ahd, is a complete roster of the members of the Arab nationalist societies before 1914" (*ibid*).

Chapter 29

1 The official breakdown of the Reform Society of Beirut was: 42 Muslims, 42 Christians and 2 Jews.
2 Those activists for whom accurate details about year of birth were not found were counted as young either if they were explicitly defined as such in the sources, or if they were students when they entered the society. Those with the title Sheikh or Pasha, as well as members of parliament, were counted as older. When there was no other alternative, photographs were used in order to determine the age of the activists, on condition that they were photographed during the events or in proximity to them.
3 Those activists for whom no exact description of family background was found were considered as belonging to the upper class if they held the title Pasha, Bek, Amir, or 'notable' in its various definitions; held a senior rank in the army or in the administration; were members of parliament; or came from wealthy families.
4 L, 'Abd al-Hamid al-Zahrawi (Istanbul) to Rashid Rida (Cairo) 13 Jan.1914, cited in *al-Manar* 19:3 29 Aug.1916, pp.178-179.
5 'Higher education' includes also the officers who had higher education beyond their military studies. 'Religious education' means advanced religious studies beyond the basic ones, which were of course common to a much larger number of activists. 'Other education' means education less than higher, which was not included in one of the other categories.
6 *Al-Mu'tamar al-'Arabi*, p.20.

Chapter 30

1 Cromer, vol.2, pp.213-216. Jamal Mohammed Ahmed, *The Intellectual Origins of Egyptian Nationalism* (London, [1960] rep.1968), pp.82-84. Jankowski, pp.245-250. Kurd 'Ali, *al-Mudhakkirat*, vol.1, pp.47-48.
2 Subayh, *al-Yaqza*, p.257. Al-Sayyid, p.137. Hartmann, *Reisebriefe*, p.93.
3 *Al-Manar* 14:1 30 Jan.1911, pp.37-40, 59-62; 14:2 1 Mar.1911, pp.121-124.
4 See chapter 22 and also *al-Mufid* 24 May 1913, cited in Baru, pp.507-508. Darwaza, *Nash'a*, p.441. Sa'id, *al-Thawra*, vol.1, p.52. *Al-Mu'tamar al-'Arabi*, p.220. Abi Zayd, p.108. MAE, NS Turquie 121: d, Ottavi (Damascus) to Pichon 22 May 1913. MAE, NS Turquie 122: d127, Coulondre (Beirut) to Pichon 20 June 1913.

5 *Al-Ra'y al-'Amm* 4 Sept.1912, cited in Baru, p.444.
6 Longrigg, p.184.
7 So wrote Anwar al-Sadat in *al-Jumhuriyya*. See Shuman, p.8.

Chapter 31

1 Darwaza, *Hawla*, vol.1, pp.29, 31. Idem, *Nash'a*, pp.484, 502-504.
   Qadri, pp.12-13. Al-Shihabi, pp.73-74. Musa, *al-Haraka*, p.136.
   Idem, "Jam'iyya", p.54. Al-'Umari, vol.3, p.26. L/P&S/10/586:
   Arabian Report N.S. No.XI 27 Sept.1916.
2 *Idahat*, p.17. Al-A'zami, vol.3, p.34. Sa'id, *al-Thawra*, vol.1, p.10.
3 Daghir, *Mudhakkirati*, p.83. Sayf al-Din al-Khatib is cited in *Idahat*, pp.18-19.
4 Qasimiyya, pp.9-11. Darwaza, *Hawla*, vol.1, p.35. Al-Shihabi,
   p.82. 131, Haqqi al-'Azm (Cairo) to Mahmud al-Mihmisani (Beirut) n.d., cited in *Idahat*, p.69 and *JB* 414 2 Sept.1915.
5 See e.g. in 1, Haqqi al-'Azm to Mahmud al-Mihmisani 16
   Apr.1914, cited in *Idahat*, p.66; 131, same to same n.d., cited in *Idahat*, p.69 and *JB* 414 2 Sept.1915; 170, same to same 20 July 1914,
   cited in *JB* 413 1 Sept.1915.
6 FO 371/2136: d41, Cumberbatch (Beirut) to Mallet 25 June 1914.
   Ha-Herut 5:189 9 May 1913. *Thawrat al-'Arab*, p.192. *Idahat*,
   pp.93-94.
7 For this role of the press see Eliezer Tauber, "The Press and the
   Journalist as a Vehicle in Spreading National Ideas in Syria in the
   Late Ottoman Period", *Die Welt des Islams*, 30 (1990), pp.163-177.
8 L/P&S/11/95: 1, Cox (Basra) to McMahon (Cairo) 18 Mar.1915.
9 A Hebrew translation of the manifesto may be found in CZA
   Z3/115.
10 MAE, NS Turquie 120: d, Couget (Beirut) to Bompard 31
   Mar.1913.
11 L32, Haqqi al-'Azm to Mahmud al-Mihmisani 24 July 1914, cited
   in *Idahat*, p.84 and *JB* 412 31 Aug.1915. The proclamations are
   cited in *Idahat*, pp.24, 29

Chapter 32

1 *Idahat*, pp.32, 34-35. 'Aziz Bek, *Suriya*, p.278. Al-A'zami, vol.4,
   pp.75-76.
2 Sa'id, *al-Thawra*, vol.1, p.10. Qadri, pp.13, 29-30. *Al-Mu'tamar
   al-'Arabi*, p.5. Hirfi, "Mudhakkirat" 12, p.97. See also end of
   chapter 13.
3 *Idahat*, pp.15, 17. Al-Shihabi, p.71. Al-A'zami, vol.3, pp.37-38.
4 *Idahat*, p.92. PRO 30/57/44: r, Intelligence Department, WO
   (Cairo) 20 Jan.1913. MAE, NS Turquie 120: d57, Couget (Beirut)

to MAE 10 Mar.1913. Salibi, "Beirut", p.208, citing p.24 of Salim 'Ali Salam's manuscript. *Al-Manar* 17:3 25 Feb.1914, p.237. Khairallah, *Problème*, p.41.
5 'Aziz Bek, *Suriya*, p.21. Faydi, pp.116, 118-123, 130.
6 *Idahat*, p.20.
7 Al-Qaysi, vol.1, p.40.

Chapter 33

1 *RMM* 6:10 Oct.1908, p.241. Al-Shihabi, p.68.
2 On the character and authority of the six leaders of the society see *Journal du Caire* 2 May 1913.
3 On Salim al-Jaza'iri see Hirfi, "al-Jaza'ir", pp.31-33. Al-A'zami, vol.3, p.33. His book *Mizan al-Haqq fil-Mantiq* was printed only in 1920, after his death. Khalil Hamada was criticized by Shafiq al-Mu'ayyad (who was not a member of the society). See 'Aziz Bek, *Suriya*, p.21.
4 See e.g. Darwaza, *Hawla*, vol.1, p.84.
5 Khadduri, pp.149-150. Baru, pp.559-561. Subayh, *Batal*, pp.74-75. All three interviewed al-Misri.
6 *Ibid*, pp.6, 83. Storrs, p.209. On Yasin al-Hashimi being a competitor for the leadership of the society and on al-Misri's lack of confidence in Nuri al-Sa'id see FO 371/2490: 1, General Commanding, Mediterranean Expeditionary Force (G.H.Q.) to WO (London) 25 Aug.1915; FO 882/15: Cairo to Lawrence (Basra) 26 Mar.1916.
7 Kurd 'Ali, *al-Mudhakkirat*, vol.1, p.114.
8 *Al-Manar* 19:3 29 Aug.1916, pp.169-186; 21:3 29 May 1919, pp.150-153; 21:4 28 June 1919, pp.207-210. *Al-Kawkab* 20 12 Dec.1916. Al-Tikriti, pp.29-35. Kedourie, *Arabic Political Memoirs*, pp.126-127.
9 Al-'Umari, vol.2, pp.227-231.
10 The data are taken mainly from 'Abd al-Razzaq al-Hasani, *Al-Usul al-Rasmiyya li-Ta'rikh al-Wizarat al-'Iraqiyya fil-'Ahd al-Mulki al-Za'il* (Sidon, 1964).

Bibliography

Documents

France

Archives du Ministère des Affaires Etrangères, Paris.
  Correspondance Politique des Consuls
      Beyrouth
      Damas
  Nouvelle Série
      Egypte
      Turquie
  Guerre 1914-1918
      Affaires Musulmanes
      Turquie
  Levant 1918-1929
      Syrie-Liban-Cilicie

Archives du Ministère de la Guerre, Service Historique de l'Armée de Terre, Vincennes.
  Série N: Première Guerre Mondiale
      6N: Fonds Particuliers
      7N: L'Etat-Major de L'Armée

Archives Nationales, Paris.
  432AP: Papiers Etienne Flandin

Britain

The Public Record Office, Kew, Richmond, Surrey.
  FO 141: Egypt — Correspondence
  FO 195: Turkey — Correspondence
  FO 371: Political
  FO 407: Egypt and the Sudan
  FO 424: Turkey
  FO 602: Basra — Correspondence
  FO 618: Damascus — Correspondence
  FO 882: Arab Bureau Papers
  PRO 30/57: Kitchener Papers

Foreign and Commonwealth Office, Library and Records Department,

London.
German Foreign Ministry
10/405: [Türkei 177] Der Libanon (Syrien)

India Office Library and Records, London.
L/P&S/10: Departmental Papers — Political and Secret Separate Files
L/P&S/11: Political and Secret Annual Files

Israel

Central Zionist Archives, Jerusalem.
A18: Nahum Sokolow Papers
L2: Zionist Office, Jaffa
Z2: Central Zionist Office, Cologne
Z3: Central Zionist Office, Berlin

Israel State Archives, Jerusalem.
67: Kaiserich Deutsches Konsulat, Jerusalem

Official Publications and Collections of Documents

[Jamal Pasha] Al-Qa'id al-'Amm lil-Jaysh al-Rabi', *Idahat 'an al-Masa'il al-Siyasiyya Allati Jarat Tadqiquha bi-Diwan al-Harb al-'Urfi al-Mutashakkil bi-'Aleyh* (Istanbul, 1916).
Al-Lajna al-'Ulya li-Hizb al-Lamarkaziyya bi-Misr [Muhibb al-Din al-Khatib], *Al-Mu'tamar al-'Arabi al-Awwal* (Cairo, 1913).
Musa, Sulayman (ed.), *Al-Thawra al-'Arabiyya al-Kubra: Watha'iq wa-Asanid* (Amman, 1966).
Shibika, Makki (ed.), *Al-'Arab wal-Siyasa al-Baritaniyya fil-Harb al-'Alamiyya al-Ula* (Beirut, 1971).

Arab Bulletin 1916-1918
[Djemal Pacha] Le Commandement de la IVe Armée Ottoman, *La Vérité sur la question syrienne* (Istanbul, 1916).
Gooch, G.P. and Temperley, Harold (eds.), *British Documents on the Origins of the War 1898-1914* (London, 1926-1936).
Handbooks prepared under the direction of the Historical Section of the Foreign Office:
No.88: *Turkey in Asia* (Mar.1919).
No.92: *Mesopotamia* (Feb.1919).
No.93: *Syria and Palestine* (Apr.1919).
No.96 a&b: *The Rise of Islam and the Caliphate — The Pan-Islamic Movement* (Jan.1919).
No.96 c&d: *The Rise of the Turks — The Pan-Turanian Movement*

(Feb.1919).

Kampffmeyer, Georg, *Damaskus — Dokumente zum Kampf der Araber um ihre Unabhängigkeit* (Berlin, 1926).

Personalities — 'Iraq (London, revised ed. Oct.1919).

Newspapers and Periodicals

Al-Hilal (Cairo) 1908-1914.
Al-Kawkab (Cairo) 1916.
Al-Manar (Cairo) 1907-1919, 1927.
Al-Muqtabas (Damascus) 1908-1913.
Al-Muqtataf (Cairo) 1908-1914.
Al-Mustaqbal (Paris) 1916.
Al-'Urwa al-Wuthqa (Beirut ed., 1970).

Ha-Herut (Jerusalem) 1909-1916.

Correspondance d'Orient (Paris) 1908-1914.
L'Echo de Paris (Paris) 1913.
L'Indépendance Arabe (Paris) 1907-1908.
Le Journal de Beyrouth (Beirut) 1913, 1915-1916.
Revue du Monde Musulman (Paris) 1908-1913.
Le Temps (Paris) 1912-1913.
The Times (London) 1913-1914.

Books, Articles and Doctoral Dissertations

Arabic

'Abdallah ibn al-Husayn, *Mudhakkirati* (Jerusalem, 1945).

Abi Zayd, Nasif, *Ta'rikh al-'Asr al-Damawi* (Damascus, 1919).

Amin, Ahmad, *Zu'ama' al-Islah fil-'Asr al-Hadith* (Cairo, 1965).

Arslan, Shakib, *Al-Sayyid Rashid Rida aw Ikha' Arba'in Sana* (Damascus, 1937).

'Awad, 'Abd al-'Aziz Muhammad, *Al-Idara al-'Uthmaniyya fi Wilayat Suriyya 1864-1914* (Cairo, 1969).

Al-A'zami, Ahmad 'Izzat, *Al-Qadiyya al-'Arabiyya: Asbabuha, Muqaddimatuha, Tatawwuratuha wa-Nata'ijuha* (Baghdad, 1931-1934).

'Aziz Bek, *Al-Istikhbarat wal-Jasusiyya fi Lubnan wa-Suriya wa-Filastin khilala al-Harb al-'Alamiyya* (Beirut, 1937).
    Suriya wa-Lubnan fil-Harb al-'Alamiyya: Al-Istikhbarat wal-Jasusiyya fil-Dawla al-'Uthmaniyya (Beirut, 1933).

"'Aziz al-Misri Yatahaddathu ila al-Ahram", *al-Ahram* (21 July 1959),

pp.3, 9.
Al-'Azm, Rafiq, *Majmu'at Athar Rafiq Bek al-'Azm* (Cairo, [1925]).
Baru, Tawfiq 'Ali, *Al-'Arab wal-Turk fil-'Ahd al-Dusturi al-'Uthmani 1908-1914* (Cairo, 1960).
Al-Basir, Muhammad al-Mahdi, *Ta'rikh al-Qadiyya al-'Iraqiyya* (Baghdad, 1923).
Bayhum, Muhammad Jamil, *Al-'Arab wal-Turk fil-Sira' bayna al-Sharq wal-Gharb* (Beirut, 1957).
Burj, M., "Tahir wa-Salim al-Jaza'iriyyan: Ra'ida al-Nahda al-Haditha fil-Mashriq", *al-Thaqafa* [Algeria], 6 (Jan.1972), pp.31-45.
Daghir, As'ad, *Mudhakkirati 'ala Hamish al-Qadiyya al-'Arabiyya* (Cairo, n.d.[1959?]).
[Daghir, As'ad] Ahad A'da' al-Jam'iyyat al-'Arabiyya, *Thawrat al-'Arab: Muqaddimatuha, Asbabuha, Nata'ijuha* (Cairo, 1916).
Al-Dahhan, Sami, *'Abd al-Rahman al-Kawakibi 1854-1902* (Cairo, 1964).
Darwaza, Muhammad 'Izzat, *Hawla al-Haraka al-'Arabiyya al-Haditha* (Sidon, 1950-1953).
Nash'at al-Haraka al-'Arabiyya al-Haditha (Sidon, Beirut, [1971]).
Al-Fayad, 'Abdallah, *Al-Thawra al-'Iraqiyya al-Kubra Sanat 1920* (Baghdad, 1963).
Faydi, Sulayman, *Fi Ghamrat al-Nidal: Mudhakkirat Sulayman Faydi* (Baghdad, 1952).
Al-Ghusayn, Fa'iz, *Mudhakkirati 'an al-Thawra al-'Arabiyya* (Damascus, 1956).
Al-Hakim, Yusuf, *Bayrut wa-Lubnan fi 'Ahd Al 'Uthman* (Beirut, 1964).
Suriyya wal-'Ahd al-'Uthmani (Beirut, 1966).
Al-Hasani, 'Abd al-Razzaq, *Al-'Iraq fi Dawray al-Ihtilal wal-Intidab* (Sidon, 1935).
Ta'rikh al-Sahafa al-'Iraqiyya (Baghdad, 1957).
Al-Thawra al-'Iraqiyya al-Kubra (Sidon, [1952] 2nd ed.1965).
Al-Usul al-Rasmiyya li-Ta'rikh al-Wizarat al-'Iraqiyya fil-'Ahd al-Mulki al-Za'il (Sidon, 1964).
Al-Hashimi, Taha, *Mudhakkirat Taha al-Hashimi 1919-1943* (Beirut, 1967).
Hirfi, Salih, "Al-Jaza'ir wa-Dawruha fil-Nahda al-'Arabiyya al-Haditha fil-Mashriq", *al-Thaqafa* [Algeria], 26 (Apr.-May 1975), pp.1-38.
"Mudhakkirat Muhibb al-Din al-Khatib", *al-Thaqafa* [Algeria], 6 (Jan.1972), pp.86-97; 7 (Mar.1972), pp.82-90; 8-9 (Apr.-May 1972), pp.92-99; 10 (Sept.1972), pp.63-69; 11 (Nov.1972), pp.97-103; 12 (Jan.1973) pp.91-97.
Al-Husri, Sati', *Al-Bilad al-'Arabiyya wal-Dawla al-'Uthmaniyya* (Beirut, 2nd rep.1960).
Muhadarat fi Nushu' al-Fikra al-Qawmiyya (Beirut, [1951] 4th rep.1959).
Jawdat, 'Ali, *Dhikrayat 'Ali Jawdat 1900-1958* (Beirut, 1967).

[Al-Kawakibi, 'Abd al-Rahman] Al-Rahhala K, *Taba'i' al-Istibdad wa-Masari' al-Isti'bad* (Cairo ed., 1931).

[Al-Kawakibi, 'Abd al-Rahman] Al-Sayyid al-Furati, *Umm al-Qura* (Cairo ed., 1931).

Al-Khatib, 'Adnan, *Al-Shaykh Tahir al-Jaza'iri: Ra'id al-Nahda al-'Ilmiyya fi Bilad al-Sha'm* (Cairo, 1971).

Al-Khatib, Muhibb al-Din (ed.), *Al-Duktur Salah al-Din al-Qasimi 1305-1334: Atharuhu — Safahat min Ta'rikh al-Nahda al-'Arabiyya fi Awa'il al-Qarn al-'Ishrin* (Cairo, 1959).

Kurd 'Ali, Muhammad, *Kitab Khitat al-Sha'm* (Damascus, 1925).

Al-Mudhakkirat (Damascus, 1948).

Musa, Sulayman, "Al-'Alam al-'Arabi", *al-'Arabi*, 138 (1970), pp.78-81.

"'Awni 'Abd al-Hadi 1889-1970", *al-'Arabi*, 153 (1971), pp.67-73.

Al-Haraka al-'Arabiyya: Sirat al-Marhala al-Ula lil-Nahda al-'Arabiyya al-Haditha 1908-1924 (Beirut, 1970).

"Jam'iyyat al-'Arabiyya al-Fatat", *al-'Arabi*, 151 (1971), pp.52-59.

Al-Najjari, 'Ali Haydar, "Mustafa al-Shihabi: 'Alam min A'lam al-Umma al-'Arabiyya", *al-'Arabi*, 138 (1970), pp.82-86.

Qadri, Ahmad, *Mudhakkirati 'an al-Thawra al-'Arabiyya al-Kubra* (Damascus, 1956).

Al-Qasimi, Zafir, *Maktab 'Anbar* (Beirut, 1964).

Qasimiyya, Khayriyya (ed.), *'Awni 'Abd al-Hadi: Awraq Khassa* (Beirut, 1974).

Al-Qaysi, Sami 'Abd al-Hafiz, *Yasin al-Hashimi wa-Dawruhu fil-Siyasa al-'Iraqiyya bayna 'Amay 1922-1936* (Basra, 1975).

Rida, Muhammad Rashid, *Al-Khilafa aw al-Imama al-'Uzma* (Cairo, [1923]).

Sa'id, Amin, *Asrar al-Thawra al-'Arabiyya al-Kubra wa-Ma'sat al-Sharif Husayn* (Beirut, [1960]).

Al-Thawra al-'Arabiyya al-Kubra (Cairo, [1934]).

Al-Sayyid, Ahmad Lutfi, *Qissat Hayati* (Cairo, 1962).

Shafiq Pasha, Ahmad, *Mudhakirrati fi Nisf Qarn* (Cairo, [1934]).

Al-Sharbasi, Ahmad, *Rashid Rida Sahib al-Manar: 'Asruhu wa-Hayatuhu wa-Masadir Thaqafatuhu* (Cairo, 1970).

Al-Shihabi, Mustafa, *Al-Qawmiyya al-'Arabiyya: Ta'rikhuha wa-Qiwamuha wa-Maramiha — Muhadarat* (Cairo, [1959] 2nd ed.1961).

Shuman, Ahmad, "'Aziz al-Misri Abu al-Thawra al-Misriyya", *al-Jarida* [Beirut] (18 Aug.1955), pp.1, 8.

Subayh, Muhammad, *Batal La Nansahu: 'Aziz al-Misri wa-'Asruhu* (Beirut, Sidon, [1971]).

Mawaqif Hasima fi Ta'rikh al-Qawmiyya al-'Arabiyya, vol.2: *Al-Yaqza khilala al-Qarnayn al-Tasi' 'Ashar wal-'Ishrin al-Miladi* (Cairo, 1964).

Al-Sulh, 'Adil, *Sutur min al-Risala: Ta'rikh Haraka Istiqlaliyya Qamat fil-Mashriq al-'Arabi Sanat 1877* (Beirut, 1966).

Al-Suwaydi, Tawfiq, *Mudhakkirati: Nisf Qarn min Ta'rikh al-'Iraq wal-Qadiyya al-'Arabiyya* (Beirut, 1969).

384   THE EMERGENCE OF THE ARAB MOVEMENTS

Tarrazi, Philippe de, *Ta'rikh al-Sahafa al-'Arabiyya* (Beirut, 1913-1914, 1933).
Al-Tikriti, Salim Taha, "Al-Sayyid 'Abd al-Hamid al-Zahrawi", *Afkar*, 16 (1967), pp.29-35.
Al-'Umari, Muhammad Tahir, *Ta'rikh Muqaddarat al-'Iraq al-Siyasiyya* (Baghdad, 1924-1925).
Wahba, Hafiz, *Jazirat al-'Arab fil-Qarn al-'Ishrin* (Cairo, 3rd ed.1956).
Al-Zirikli, Khayr al-Din, *Al-A'lam: Qamus Tarajim li-Ashhur al-Rijal wal-Nisa' min al-'Arab wal-Musta'ribin wal-Mustashriqin* (Beirut, 3rd ed.1969).

European Languages

Abbott, G.F., *Turkey in Transition* (London, 1909).
Abu-Manneh, Butrus, "The Christians between Ottomanism and Syrian Nationalism: The Ideas of Butrus al-Bustani", *IJMES*, 11:3 (1980), pp.287-304.
Adams, Charles C., *Islam and Modernization in Egypt: A Study of the Modern Reform Movement Inagurated by Muhammad 'Abduh* (New York, [1933] 1968).
Ahmad, Feroz, *The Young Turks: The Committee of Union and Progress in Turkish Politics 1908-1914* (London, 1969).
Ahmed, Jamal Mohammed, *The Intellectual Origins of Egyptian Nationalism* (London, [1960] rep.1968).
Andrew, Christopher M. and Kanya-Forstner, A.S., *The Climax of French Imperial Expansion 1914-1924* (Stanford, 1981).
Antonius, George, *The Arab Awakening: The Story of The Arab National Movement* (London, [1938] rep.1945).
Atiyyah, Ghassan R., *Iraq 1908-1921: A Socio-Political Study* (Beirut, 1973).
Azoury, Nejib, *Le Réveil de la Nation Arabe dans l'Asie Turque* (Paris, 1905).
Birdwood, Lord, *Nuri as-Said: A Study in Arab Leadership* (London, 1959).
Blanckenhorn, Max, *Syrien und die deutsche Arbeit* (Weimar, 1916).
Bray, Norman N.E. *Shifting Sands* (London, 1934).
Busch, Briton Cooper, *Britain, India and the Arabs 1914-1921* (Berkeley, 1971).
Buxton, Charles Roden, *Turkey in Transition* (New York, London, 1909).
Cioeta, Donald J., "Ottoman Censorship in Lebanon and Syria 1876-1908", *IJMES*, 10:2 (1979), pp.167-186.
Cleveland, William L., *The Making of an Arab Nationalist: Ottomanism and Arabism in the Life and Thought of Sati' Al-Husri* (Princeton, 1971).
Cohen, Stuart A., *British Policy in Mesopotamia 1903-1914* (London, 1976).

Colombe, Marcel, "Islam et nationalisme arabe à la veille de la première guerre mondiale", *Revue Historique*, 223:1 (1960), pp.85-98.
Contenson, Ludovic de, *Les Réformes en Turquie d'Asie: La Question arménienne, la question syrienne* (Paris, 1913).
Cressaty (de Damas), Le Comte, *La Question syrienne et la France* (Paris, 1920).
La Syrie française (Paris, 1915).
Cromer, Earl of, *Modern Egypt* (London, 1908).
Dawn, C. Ernest, *From Ottomanism to Arabism: Essays on the Origins of Arab Nationalism* (Urbana, 1973).
Djemal Pasha, *Memories of a Turkish Statesman* (New York, [1922] rep.1973).
Edib, Halide, *Conflict of East and West in Turkey* (Lahore, [1935] rep.1963).
Fargo, Mumtaz Ayoub, *Arab-Turkish Relations from the Emergence Of Arab Nationalism to the Arab Revolt 1848-1916* (Ph.D. Dissertation, University of Utah, 1969).
Fatemi, Nasrollah S., "The Roots of Arab Nationalism", *Orbis*, 2:4 (1959), pp.437-456.
Gabrieli, Francesco, *The Arab Revival* (London, 1961).
Goldner, Werner Ernst, *The Role of Abdullah Ibn Husain, King of Jordan, in Arab Politics 1914-1951* (Ph.D. Dissertation, Stanford University, 1954).
Graves, Philip P., *Briton and Turk* (London, 1941).
Gross, Max L., *Ottoman Rule in the Province of Damascus 1860-1909* (Ph.D. Dissertation, Georgetown University, 1979).
Grothe, Hugo, *Die asiatische Türkei und die deutsche Interessen* (Halle, 1913).
Haddad, George, *Fifty Years of Modern Syria and Lebanon* (Beirut, 1950).
Haim, Sylvia G. (ed.), *Arab Nationalism: An Anthology* (Berkeley, [1962] ed.1976).
"'The Arab Awakening' — A Source for the Historian?", *Die Welt des Islams*, N.S. 2:4 (1953), pp.237-250.
Harran, Taj Elsir Ahmad, "The Young Turks and the Arabs 1909-1912" in *Arabic and Islamic Garland: Historical, Educational and Literary Papers presented to Abdul-Latif Tibawi* (London, 1977), pp.111-119.
"The Young Turks and the Arabs: The Role of Arab Societies in the Turkish-Arab Relations in the Period 1908-1914" in *Türk-Arap Iskileri: Geçmişte, Bugün ve Gelecekte*, Proceedings of an International Conference on Turkish-Arab Relations, Ankara, Hacettepe University, 18-22 June 1979 (Ankara, 1980), pp.182-202.
Hartmann, Martin, *Reisebriefe aus Syrien* (Berlin, 1913).
Hartmann, Richard, *Die arabische Frage und das türkische Reich* (Halle, 1919).
"Arabische politische Gesellschaften bis 1914: Ein Beitrag zur

386   THE EMERGENCE OF THE ARAB MOVEMENTS

Entwicklung des arabischen Nationalismus" in Hartmann, Richard and Scheel, Helmuth (eds.) *Beitrage zur Arabistik, Semitistik und Islamwissenschaft* (Leipzig, 1944), pp.439-467.

Heller, Joseph, "Sir Louis Mallet and the Ottoman Empire: The Road to War", *MES*, 12:1 (1976), pp.3-44.

Heyd, Uriel, *Foundations of Turkish Nationalism: The Life and Teachings of Ziya Gökalp* (London, 1950).

Hourani, Albert, *Arabic Thought in the Liberal Age 1798-1939* (London, [1962] 1970).

Syria and Lebanon (Beirut, [1946] 1968).

Ireland, Philip Willard, *'Iraq: A Study of Political Development* ([London, 1937] rep. New York, 1970).

Jankowski, James, "Ottomanism and Arabism in Egypt 1860-1914", *MW*, 70:3-4 (1980), pp.226-259.

Jessup, Henry Harris, *Fifty-Three Years in Syria* (New York, 1910).

Jomier, J., "Les Raisons de l'adhésion du Sayyed Rashid Rida au nationalisme arabe", *Bulletin de l'Institut d'Egypte*, 53-54 (1971-72/1972-73), pp.53-61.

Jung, Eugène, *Les Puissances devant la révolte arabe: La Crise mondiale de demain* (Paris, 1906).

La Révolte arabe (Paris, 1924-1925).

Keddie, Nikki R., "Pan-Islam as Proto-Nationalism", *Journal of Modern History*, 41:1 (1969), pp.17-28.

Kedourie, Elie, *Arabic Political Memoirs and Other Studies* (London, 1974).

England and the Middle East: The Destruction of the Ottoman Empire 1914-1921 (London, [1956] 1978).

Khadduri, Majid, "'Aziz 'Ali Misri and the Arab Nationalist Movement" in Hourani, Albert (ed.), *St Antony's Papers No.17 — Middle Eastern Affairs No.4* (London, 1965), pp.140-163.

Khairallah, K.T., *Le Problème du Levant: Les Régions Arabes Libérées — Syrie-Irak-Liban* (Paris, 1919).

La Question du Liban (Paris, 1915).

La Syrie (Paris, 1912).

Khalidi, Rashid I., "Arab Nationalism in Syria: The Formative Years 1908-1914", in Haddad, William W. and Ochsenwald, William (eds.), *Nationalism in a Non-National State* (Columbus, 1977), pp.207-237.

British Policy towards Syria and Palestine 1906-1914 (London, 1980).

"The Press as a Source for Modern Arab Political History: 'Abd al-Ghani al-'Uraisi and al-Mufid", *Arab Studies Quarterly*, 3:1 (1981), pp.22-42.

Khan, Rasheeduddin, "The Rise of Arab Nationalism and European Diplomacy 1908-1916", *Islamic Culture*, 36:3,4 (1962), pp.196-206, 245-255.

Khoury, Philip S., *Urban Notables and Arab Nationalism: The Politics of Damascus 1860-1920* (Cambridge, 1983).

Kirk, George E., "'The Arab Awakening' Reconsidered", *Middle Eastern Affairs*, 13:6 (1962), pp.162-173.

Kohn, Hans, *A History of Nationalism in the East* (New York, [1929] rep.1969).

Lammens H., *La Syrie: Précis historique* (Beirut, 1921).

Landau, Jacob M., "An Arab Anti-Turk Handbill, 1881", *Turcica*, 9:1 (1977), pp.215-227.

Pan-Turkism in Turkey (London, 1981).

"Prolegomena to a Study of Secret Societies in Modern Egypt", *MES*, 1:2 (1965), pp.135-168.

Laoust, Henry, *Essai sur les doctrines sociales et politiques de Taki-D-Din Ahmad B. Taimiya* (Cairo, 1939).

Lavan, Spencer, "Four Christian Arab Nationalists: A Comparative Study", *MW*, 57:2 (1967), pp.114-125.

Lawrence, T.E., *Seven Pillars of Wisdom* (New York, 1938).

Lesch, Ann, "The Origins of Palestine Arab Nationalism" in Haddad, William W. and Ochsenwald, William (eds.), *Nationalism in a Non-National State* (Columbus, 1977), pp.265-290.

Lewis, Bernard, *The Emergence of Modern Turkey* (London, 1961).

Liman von Sanders, [Otto], *Fünf Jahre Türkei* (Berlin, 1920).

Longrigg, Stephen Hemsley, *Iraq 1900-1950: A Political, Social and Economic History* (Beirut, [1953] 3rd imp.1968).

MacCallum, Elizabeth P., "The Arab Nationalist Movement", *MW*, 25:4 (1935), pp.359-374.

Mandel, Neville J., *The Arabs the Zionism before World War I* (Berkeley, 1976).

"Attempts at an Arab-Zionist Entente 1913-1914", *MES*, 1:3 (1965), pp.238-267.

"Turks, Arabs and Jewish Immigration into Palestine 1882-1914" in Hourani, Albert (ed.), *St Antony's Papers No.17 — Middle Eastern Affairs No.4* (London, 1965), pp.77-108.

Mandelstam, André, *Le Sort de l'empire ottoman* (Lausanne, 1917).

Ma'oz, Moshe, "Attempts at Creating a Political Community in Modern Syria", *MEJ*, 26:4 (1972), pp.389-404.

Miller, William, *The Ottoman Empire and its Successors 1801-1927* (London, imp.1966).

Mousa, Suleiman, "The Rise of Arab Nationalism and the Emergence of Transjordan" in Haddad, William W. and Ochsenwald, William (eds.), *Nationalism in a Non-National State* (Columbus, 1977), pp.239-263.

Moutran, Nadra, *La Syrie de demain* (Paris, 1916).

Nadhmi, Wamidh J.O., *The Political, Intellectual and Social Roots of the Iraqi Independence Movement, 1920* (Ph.D. Dissertation, Durham University, 1974).

[Nujaym, Paul] M. Jouplain, *La Question du Liban: Etude d'Histoire Diplomatique et de Droit International* (Paris, 1908).

Pears, Edwin, *Forty Years in Constantinople: The Recollections of Sir Edwin Pears 1873-1915* (New York, 1916).

Ramsaur, Ernest Edmondson, *The Young Turks: Prelude to the Revolution of 1908* (New York, [1957] 1970).

Rémond, Georges, *Aux Camps Turco-Arabes: Notes de Route et de Guerre en Cyrénaïque et en Tripolitaine* (Paris, 1913).

Richard, Henry, *La Syrie et la Guerre* (Paris, 1916).

Ristelhueber, René, "Liban, Cher Liban! (Souvenirs)", *Revue d'Histoire Diplomatique*, 74:1 (1960), pp.9-32.

Roded, Ruth, "Ottoman Service as a Vehicle for the Rise of New Upstarts among the Urban Elite Families of Syria in the Last Decades of Ottoman Rule", *Asian and African Studies*, 17 (1983), pp.63-94.

Saab, Hassan, *The Arab Federalists of the Ottoman Empire* (Amsterdam, 1958).

Sachar, Howard M., *The Emergence of the Middle East 1914-1924* (New York, 1969).

Saleh, Zaki, *Britain and Mesopotamia (Iraq to 1914)* (Baghdad, 1966).

Saliba, Najib E., "Emigration from Syria", *Arab Studies Quarterly*, 3:1 (1981), pp.56-67.

Wilayat Suriyya 1876-1909 (Ph.D. Dissertation, The University of Michigan, 1971).

Salibi, Kamal S., "Beirut Under the Young Turks as Depicted in the Political Memoirs of Salim 'Ali Salam (1868-1938)" in Berque, Jacques and Chevallier, Dominique (eds.), *Les Arabes par leur archives (XVIe-XXe siècles)* (Paris, 1976), pp.193-215.

The Modern History of Lebanon (London, [1965] 1968).

Samné, Georges, *Le Liban Autonome (de 1864 à nos jours)* (Paris, 1919).

La Syrie (Paris, 1920).

Serauky, Eberhard, "Nationale Aspekte der syrische-libanesischen Entwicklung von Literatur und Publizistik im 19. Jahrhundert", *Mitteilungen des Instituts für Orientforschung*, 13:1 (1967), pp.59-81.

Shamir, Shimon, "Midhat Pasha and Anti-Turk Agitation in Syria", *MES*, 10:2 (1974), pp.115-141.

Shorrock, William I., *French Imperialism in the Middle East: The Failure of Policy in Syria and Lebanon 1900-1914* (Madison, 1976).

"The French Presence in Syria and Lebanon Before the First World War, 1900-1914", *The Historian*, 34:2 (1972), pp.293-303.

"French Suspicion of British Policy in Syria 1900-1914", *Journal of European Studies*, 6:3 (1976), pp.190-208.

Spagnolo, John P., *France and Ottoman Lebanon 1861-1914* (London, 1977).

"French Influence in Syria Prior to World War I: The Functional Weakness of Imperialism", *MEJ*, 23:1 (1969), pp.45-62.

Stoddard, Lothrop, *The New World of Islam* (New York, 1922).

Stoddard, Philip Hendrick, *The Ottoman Government and the Arabs 1911 to 1918: A Preliminary Study of the Teskilât-i Mahsusa* (Ph.D. Dissertation, Princeton University, 1963).

Storrs, Ronald, *Orientations* (London, 1937).

Tauber, Eliezer, "Four Syrian Manifestos after the Young Turk Revolution", *Turcica*, 19 (1987), pp.195-213.

"The Press and the Journalist as a Vehicle in Spreading National Ideas in Syria in the Late Ottoman Period", *Die Welt des Islams*, 30 (1990), pp.163-177.

"Rashid Rida as Pan-Arabist before World War I", *Muslim World*, 79 (1989), pp.102-112.

"Sayyid Talib and the Young Turks in Basra", *Middle Eastern Studies*, 25 (1989), pp.3-22.

Tibawi, A.L., *A Modern History of Syria* (London, 1969).

Tlili, Bechir, "Les Rapports arabo-turcs à la veille de la Grande Guerre (1907-1913)", *Cahiers de Tunisie*, 23 (nos.89-90, 1975), pp.33-140.

Wilson, Arnold T., *Loyalties: Mesopotamia 1914-1917* (London, [1930] 1936).

Winstone, H.V.F., *The Illicit Adventure: The Story of Political and Military Intelligence in the Middle East from 1898 to 1926* (London, 1982).

X., "Les Courants politiques dans la Turquie contemporaine", *RMM*, 21 (Dec.1912), pp.158-221.

X., "Les Courants politiques dans le milieu arabe", *RMM*, 25 (Dec.1913), pp.236-281.

X., "Le Panislamisme et le Panturquisme", *RMM*, 22 (Mar.1913), pp.179-220.

Yaphe, Judith Share, *The Arab Revolt in Iraq of 1920* (Ph.D. Dissertation, University of Illinois, 1972).

Zeine, Zeine N., *The Emergence of Arab Nationalism with a Background Study of Arab-Turkish Relations in the Near East* (New York, [1958] 3rd ed.1973).

"Unpublished Documents Concerning Independence Movements in the Arab Provinces of the Ottoman Empire", *Actes du premier congrès international des études balkaniques et sud-est européenes*, 4 (1969), pp.693-697.

Ziadeh, Nicola A., *Syria and Lebanon* (London, 1957).

Index

404 THE EMERGENCE OF THE ARAB MOVEMENTS

al-Shihabi, 'Arif, 45-47, 55, 93, 99-100, 195, 320, 351
al-Shihabi, Bahjat, 375
al-Shihabi, Mustafa, 93, 350
Shi'ites, 11, 174, 183, 275, 278, 296
Shu'ayba, 161
Shukri, Midhat, 107, 199-200, 207
Shumayyil, Shibli, 105, 123
Shuqayr, As'ad, 203, 306
Shuqayr, Najib, 201, 211
al-Shurayqi, Muhammad, 95
al-Shurbaji, Shukri, 282
Shuwaymar, 231
Sidon, 10-11, 16-18, 71, 84, 87, 122, 135, 254-255, 290, 292, 348
Sidqi, Bakr, 196, 330
Simisma, Mustafa, 288
al-Siyadi, Abu al-Huda, 90, 152-153, 328
Small Circle of Damascus, 44-45, 247
Smyrna, 20, 216, 220
Society for the Protection of the Rights of the Arab Nation, 20, 338
Society of Good Intentions, 18-19, 43
Society of Knowledge and Guidance, 112
Society of Propaganda and Guidance, 113, 115
Society of the Arab Association, 109, 114-115, 118, 246, 251, 253, 268, 288-289, 303, 305, 312
Society of the Arab Revival, 43, 46-49, 57, 101, 246-248, 287, 289-291, 293-295, 297, 300, 320, 342, 372
Society of the Lebanese Revival, 1, 70-90, 109, 132, 140, 181-182, 185-186, 196, 199, 254-256, 258-259, 268-270, 272-275, 277, 280, 285, 287, 289, 292-293, 295, 298, 301, 308, 311, 315, 318, 320-322, 330, 333, 347, 358, 373
Society of the Ottoman Council, 51-53, 110
Society of the Young Arabs, 216
Society of Young Zahla, 196
Sollum, 219
Sublime Porte, 75, 80-81, 115, 122, 129, 131-132, 137-138, 177, 185, 201, 209-210, 228, 255, 337, see also Ottoman government
Sudan, 221, 250, 326
Suez, 134
Suez Canal, 34, 37, 247, 265, 278
Sufayr, 'Abdallah, 373
al-Sulh, Ahmad, 10-12, 336
al-Sulh, Kamil, 136, 140
al-Sulh, Mukhtar, 327
al-Sulh, Munah, 11
al-Sulh, Rida, 327
al-Sulh, Riyad, 327
al-Sulh, Sami, 102, 327
Sursuq, Albert, 181-182
Sursuq, Yusuf, 137, 144-145, 209
al-Suwaydi, Naji, 174
al-Suwaydi, Tawfiq, 93-94, 178, 185, 189, 247, 260
al-Suwaydi, Yusuf, 174, 176-177
Switzerland, 123, 285
Sykes, Mark, 282
Syria, 7-8, 10-12, 15-20, 23, 26, 33, 35, 37-39, 41-43, 45, 50, 57, 62-64, 66-68, 82, 84-85, 88, 93, 95-97, 100, 103, 106, 108, 111, 114-117, 121-122, 125-129, 132, 134-135, 138, 141, 147, 150, 167, 173, 176, 178-181, 184-185, 188, 190, 195-197, 200, 203, 207, 210, 214, 219, 223, 233, 245, 251-252, 255, 257-262, 264, 266, 268, 270-283, 285, 289-293, 305-308, 310-311, 316-318, 321, 326, 330-333, 335, 343-346, 375
Syrian Catholics, 364
Syrian Central Society, 66-68, 258-259, 270, 287, 289, 307
Syrian Nationalist Society, 196

Syrian Protestant College (Beirut), 15, 45, 143, 337
Syrian Reform Society, 196
Syrian Scientific Society, 336
Syrian Union Party, 134
Syrian Union Society, 88, 186, 188, 258, 287, 289

Ta'rikh al-Mustaqbal, 57
Taba'i' al-Istibdad, 26-27, 339
al-Tabaqjali, Muhammad Kamil, 176
al-Tabataba'i, 'Abd al-Wahhab, 282
Tabbara, Ahmad Hasan, 78, 137-138, 146, 181-182, 185-186, 189-191, 196-197, 202-203, 261, 324
Tabbara, Zakarya, 143, 146-147, 182
Tal'at, 104-105, 107, 112, 132, 153, 158, 160, 168-170, 198-199, 202, 225-226, 230, 317
Talib, Sayyid, *see* al-Naqib, Sayyid Talib
Tallu, Na'if, 125
al-Tamimi, Rafiq, 90, 92, 208
Tanin, 56, 65, 183, 200, 260
Tariq ibn Ziyad, 105
Tarrad, Pietro, 136-137, 140, 142, 324
Taurus Mts., 47, 247
Tawfiq, Khedive, 22, 31, 339
Taymur, Ahmad, 105
Tayyara, Salim, 143
Temps, 82, 84, 185, 273, 278
Ten Brothers Society, 95
Teşkilât-i Mahsusa, 217, 369
al-Thabat, 78, 274
Thabit, Ayyub, 85, 137, 140, 146, 181-183, 185, 189, 197, 199, 206-207, 257, 324
Thabit, Ibrahim, 136, 225, 227
Thabit, Salim, 99-100, 266, 279, 305, 318-319
Thessalia, 38
Thrace, 218, 225

Tiberias, 306
Tigris, 34, 247, 265
Timerlane, 56
Times, 231, 235, 273, 343
Tonkin, 341
Transjordan, 11, 257, 330, 333
Tripoli (East), 16-17, 49, 71, 84, 87, 95, 102, 109-111, 135, 150, 241, 254-255, 260, 269, 290, 292, 347
Tripoli (West), 61, 104, 106, 183, 218, 229, 260
Tripolitania, *see* Tripoli (West)
True Reform Party, 184, 307
Tul Karm, 292
Tunisia, 24, 38, 81, 183, 221, 241, 250, 260, 282, 326
Turanian nationalism, 56, 111, 224, 344
Turkey, *see* Ottoman Empire
Turkification policy, 1, 48, 57-58, 64, 69, 104, 113, 135, 167, 213, 215, 225, 266, 268, 308, 331
al-Tuwayni, Michel, 128, 140
Tyre, 348

'Ubaydallah, Sheikh, 238, 240
'Ujaymi ibn Sa'dun, 155-156, 158, 160-162, 164-166, 168-170, 309
'Uman, 282
'Uman, Sea of, 34, 247
'Umar ibn 'Abd al-'Aziz, Caliph, 31
al-'Umar, Ibrahim Hilmi, 174, 176, 223
'Umar Tusun, Prince, 214, 260
Umayyads, 95
Umm al-Qura, 26, 28-33, 45, 110, 249
United States, 27, 37, 68, 76, 87-88, 125, 196, 205, 285
al-'Uraysi, 'Abd al-Ghani, 45, 92-94, 178, 180, 182, 186-187, 191-193, 249, 284, 325, 357
Urfa, 261
al-'Urwa al-Wuthqa, 22-24, 109, 271, 282

CPSIA information can be obtained at www.ICGtesting.com
Printed in the USA
LVOW031241210911

247244LV00004B/75/P